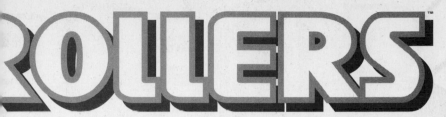

ROLLERS™

by

Matthew Loux

Lettered by
Douglas E. Sherwood

Designed by
Matthew Loux
Steven Birch

Edited by
Randal C. Jarrell
Douglas E. Sherwood

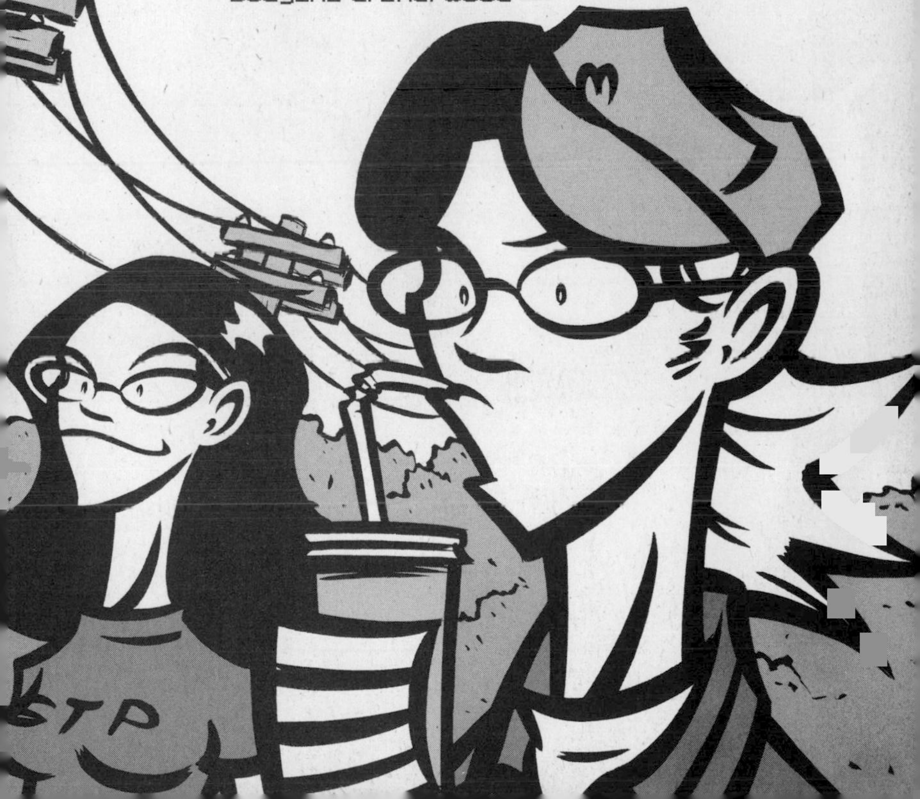
STP

Published by Oni Press, Inc.
Joe Nozemack, publisher
James Lucas Jones, editor in chief
Randal C. Jarrell, managing editor
Douglas E. Sherwood, editorial assistant

ONI PRESS, INC.
1305 SE Martin Luther King Jr. Blvd.
Suite A
Portland, OR 97214
USA

www.onipress.com

First edition: september 2006

ISBN: 1-978-932664-50-8

10 9 8 7 6 5 4 3

PRINTED IN U.S.A.

SIDESCROLLERS™

ONI PRESS

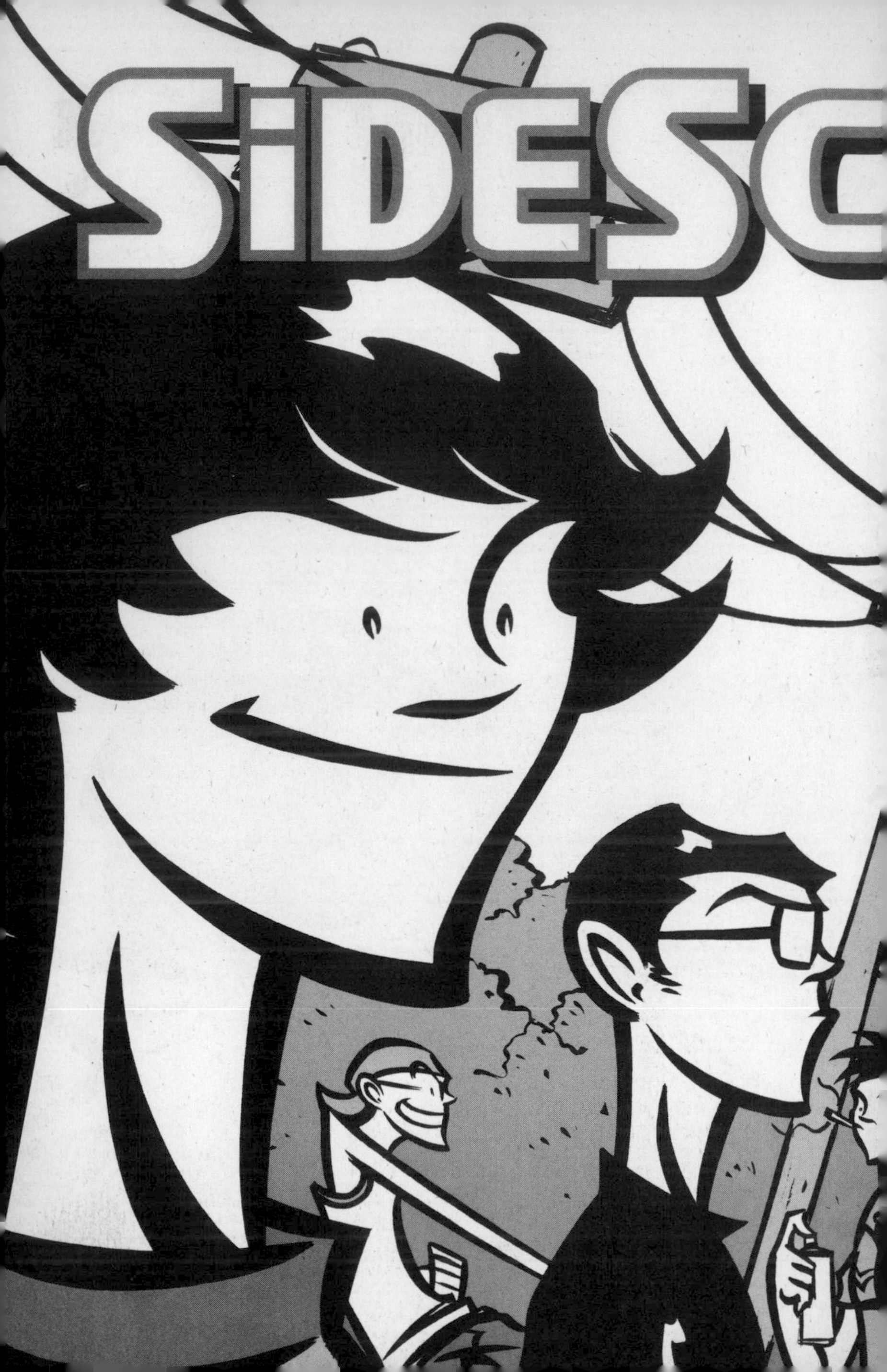
SiDESC

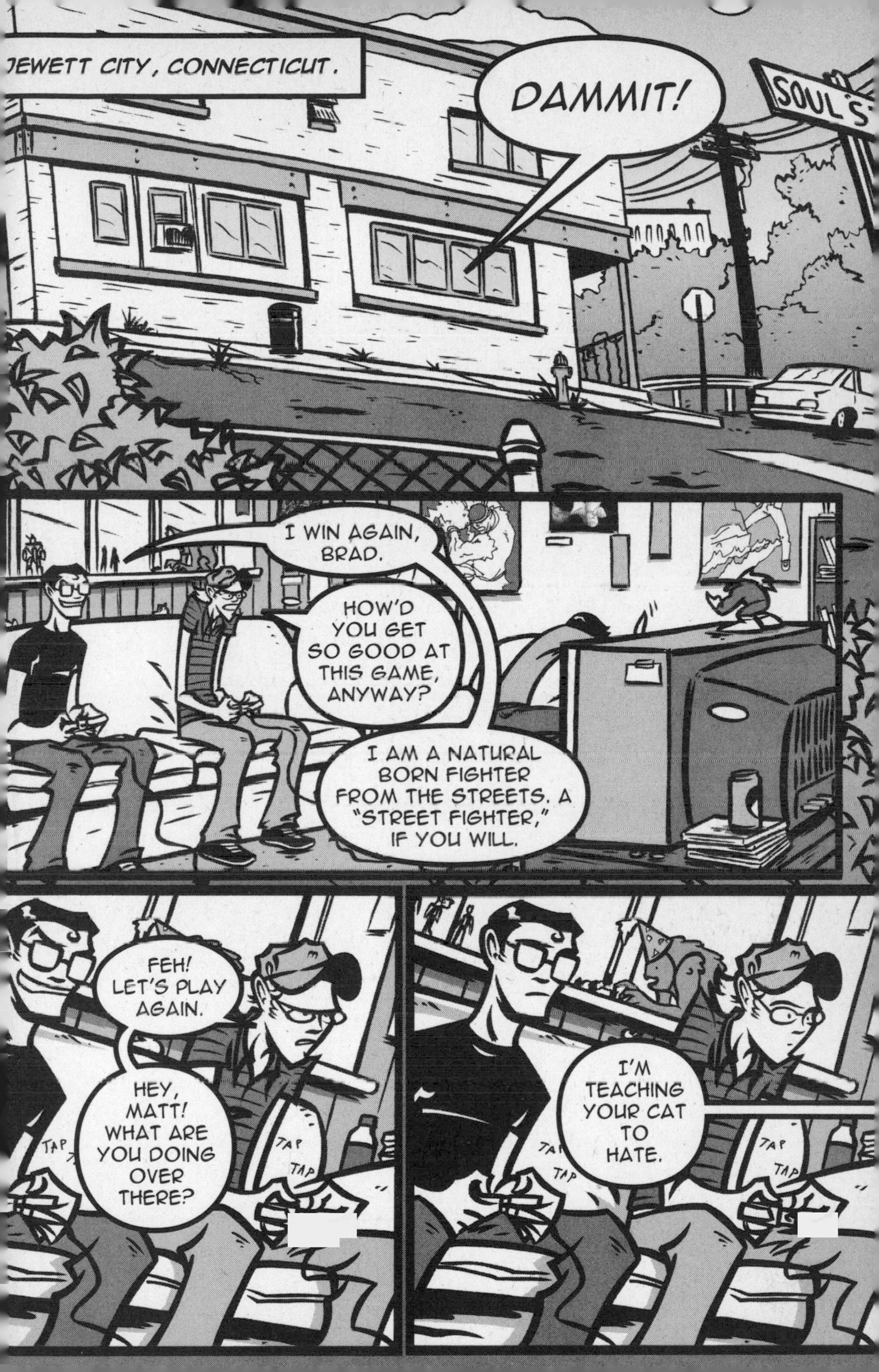

JEWETT CITY, CONNECTICUT.
DAMMIT!
SOUL'S
I WIN AGAIN, BRAD.
HOW'D YOU GET SO GOOD AT THIS GAME, ANYWAY?
I AM A NATURAL BORN FIGHTER FROM THE STREETS. A "STREET FIGHTER," IF YOU WILL.
FEH! LET'S PLAY AGAIN.
HEY, MATT! WHAT ARE YOU DOING OVER THERE?
TAP
TAP
TAP
I'M TEACHING YOUR CAT TO HATE.
TAP
TAP
TAP
TAP

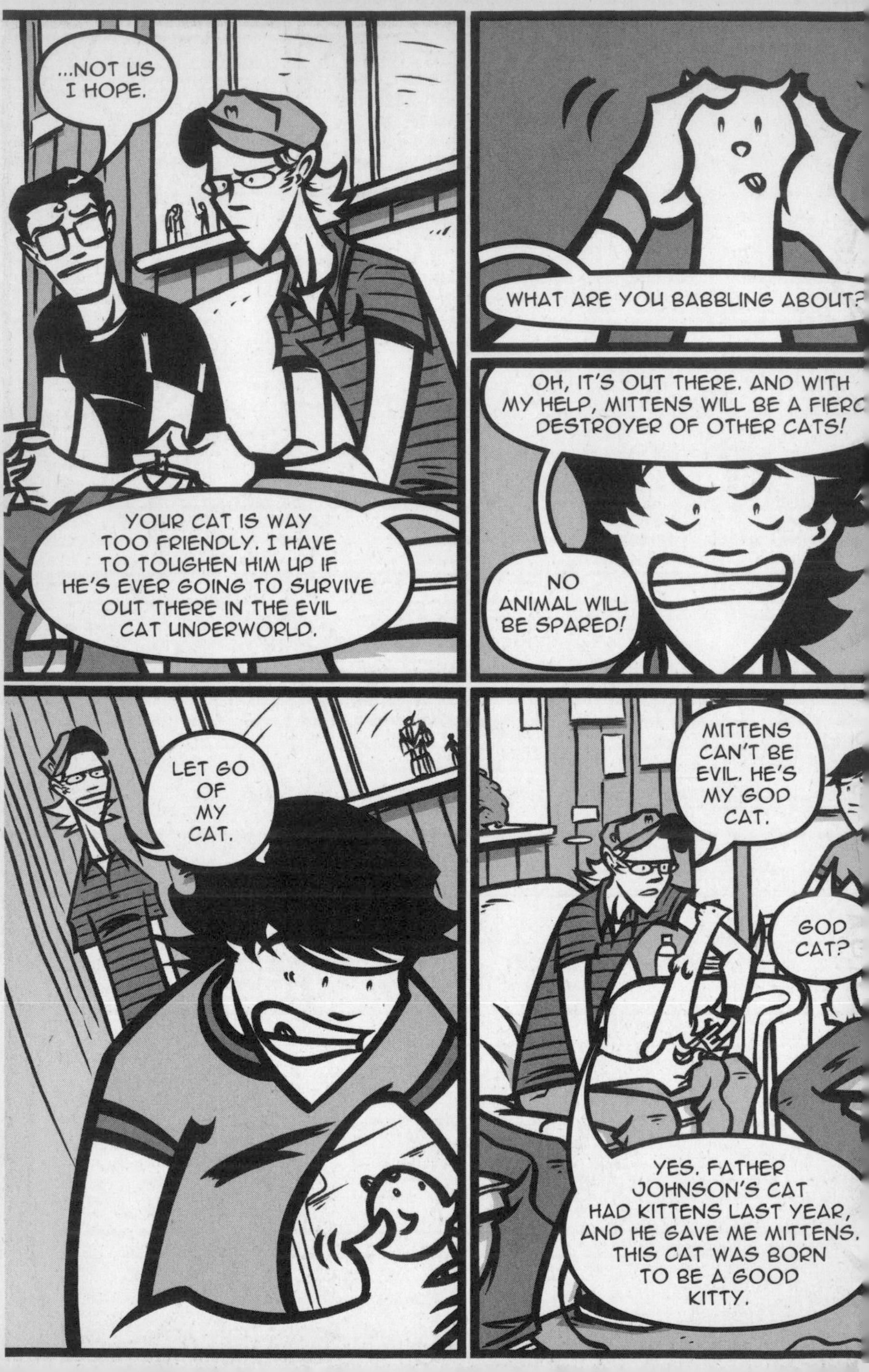

...NOT US I HOPE.
YOUR CAT IS WAY TOO FRIENDLY. I HAVE TO TOUGHEN HIM UP IF HE'S EVER GOING TO SURVIVE OUT THERE IN THE EVIL CAT UNDERWORLD.
WHAT ARE YOU BABBLING ABOUT?
OH, IT'S OUT THERE. AND WITH MY HELP, MITTENS WILL BE A FIERC DESTROYER OF OTHER CATS!
NO ANIMAL WILL BE SPARED!
LET GO OF MY CAT.
MITTENS CAN'T BE EVIL. HE'S MY GOD CAT.
GOD CAT?
YES. FATHER JOHNSON'S CAT HAD KITTENS LAST YEAR, AND HE GAVE ME MITTENS. THIS CAT WAS BORN TO BE A GOOD KITTY.

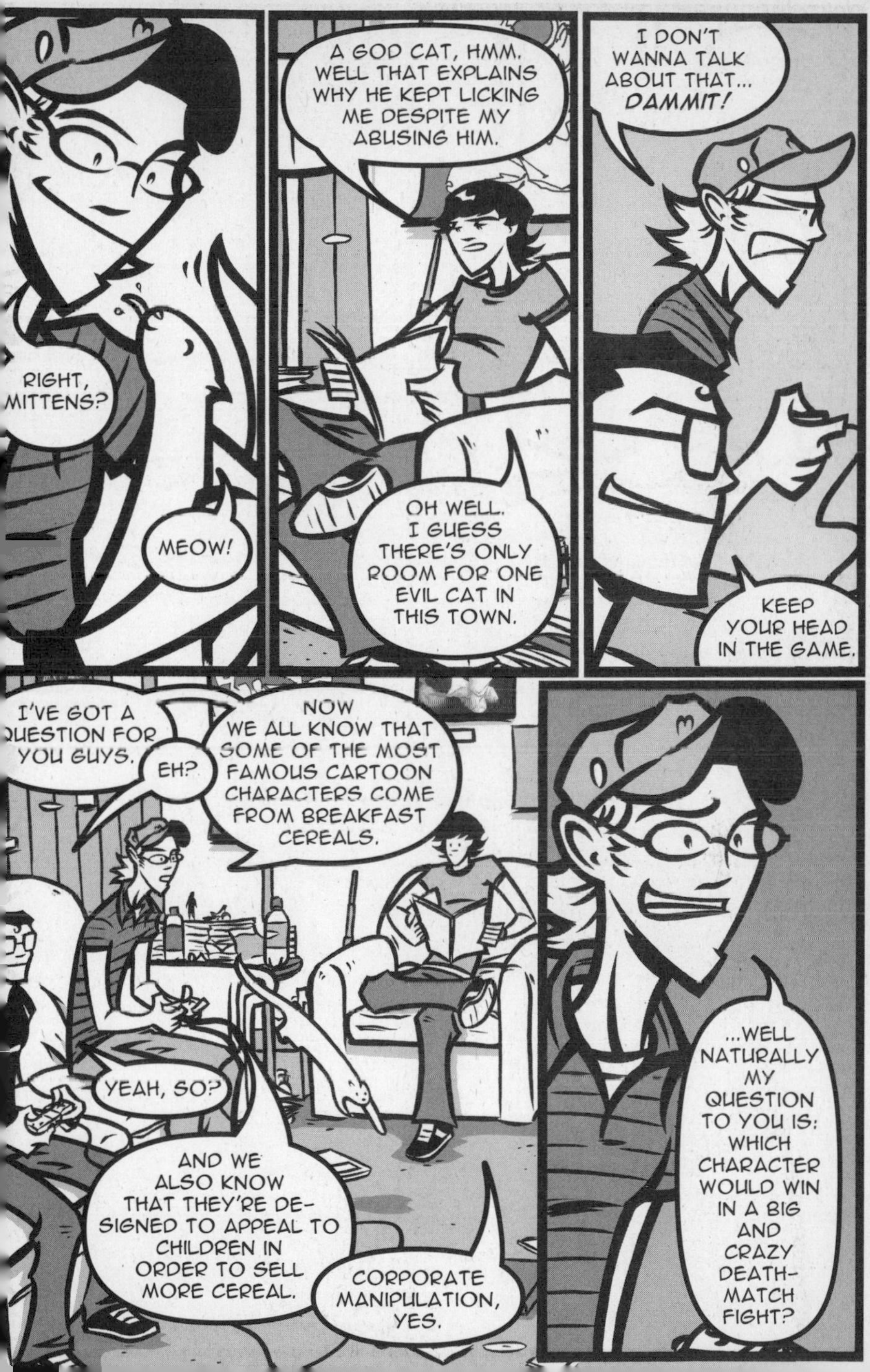
A GOD CAT, HMM. WELL THAT EXPLAINS WHY HE KEPT LICKING ME DESPITE MY ABUSING HIM.
RIGHT, MITTENS?
MEOW!
OH WELL. I GUESS THERE'S ONLY ROOM FOR ONE EVIL CAT IN THIS TOWN.
I DON'T WANNA TALK ABOUT THAT... *DAMMIT!*
KEEP YOUR HEAD IN THE GAME.
I'VE GOT A QUESTION FOR YOU GUYS.
EH?
NOW WE ALL KNOW THAT SOME OF THE MOST FAMOUS CARTOON CHARACTERS COME FROM BREAKFAST CEREALS.
YEAH, SO?
AND WE ALSO KNOW THAT THEY'RE DE-SIGNED TO APPEAL TO CHILDREN IN ORDER TO SELL MORE CEREAL.
CORPORATE MANIPULATION, YES.
...WELL NATURALLY MY QUESTION TO YOU IS: WHICH CHARACTER WOULD WIN IN A BIG AND CRAZY DEATH-MATCH FIGHT?

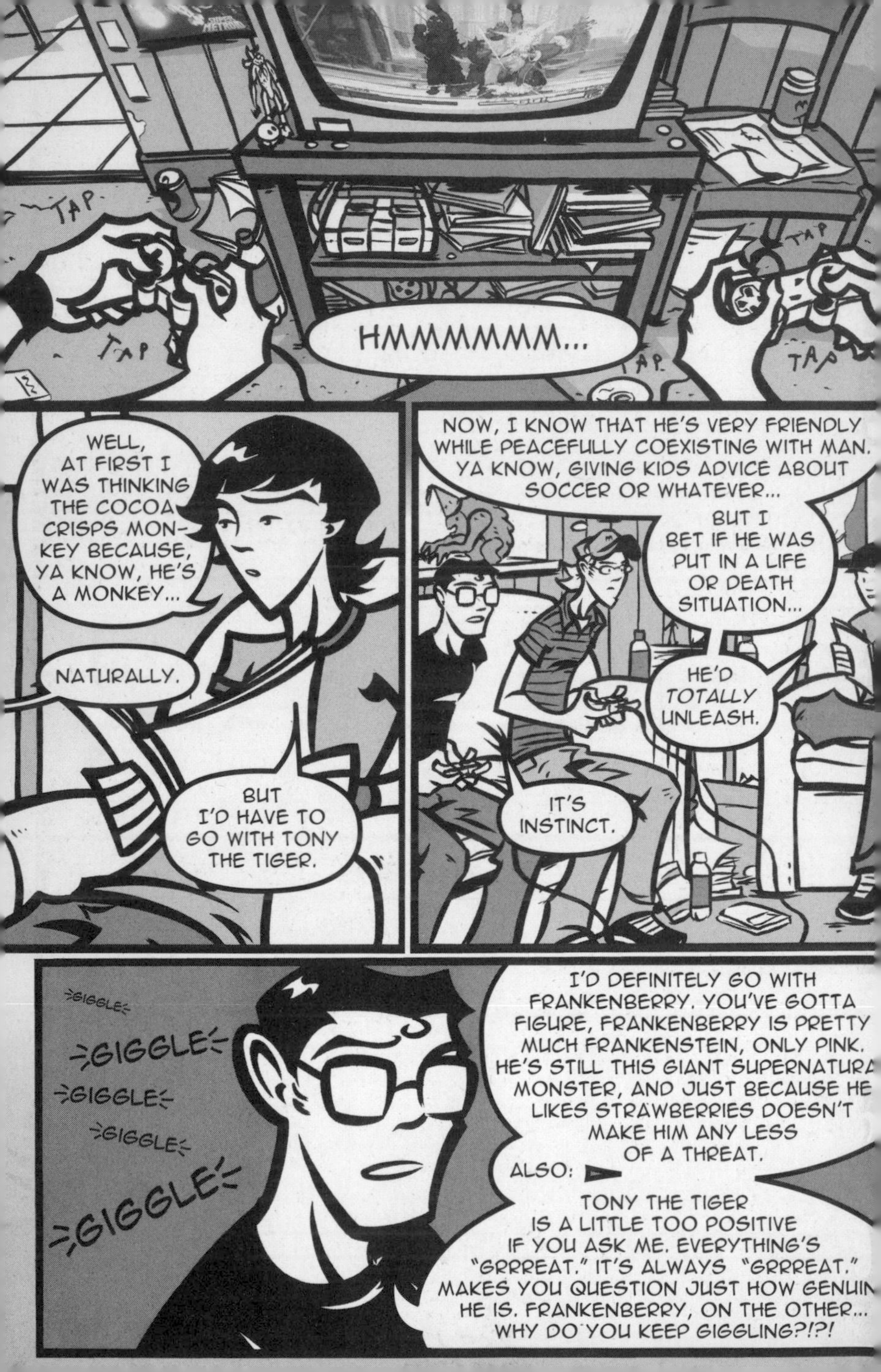
TAP
TAP
HMMMMMM...
TAP
TAP
TAP
WELL, AT FIRST I WAS THINKING THE COCOA CRISPS MON-KEY BECAUSE, YA KNOW, HE'S A MONKEY...
NATURALLY.
BUT I'D HAVE TO GO WITH TONY THE TIGER.
NOW, I KNOW THAT HE'S VERY FRIENDLY WHILE PEACEFULLY COEXISTING WITH MAN. YA KNOW, GIVING KIDS ADVICE ABOUT SOCCER OR WHATEVER...
BUT I BET IF HE WAS PUT IN A LIFE OR DEATH SITUATION...
HE'D *TOTALLY* UNLEASH.
IT'S INSTINCT.
GIGGLE
GIGGLE
GIGGLE
GIGGLE
GIGGLE
I'D DEFINITELY GO WITH FRANKENBERRY. YOU'VE GOTTA FIGURE, FRANKENBERRY IS PRETTY MUCH FRANKENSTEIN, ONLY PINK. HE'S STILL THIS GIANT SUPERNATURA MONSTER, AND JUST BECAUSE HE LIKES STRAWBERRIES DOESN'T MAKE HIM ANY LESS OF A THREAT.
ALSO:
TONY THE TIGER IS A LITTLE TOO POSITIVE IF YOU ASK ME. EVERYTHING'S "GRRREAT." IT'S ALWAYS "GRRREAT." MAKES YOU QUESTION JUST HOW GENUIN HE IS. FRANKENBERRY, ON THE OTHER... WHY DO YOU KEEP GIGGLING?!?!

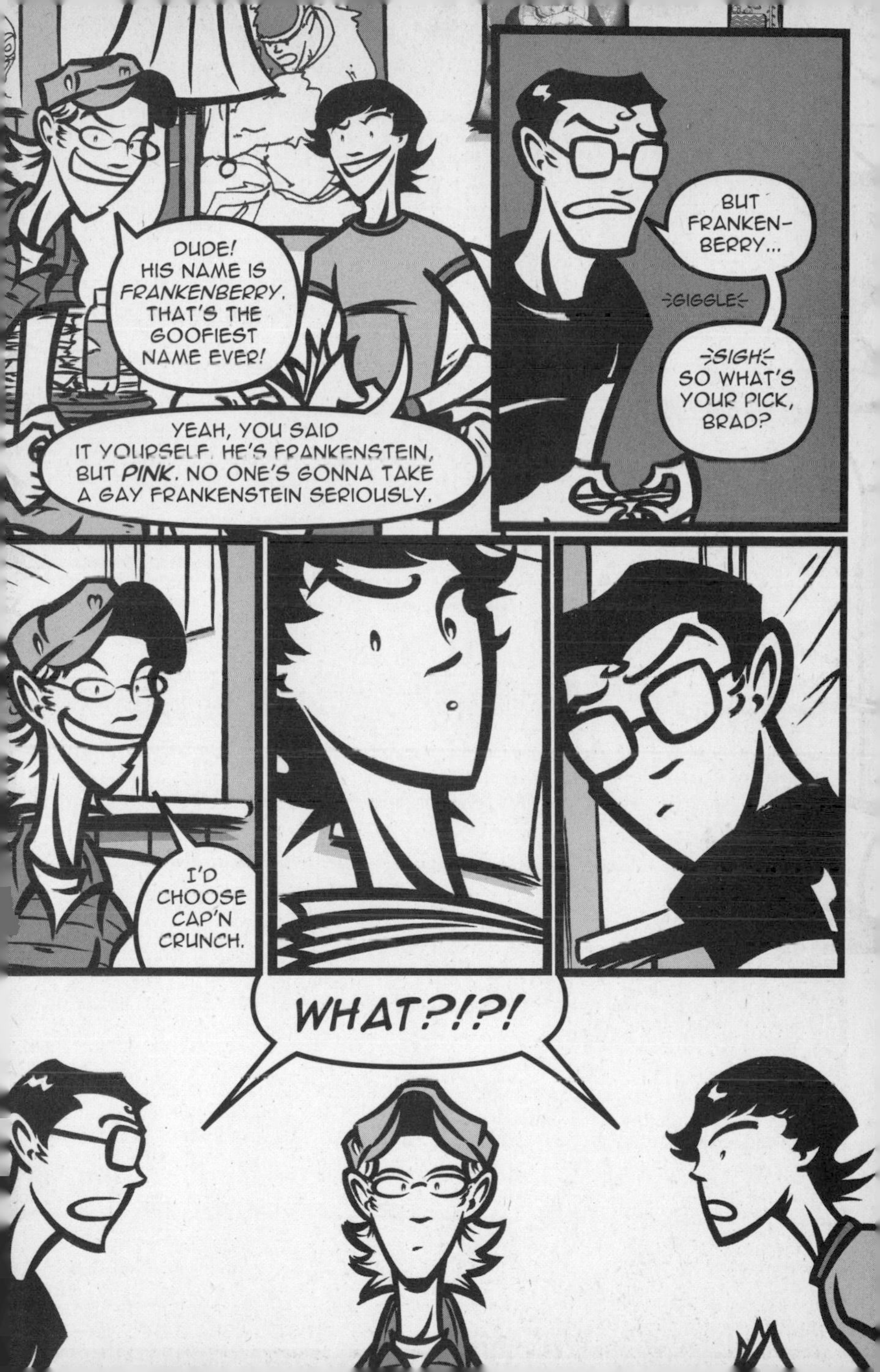
DUDE! HIS NAME IS FRANKENBERRY. THAT'S THE GOOFIEST NAME EVER!
YEAH, YOU SAID IT YOURSELF. HE'S FRANKENSTEIN, BUT PINK. NO ONE'S GONNA TAKE A GAY FRANKENSTEIN SERIOUSLY.
BUT FRANKEN-BERRY...
GIGGLE
SIGH SO WHAT'S YOUR PICK, BRAD?
I'D CHOOSE CAP'N CRUNCH.
WHAT?!?!

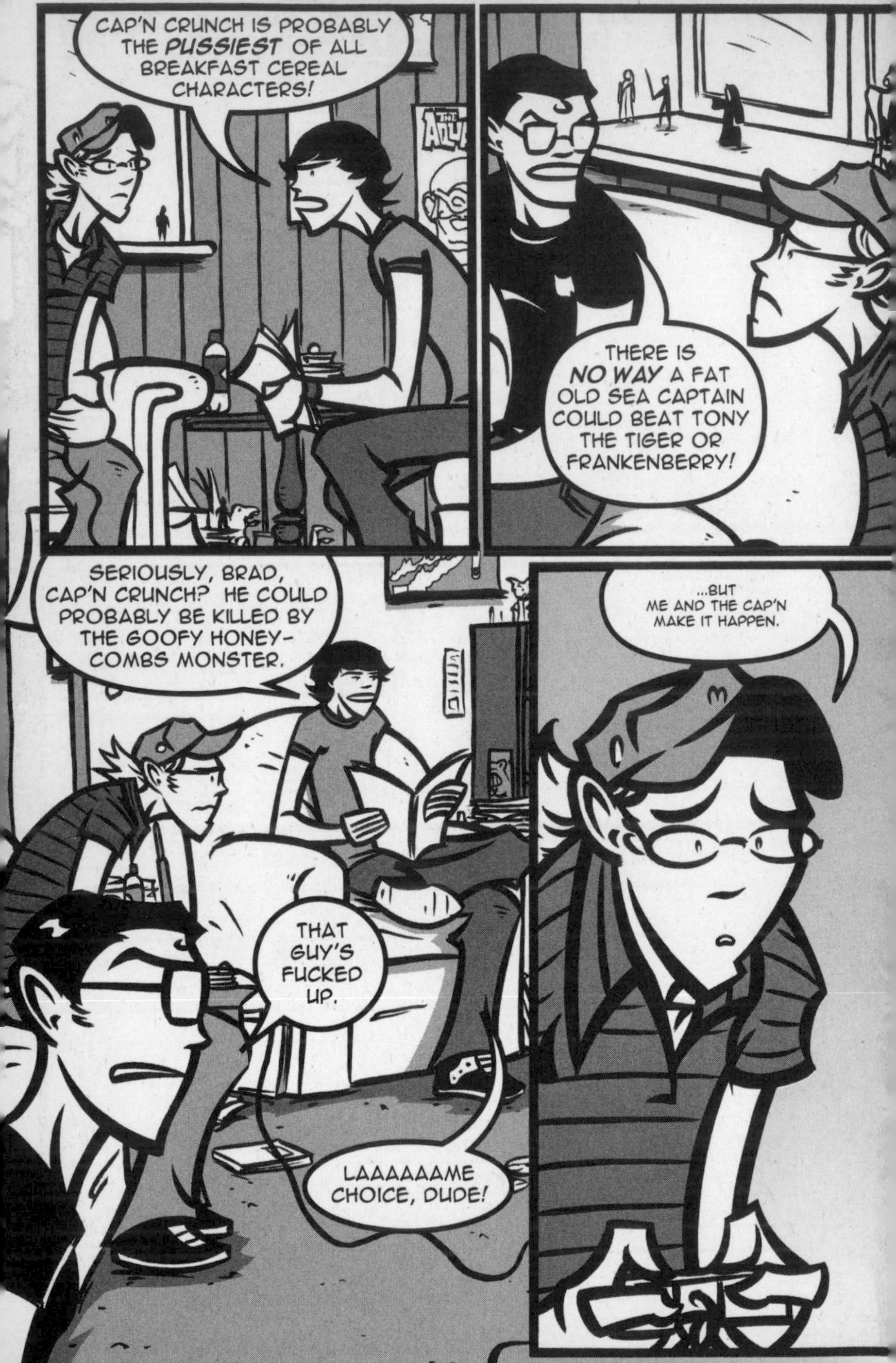
CAP'N CRUNCH IS PROBABLY THE PUSSIEST OF ALL BREAKFAST CEREAL CHARACTERS!
THE AQU
THERE IS NO WAY A FAT OLD SEA CAPTAIN COULD BEAT TONY THE TIGER OR FRANKENBERRY!
SERIOUSLY, BRAD, CAP'N CRUNCH? HE COULD PROBABLY BE KILLED BY THE GOOFY HONEY-COMBS MONSTER.
THAT GUY'S FUCKED UP.
LAAAAAAME CHOICE, DUDE!
...BUT ME AND THE CAP'N MAKE IT HAPPEN.

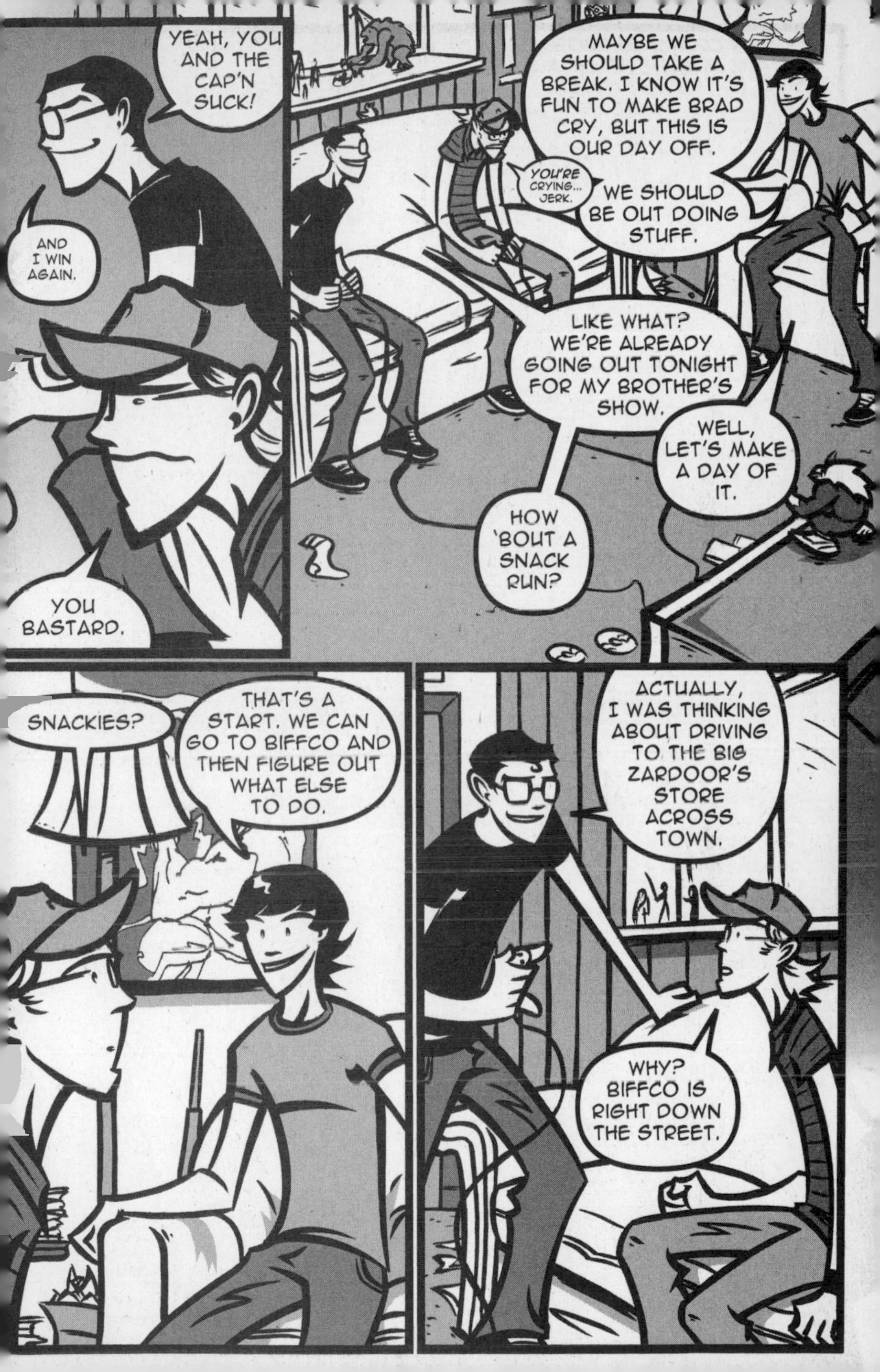

YEAH, YOU AND THE CAP'N SUCK!
AND I WIN AGAIN.
YOU BASTARD.
MAYBE WE SHOULD TAKE A BREAK. I KNOW IT'S FUN TO MAKE BRAD CRY, BUT THIS IS OUR DAY OFF.
YOU'RE CRYING... JERK.
WE SHOULD BE OUT DOING STUFF.
LIKE WHAT? WE'RE ALREADY GOING OUT TONIGHT FOR MY BROTHER'S SHOW.
WELL, LET'S MAKE A DAY OF IT.
HOW 'BOUT A SNACK RUN?
SNACKIES?
THAT'S A START. WE CAN GO TO BIFFCO AND THEN FIGURE OUT WHAT ELSE TO DO.
ACTUALLY, I WAS THINKING ABOUT DRIVING TO THE BIG ZARDOOR'S STORE ACROSS TOWN.
WHY? BIFFCO IS RIGHT DOWN THE STREET.

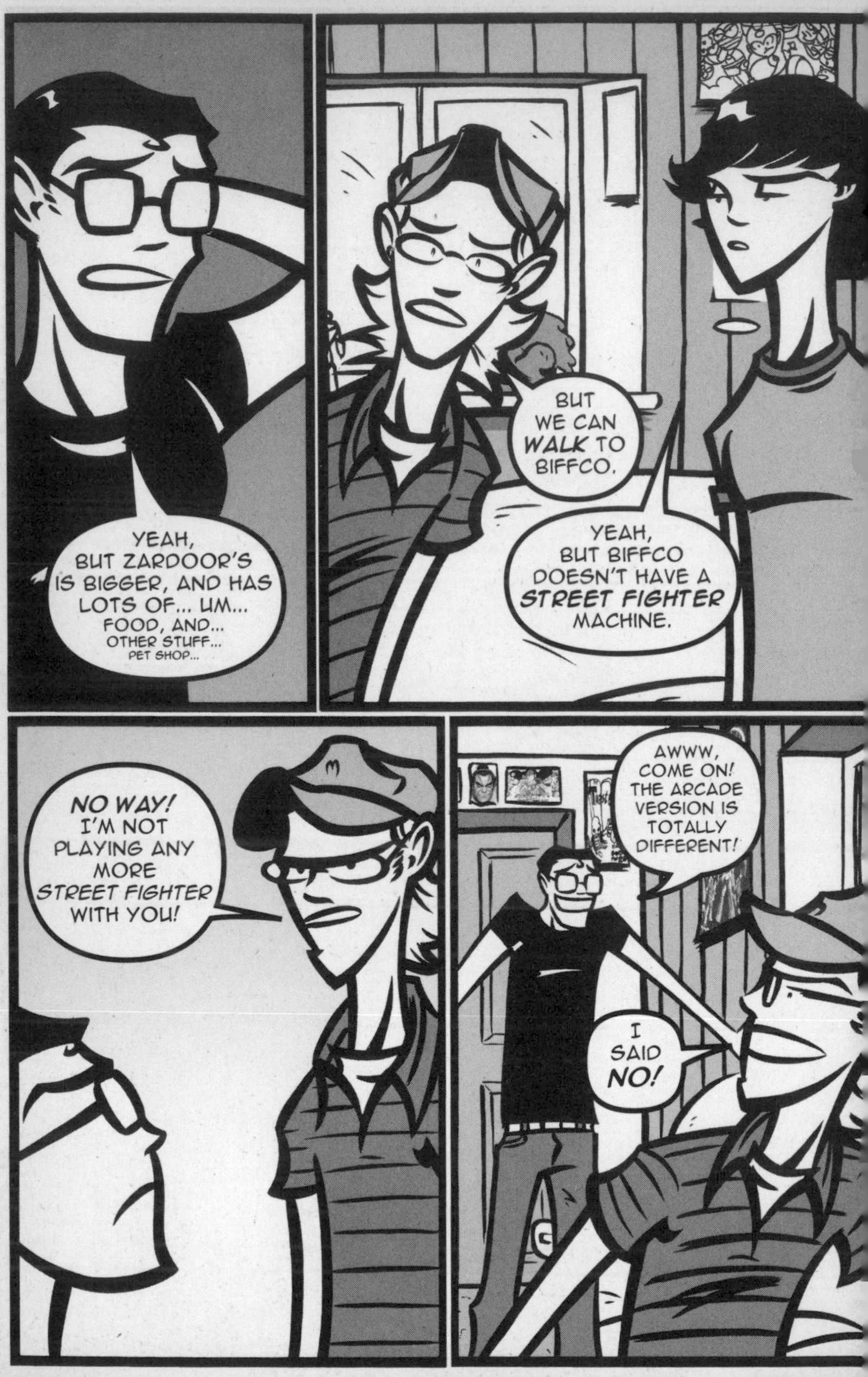
YEAH, BUT ZARDOOR'S IS BIGGER, AND HAS LOTS OF... UM... FOOD, AND... OTHER STUFF... PET SHOP...
BUT WE CAN WALK TO BIFFCO.
YEAH, BUT BIFFCO DOESN'T HAVE A STREET FIGHTER MACHINE.
NO WAY! I'M NOT PLAYING ANY MORE STREET FIGHTER WITH YOU!
AWWW, COME ON! THE ARCADE VERSION IS TOTALLY DIFFERENT!
I SAID NO!

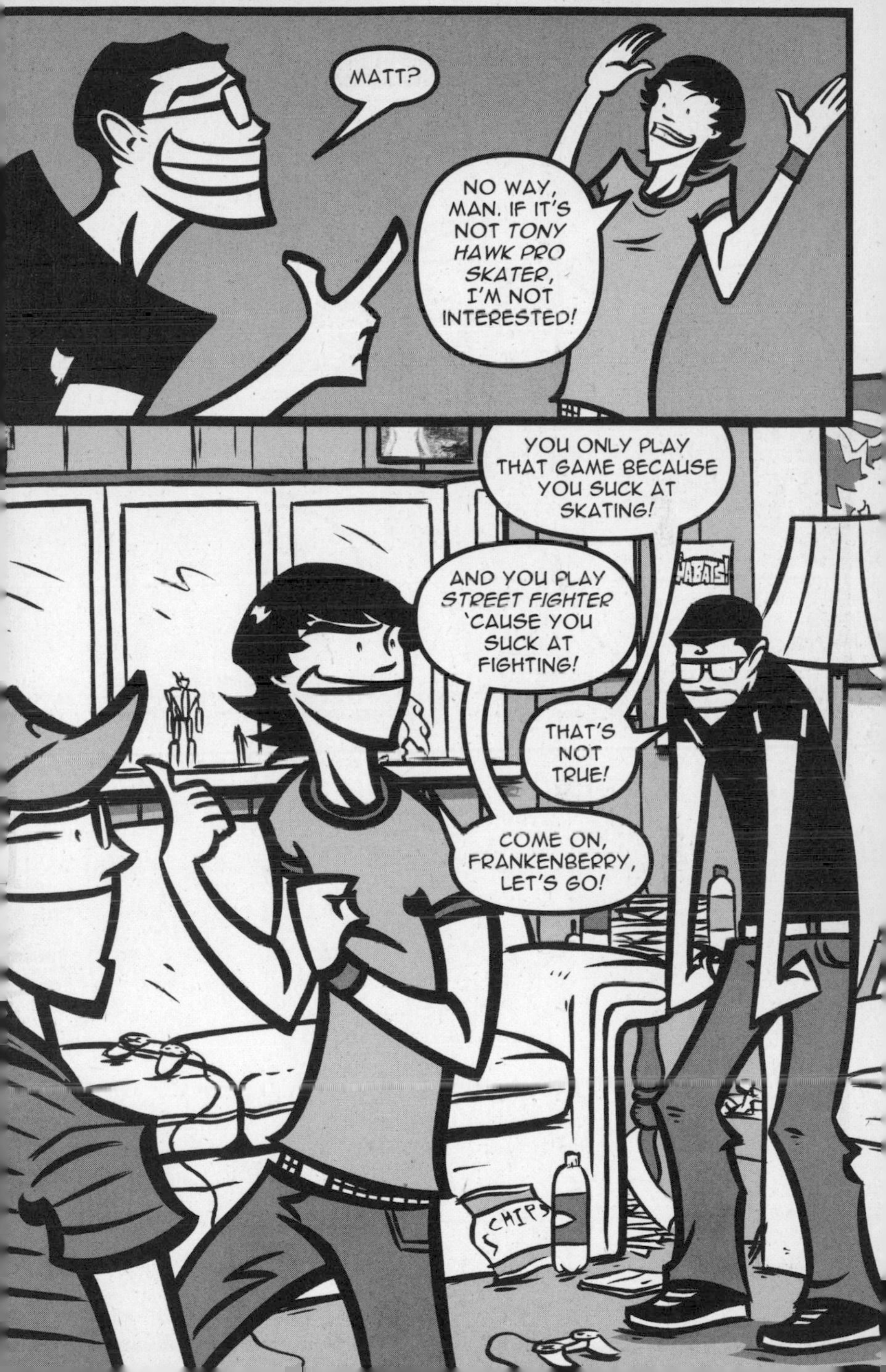
MATT?
NO WAY, MAN. IF IT'S NOT *TONY HAWK PRO SKATER*, I'M NOT INTERESTED!
YOU ONLY PLAY THAT GAME BECAUSE YOU SUCK AT SKATING!
AND YOU PLAY *STREET FIGHTER* 'CAUSE YOU SUCK AT FIGHTING!
THAT'S NOT TRUE!
COME ON, FRANKENBERRY, LET'S GO!
CHIPS

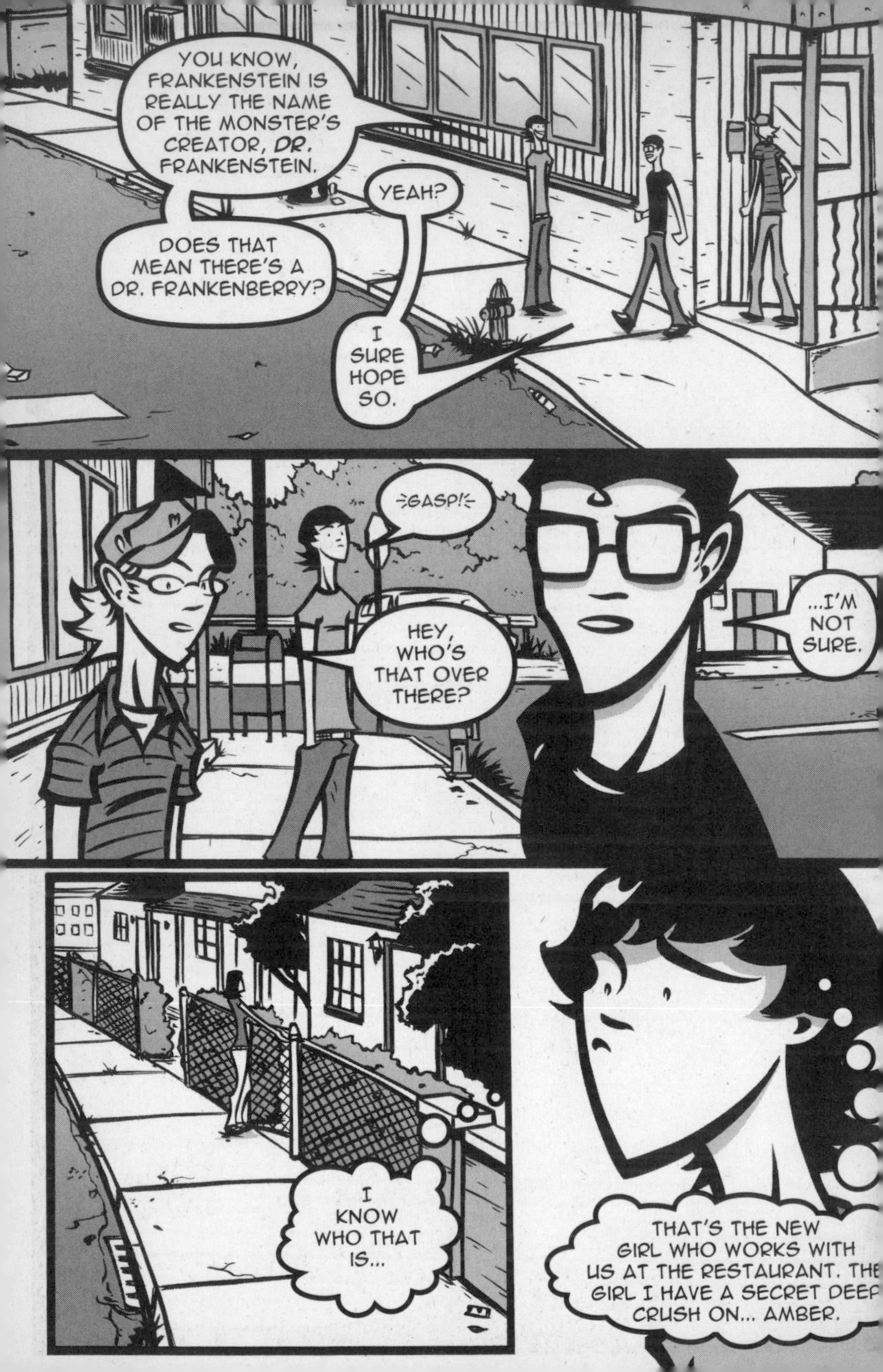
YOU KNOW, FRANKENSTEIN IS REALLY THE NAME OF THE MONSTER'S CREATOR, DR. FRANKENSTEIN.
YEAH?
DOES THAT MEAN THERE'S A DR. FRANKENBERRY?
I SURE HOPE SO.
GASP!
HEY, WHO'S THAT OVER THERE?
...I'M NOT SURE.
I KNOW WHO THAT IS...
THAT'S THE NEW GIRL WHO WORKS WITH US AT THE RESTAURANT. THE GIRL I HAVE A SECRET DEEP CRUSH ON... AMBER.

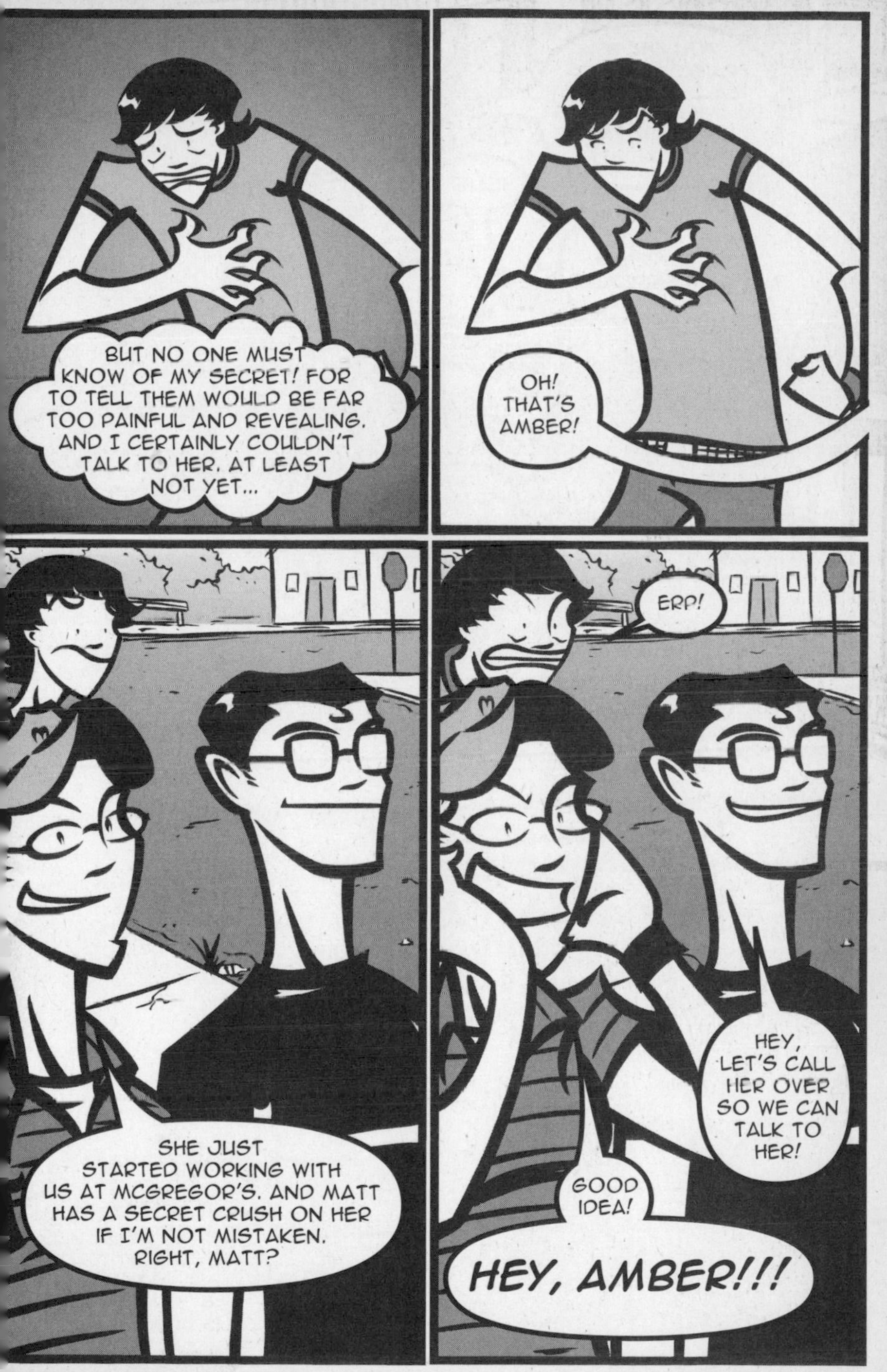
BUT NO ONE MUST KNOW OF MY SECRET! FOR TO TELL THEM WOULD BE FAR TOO PAINFUL AND REVEALING. AND I CERTAINLY COULDN'T TALK TO HER. AT LEAST NOT YET...
OH! THAT'S AMBER!
SHE JUST STARTED WORKING WITH US AT MCGREGOR'S. AND MATT HAS A SECRET CRUSH ON HER IF I'M NOT MISTAKEN. RIGHT, MATT?
ERP!
HEY, LET'S CALL HER OVER SO WE CAN TALK TO HER!
GOOD IDEA!
HEY, AMBER!!!

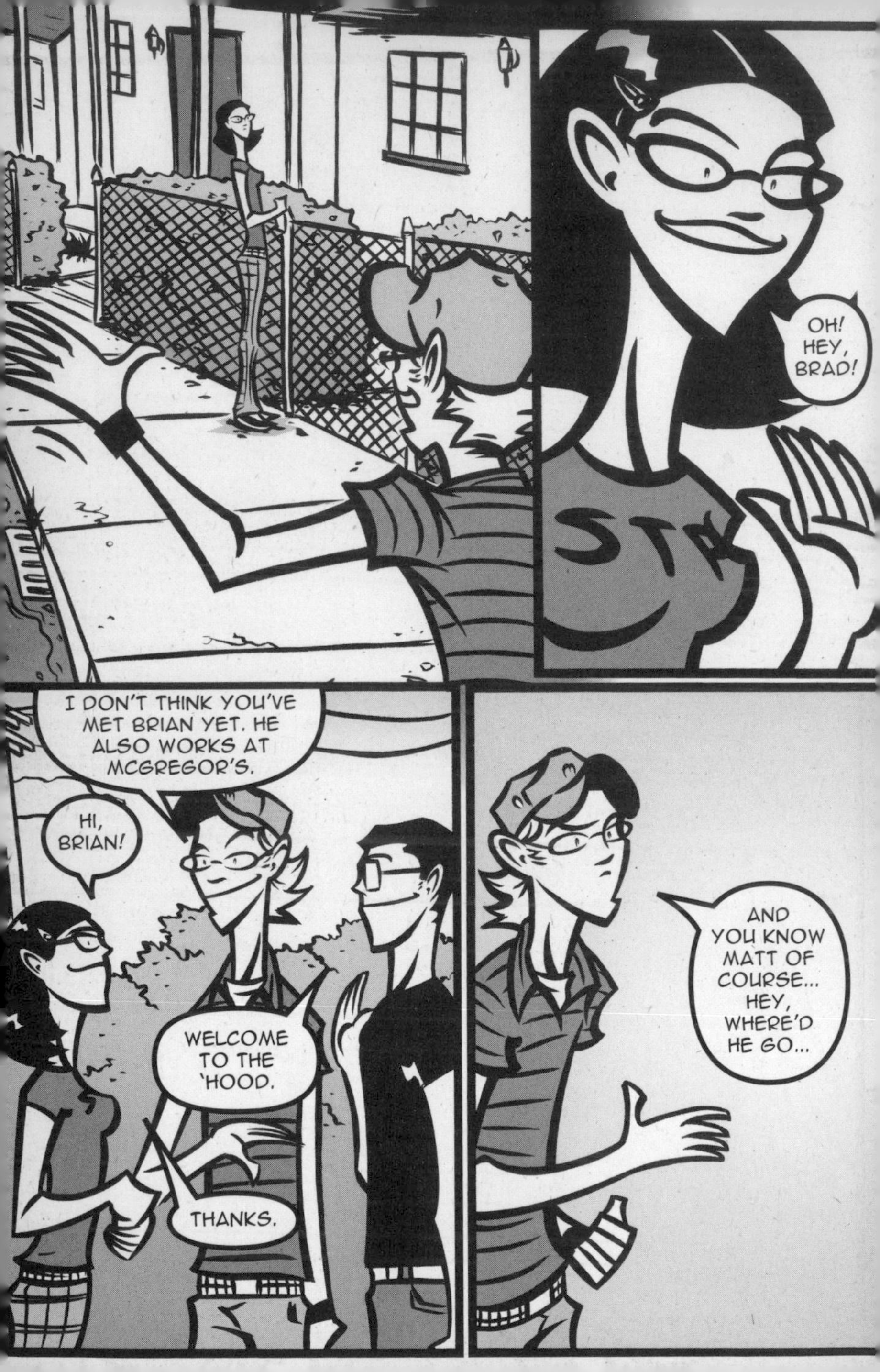
OH! HEY, BRAD!
I DON'T THINK YOU'VE MET BRIAN YET. HE ALSO WORKS AT MCGREGOR'S.
HI, BRIAN!
WELCOME TO THE 'HOOD.
THANKS.
AND YOU KNOW MATT OF COURSE... HEY, WHERE'D HE GO...

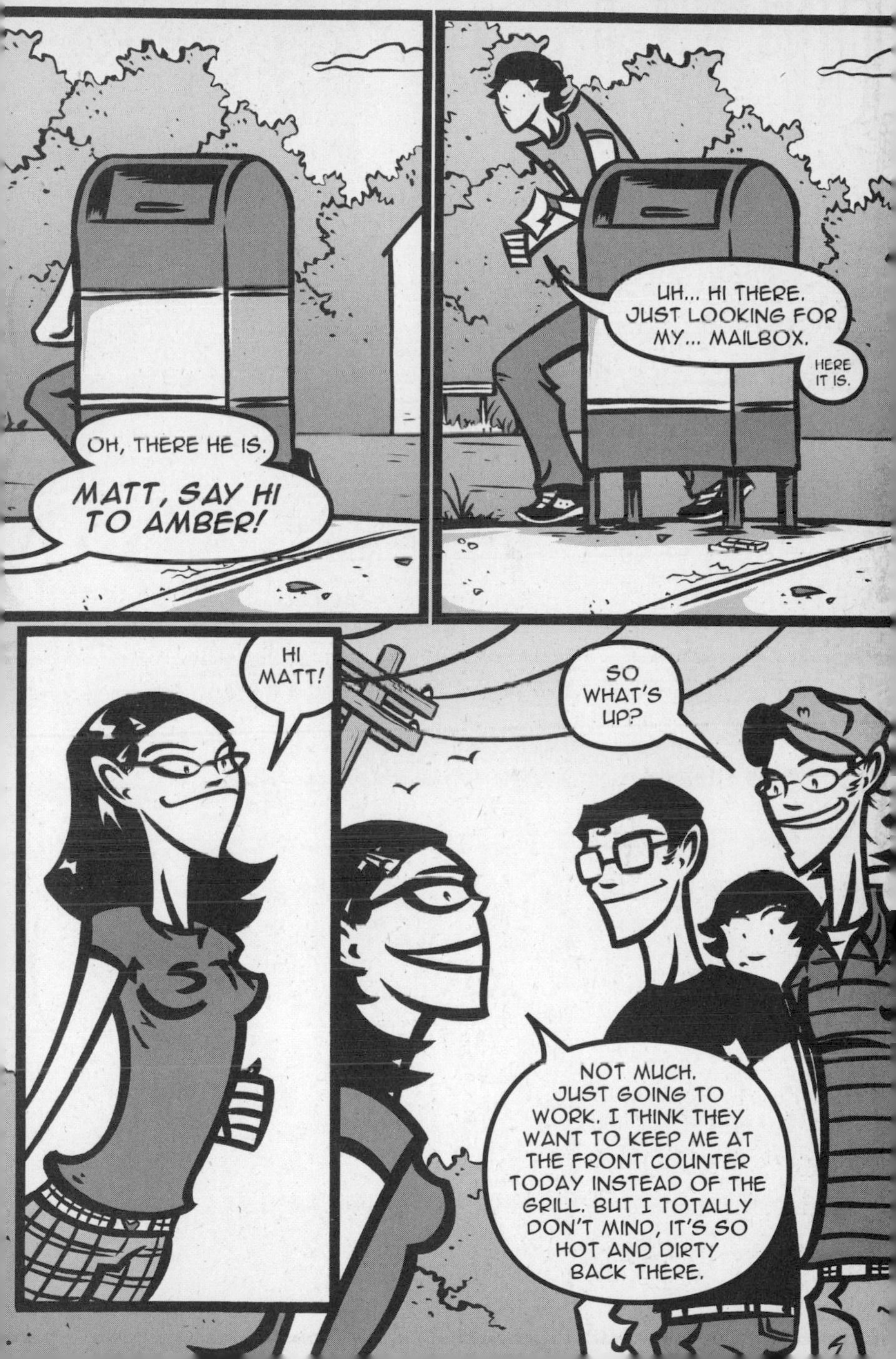
OH, THERE HE IS.
MATT, SAY HI TO AMBER!
UH... HI THERE. JUST LOOKING FOR MY... MAILBOX.
HERE IT IS.
HI MATT!
SO WHAT'S UP?
NOT MUCH. JUST GOING TO WORK. I THINK THEY WANT TO KEEP ME AT THE FRONT COUNTER TODAY INSTEAD OF THE GRILL. BUT I TOTALLY DON'T MIND, IT'S SO HOT AND DIRTY BACK THERE.

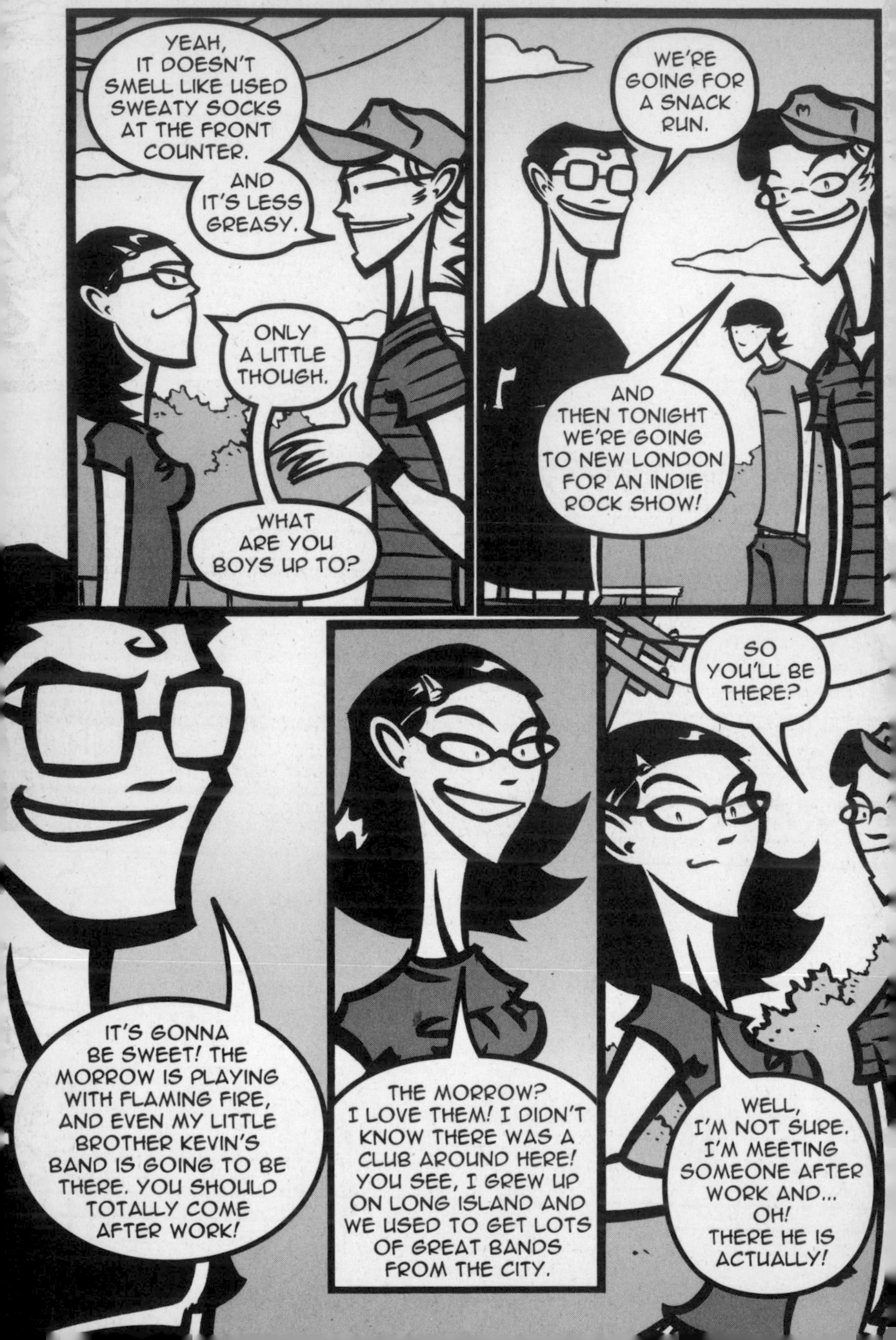
YEAH, IT DOESN'T SMELL LIKE USED SWEATY SOCKS AT THE FRONT COUNTER.
AND IT'S LESS GREASY.
ONLY A LITTLE THOUGH.
WHAT ARE YOU BOYS UP TO?
WE'RE GOING FOR A SNACK RUN.
AND THEN TONIGHT WE'RE GOING TO NEW LONDON FOR AN INDIE ROCK SHOW!
IT'S GONNA BE SWEET! THE MORROW IS PLAYING WITH FLAMING FIRE, AND EVEN MY LITTLE BROTHER KEVIN'S BAND IS GOING TO BE THERE. YOU SHOULD TOTALLY COME AFTER WORK!
THE MORROW? I LOVE THEM! I DIDN'T KNOW THERE WAS A CLUB AROUND HERE! YOU SEE, I GREW UP ON LONG ISLAND AND WE USED TO GET LOTS OF GREAT BANDS FROM THE CITY.
SO YOU'LL BE THERE?
WELL, I'M NOT SURE. I'M MEETING SOMEONE AFTER WORK AND... OH! THERE HE IS ACTUALLY!

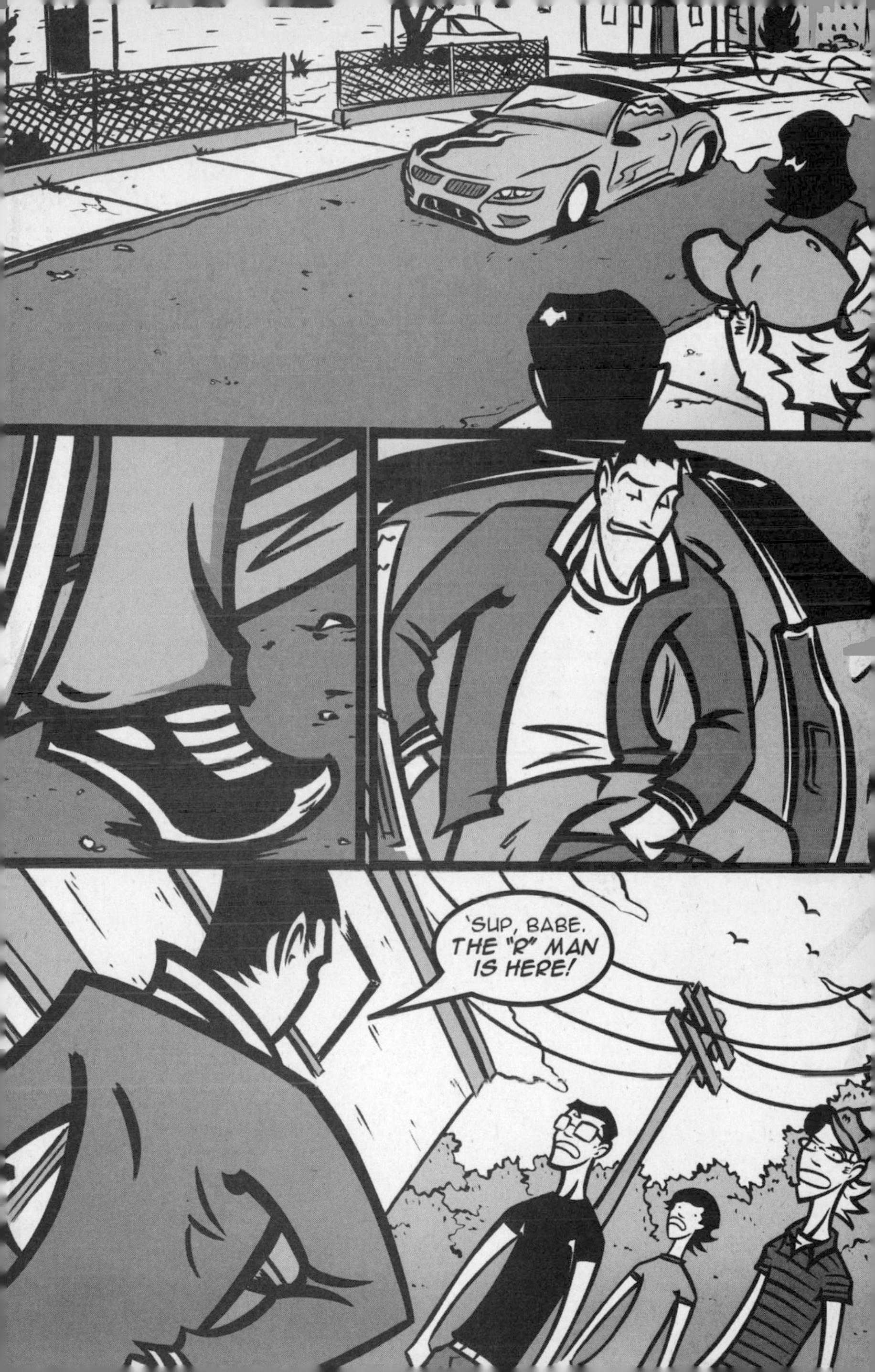
'SUP, BABE. THE "R" MAN IS HERE!

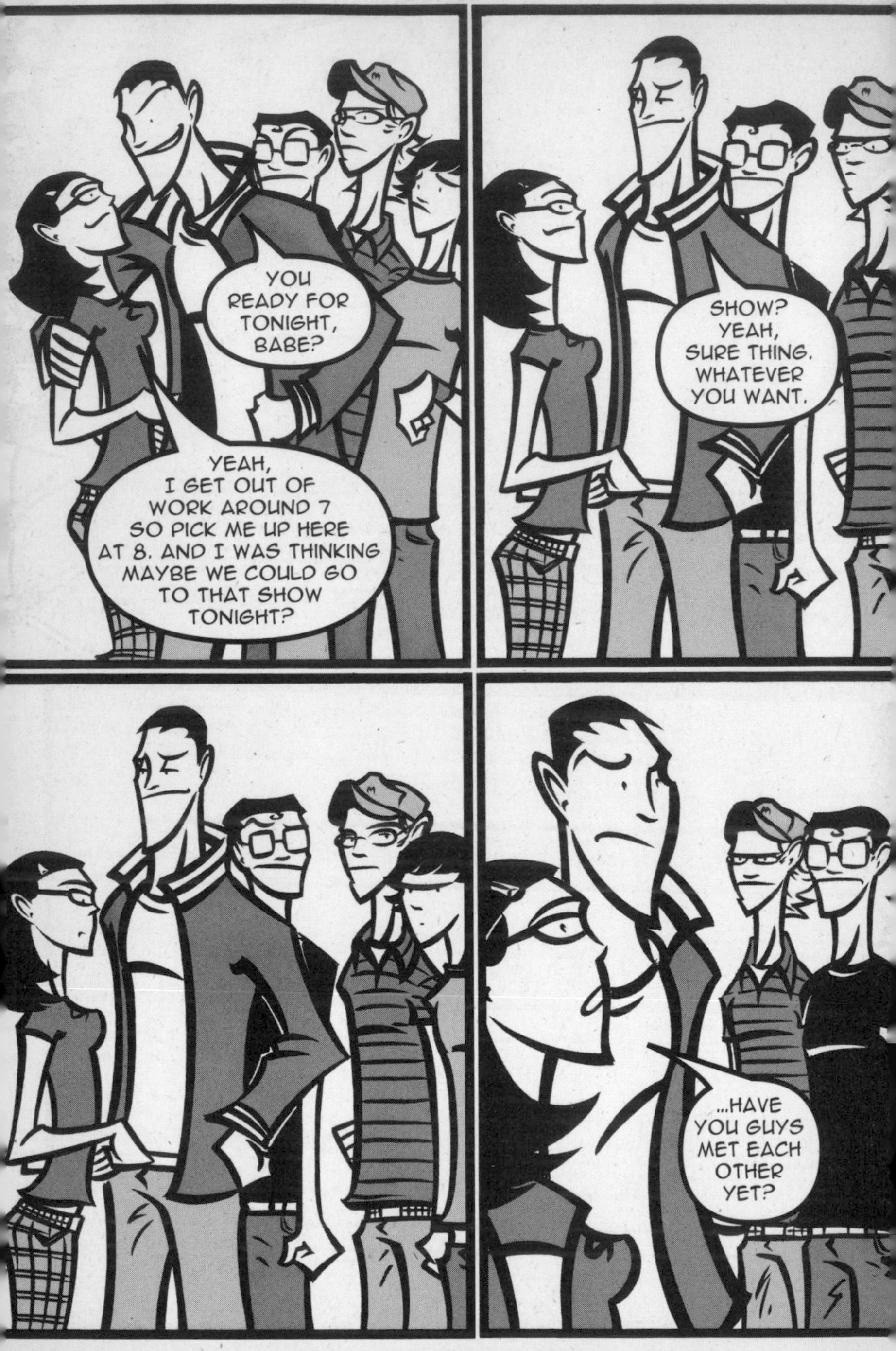
YOU READY FOR TONIGHT, BABE?
YEAH, I GET OUT OF WORK AROUND 7 SO PICK ME UP HERE AT 8. AND I WAS THINKING MAYBE WE COULD GO TO THAT SHOW TONIGHT?
SHOW? YEAH, SURE THING. WHATEVER YOU WANT.
...HAVE YOU GUYS MET EACH OTHER YET?

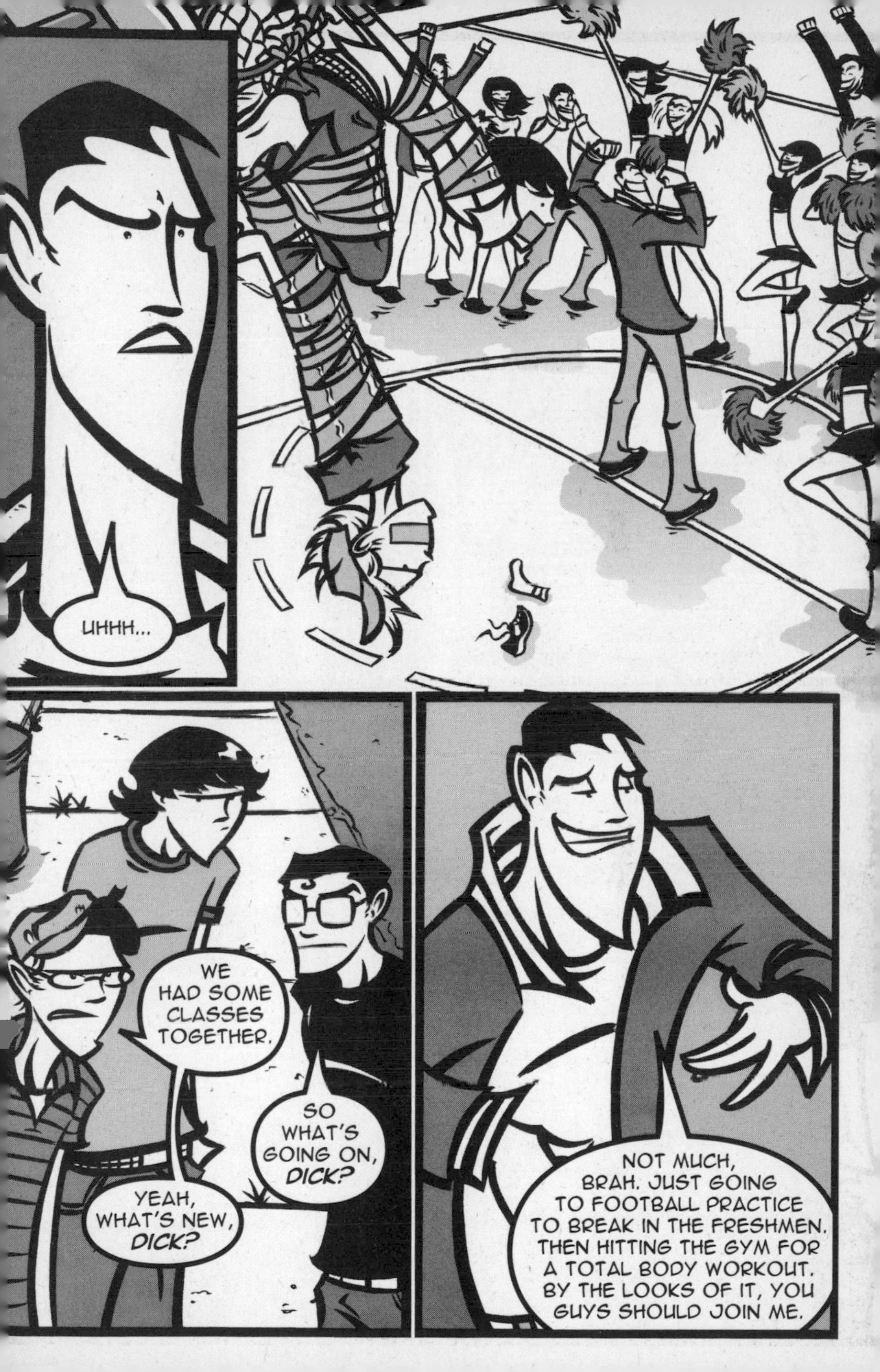
UHHH...
WE HAD SOME CLASSES TOGETHER.
SO WHAT'S GOING ON, *DICK?*
YEAH, WHAT'S NEW, *DICK?*
NOT MUCH, BRAH. JUST GOING TO FOOTBALL PRACTICE TO BREAK IN THE FRESHMEN. THEN HITTING THE GYM FOR A TOTAL BODY WORKOUT. BY THE LOOKS OF IT, YOU GUYS SHOULD JOIN ME.

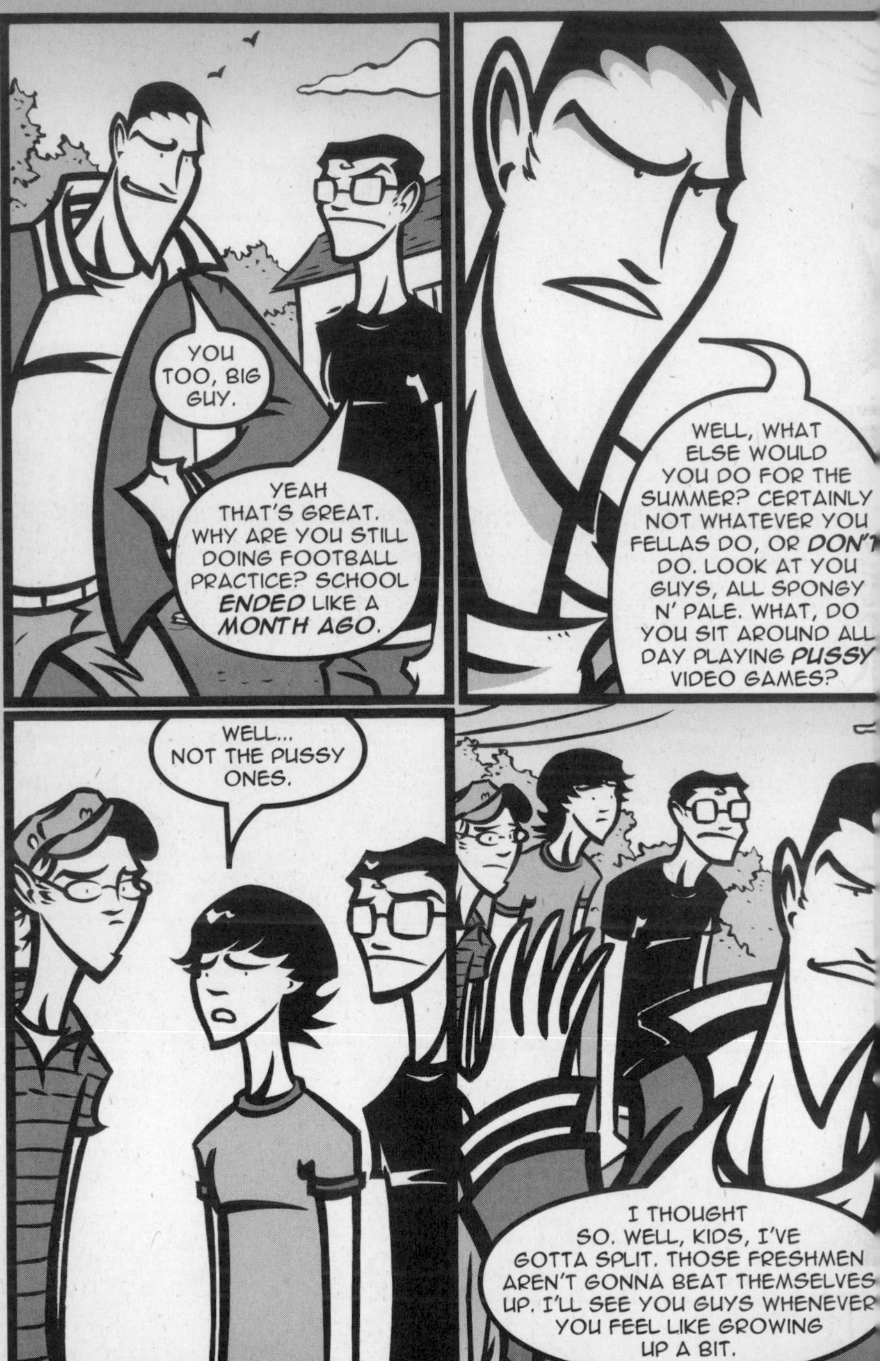
YOU TOO, BIG GUY.
YEAH THAT'S GREAT. WHY ARE YOU STILL DOING FOOTBALL PRACTICE? SCHOOL ENDED LIKE A MONTH AGO.
WELL, WHAT ELSE WOULD YOU DO FOR THE SUMMER? CERTAINLY NOT WHATEVER YOU FELLAS DO, OR DON'T DO. LOOK AT YOU GUYS, ALL SPONGY N' PALE. WHAT, DO YOU SIT AROUND ALL DAY PLAYING PUSSY VIDEO GAMES?
WELL... NOT THE PUSSY ONES.
I THOUGHT SO. WELL, KIDS, I'VE GOTTA SPLIT. THOSE FRESHMEN AREN'T GONNA BEAT THEMSELVES UP. I'LL SEE YOU GUYS WHENEVER YOU FEEL LIKE GROWING UP A BIT.

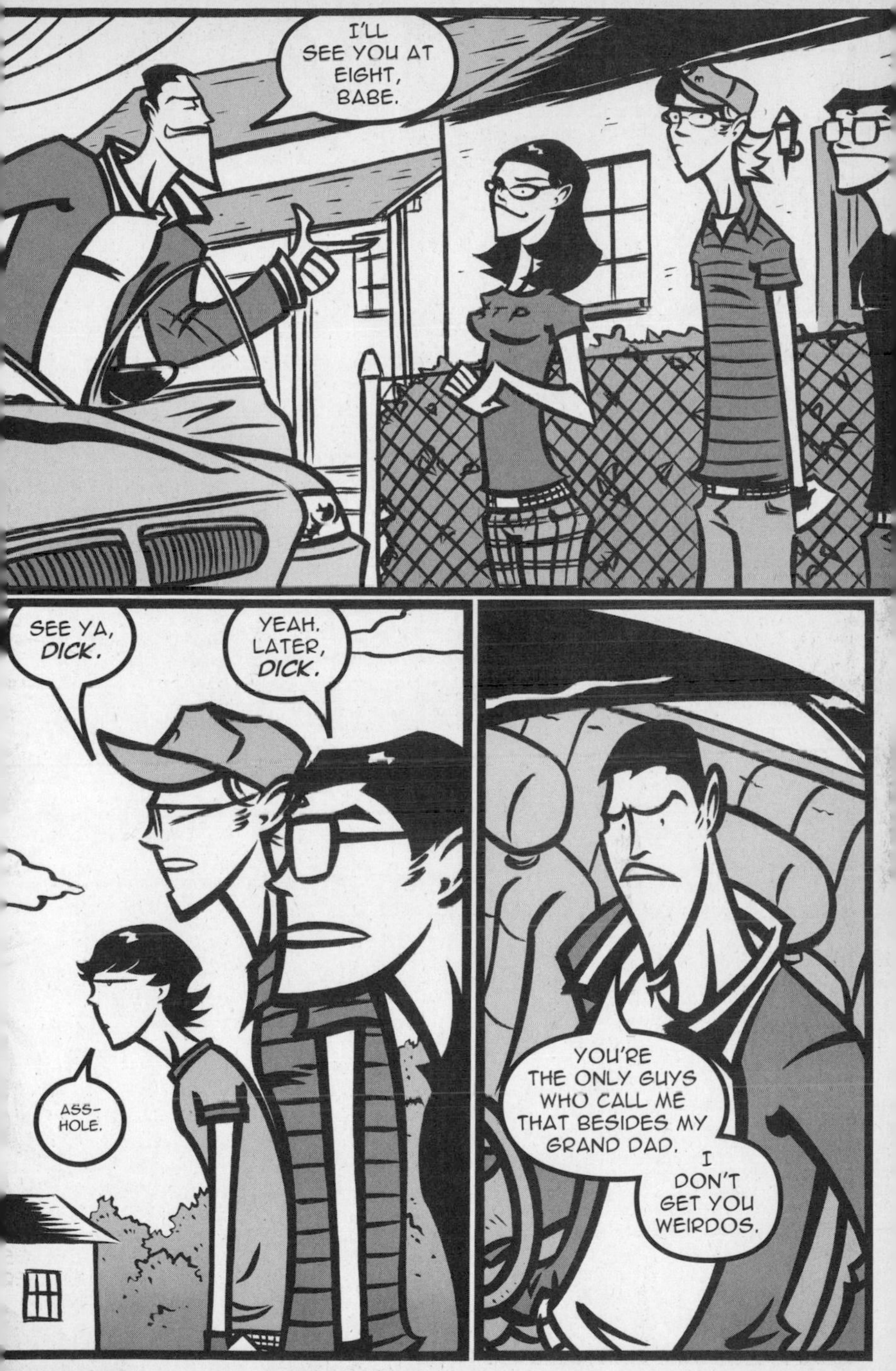
I'LL SEE YOU AT EIGHT, BABE.
SEE YA, DICK.
YEAH. LATER, DICK.
ASS-HOLE.
YOU'RE THE ONLY GUYS WHO CALL ME THAT BESIDES MY GRAND DAD.
I DON'T GET YOU WEIRDOS.

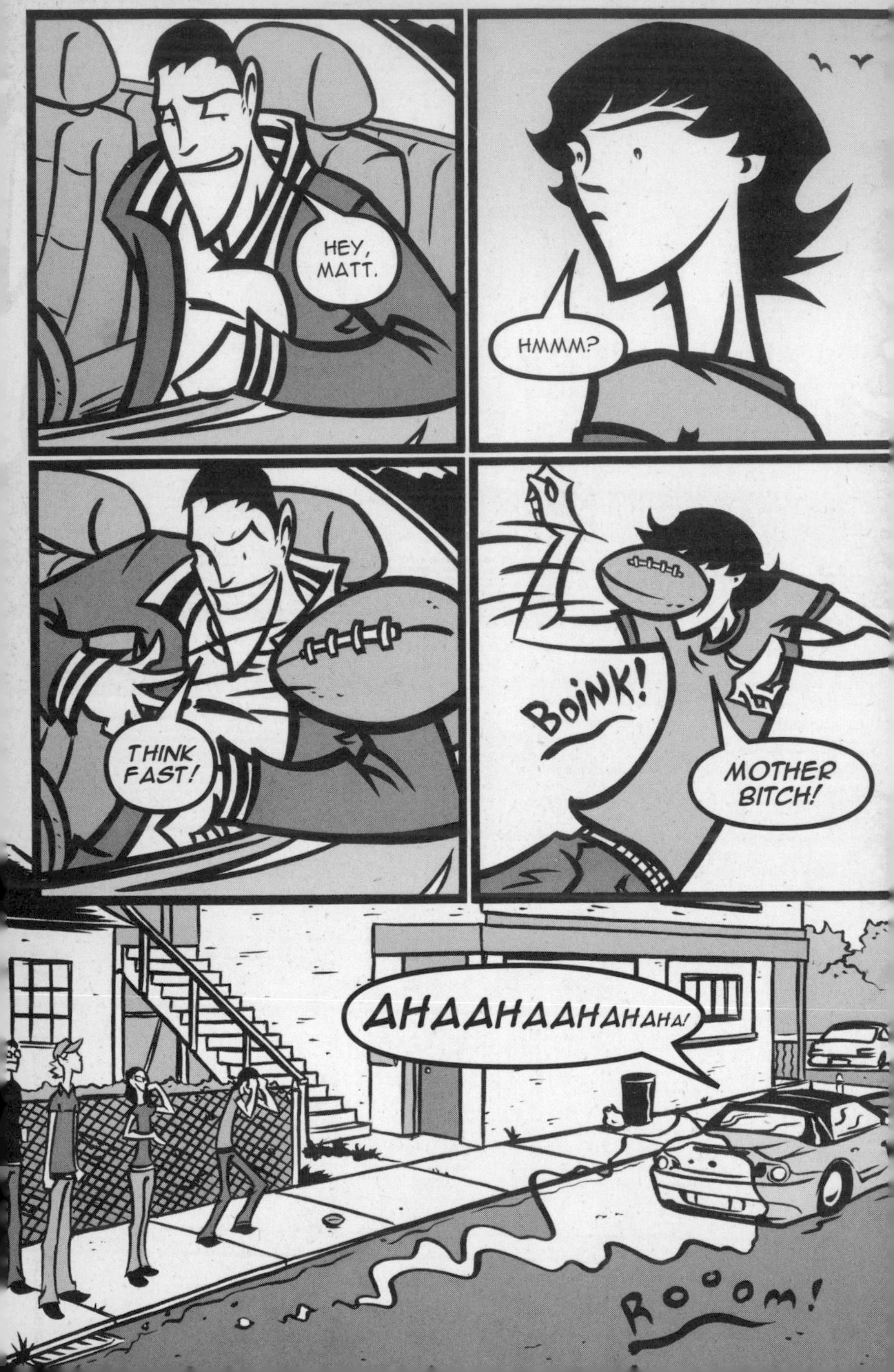
HEY, MATT.
HMMM?
THINK FAST!
BOINK!
MOTHER BITCH!
AHAAHAAHAHAHA!
ROOOM!

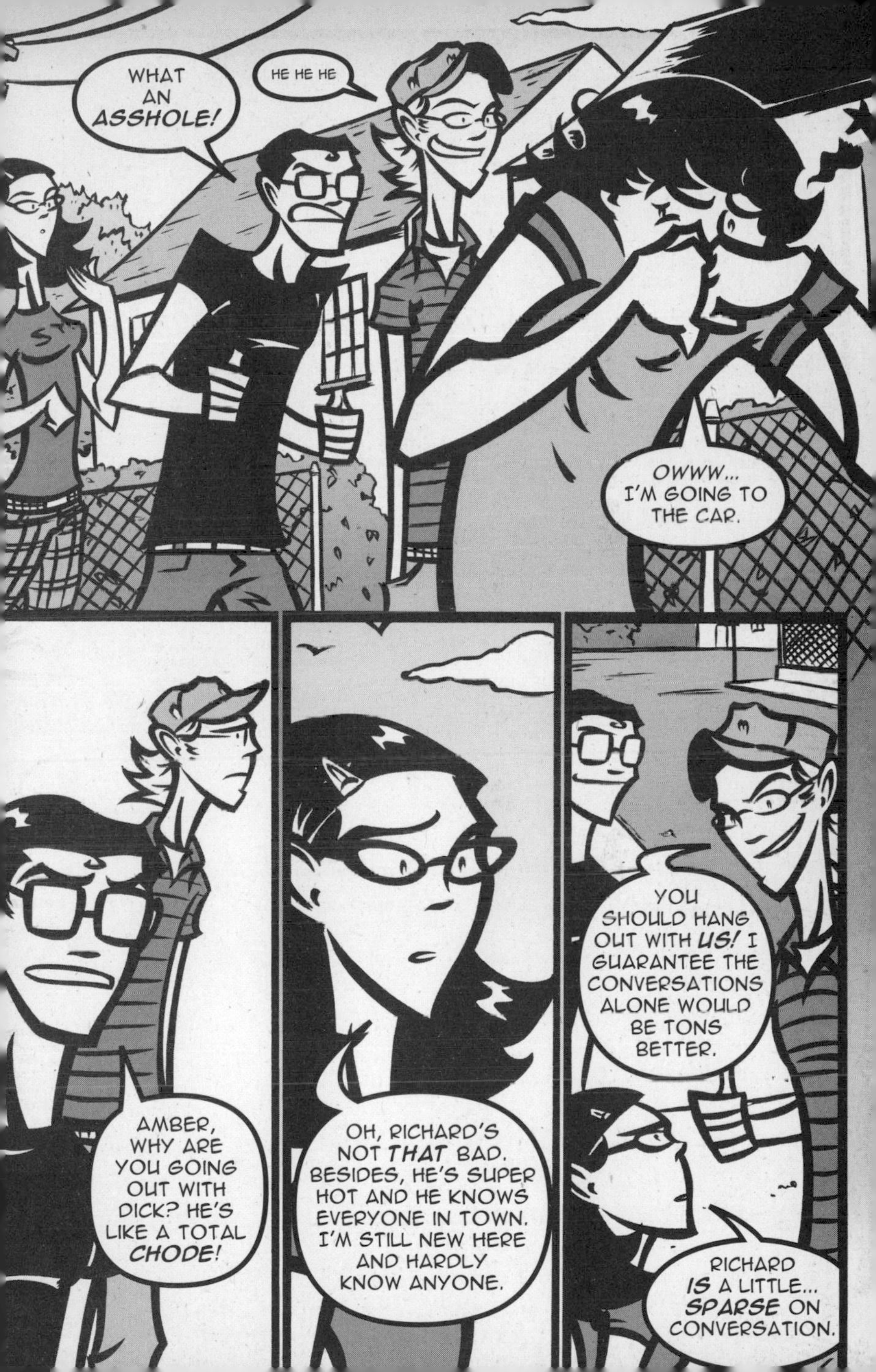
WHAT AN ASSHOLE!
HE HE HE
OWWW... I'M GOING TO THE CAR.
AMBER, WHY ARE YOU GOING OUT WITH DICK? HE'S LIKE A TOTAL CHODE!
OH, RICHARD'S NOT THAT BAD. BESIDES, HE'S SUPER HOT AND HE KNOWS EVERYONE IN TOWN. I'M STILL NEW HERE AND HARDLY KNOW ANYONE.
YOU SHOULD HANG OUT WITH US! I GUARANTEE THE CONVERSATIONS ALONE WOULD BE TONS BETTER.
RICHARD IS A LITTLE... SPARSE ON CONVERSATION.

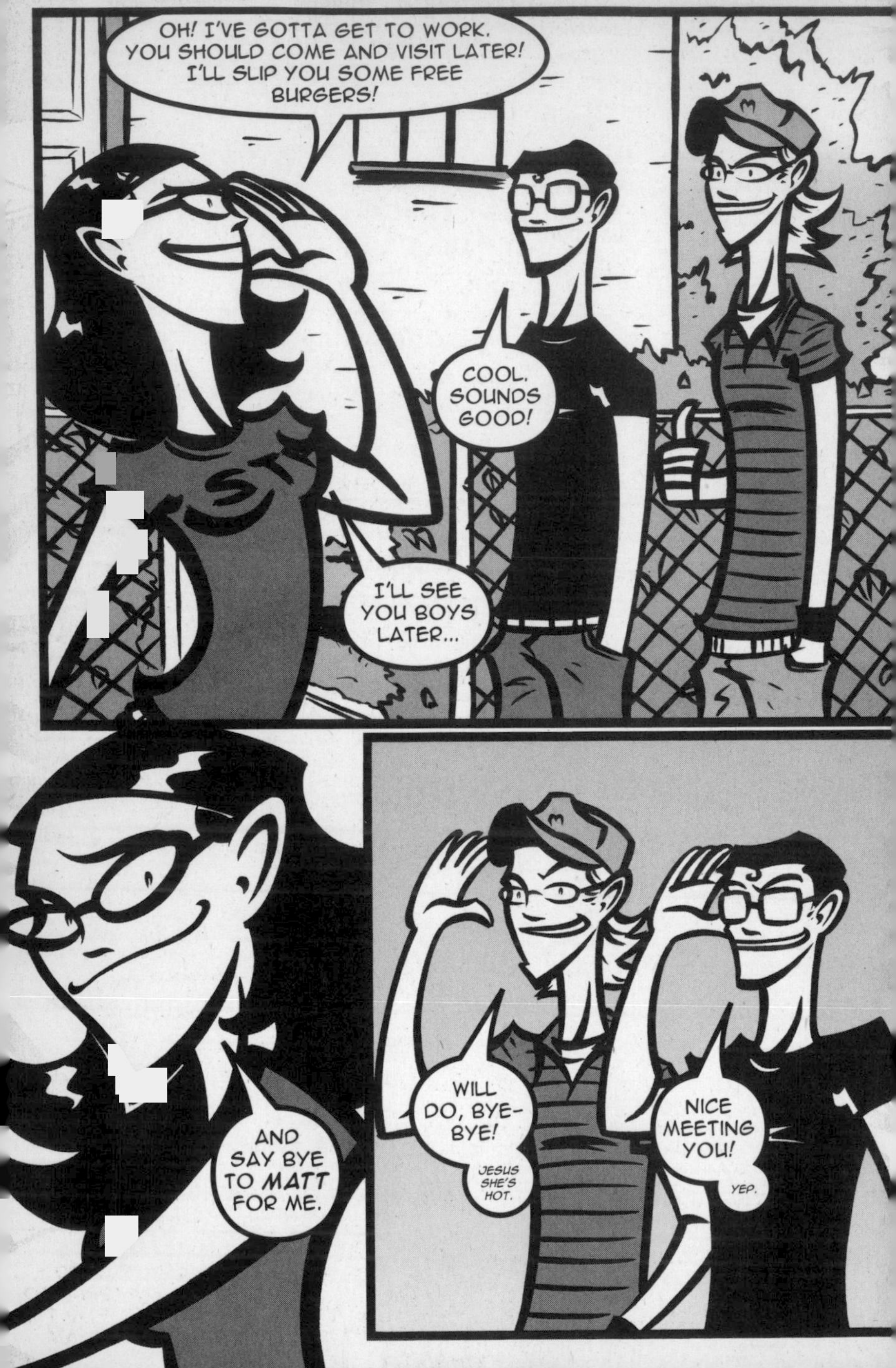
OH! I'VE GOTTA GET TO WORK. YOU SHOULD COME AND VISIT LATER! I'LL SLIP YOU SOME FREE BURGERS!
COOL. SOUNDS GOOD!
I'LL SEE YOU BOYS LATER...
AND SAY BYE TO MATT FOR ME.
WILL DO, BYE-BYE!
JESUS SHE'S HOT.
NICE MEETING YOU!
YEP.

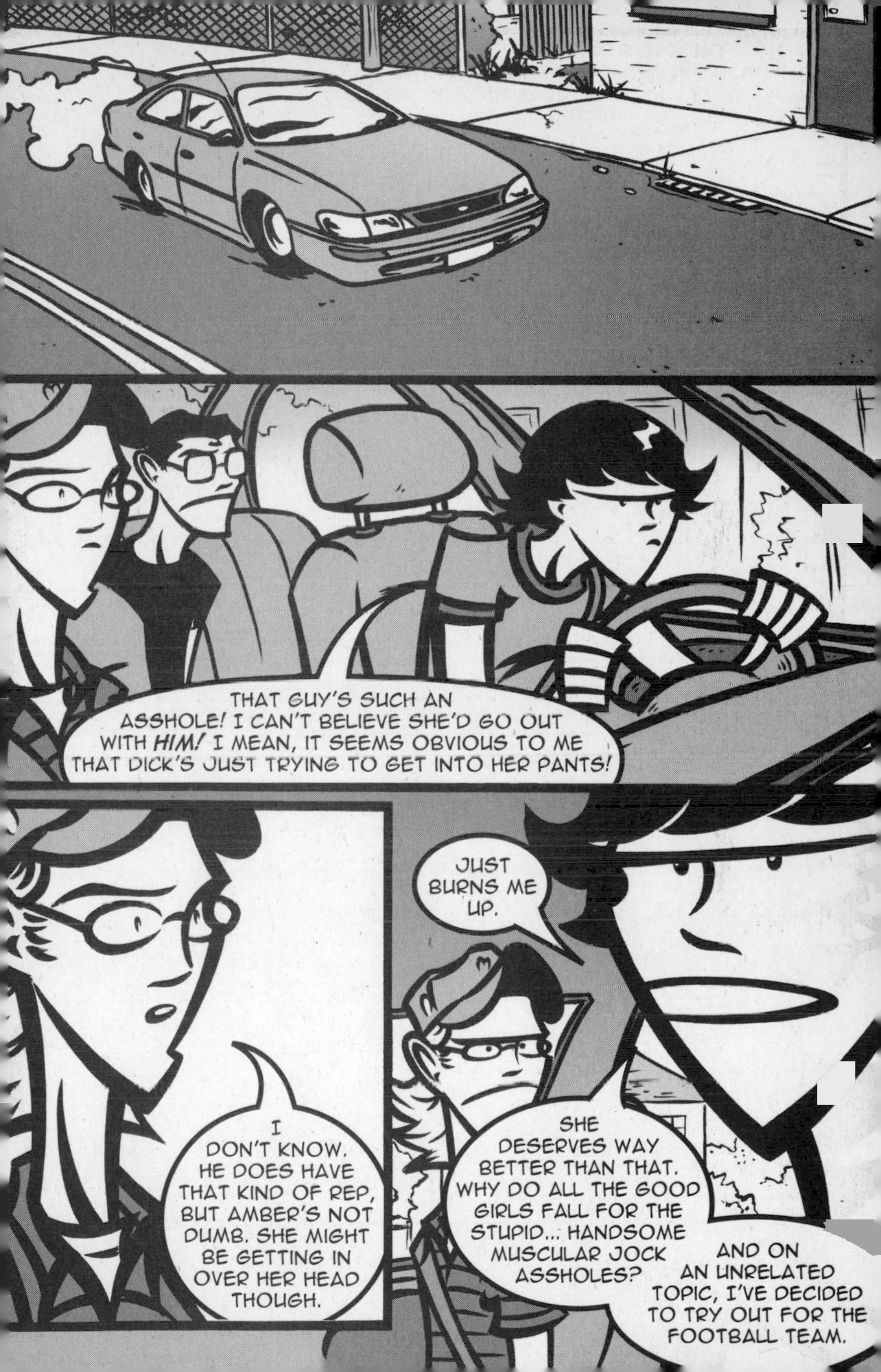
THAT GUY'S SUCH AN ASSHOLE! I CAN'T BELIEVE SHE'D GO OUT WITH *HIM!* I MEAN, IT SEEMS OBVIOUS TO ME THAT DICK'S JUST TRYING TO GET INTO HER PANTS!
I DON'T KNOW. HE DOES HAVE THAT KIND OF REP, BUT AMBER'S NOT DUMB. SHE MIGHT BE GETTING IN OVER HER HEAD THOUGH.
JUST BURNS ME UP.
SHE DESERVES WAY BETTER THAN THAT. WHY DO ALL THE GOOD GIRLS FALL FOR THE STUPID... HANDSOME MUSCULAR JOCK ASSHOLES?
AND ON AN UNRELATED TOPIC, I'VE DECIDED TO TRY OUT FOR THE FOOTBALL TEAM.

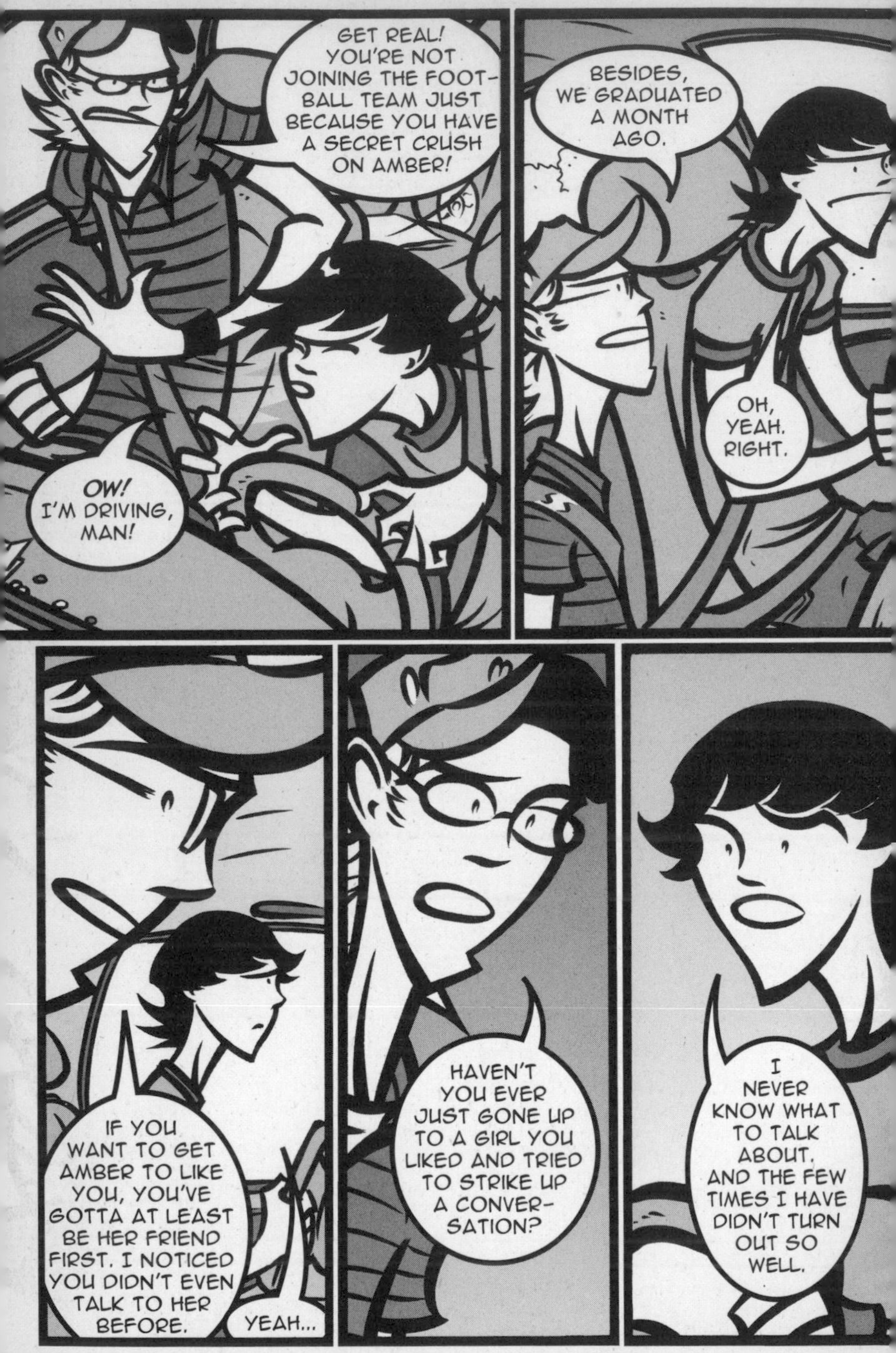
GET REAL! YOU'RE NOT JOINING THE FOOT-BALL TEAM JUST BECAUSE YOU HAVE A SECRET CRUSH ON AMBER!
OW! I'M DRIVING, MAN!
BESIDES, WE GRADUATED A MONTH AGO.
OH, YEAH. RIGHT.
IF YOU WANT TO GET AMBER TO LIKE YOU, YOU'VE GOTTA AT LEAST BE HER FRIEND FIRST. I NOTICED YOU DIDN'T EVEN TALK TO HER BEFORE.
YEAH...
HAVEN'T YOU EVER JUST GONE UP TO A GIRL YOU LIKED AND TRIED TO STRIKE UP A CONVER-SATION?
I NEVER KNOW WHAT TO TALK ABOUT. AND THE FEW TIMES I HAVE DIDN'T TURN OUT SO WELL.

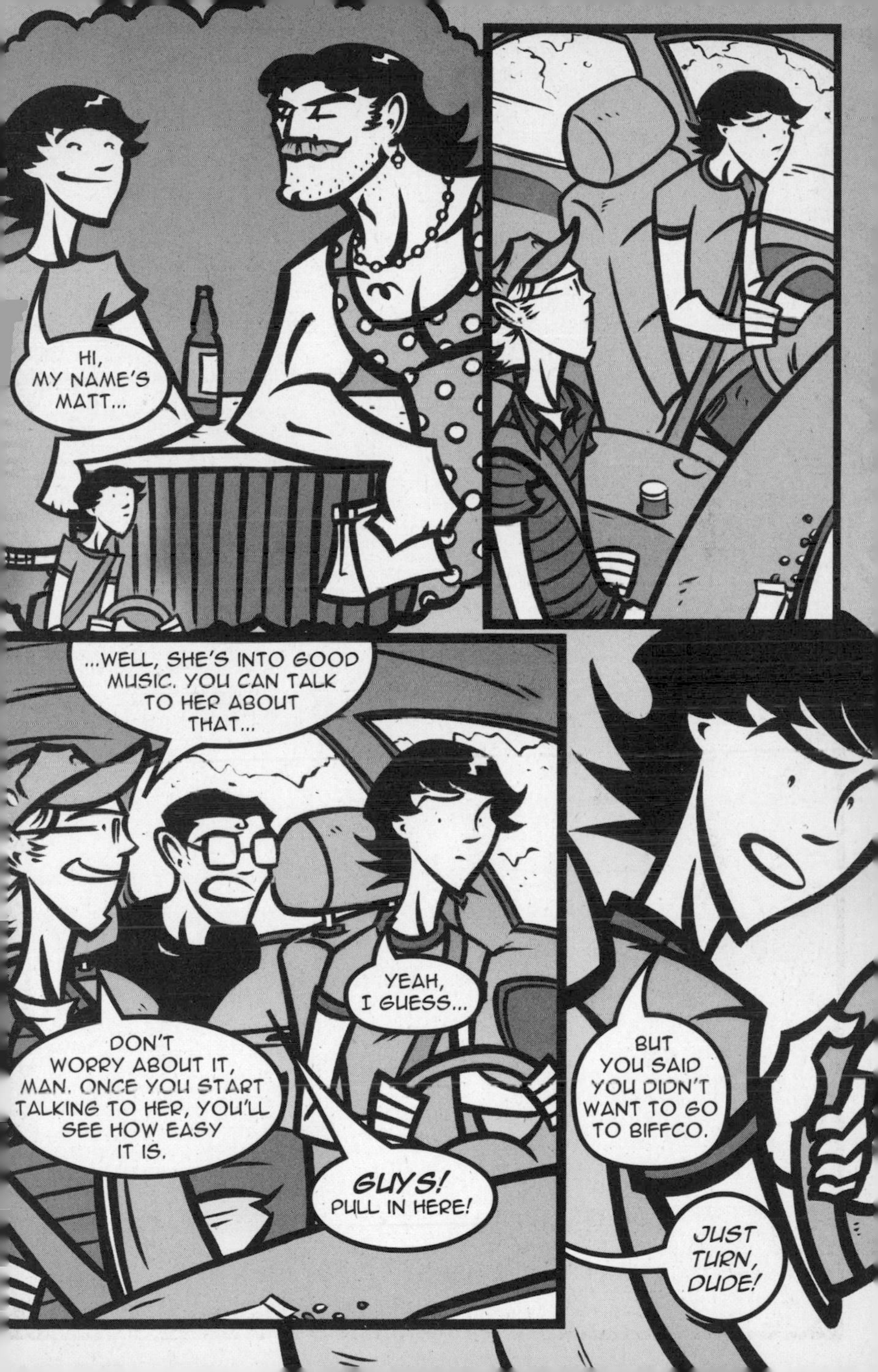
HI, MY NAME'S MATT...
...WELL, SHE'S INTO GOOD MUSIC. YOU CAN TALK TO HER ABOUT THAT...
YEAH, I GUESS...
DON'T WORRY ABOUT IT, MAN. ONCE YOU START TALKING TO HER, YOU'LL SEE HOW EASY IT IS.
GUYS! PULL IN HERE!
BUT YOU SAID YOU DIDN'T WANT TO GO TO BIFFCO.
JUST TURN, DUDE!

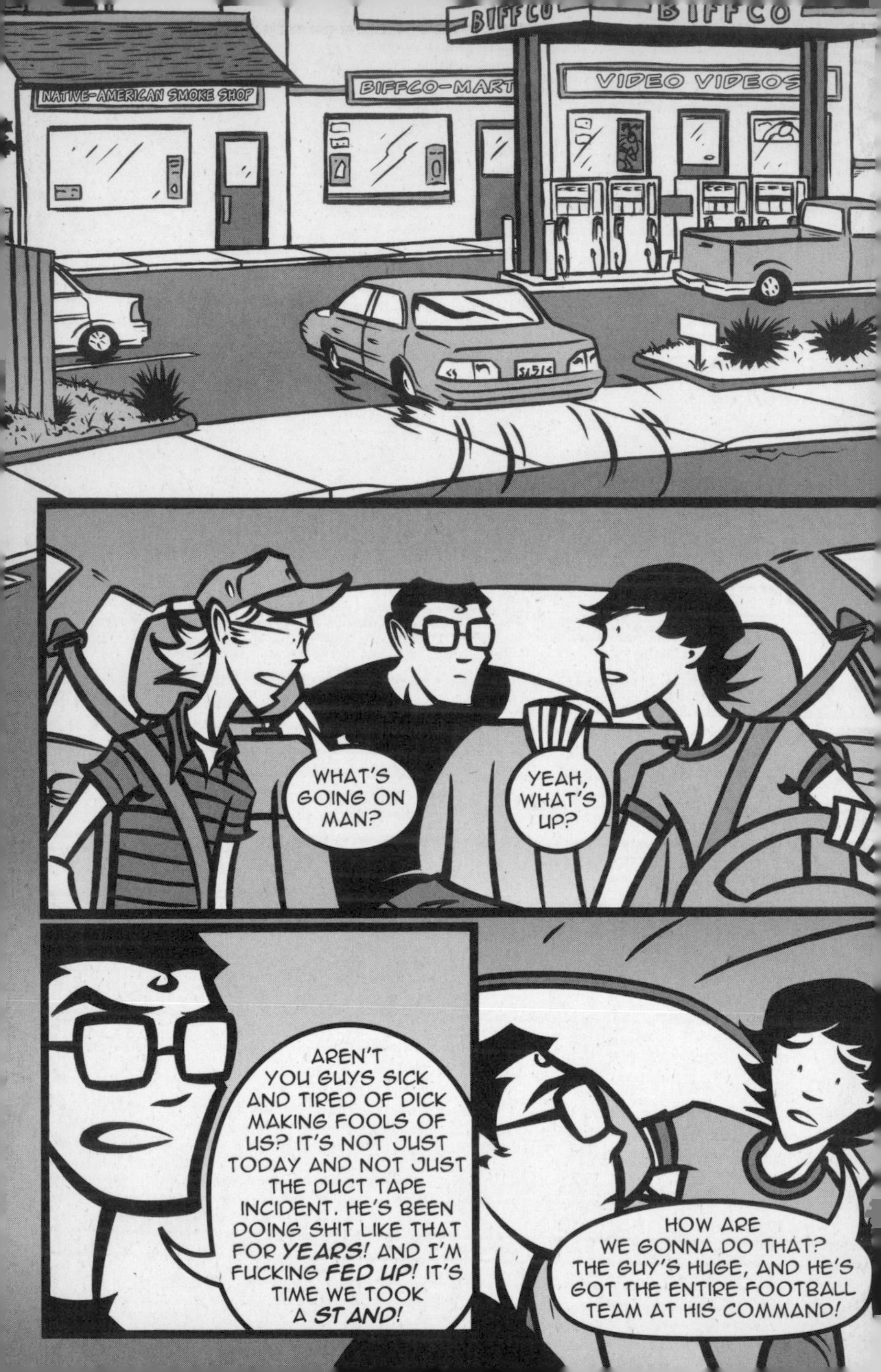
BIFFCO
BIFFCO
NATIVE-AMERICAN SMOKE SHOP
BIFFCO-MART
VIDEO VIDEOS
WHAT'S GOING ON MAN?
YEAH, WHAT'S UP?
AREN'T YOU GUYS SICK AND TIRED OF DICK MAKING FOOLS OF US? IT'S NOT JUST TODAY AND NOT JUST THE DUCT TAPE INCIDENT. HE'S BEEN DOING SHIT LIKE THAT FOR *YEARS!* AND I'M FUCKING *FED UP!* IT'S TIME WE TOOK A *STAND!*
HOW ARE WE GONNA DO THAT? THE GUY'S HUGE, AND HE'S GOT THE ENTIRE FOOTBALL TEAM AT HIS COMMAND!

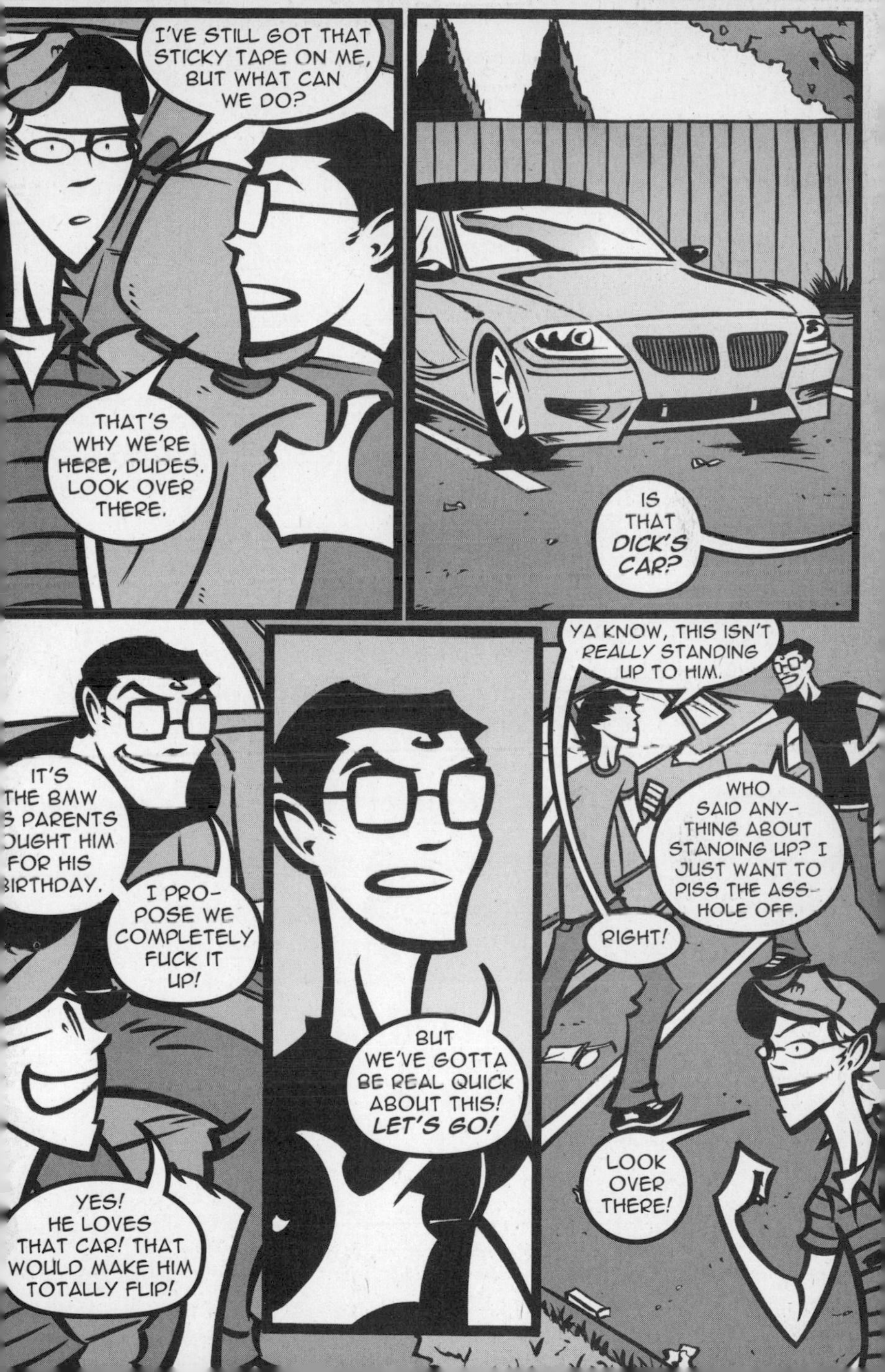
I'VE STILL GOT THAT STICKY TAPE ON ME, BUT WHAT CAN WE DO?
THAT'S WHY WE'RE HERE, DUDES. LOOK OVER THERE.
IS THAT DICK'S CAR?
IT'S THE BMW
I PRO-POSE WE COMPLETELY FUCK IT UP!
YES! HE LOVES THAT CAR! THAT WOULD MAKE HIM TOTALLY FLIP!
BUT WE'VE GOTTA BE REAL QUICK ABOUT THIS! LET'S GO!
YA KNOW, THIS ISN'T REALLY STANDING UP TO HIM.
WHO SAID ANY-THING ABOUT STANDING UP? I JUST WANT TO PISS THE ASS-HOLE OFF.
RIGHT!
LOOK OVER THERE!

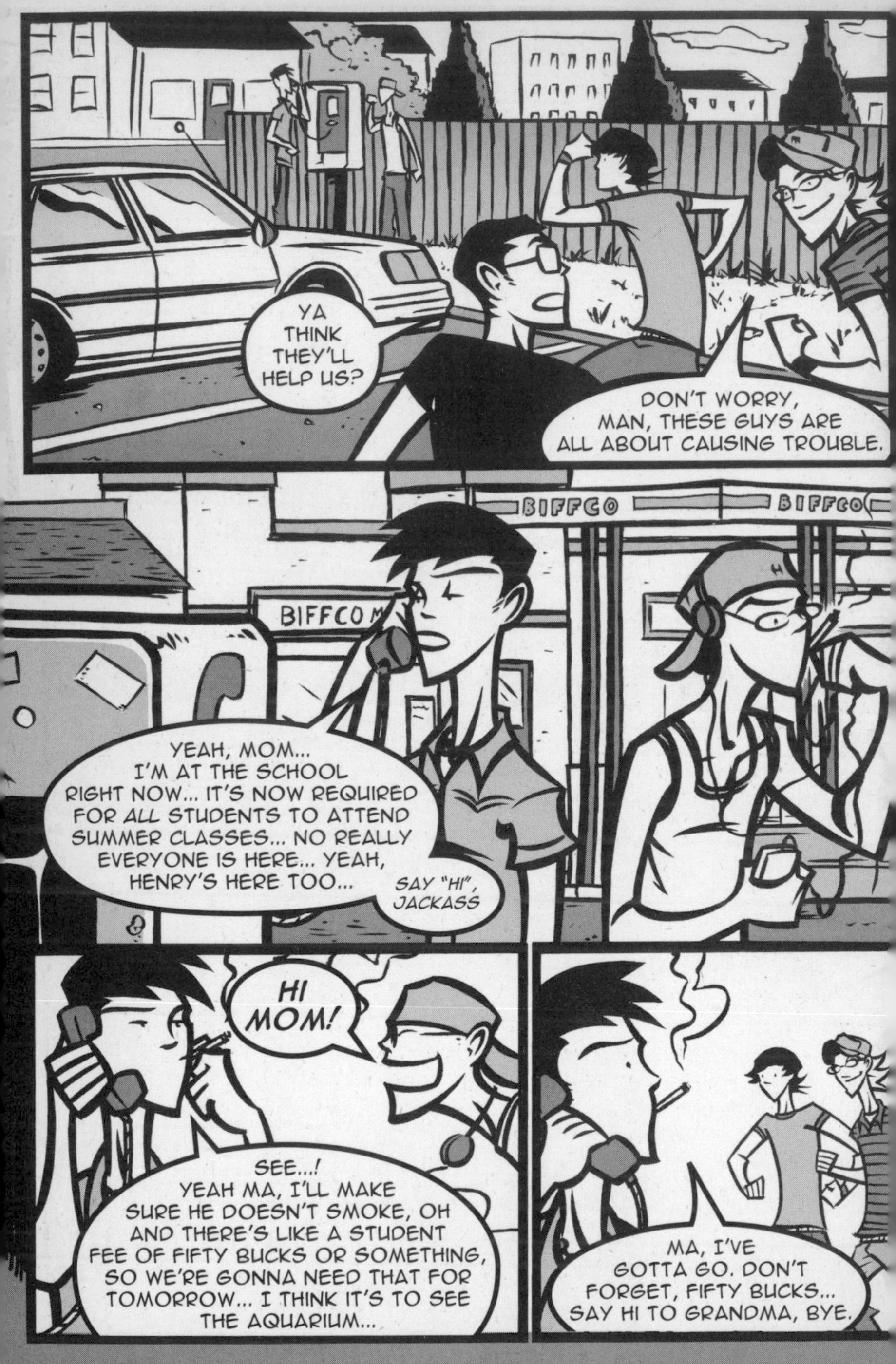
YA THINK THEY'LL HELP US?
DON'T WORRY, MAN, THESE GUYS ARE ALL ABOUT CAUSING TROUBLE.
BIFFCO
BIFFCO
BIFFCO
YEAH, MOM... I'M AT THE SCHOOL RIGHT NOW... IT'S NOW REQUIRED FOR ALL STUDENTS TO ATTEND SUMMER CLASSES... NO REALLY EVERYONE IS HERE... YEAH, HENRY'S HERE TOO...
SAY "HI", JACKASS
HI MOM!
SEE...! YEAH MA, I'LL MAKE SURE HE DOESN'T SMOKE, OH AND THERE'S LIKE A STUDENT FEE OF FIFTY BUCKS OR SOMETHING, SO WE'RE GONNA NEED THAT FOR TOMORROW... I THINK IT'S TO SEE THE AQUARIUM...
MA, I'VE GOTTA GO. DON'T FORGET, FIFTY BUCKS... SAY HI TO GRANDMA, BYE.

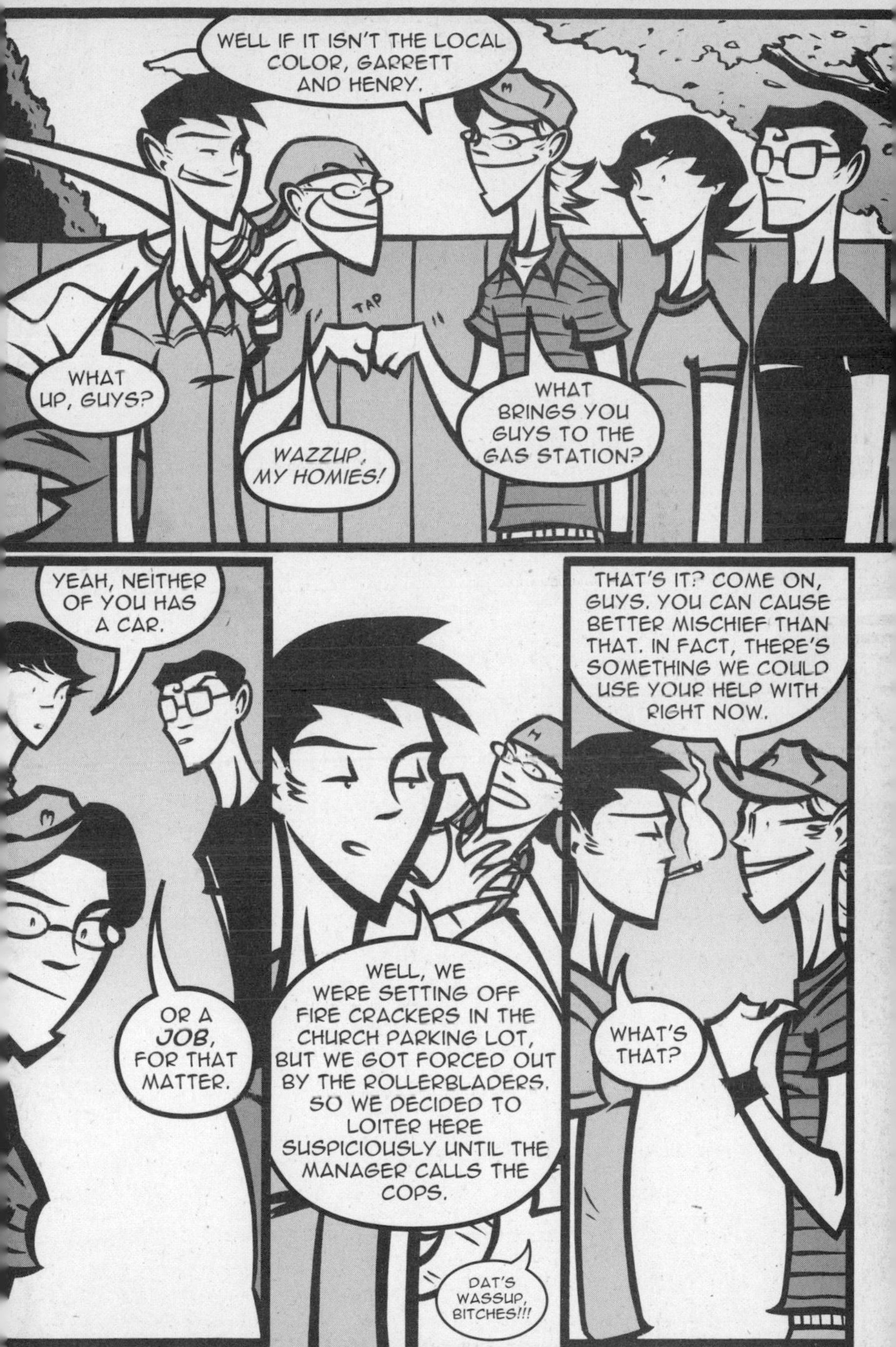
WELL IF IT ISN'T THE LOCAL COLOR, GARRETT AND HENRY.
TAP
WHAT UP, GUYS?
WAZZUP, MY HOMIES!
WHAT BRINGS YOU GUYS TO THE GAS STATION?
YEAH, NEITHER OF YOU HAS A CAR.
OR A *JOB*, FOR THAT MATTER.
WELL, WE WERE SETTING OFF FIRE CRACKERS IN THE CHURCH PARKING LOT, BUT WE GOT FORCED OUT BY THE ROLLERBLADERS. SO WE DECIDED TO LOITER HERE SUSPICIOUSLY UNTIL THE MANAGER CALLS THE COPS.
DAT'S WASSUP, BITCHES!!!
THAT'S IT? COME ON, GUYS. YOU CAN CAUSE BETTER MISCHIEF THAN THAT. IN FACT, THERE'S SOMETHING WE COULD USE YOUR HELP WITH RIGHT NOW.
WHAT'S THAT?

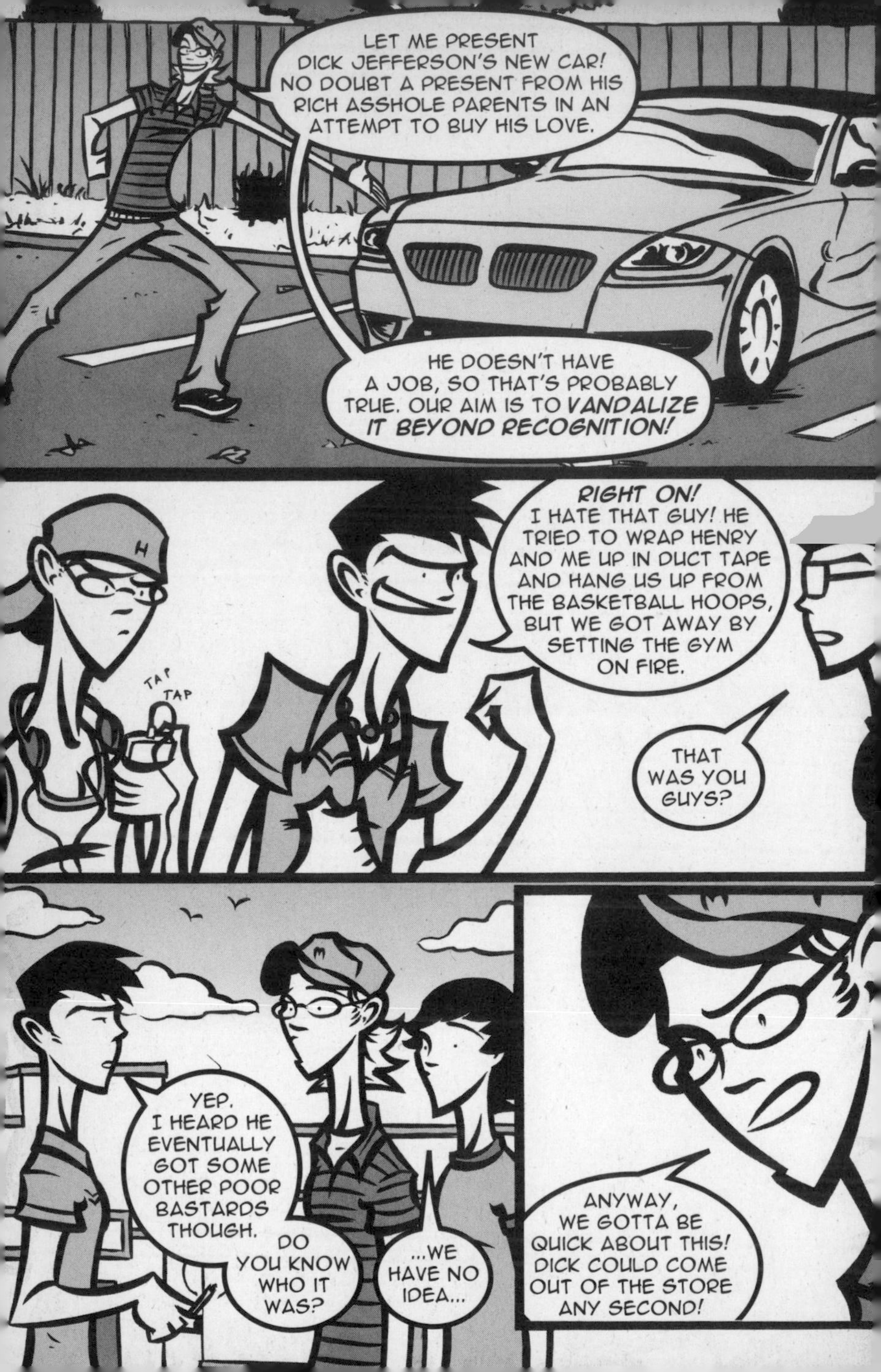
LET ME PRESENT DICK JEFFERSON'S NEW CAR! NO DOUBT A PRESENT FROM HIS RICH ASSHOLE PARENTS IN AN ATTEMPT TO BUY HIS LOVE.
HE DOESN'T HAVE A JOB, SO THAT'S PROBABLY TRUE. OUR AIM IS TO *VANDALIZE IT BEYOND RECOGNITION!*
RIGHT ON! I HATE THAT GUY! HE TRIED TO WRAP HENRY AND ME UP IN DUCT TAPE AND HANG US UP FROM THE BASKETBALL HOOPS, BUT WE GOT AWAY BY SETTING THE GYM ON FIRE.
TAP TAP
THAT WAS YOU GUYS?
YEP. I HEARD HE EVENTUALLY GOT SOME OTHER POOR BASTARDS THOUGH.
DO YOU KNOW WHO IT WAS?
...WE HAVE NO IDEA...
ANYWAY, WE GOTTA BE QUICK ABOUT THIS! DICK COULD COME OUT OF THE STORE ANY SECOND!

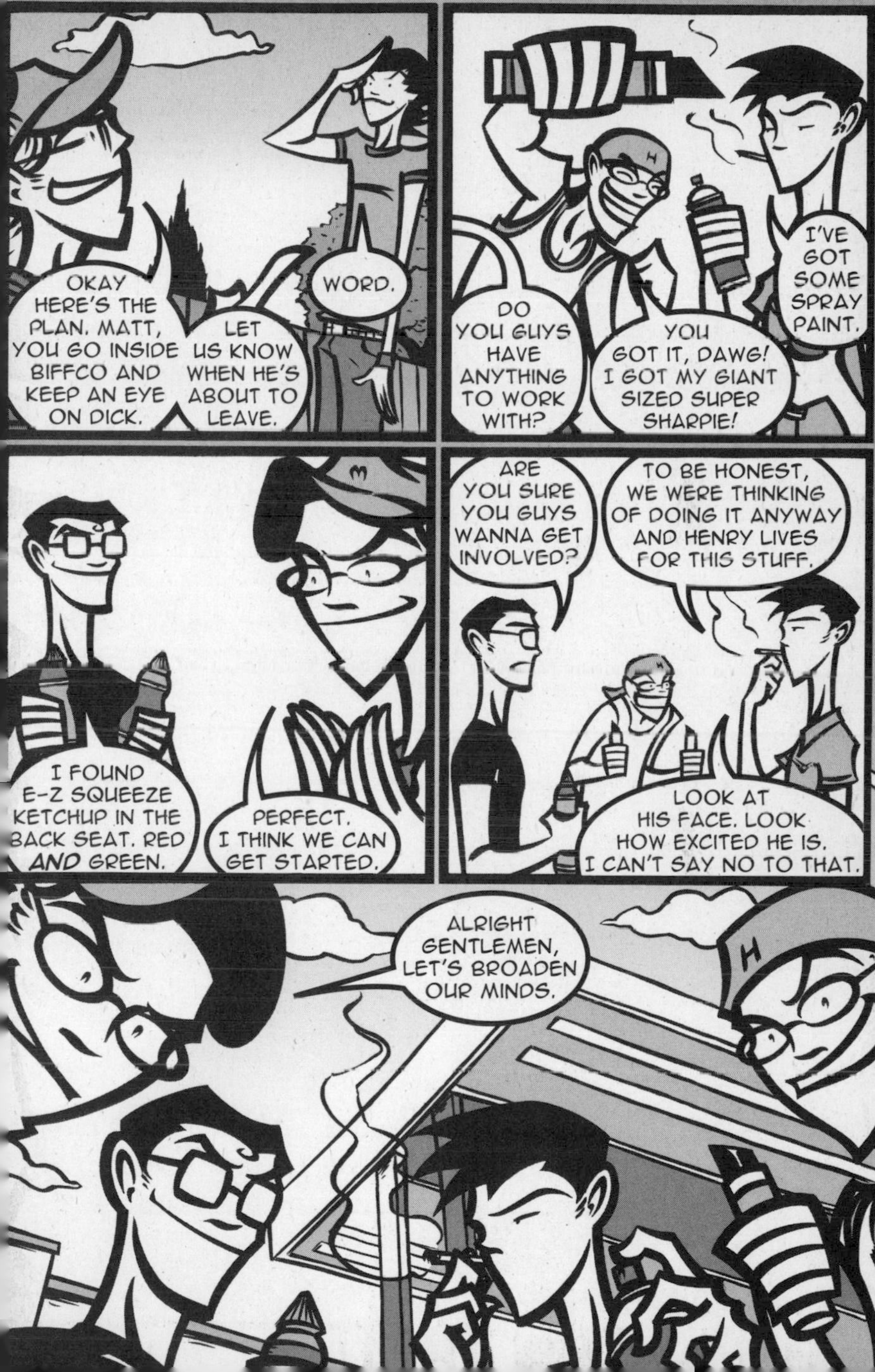
OKAY HERE'S THE PLAN. MATT, YOU GO INSIDE BIFFCO AND KEEP AN EYE ON DICK.
LET US KNOW WHEN HE'S ABOUT TO LEAVE.
WORD.
DO YOU GUYS HAVE ANYTHING TO WORK WITH?
YOU GOT IT, DAWG! I GOT MY GIANT SIZED SUPER SHARPIE!
I'VE GOT SOME SPRAY PAINT.
I FOUND E-Z SQUEEZE KETCHUP IN THE BACK SEAT. RED AND GREEN.
PERFECT. I THINK WE CAN GET STARTED.
ARE YOU SURE YOU GUYS WANNA GET INVOLVED?
TO BE HONEST, WE WERE THINKING OF DOING IT ANYWAY AND HENRY LIVES FOR THIS STUFF.
LOOK AT HIS FACE. LOOK HOW EXCITED HE IS. I CAN'T SAY NO TO THAT.
ALRIGHT GENTLEMEN, LET'S BROADEN OUR MINDS.

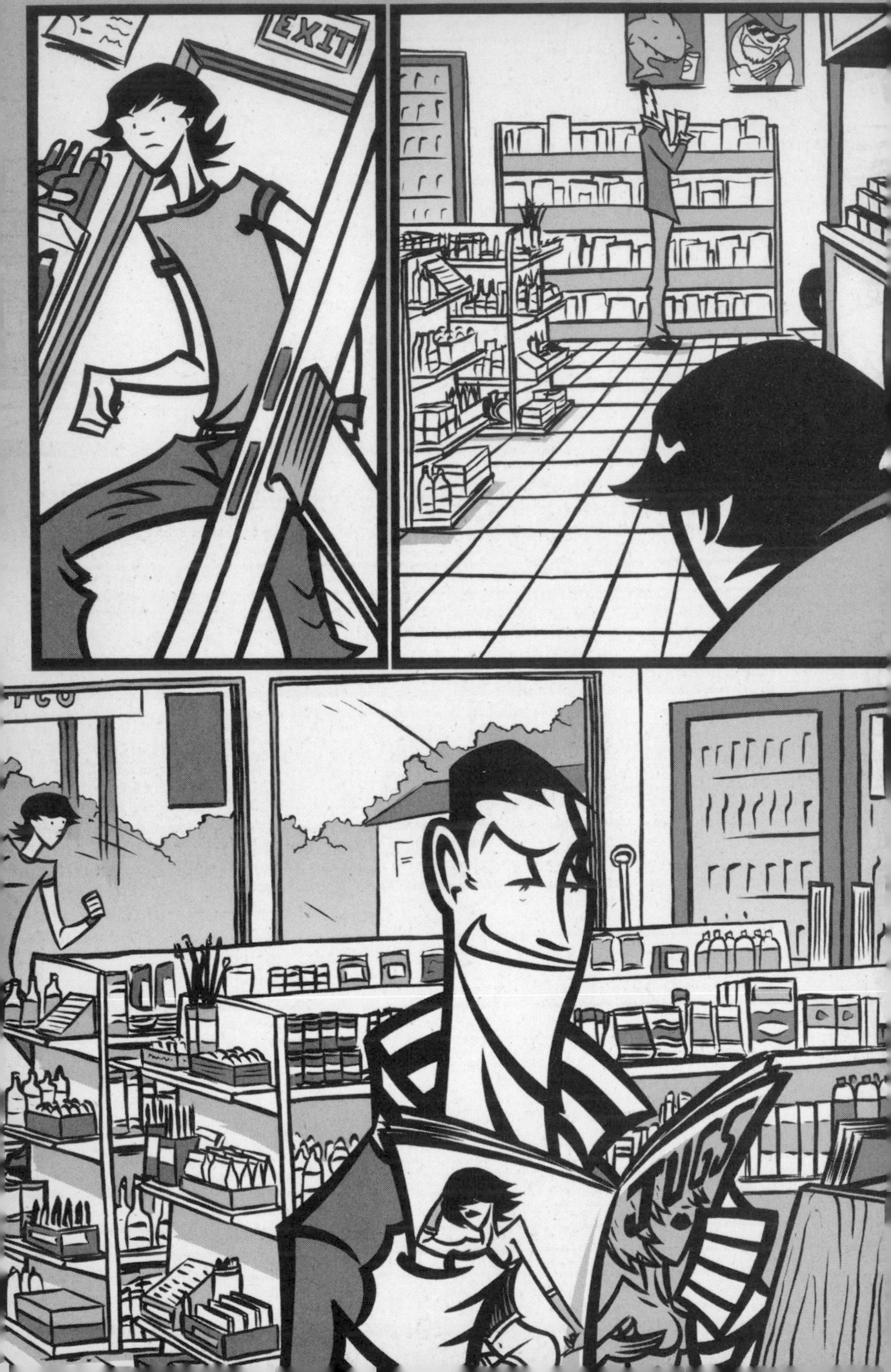
EXIT
JUGS

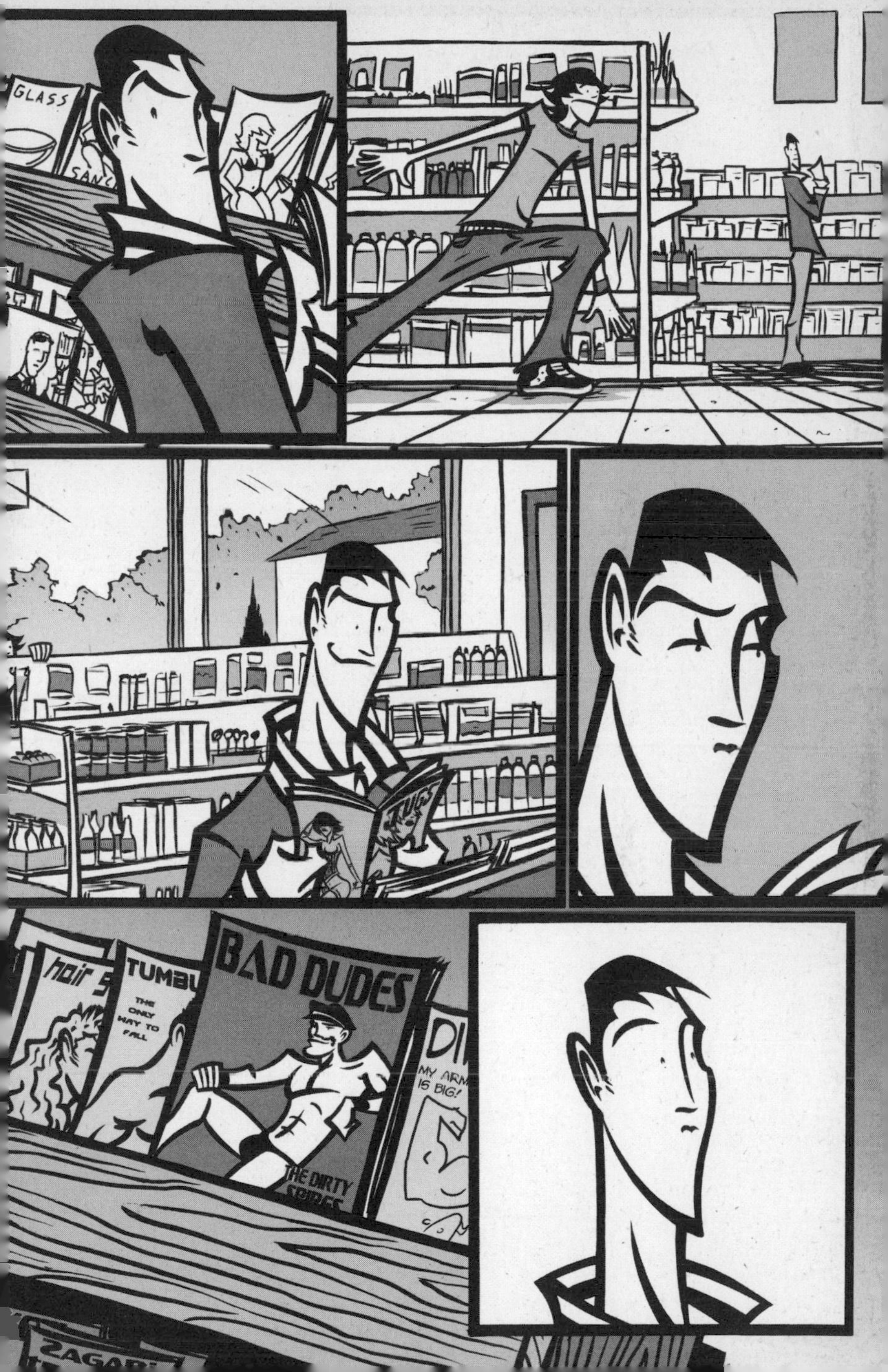
GLASS
BAD DUDES
THE ONLY WAY TO FALL
THE DIRTY
MY ARM IS BIG!

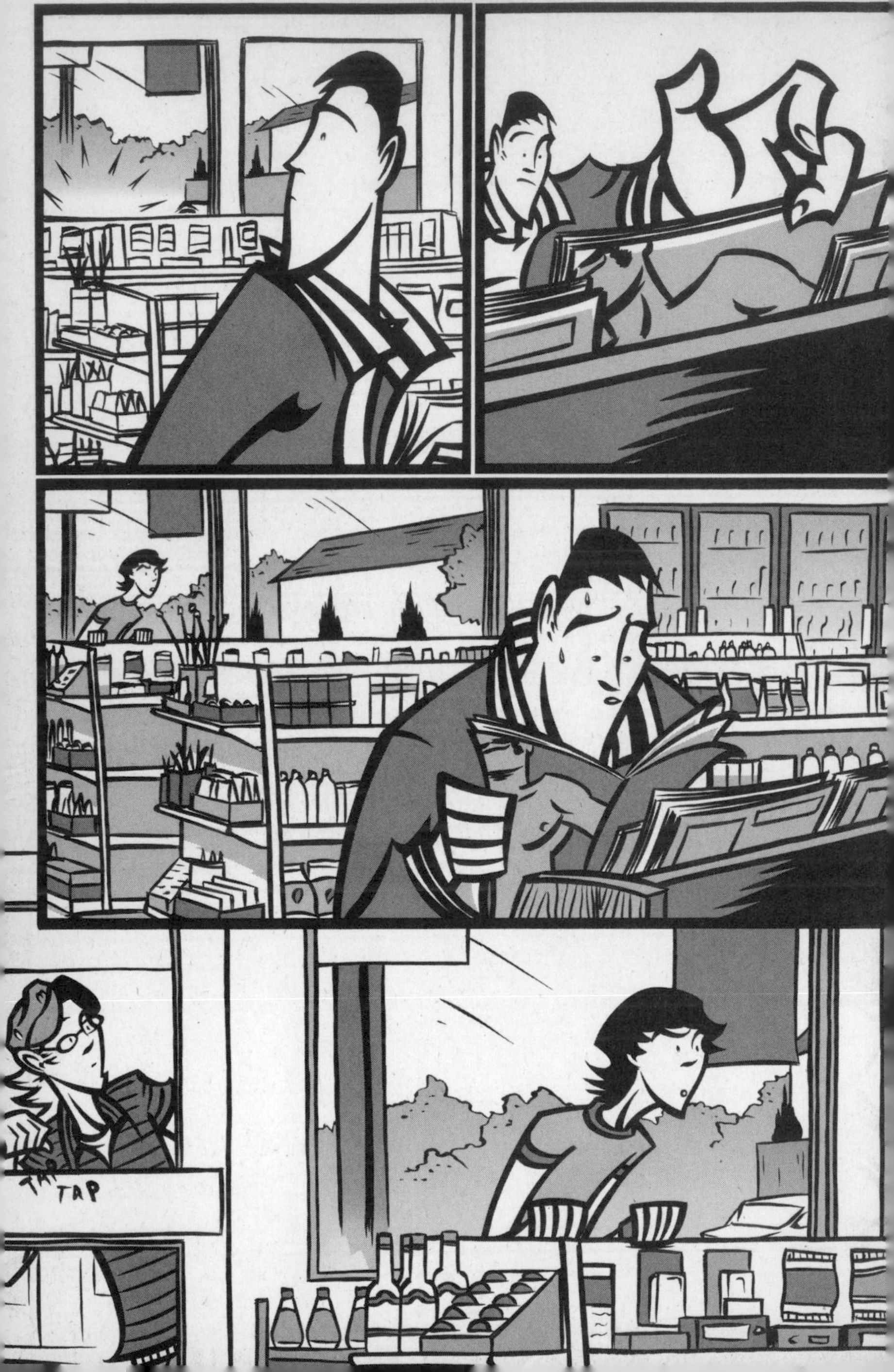
TAP TAP

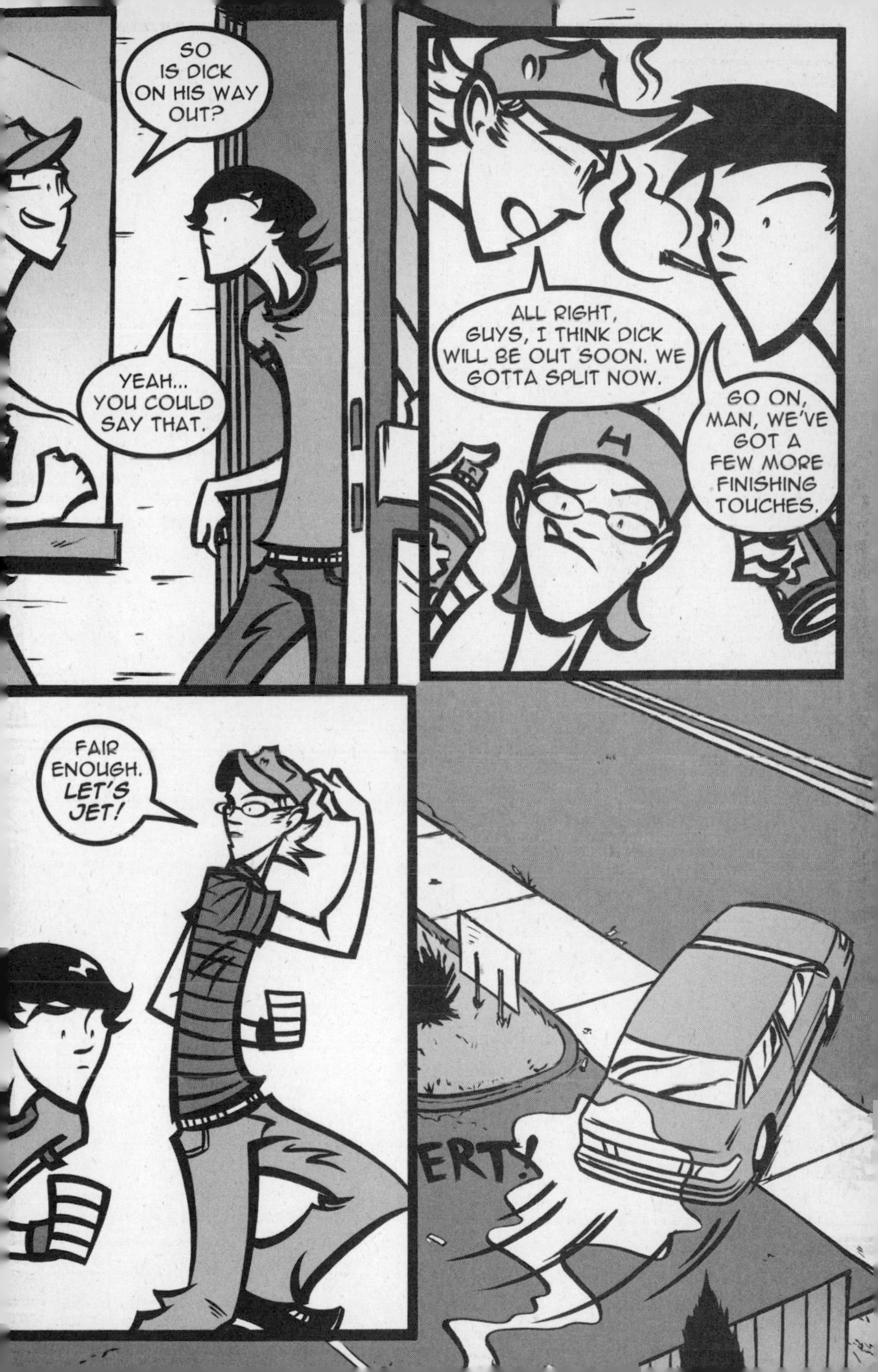
SO IS DICK ON HIS WAY OUT?
YEAH... YOU COULD SAY THAT.
ALL RIGHT, GUYS, I THINK DICK WILL BE OUT SOON. WE GOTTA SPLIT NOW.
GO ON, MAN, WE'VE GOT A FEW MORE FINISHING TOUCHES.
FAIR ENOUGH. LET'S JET!
ERT!

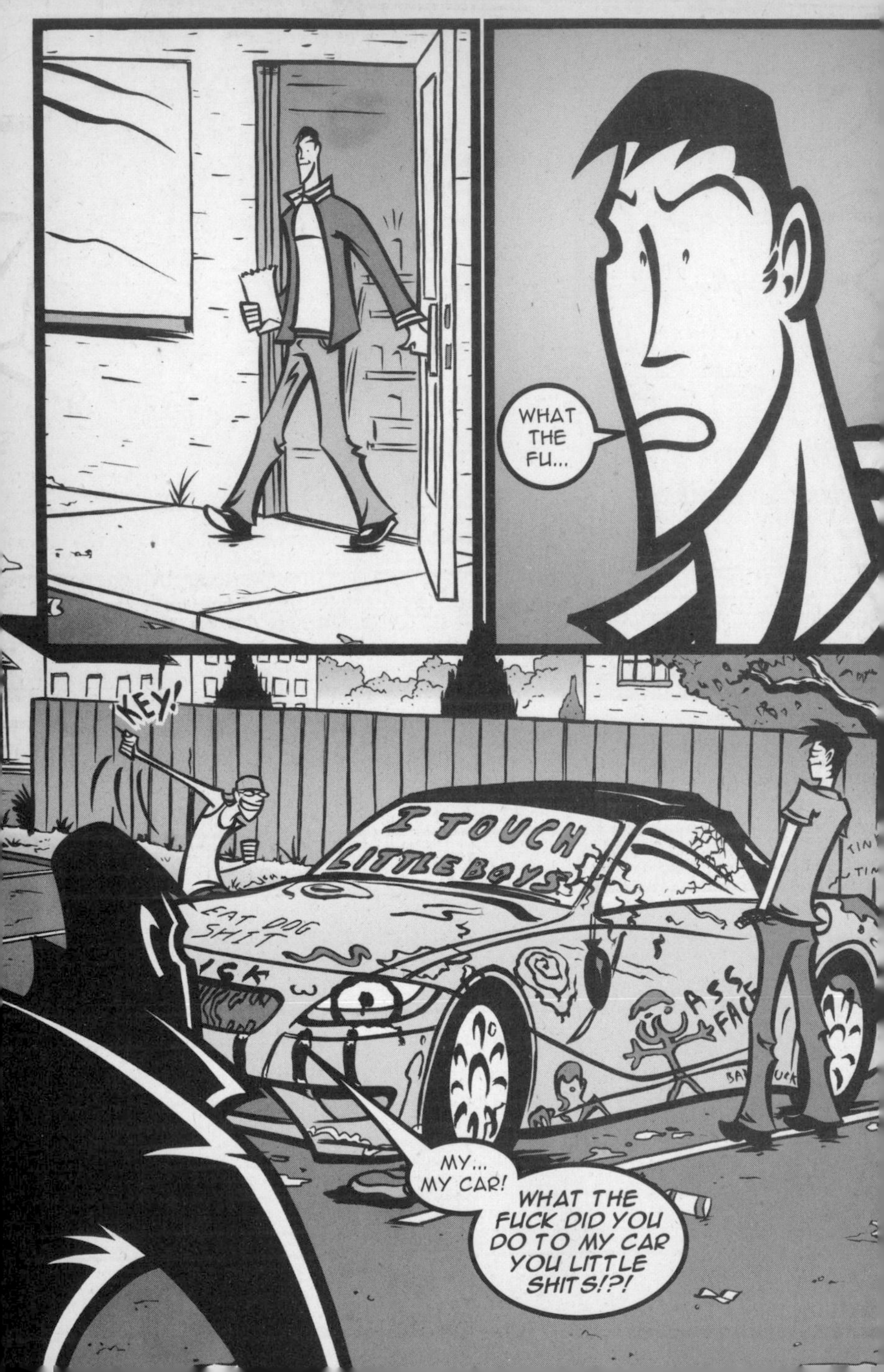
WHAT THE FU...
KEY!
I TOUCH LITTLE BOYS
EAT DOG SHIT
ASS FACE
MY... MY CAR!
WHAT THE FUCK DID YOU DO TO MY CAR YOU LITTLE SHITS!?!

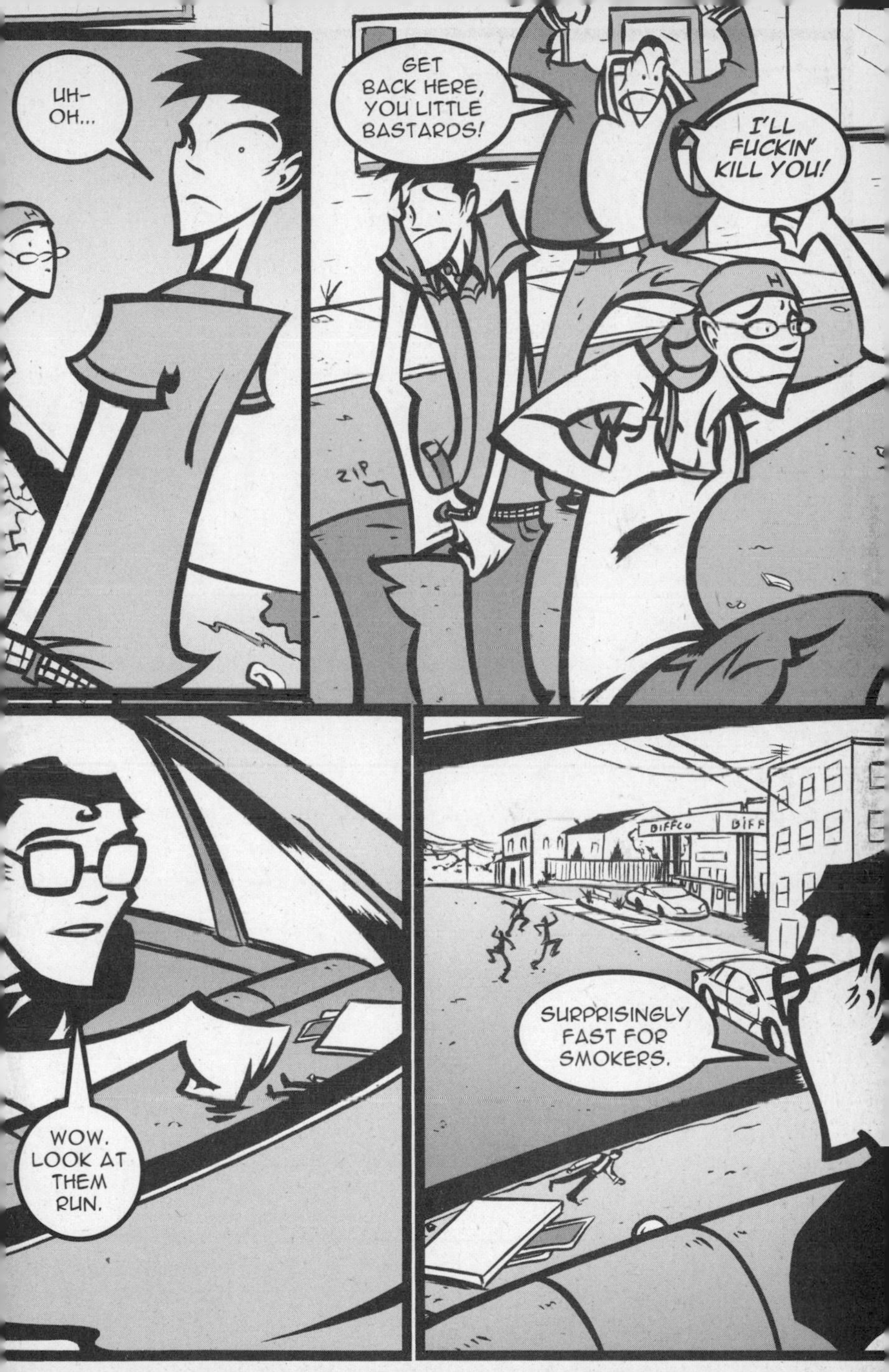
UH-OH...
GET BACK HERE, YOU LITTLE BASTARDS!
I'LL FUCKIN' KILL YOU!
ZIP
WOW. LOOK AT THEM RUN.
BIFFCO
BIFF
SURPRISINGLY FAST FOR SMOKERS.

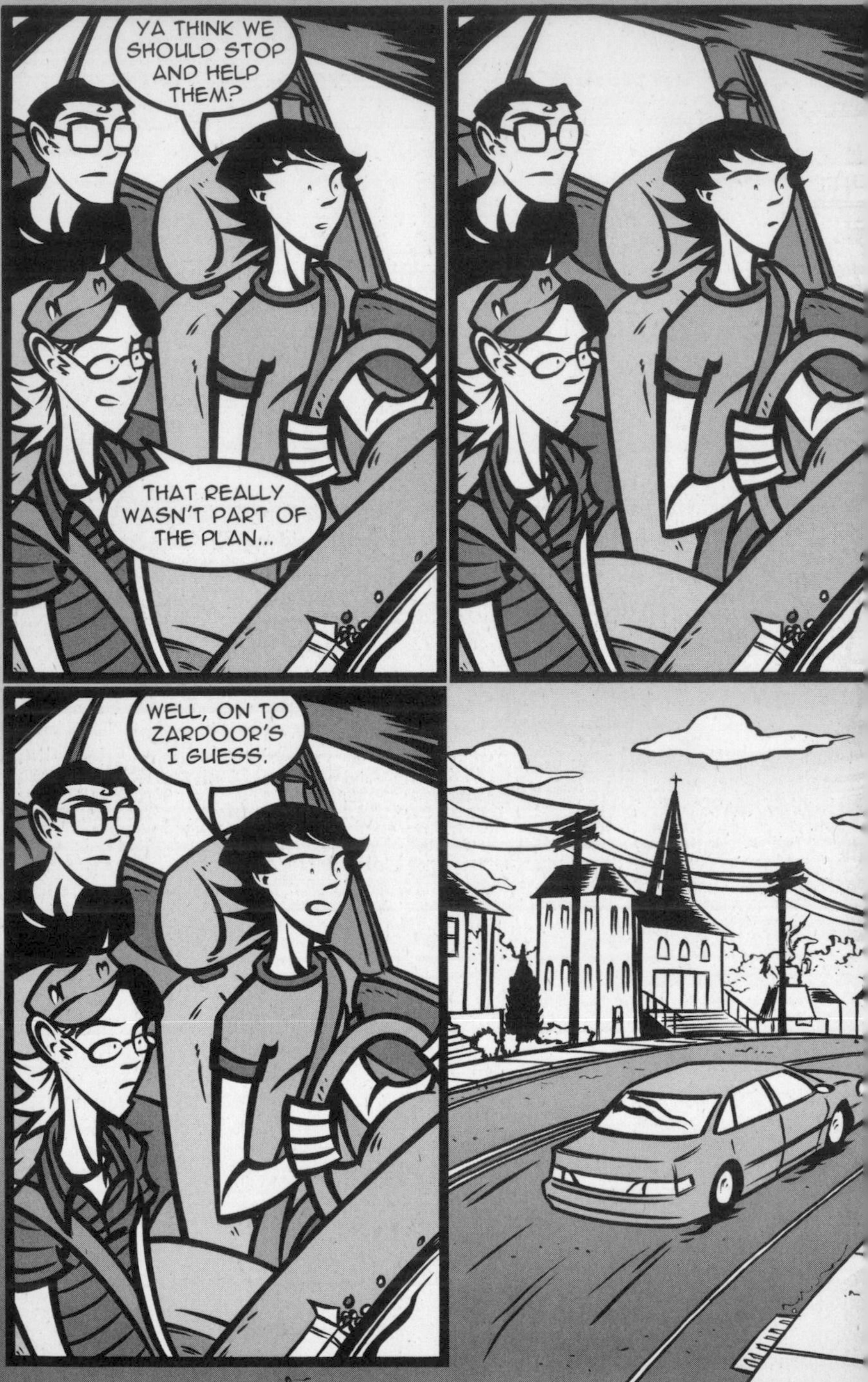
YA THINK WE SHOULD STOP AND HELP THEM?
THAT REALLY WASN'T PART OF THE PLAN...
WELL, ON TO ZARDOOR'S I GUESS.

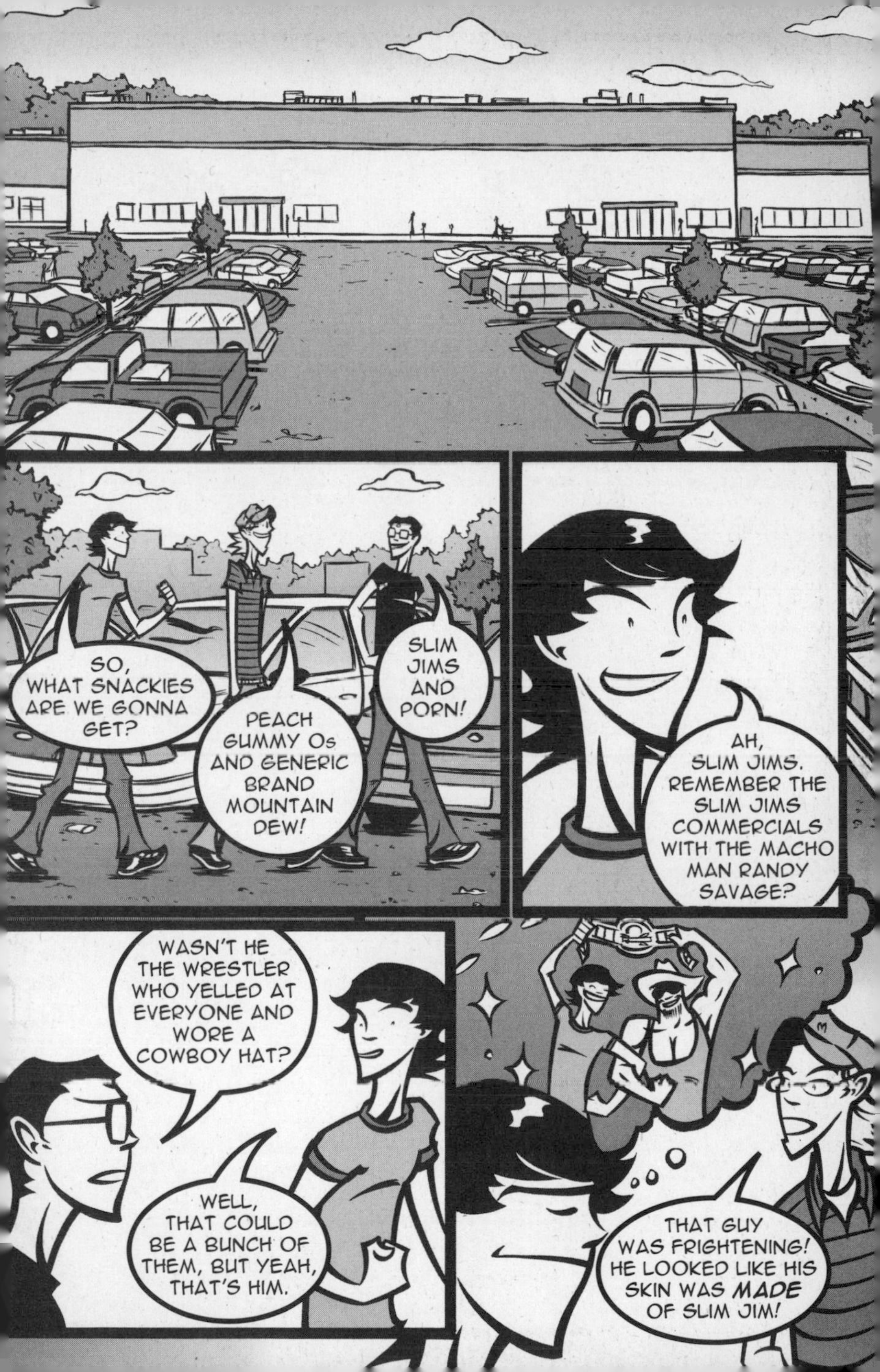

SO, WHAT SNACKIES ARE WE GONNA GET?
PEACH GUMMY Os AND GENERIC BRAND MOUNTAIN DEW!
SLIM JIMS AND PORN!
AH, SLIM JIMS. REMEMBER THE SLIM JIMS COMMERCIALS WITH THE MACHO MAN RANDY SAVAGE?
WASN'T HE THE WRESTLER WHO YELLED AT EVERYONE AND WORE A COWBOY HAT?
WELL, THAT COULD BE A BUNCH OF THEM, BUT YEAH, THAT'S HIM.
THAT GUY WAS FRIGHTENING! HE LOOKED LIKE HIS SKIN WAS *MADE* OF SLIM JIM!

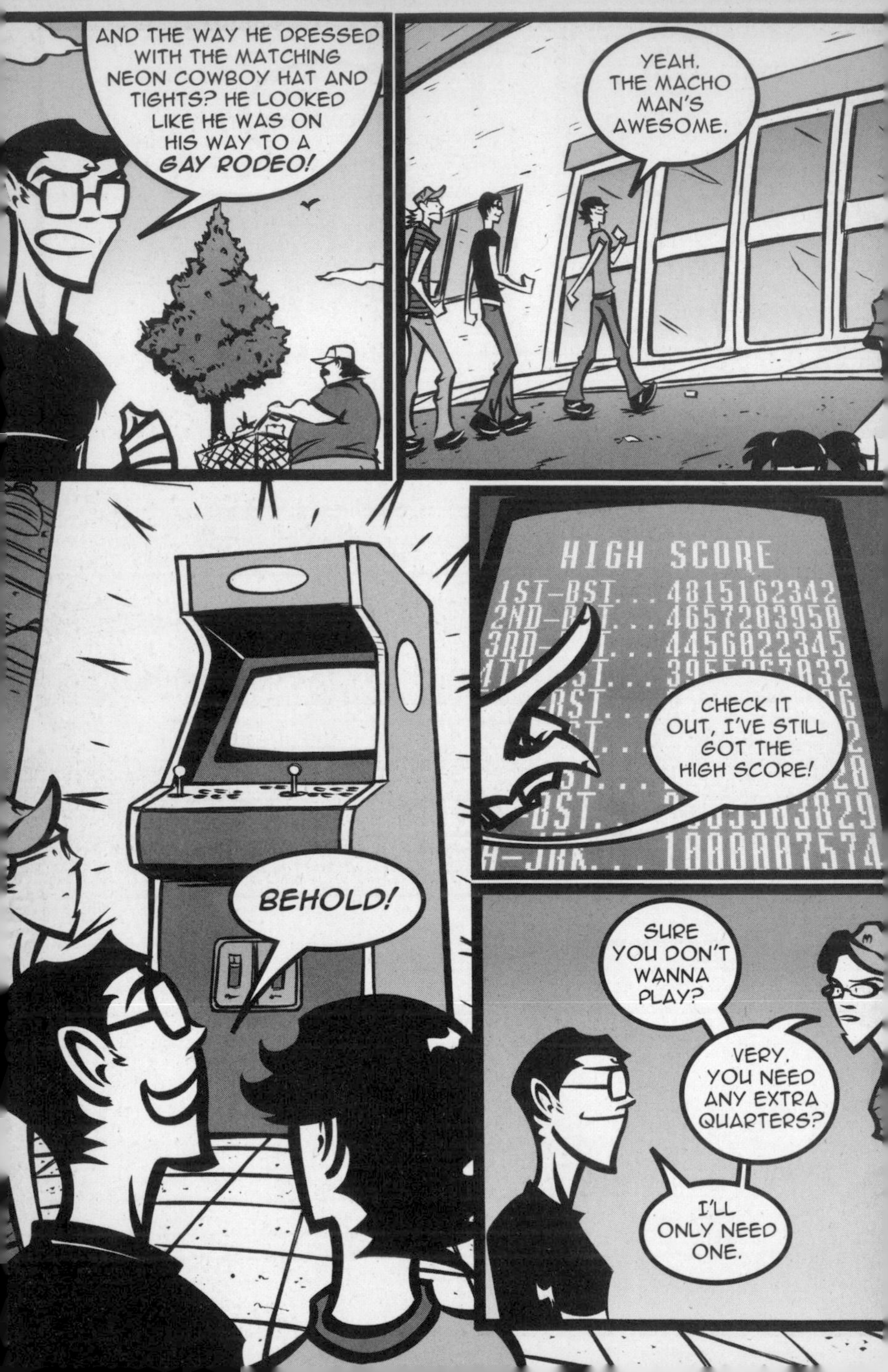
AND THE WAY HE DRESSED WITH THE MATCHING NEON COWBOY HAT AND TIGHTS? HE LOOKED LIKE HE WAS ON HIS WAY TO A GAY RODEO!
YEAH. THE MACHO MAN'S AWESOME.
BEHOLD!
HIGH SCORE
1ST-BST. . . 4815162342
CHECK IT OUT, I'VE STILL GOT THE HIGH SCORE!
SURE YOU DON'T WANNA PLAY?
VERY. YOU NEED ANY EXTRA QUARTERS?
I'LL ONLY NEED ONE.

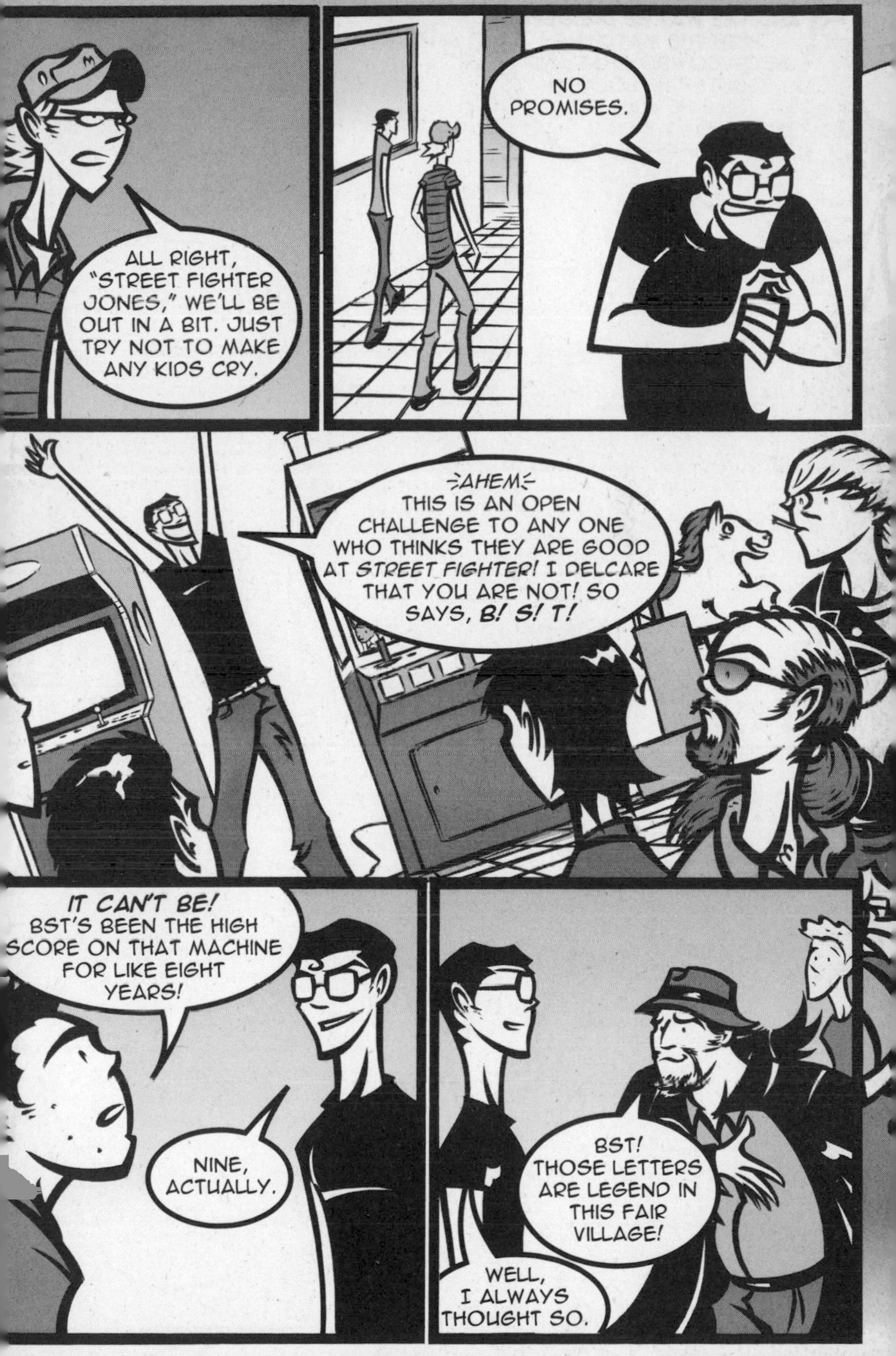
ALL RIGHT, "STREET FIGHTER JONES," WE'LL BE OUT IN A BIT. JUST TRY NOT TO MAKE ANY KIDS CRY.
NO PROMISES.
AHEM
THIS IS AN OPEN CHALLENGE TO ANY ONE WHO THINKS THEY ARE GOOD AT STREET FIGHTER! I DELCARE THAT YOU ARE NOT! SO SAYS, B! S! T!
IT CAN'T BE! BST'S BEEN THE HIGH SCORE ON THAT MACHINE FOR LIKE EIGHT YEARS!
NINE, ACTUALLY.
BST! THOSE LETTERS ARE LEGEND IN THIS FAIR VILLAGE!
WELL, I ALWAYS THOUGHT SO.

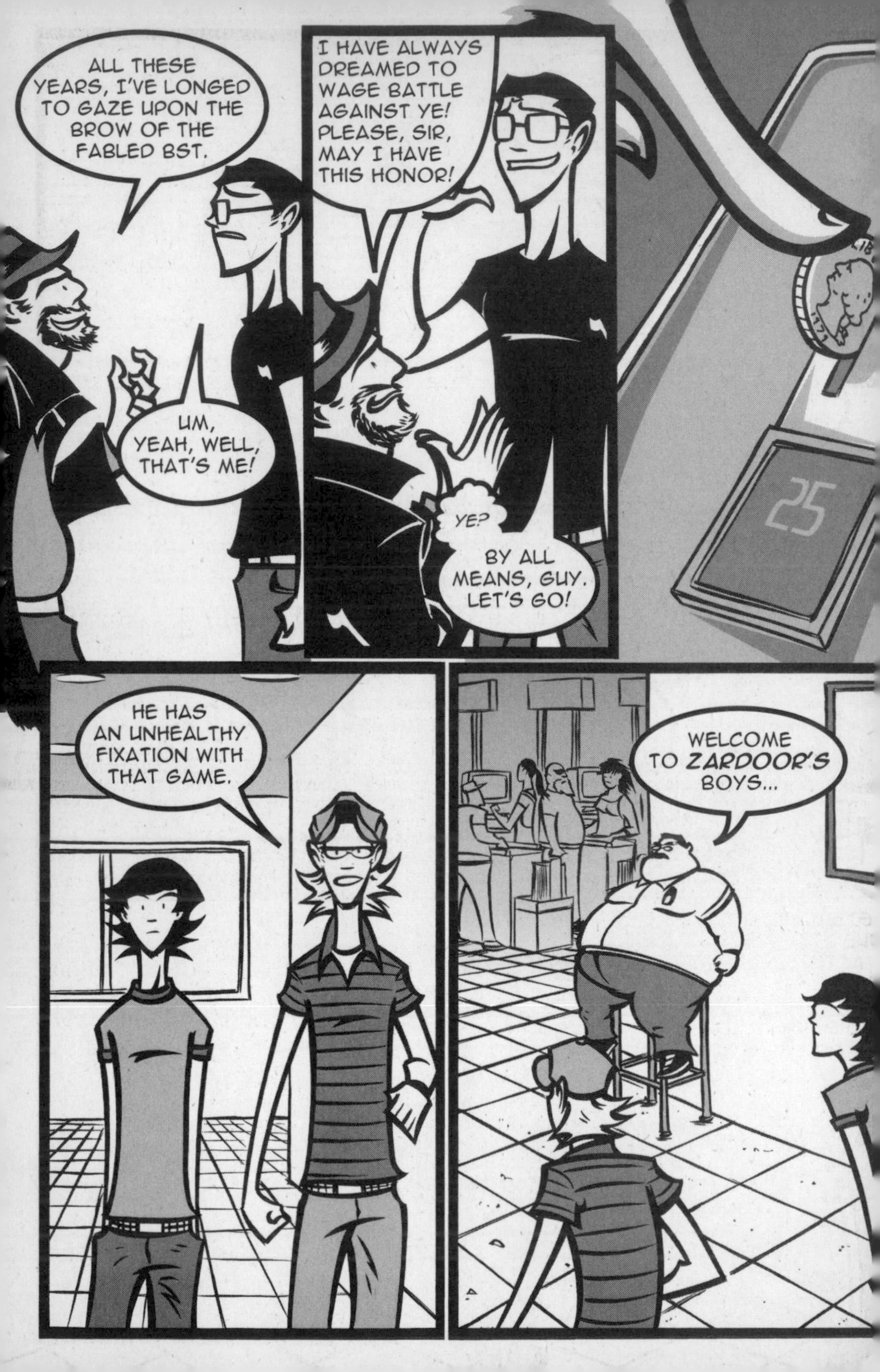
ALL THESE YEARS, I'VE LONGED TO GAZE UPON THE BROW OF THE FABLED BST.
UM, YEAH, WELL, THAT'S ME!
I HAVE ALWAYS DREAMED TO WAGE BATTLE AGAINST YE! PLEASE, SIR, MAY I HAVE THIS HONOR!
YE?
BY ALL MEANS, GUY. LET'S GO!
25
HE HAS AN UNHEALTHY FIXATION WITH THAT GAME.
WELCOME TO ZARDOOR'S BOYS...

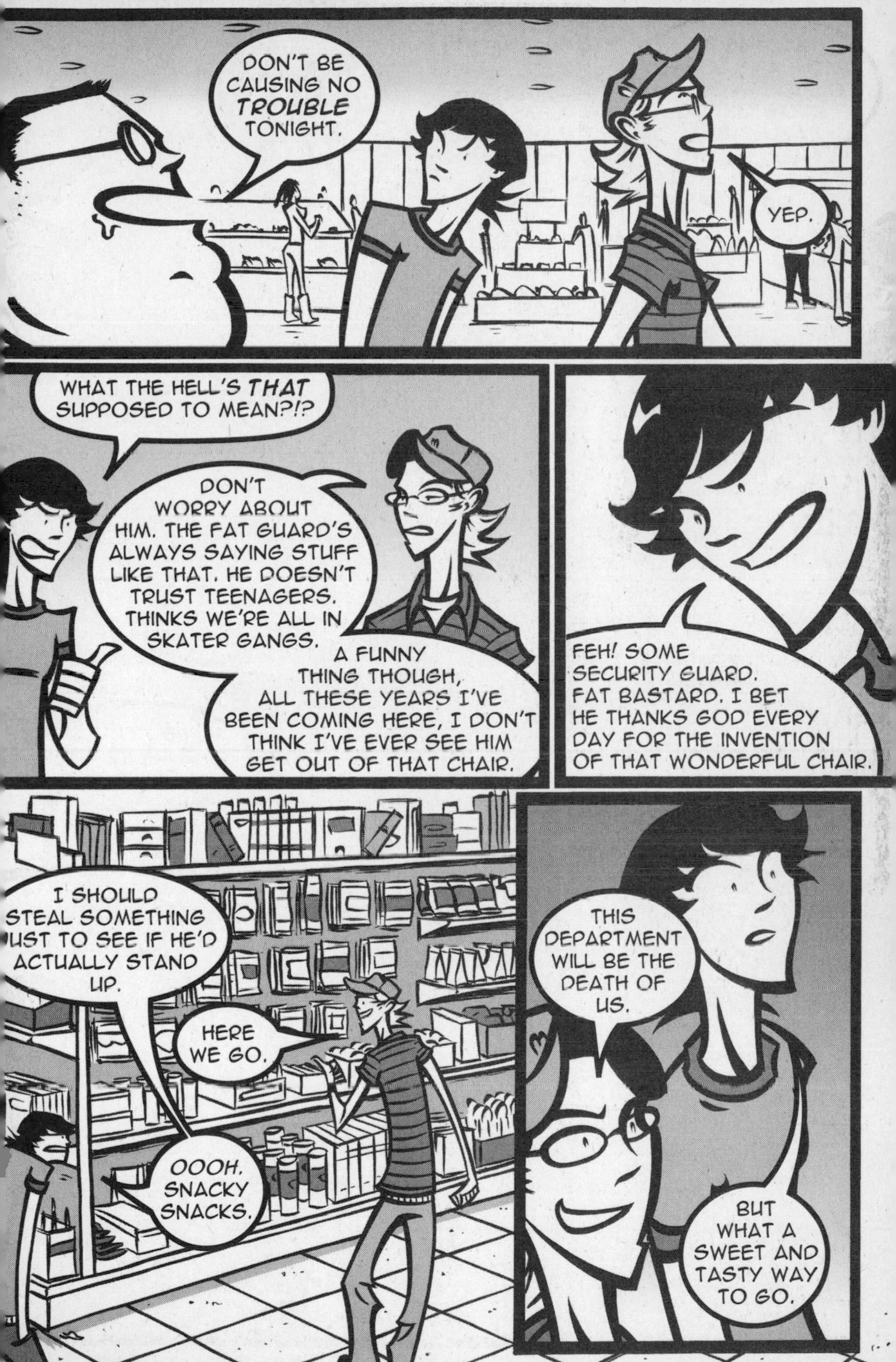
DON'T BE CAUSING NO *TROUBLE* TONIGHT.
YEP.
WHAT THE HELL'S *THAT* SUPPOSED TO MEAN?!?
DON'T WORRY ABOUT HIM. THE FAT GUARD'S ALWAYS SAYING STUFF LIKE THAT. HE DOESN'T TRUST TEENAGERS. THINKS WE'RE ALL IN SKATER GANGS.
A FUNNY THING THOUGH, ALL THESE YEARS I'VE BEEN COMING HERE, I DON'T THINK I'VE EVER SEE HIM GET OUT OF THAT CHAIR.
FEH! SOME SECURITY GUARD. FAT BASTARD. I BET HE THANKS GOD EVERY DAY FOR THE INVENTION OF THAT WONDERFUL CHAIR.
I SHOULD STEAL SOMETHING JUST TO SEE IF HE'D ACTUALLY STAND UP.
HERE WE GO.
OOOH. SNACKY SNACKS.
THIS DEPARTMENT WILL BE THE DEATH OF US.
BUT WHAT A SWEET AND TASTY WAY TO GO.

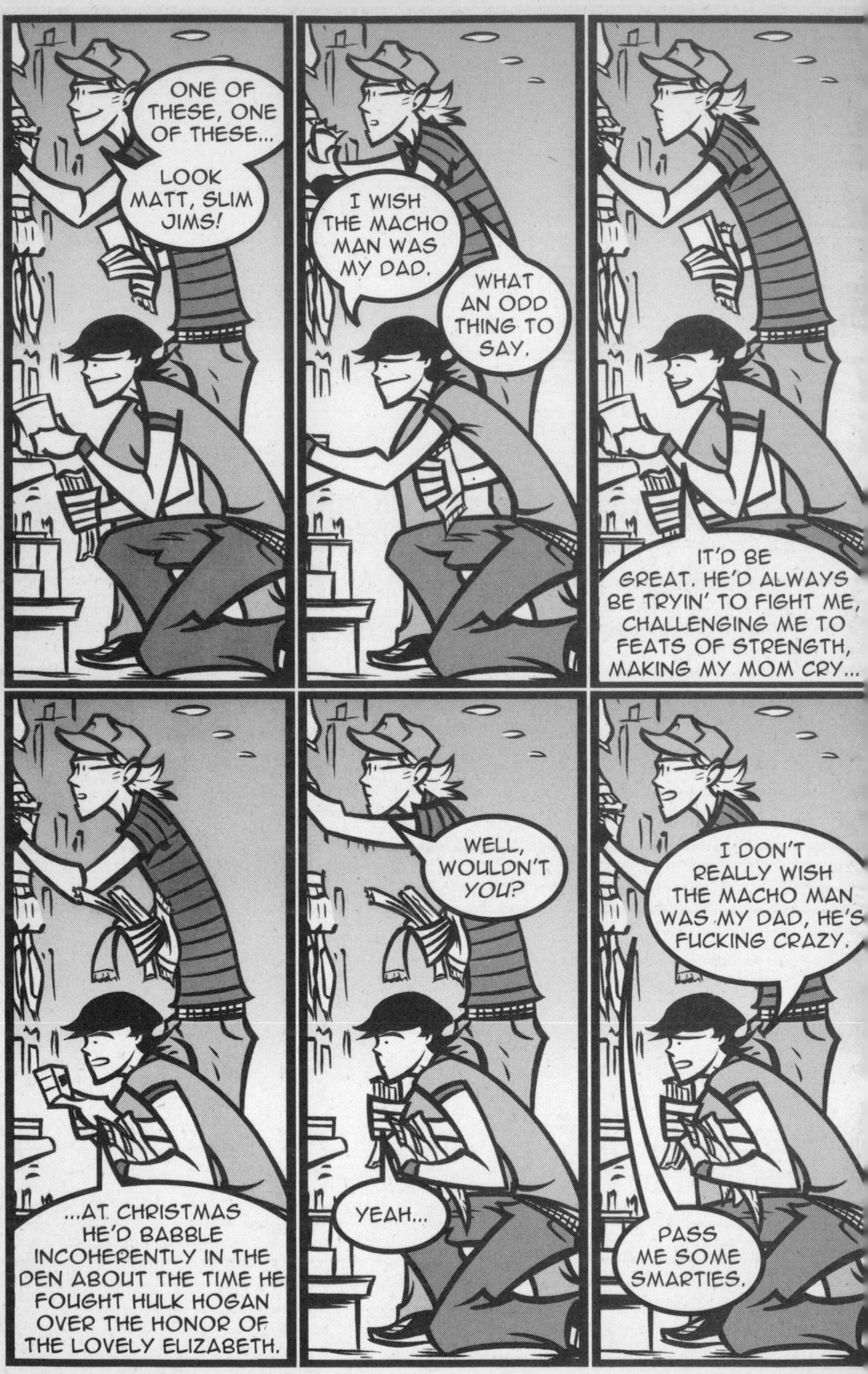
ONE OF THESE, ONE OF THESE...
LOOK MATT, SLIM JIMS!
I WISH THE MACHO MAN WAS MY DAD.
WHAT AN ODD THING TO SAY.
IT'D BE GREAT. HE'D ALWAYS BE TRYIN' TO FIGHT ME, CHALLENGING ME TO FEATS OF STRENGTH, MAKING MY MOM CRY...
...AT CHRISTMAS HE'D BABBLE INCOHERENTLY IN THE DEN ABOUT THE TIME HE FOUGHT HULK HOGAN OVER THE HONOR OF THE LOVELY ELIZABETH.
WELL, WOULDN'T *YOU?*
YEAH...
I DON'T REALLY WISH THE MACHO MAN WAS MY DAD, HE'S FUCKING CRAZY.
PASS ME SOME SMARTIES.

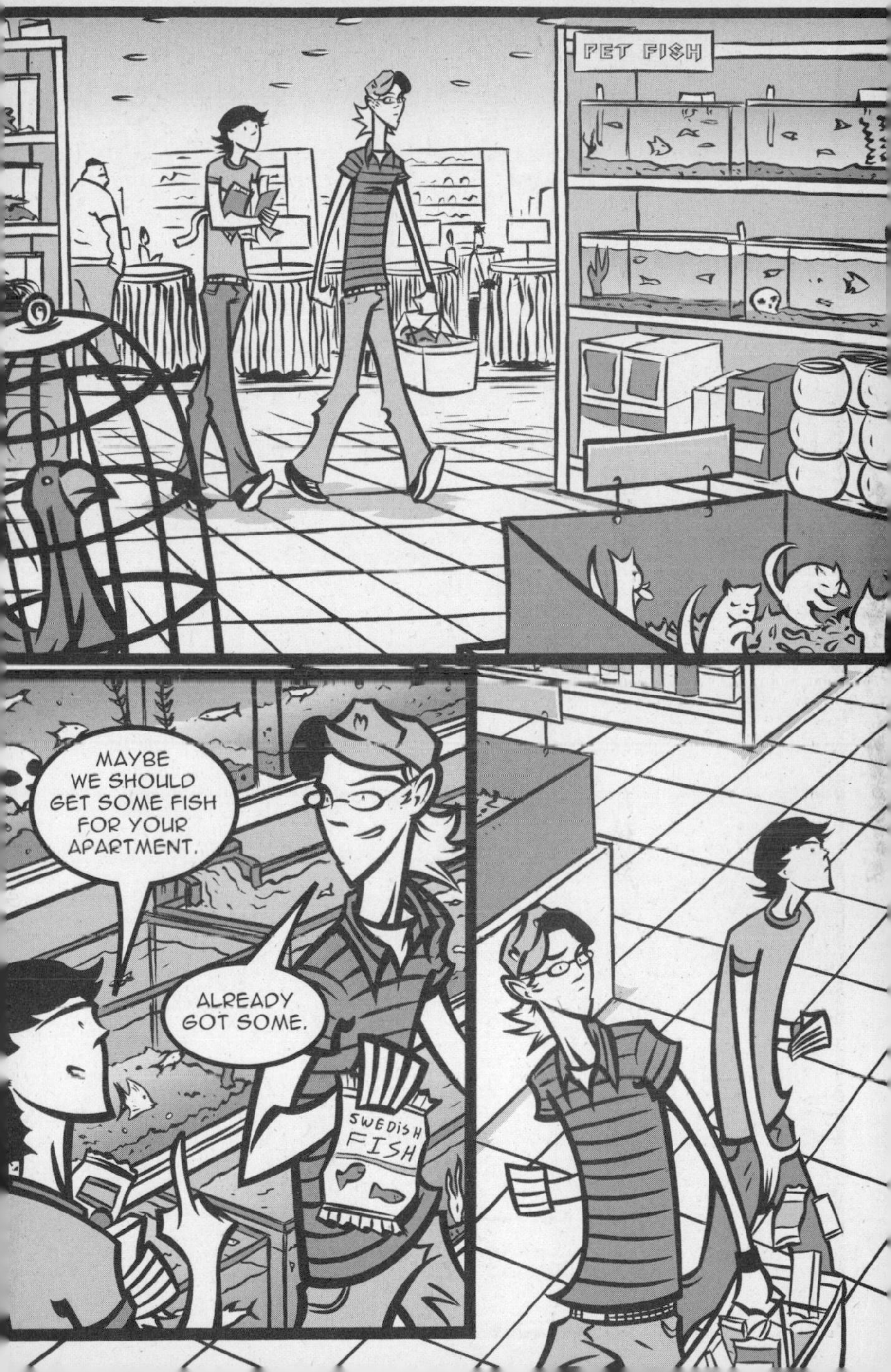
PET FISH
MAYBE WE SHOULD GET SOME FISH FOR YOUR APARTMENT.
ALREADY GOT SOME.
SWEDISH FISH

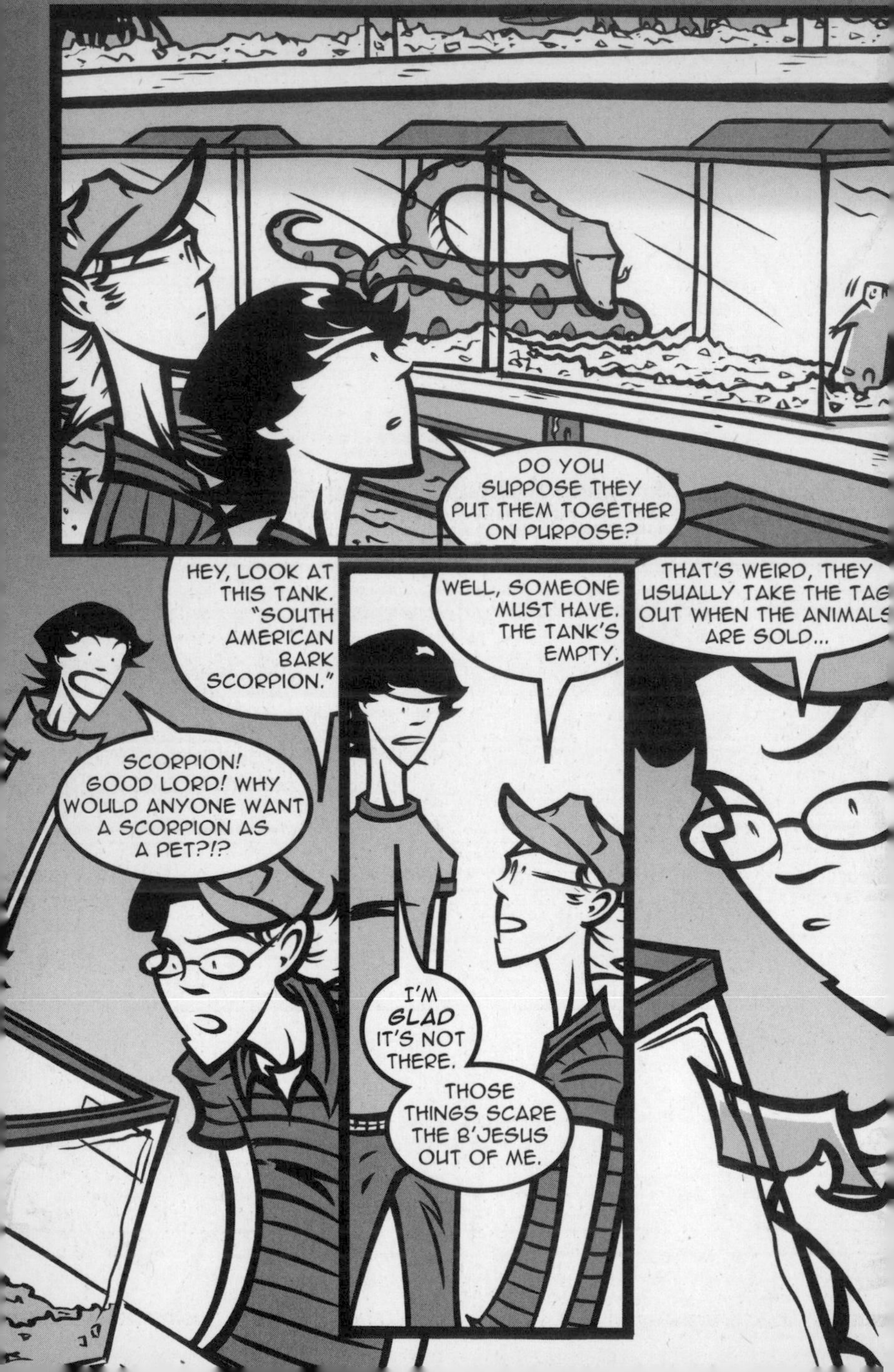
DO YOU SUPPOSE THEY PUT THEM TOGETHER ON PURPOSE?
HEY, LOOK AT THIS TANK. "SOUTH AMERICAN BARK SCORPION."
SCORPION! GOOD LORD! WHY WOULD ANYONE WANT A SCORPION AS A PET?!?
WELL, SOMEONE MUST HAVE. THE TANK'S EMPTY.
I'M *GLAD* IT'S NOT THERE.
THOSE THINGS SCARE THE B'JESUS OUT OF ME.
THAT'S WEIRD, THEY USUALLY TAKE THE TAG OUT WHEN THE ANIMALS ARE SOLD...

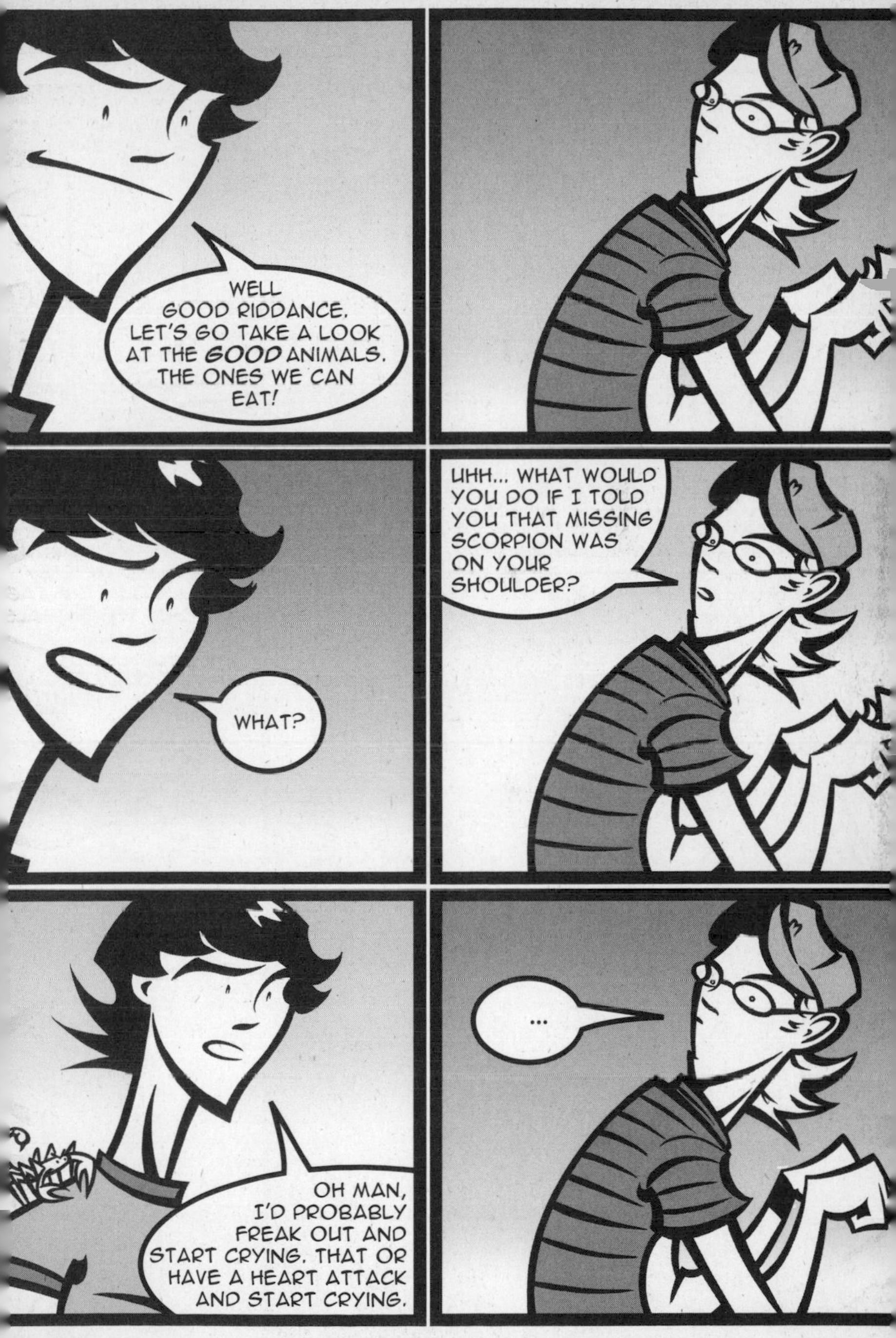
WELL GOOD RIDDANCE. LET'S GO TAKE A LOOK AT THE GOOD ANIMALS. THE ONES WE CAN EAT!
UHH... WHAT WOULD YOU DO IF I TOLD YOU THAT MISSING SCORPION WAS ON YOUR SHOULDER?
WHAT?
OH MAN, I'D PROBABLY FREAK OUT AND START CRYING. THAT OR HAVE A HEART ATTACK AND START CRYING.
...

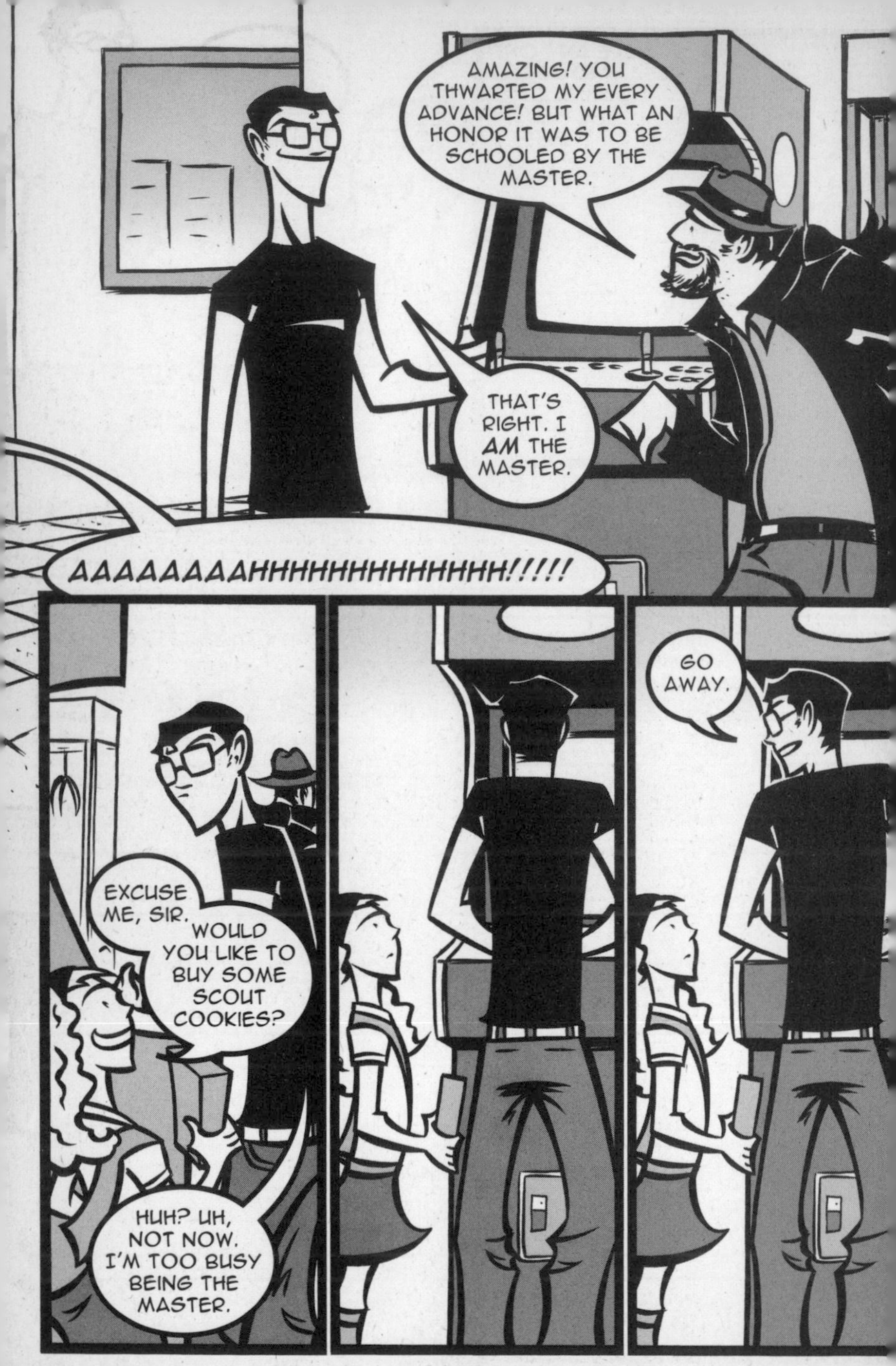
AMAZING! YOU THWARTED MY EVERY ADVANCE! BUT WHAT AN HONOR IT WAS TO BE SCHOOLED BY THE MASTER.
THAT'S RIGHT. I AM THE MASTER.
AAAAAAAAAHHHHHHHHHHHHHHH!!!!!
EXCUSE ME, SIR.
WOULD YOU LIKE TO BUY SOME SCOUT COOKIES?
HUH? UH, NOT NOW. I'M TOO BUSY BEING THE MASTER.
GO AWAY.

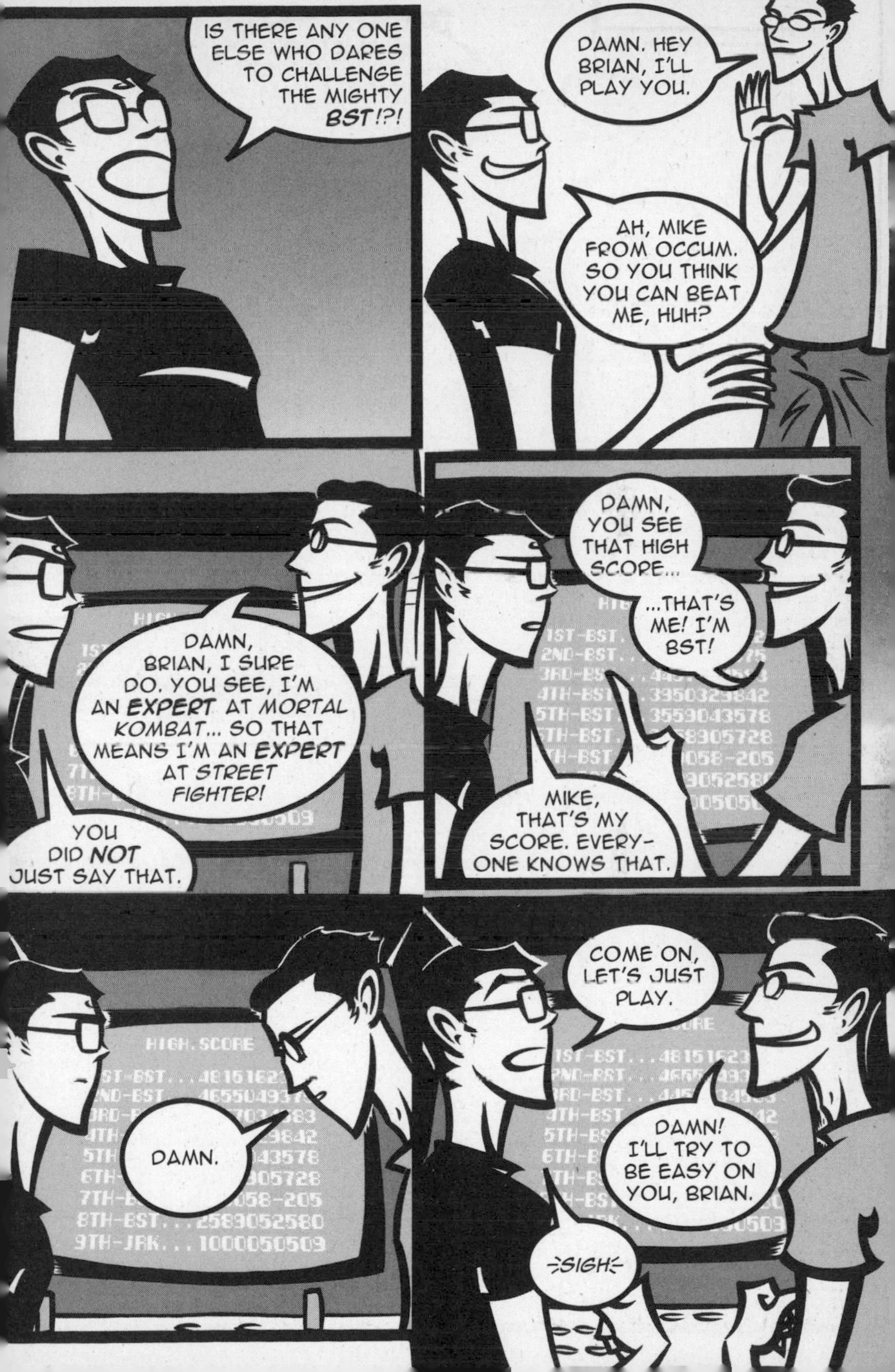
IS THERE ANY ONE ELSE WHO DARES TO CHALLENGE THE MIGHTY *BST*!?!
DAMN. HEY BRIAN, I'LL PLAY YOU.
AH, MIKE FROM OCCUM. SO YOU THINK YOU CAN BEAT ME, HUH?
DAMN, BRIAN, I SURE DO. YOU SEE, I'M AN *EXPERT* AT *MORTAL KOMBAT*... SO THAT MEANS I'M AN *EXPERT* AT *STREET FIGHTER*!
YOU DID ***NOT*** JUST SAY THAT.
DAMN, YOU SEE THAT HIGH SCORE...
...THAT'S ME! I'M BST!
MIKE, THAT'S MY SCORE. EVERY-ONE KNOWS THAT.
HIGH.SCORE
8TH-BST...2583052580
9TH-JRK...1000050509
DAMN.
COME ON, LET'S JUST PLAY.
DAMN! I'LL TRY TO BE EASY ON YOU, BRIAN.
SIGH

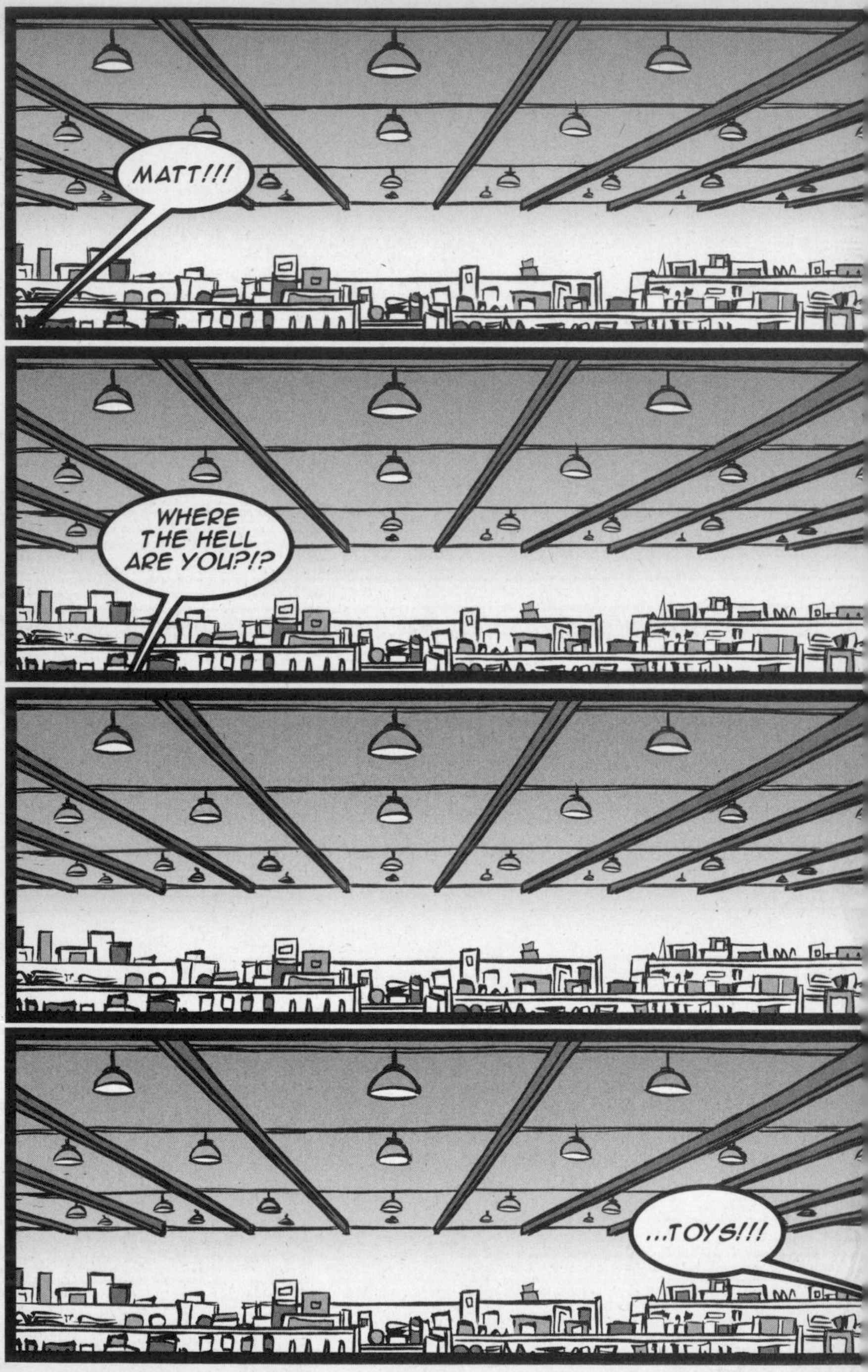
MATT!!!
WHERE THE HELL ARE YOU?!?
...TOYS!!!

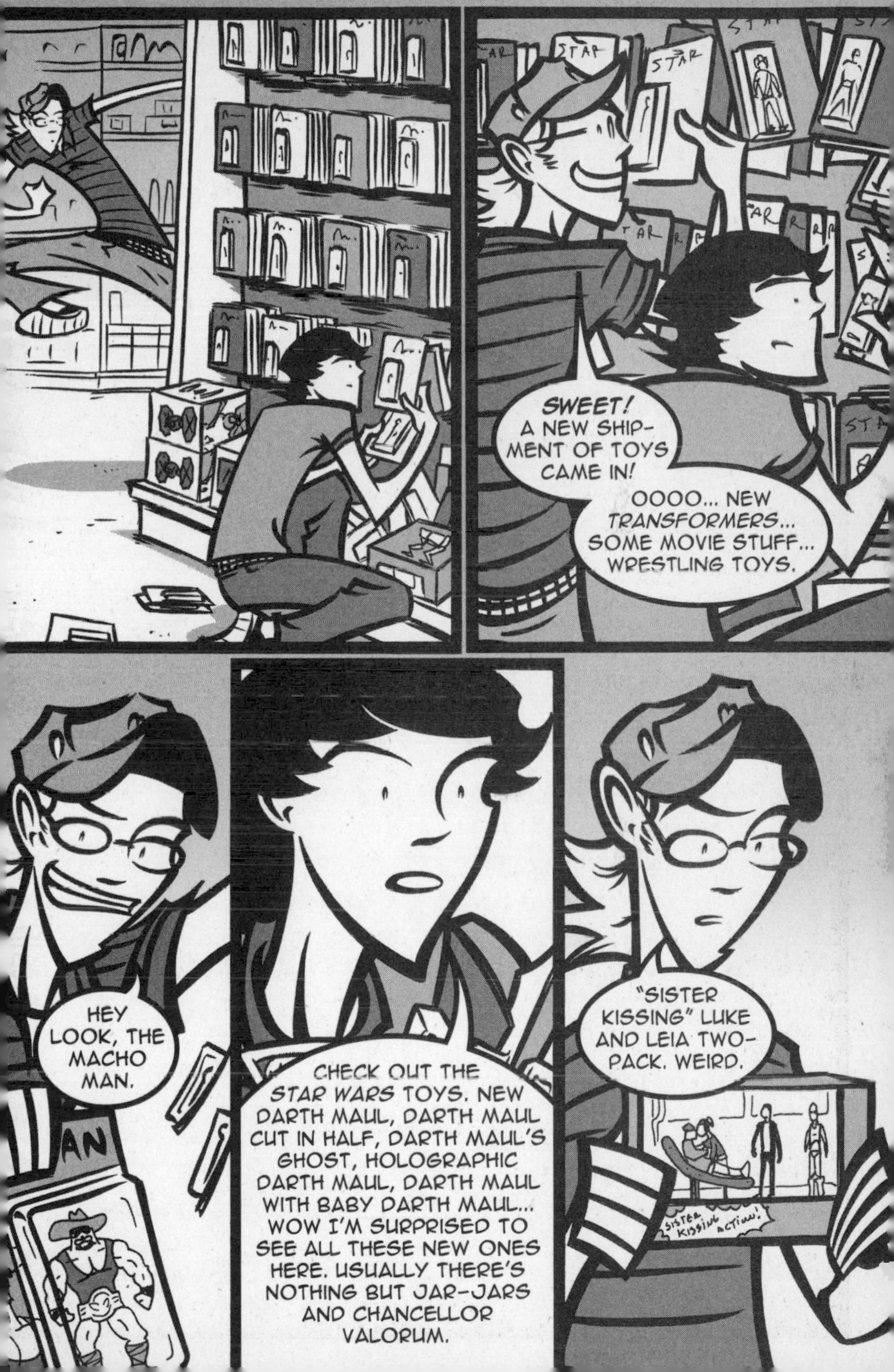
SWEET! A NEW SHIPMENT OF TOYS CAME IN!
OOOO... NEW TRANSFORMERS... SOME MOVIE STUFF... WRESTLING TOYS.
HEY LOOK, THE MACHO MAN.
CHECK OUT THE STAR WARS TOYS. NEW DARTH MAUL, DARTH MAUL CUT IN HALF, DARTH MAUL'S GHOST, HOLOGRAPHIC DARTH MAUL, DARTH MAUL WITH BABY DARTH MAUL... WOW I'M SURPRISED TO SEE ALL THESE NEW ONES HERE. USUALLY THERE'S NOTHING BUT JAR-JARS AND CHANCELLOR VALORUM.
"SISTER KISSING" LUKE AND LEIA TWO-PACK. WEIRD.
SISTER KISSING ACTION!

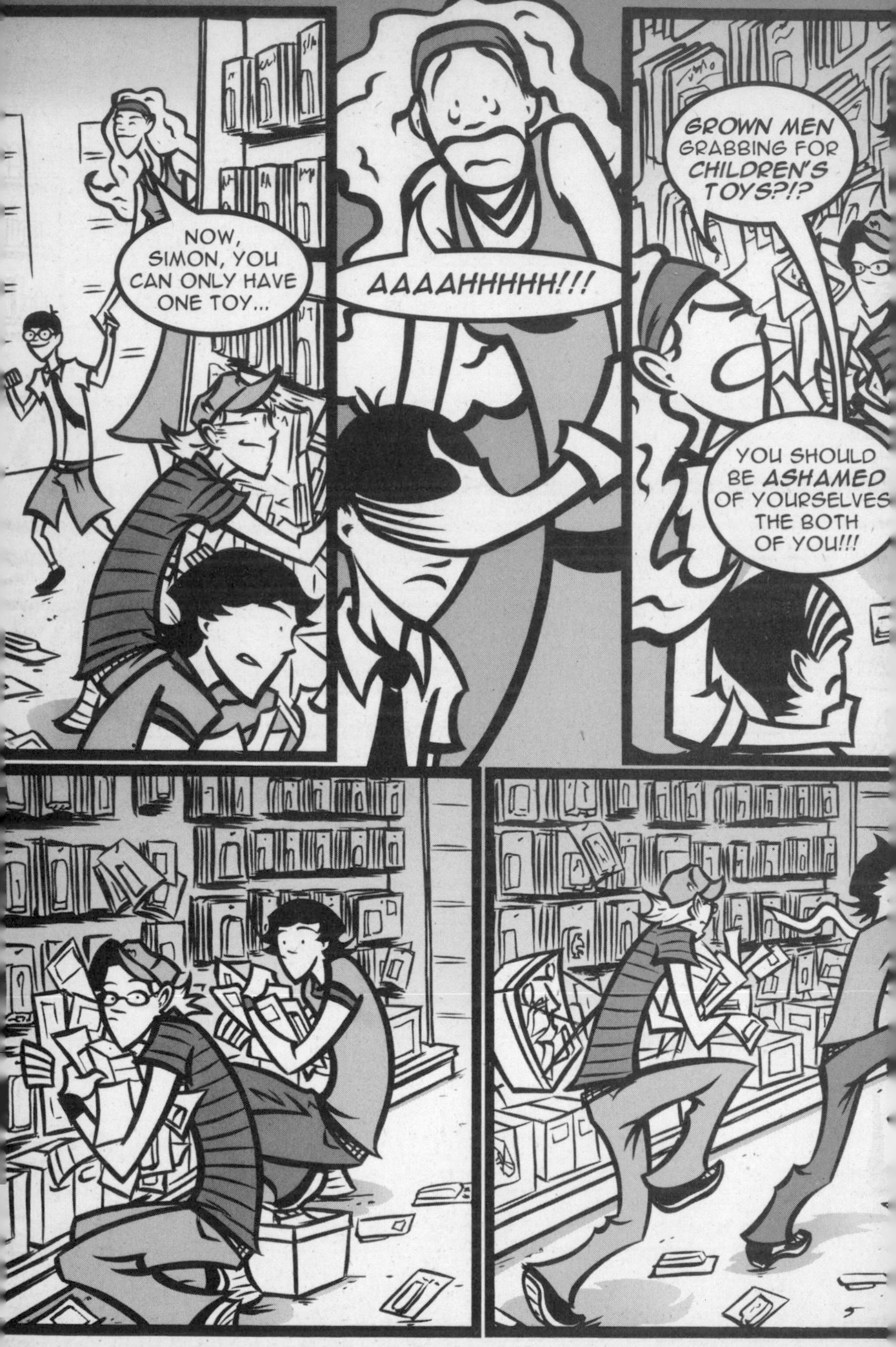
NOW, SIMON, YOU CAN ONLY HAVE ONE TOY...
AAAAHHHHH!!!
GROWN MEN GRABBING FOR CHILDREN'S TOYS?!?
YOU SHOULD BE ASHAMED OF YOURSELVES THE BOTH OF YOU!!!

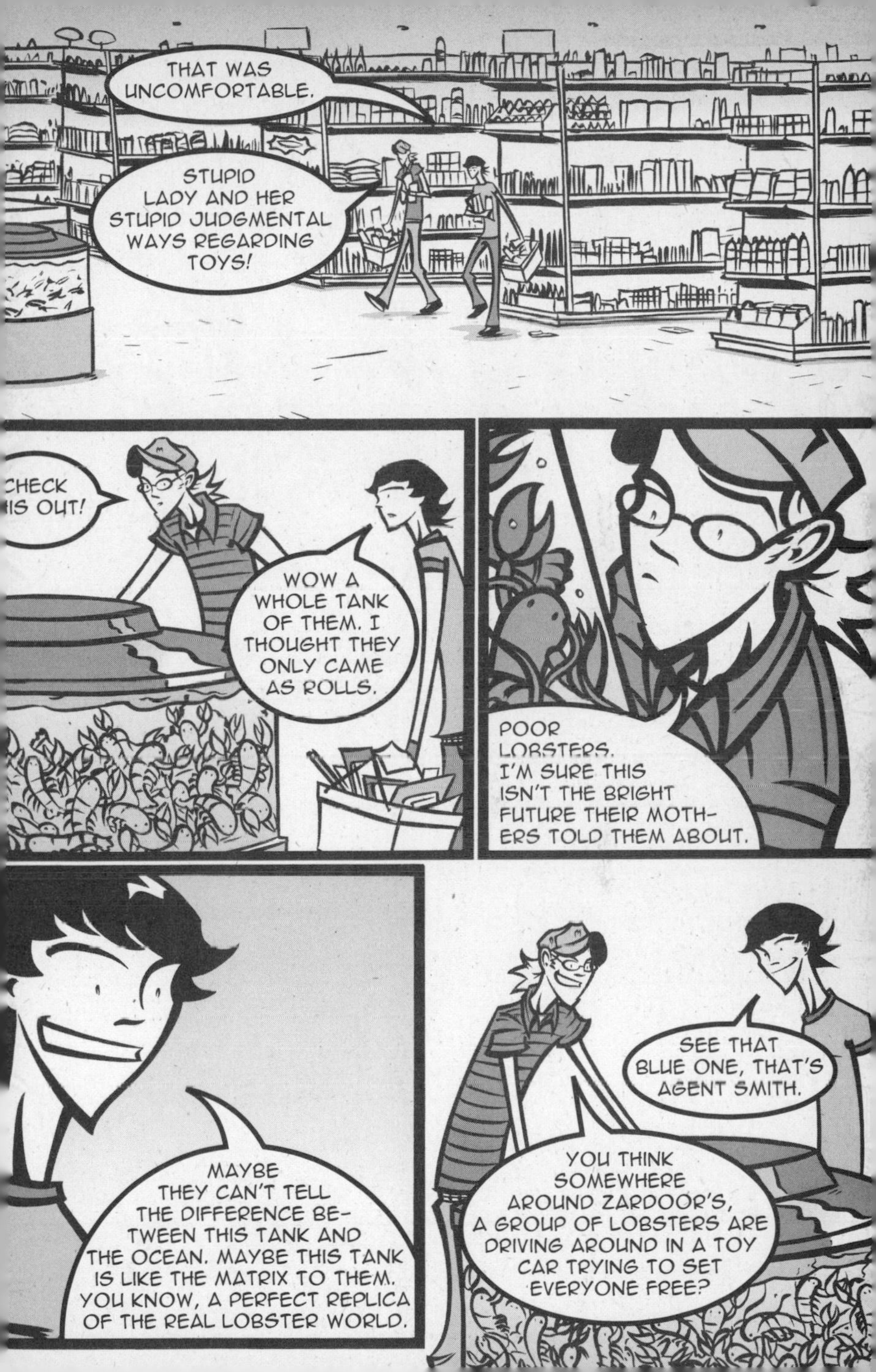
THAT WAS UNCOMFORTABLE.
STUPID LADY AND HER STUPID JUDGMENTAL WAYS REGARDING TOYS!
CHECK THIS OUT!
WOW A WHOLE TANK OF THEM. I THOUGHT THEY ONLY CAME AS ROLLS.
POOR LOBSTERS. I'M SURE THIS ISN'T THE BRIGHT FUTURE THEIR MOTH-ERS TOLD THEM ABOUT.
MAYBE THEY CAN'T TELL THE DIFFERENCE BE-TWEEN THIS TANK AND THE OCEAN. MAYBE THIS TANK IS LIKE THE MATRIX TO THEM. YOU KNOW, A PERFECT REPLICA OF THE REAL LOBSTER WORLD.
SEE THAT BLUE ONE, THAT'S AGENT SMITH.
YOU THINK SOMEWHERE AROUND ZARDOOR'S, A GROUP OF LOBSTERS ARE DRIVING AROUND IN A TOY CAR TRYING TO SET EVERYONE FREE?

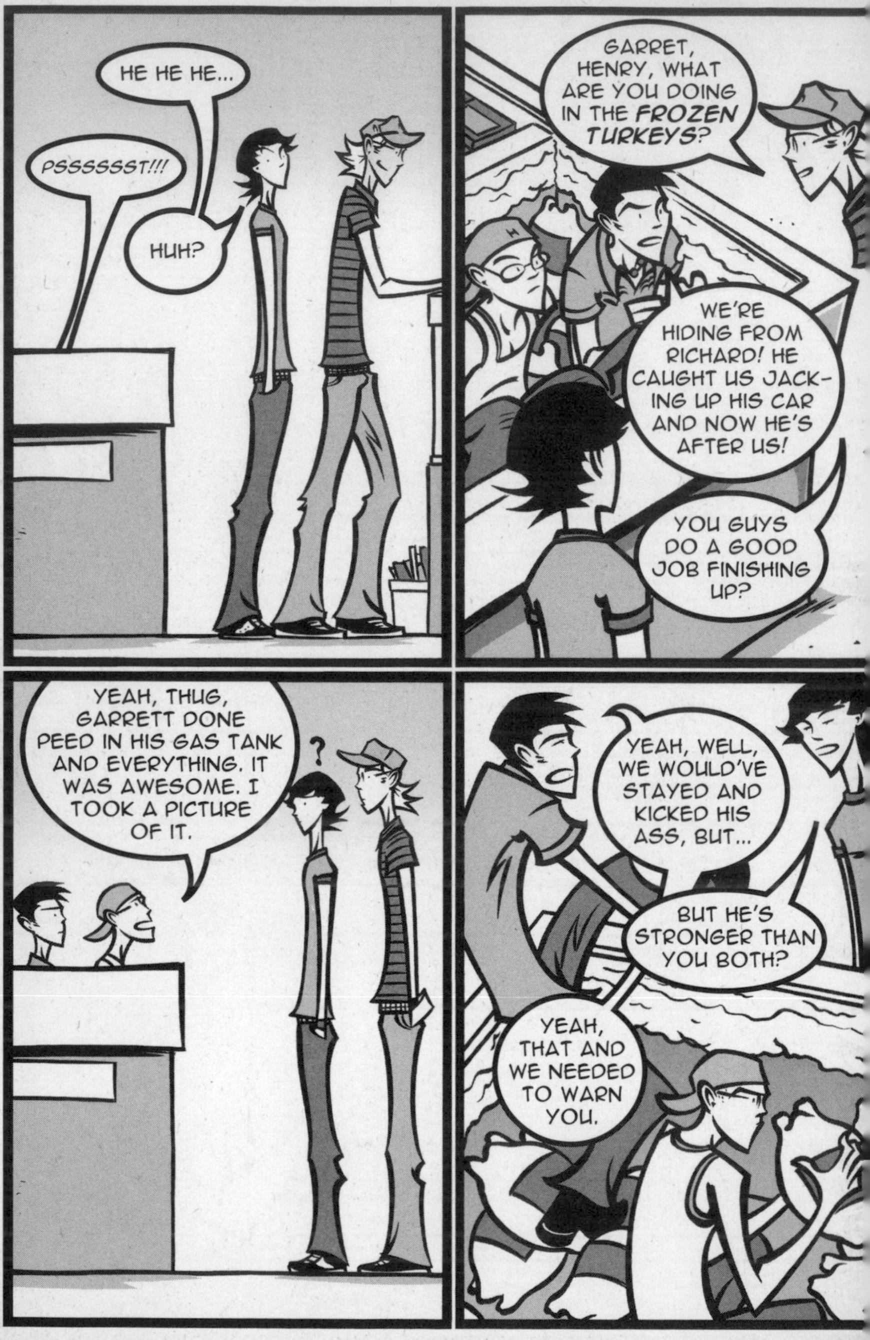
HE HE HE...
PSSSSSST!!!
HUH?
GARRET, HENRY, WHAT ARE YOU DOING IN THE *FROZEN TURKEYS*?
WE'RE HIDING FROM RICHARD! HE CAUGHT US JACK-ING UP HIS CAR AND NOW HE'S AFTER US!
YOU GUYS DO A GOOD JOB FINISHING UP?
YEAH, THUG, GARRETT DONE PEED IN HIS GAS TANK AND EVERYTHING. IT WAS AWESOME. I TOOK A PICTURE OF IT.
?
YEAH, WELL, WE WOULD'VE STAYED AND KICKED HIS ASS, BUT...
BUT HE'S STRONGER THAN YOU BOTH?
YEAH, THAT AND WE NEEDED TO WARN YOU.

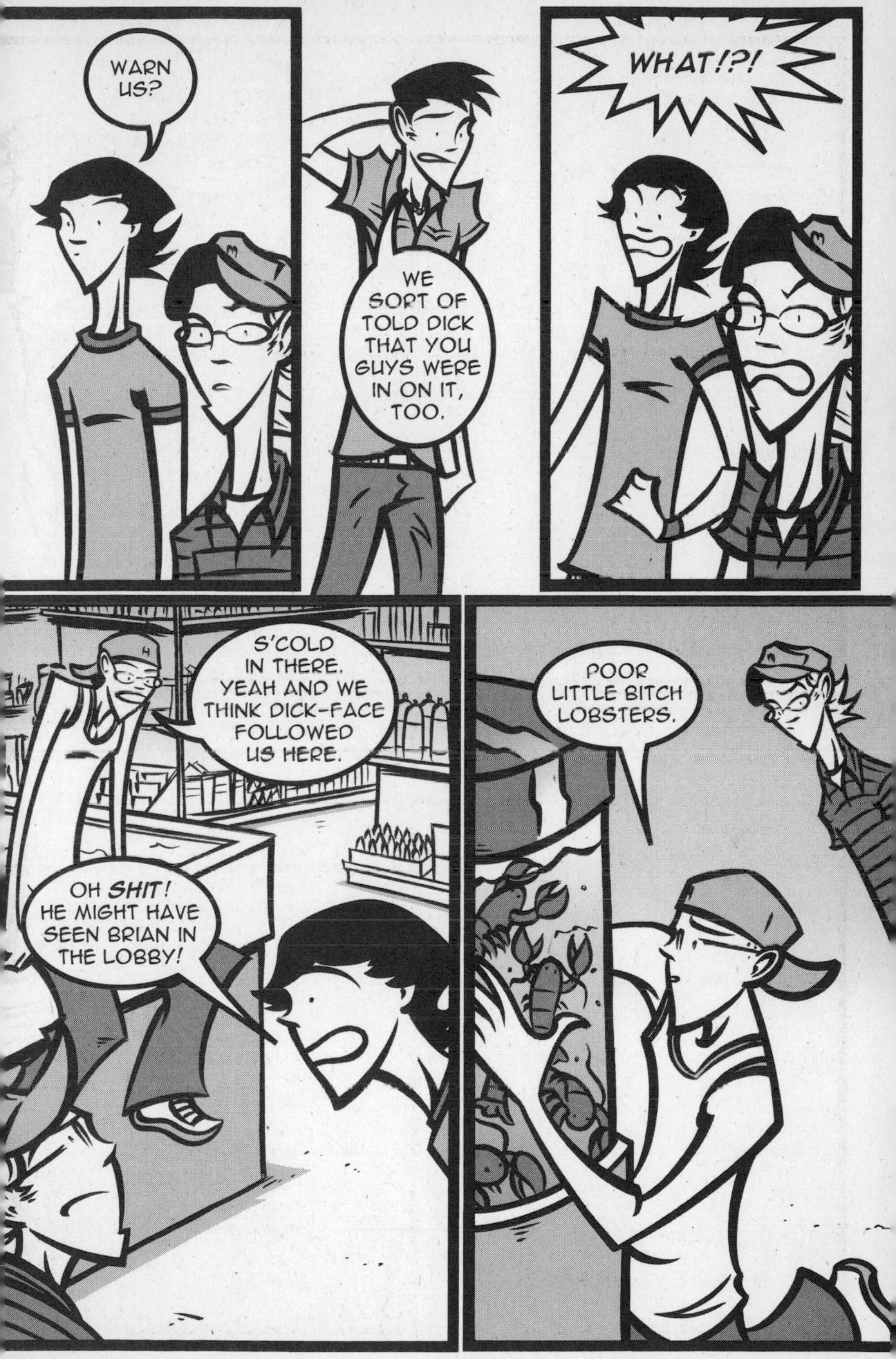
WARN US?
WE SORT OF TOLD DICK THAT YOU GUYS WERE IN ON IT, TOO.
WHAT!?!
S'COLD IN THERE. YEAH AND WE THINK DICK-FACE FOLLOWED US HERE.
OH SHIT! HE MIGHT HAVE SEEN BRIAN IN THE LOBBY!
POOR LITTLE BITCH LOBSTERS.

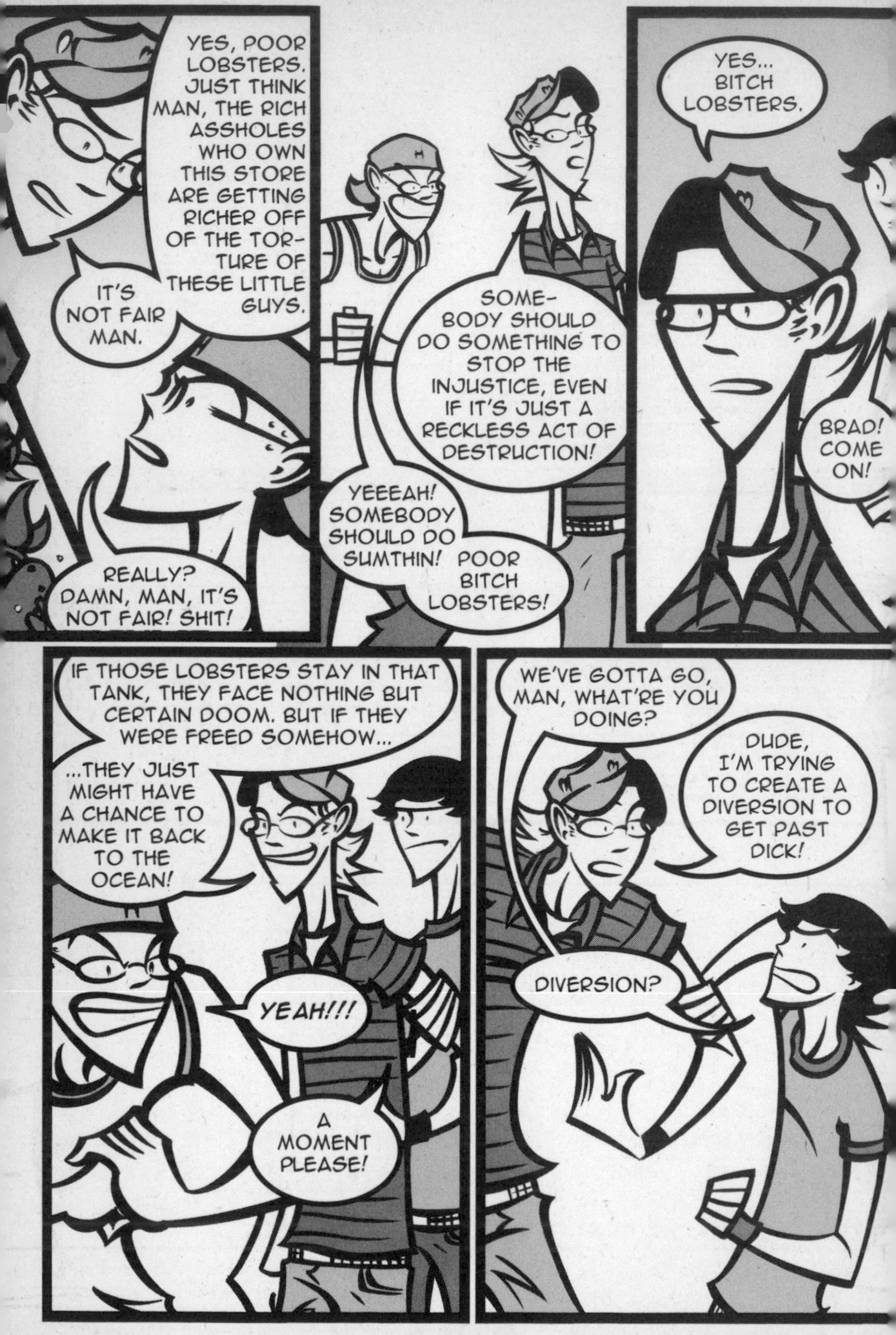
YES, POOR LOBSTERS. JUST THINK MAN, THE RICH ASSHOLES WHO OWN THIS STORE ARE GETTING RICHER OFF OF THE TORTURE OF THESE LITTLE GUYS.
IT'S NOT FAIR MAN.
REALLY? DAMN, MAN, IT'S NOT FAIR! SHIT!
SOMEBODY SHOULD DO SOMETHING TO STOP THE INJUSTICE, EVEN IF IT'S JUST A RECKLESS ACT OF DESTRUCTION!
YEEEAH! SOMEBODY SHOULD DO SUMTHIN! POOR BITCH LOBSTERS!
YES... BITCH LOBSTERS.
BRAD! COME ON!
IF THOSE LOBSTERS STAY IN THAT TANK, THEY FACE NOTHING BUT CERTAIN DOOM. BUT IF THEY WERE FREED SOMEHOW...
...THEY JUST MIGHT HAVE A CHANCE TO MAKE IT BACK TO THE OCEAN!
YEAH!!!
A MOMENT PLEASE!
WE'VE GOTTA GO, MAN, WHAT'RE YOU DOING?
DUDE, I'M TRYING TO CREATE A DIVERSION TO GET PAST DICK!
DIVERSION?

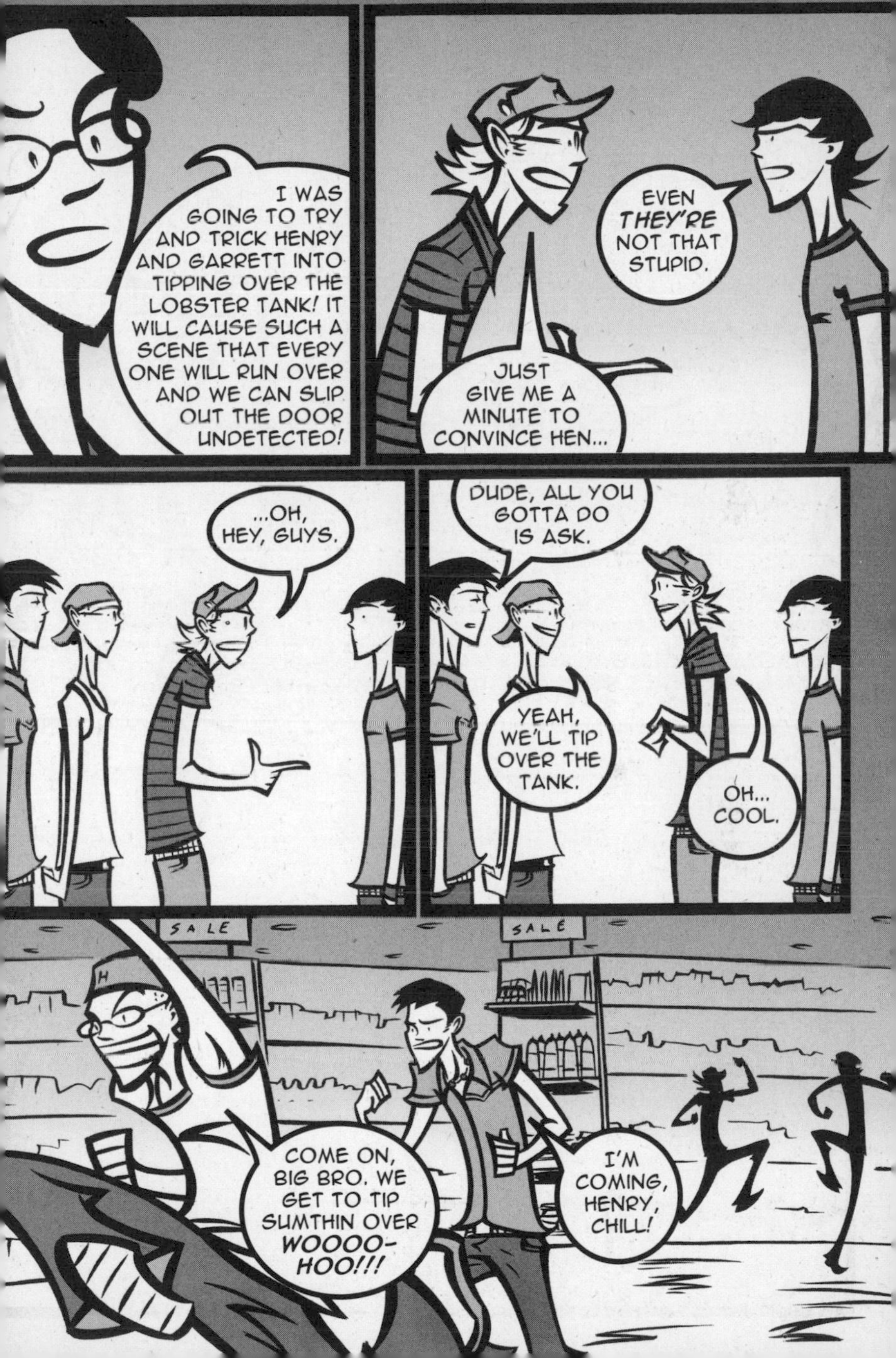
I WAS GOING TO TRY AND TRICK HENRY AND GARRETT INTO TIPPING OVER THE LOBSTER TANK! IT WILL CAUSE SUCH A SCENE THAT EVERY ONE WILL RUN OVER AND WE CAN SLIP OUT THE DOOR UNDETECTED!
EVEN *THEY'RE* NOT THAT STUPID.
JUST GIVE ME A MINUTE TO CONVINCE HEN...
...OH, HEY, GUYS.
DUDE, ALL YOU GOTTA DO IS ASK.
YEAH, WE'LL TIP OVER THE TANK.
OH... COOL.
SALE
SALE
COME ON, BIG BRO. WE GET TO TIP SUMTHIN OVER *WOOOO-HOO!!!*
I'M COMING, HENRY, CHILL!

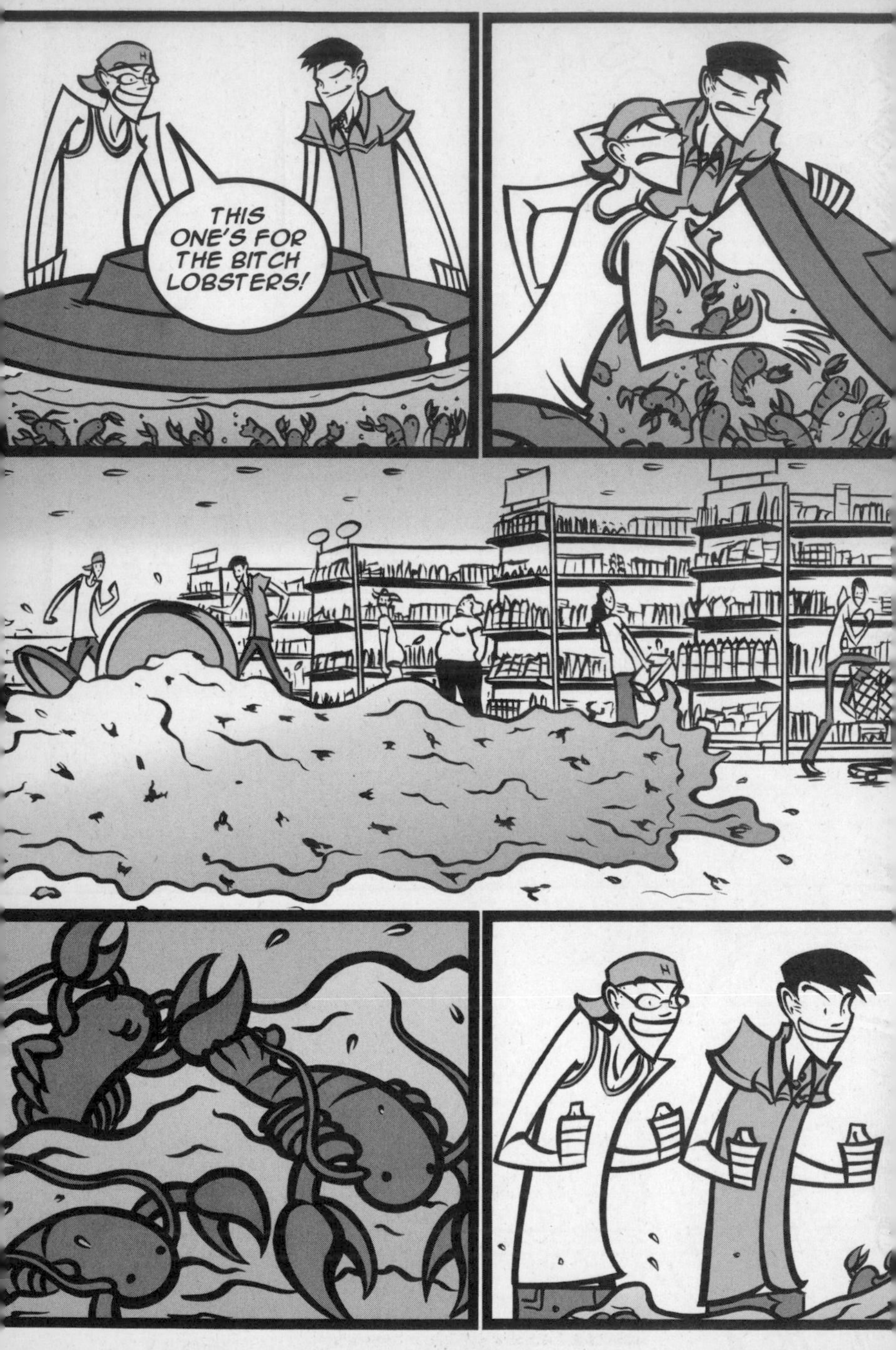
THIS ONE'S FOR THE BITCH LOBSTERS!

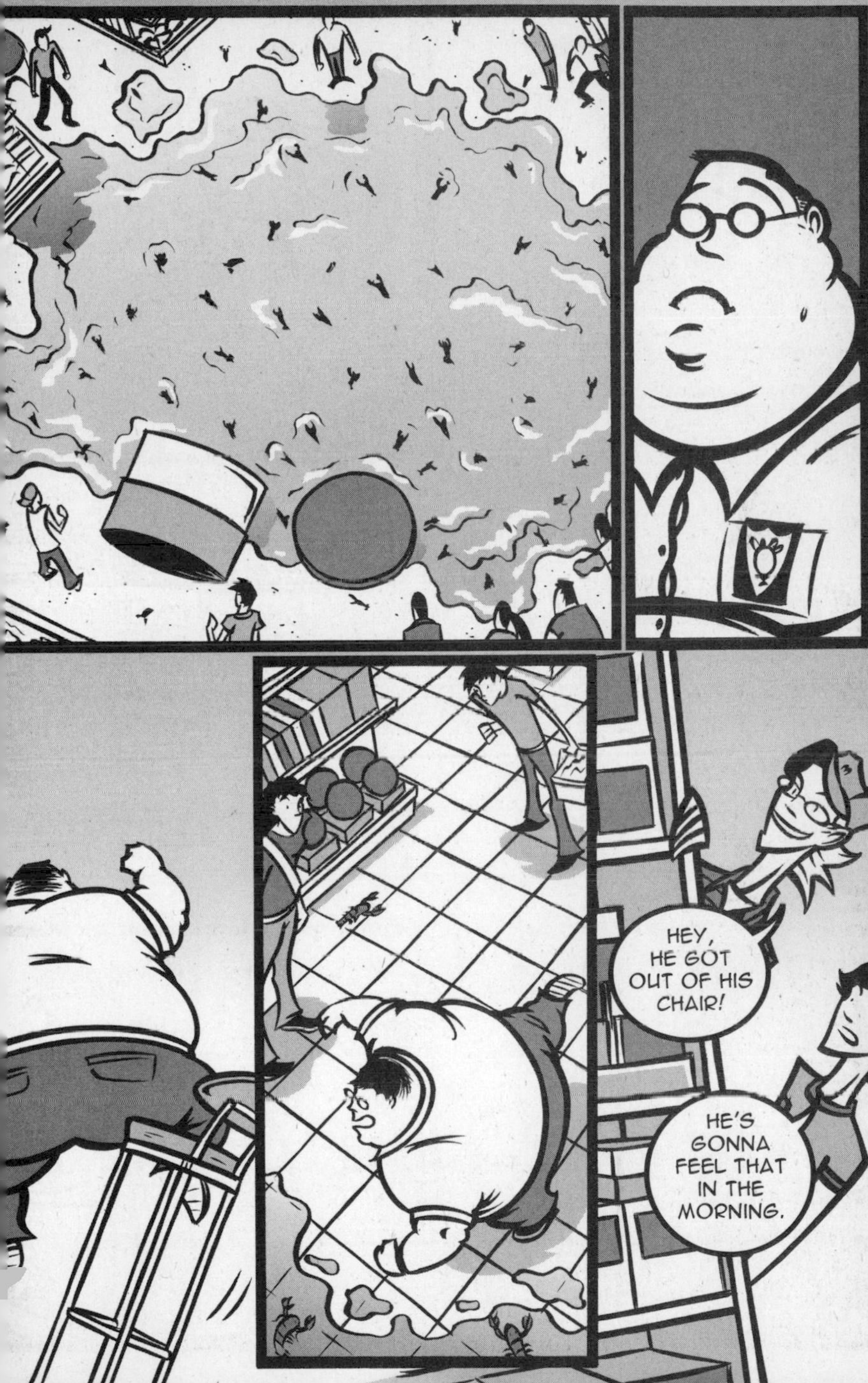
HEY, HE GOT OUT OF HIS CHAIR!
HE'S GONNA FEEL THAT IN THE MORNING.

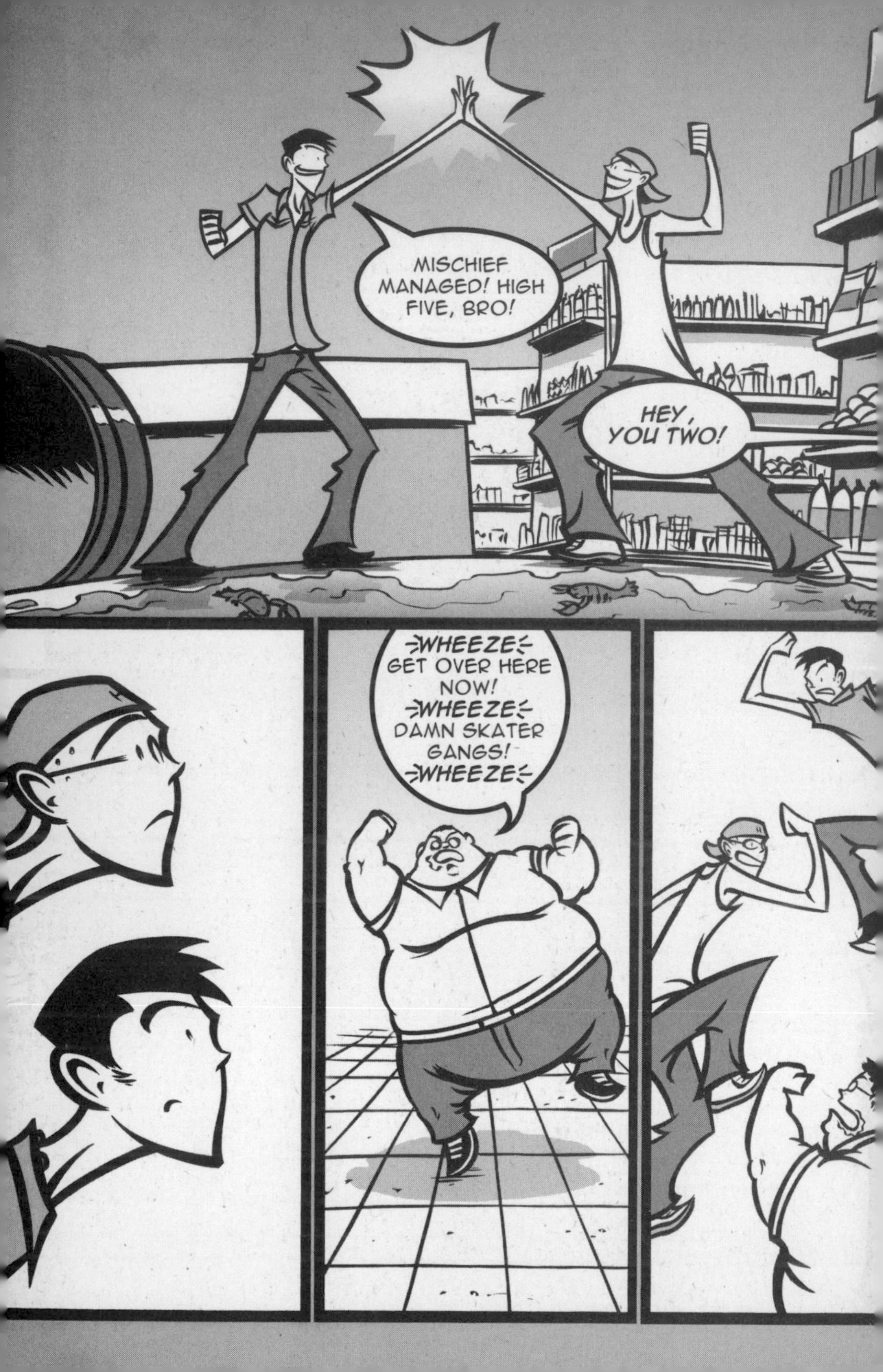
MISCHIEF MANAGED! HIGH FIVE, BRO!
HEY, YOU TWO!
-WHEEZE- GET OVER HERE NOW! -WHEEZE- DAMN SKATER GANGS! -WHEEZE-

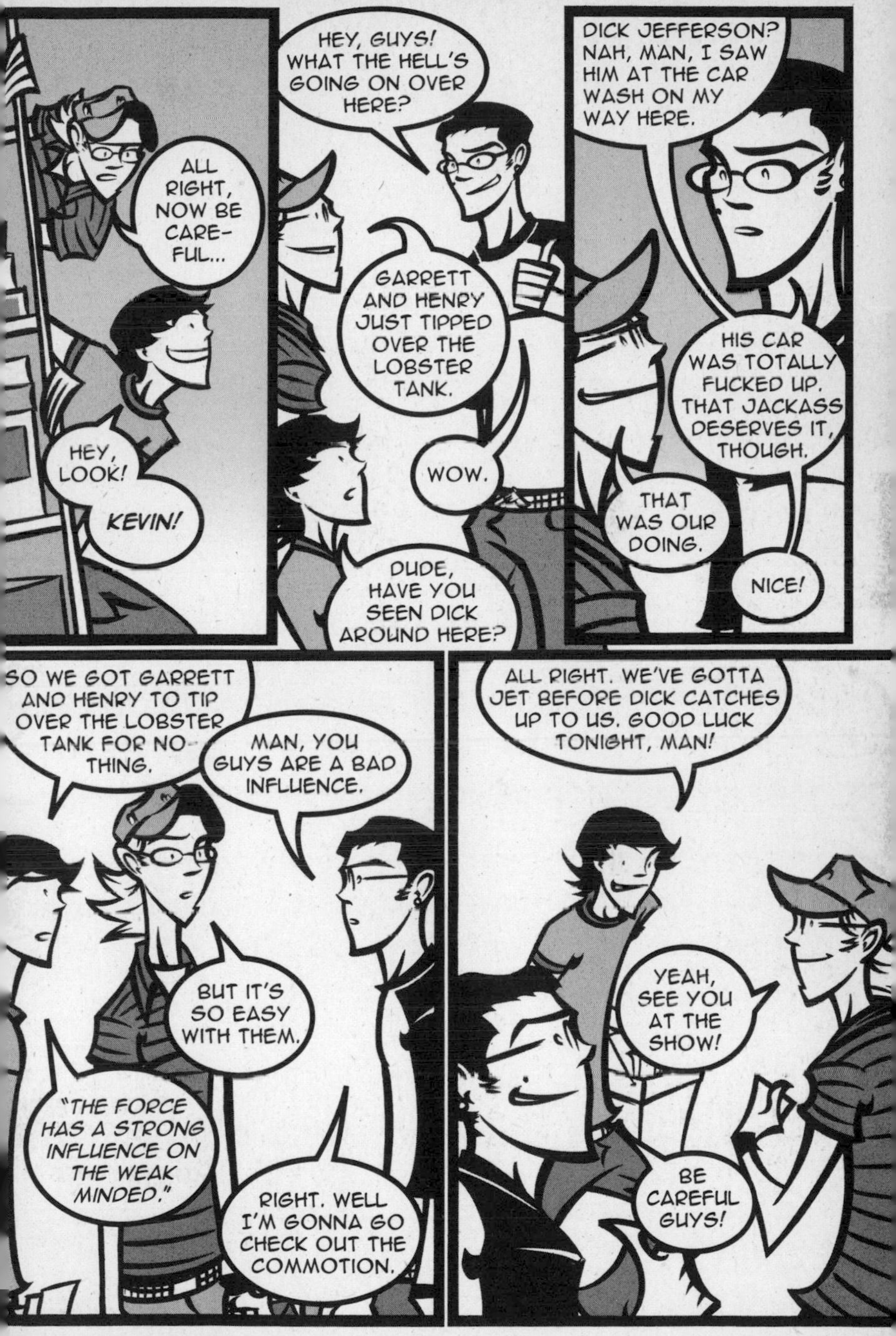
ALL RIGHT, NOW BE CARE-FUL...
HEY, LOOK!
KEVIN!
HEY, GUYS! WHAT THE HELL'S GOING ON OVER HERE?
GARRETT AND HENRY JUST TIPPED OVER THE LOBSTER TANK.
WOW.
DUDE, HAVE YOU SEEN DICK AROUND HERE?
DICK JEFFERSON? NAH, MAN, I SAW HIM AT THE CAR WASH ON MY WAY HERE.
HIS CAR WAS TOTALLY FUCKED UP. THAT JACKASS DESERVES IT, THOUGH.
THAT WAS OUR DOING.
NICE!
SO WE GOT GARRETT AND HENRY TO TIP OVER THE LOBSTER TANK FOR NO-THING.
MAN, YOU GUYS ARE A BAD INFLUENCE.
BUT IT'S SO EASY WITH THEM.
"THE FORCE HAS A STRONG INFLUENCE ON THE WEAK MINDED."
RIGHT. WELL I'M GONNA GO CHECK OUT THE COMMOTION.
ALL RIGHT. WE'VE GOTTA JET BEFORE DICK CATCHES UP TO US. GOOD LUCK TONIGHT, MAN!
YEAH, SEE YOU AT THE SHOW!
BE CAREFUL GUYS!

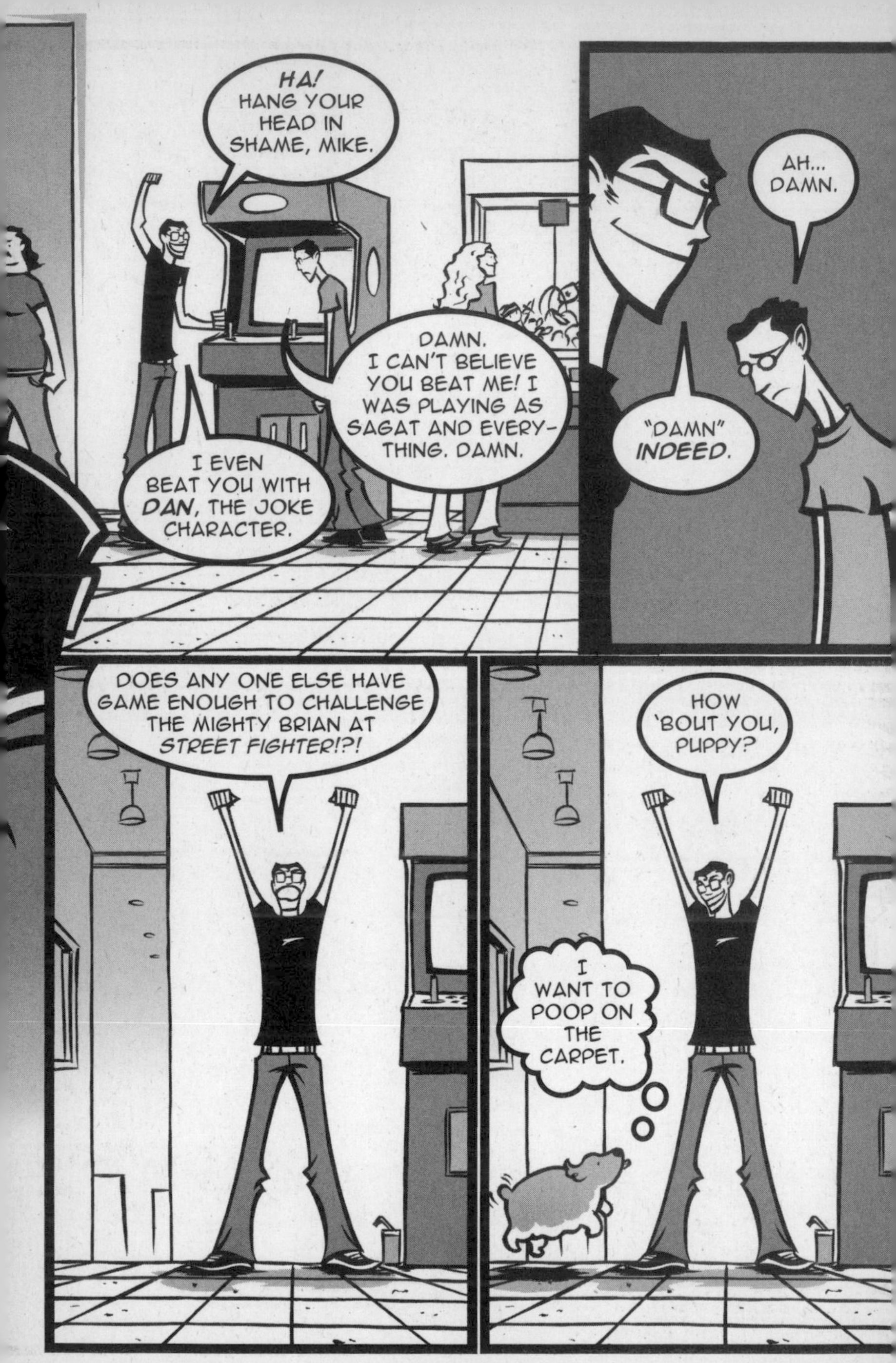
HA! HANG YOUR HEAD IN SHAME, MIKE.
DAMN. I CAN'T BELIEVE YOU BEAT ME! I WAS PLAYING AS SAGAT AND EVERY-THING. DAMN.
I EVEN BEAT YOU WITH DAN, THE JOKE CHARACTER.
AH... DAMN.
"DAMN" INDEED.
DOES ANY ONE ELSE HAVE GAME ENOUGH TO CHALLENGE THE MIGHTY BRIAN AT STREET FIGHTER!?!
HOW 'BOUT YOU, PUPPY?
I WANT TO POOP ON THE CARPET.

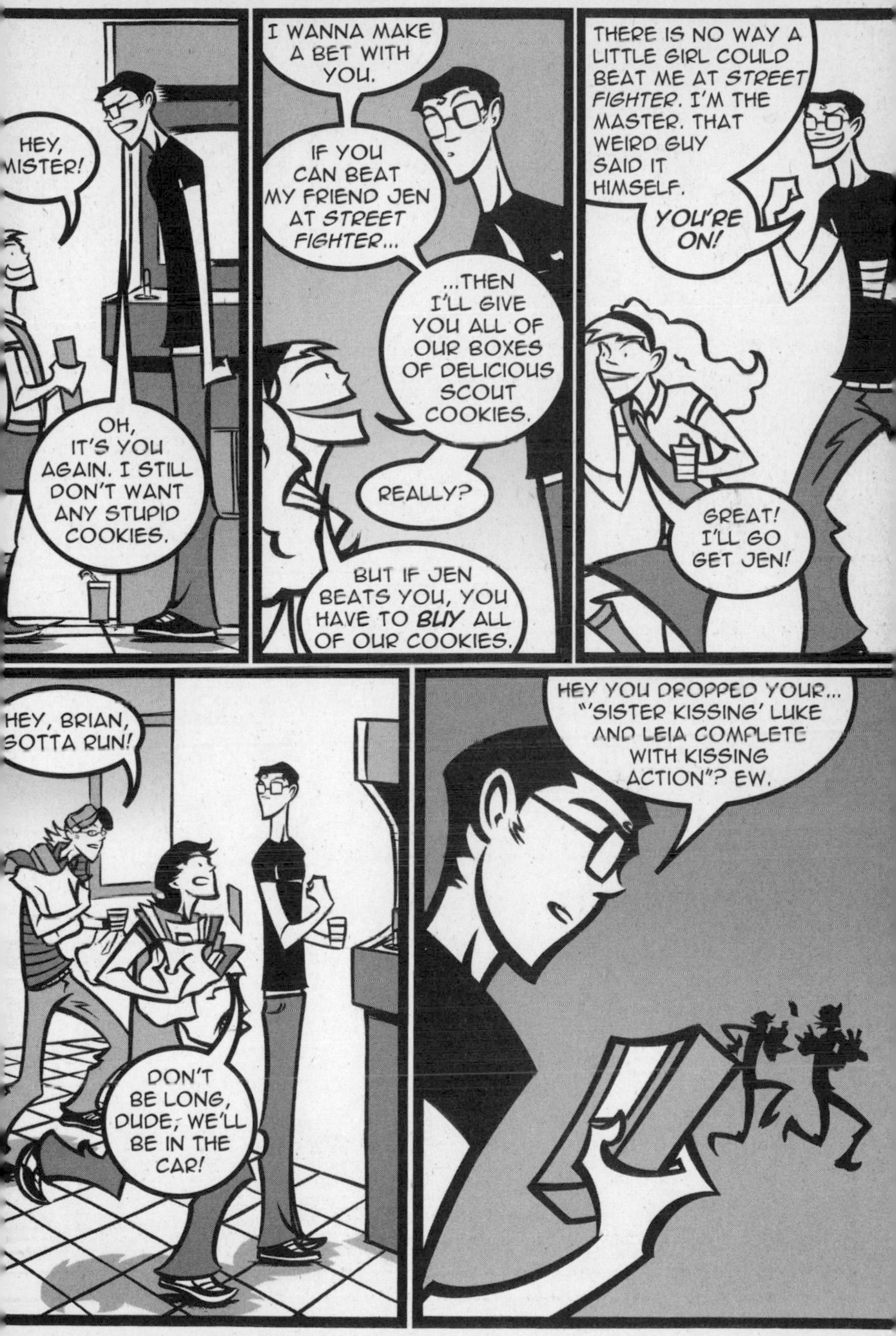
HEY, MISTER!
OH, IT'S YOU AGAIN. I STILL DON'T WANT ANY STUPID COOKIES.
I WANNA MAKE A BET WITH YOU.
IF YOU CAN BEAT MY FRIEND JEN AT STREET FIGHTER...
...THEN I'LL GIVE YOU ALL OF OUR BOXES OF DELICIOUS SCOUT COOKIES.
REALLY?
BUT IF JEN BEATS YOU, YOU HAVE TO BUY ALL OF OUR COOKIES.
THERE IS NO WAY A LITTLE GIRL COULD BEAT ME AT STREET FIGHTER. I'M THE MASTER. THAT WEIRD GUY SAID IT HIMSELF.
YOU'RE ON!
GREAT! I'LL GO GET JEN!
HEY, BRIAN, GOTTA RUN!
DON'T BE LONG, DUDE, WE'LL BE IN THE CAR!
HEY YOU DROPPED YOUR... "'SISTER KISSING' LUKE AND LEIA COMPLETE WITH KISSING ACTION"? EW.

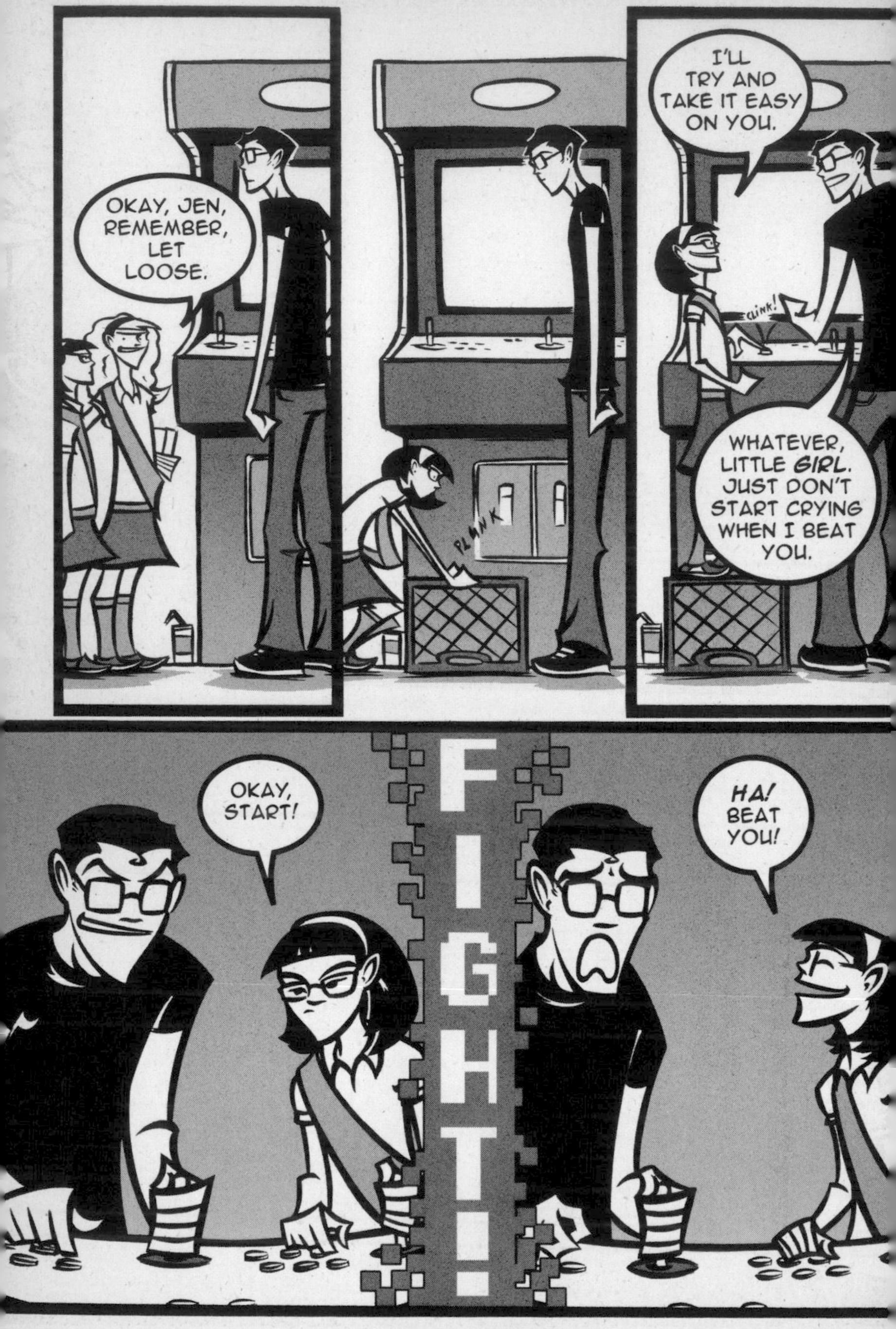

OKAY, JEN, REMEMBER, LET LOOSE.
PLUNK
I'LL TRY AND TAKE IT EASY ON YOU.
CLINK!
WHATEVER, LITTLE GIRL. JUST DON'T START CRYING WHEN I BEAT YOU.
OKAY, START!
FIGHT!
HA! BEAT YOU!

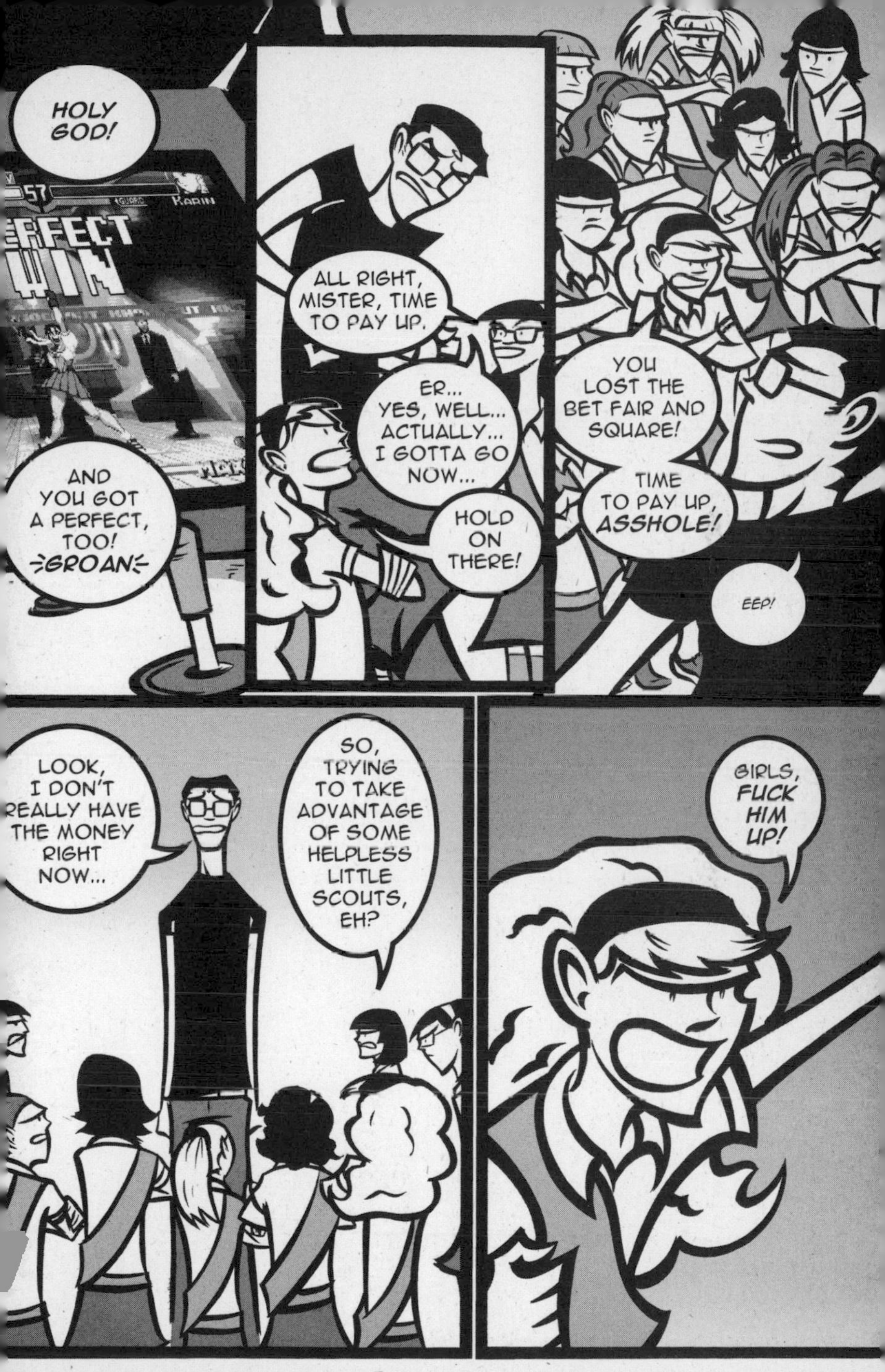
HOLY GOD!
57
GUARD
KARIN
ERFECT WIN
AND YOU GOT A PERFECT, TOO! GROAN
ALL RIGHT, MISTER, TIME TO PAY UP.
ER... YES, WELL... ACTUALLY... I GOTTA GO NOW...
HOLD ON THERE!
YOU LOST THE BET FAIR AND SQUARE!
TIME TO PAY UP, ASSHOLE!
EEP!
LOOK, I DON'T REALLY HAVE THE MONEY RIGHT NOW...
SO, TRYING TO TAKE ADVANTAGE OF SOME HELPLESS LITTLE SCOUTS, EH?
GIRLS, FUCK HIM UP!

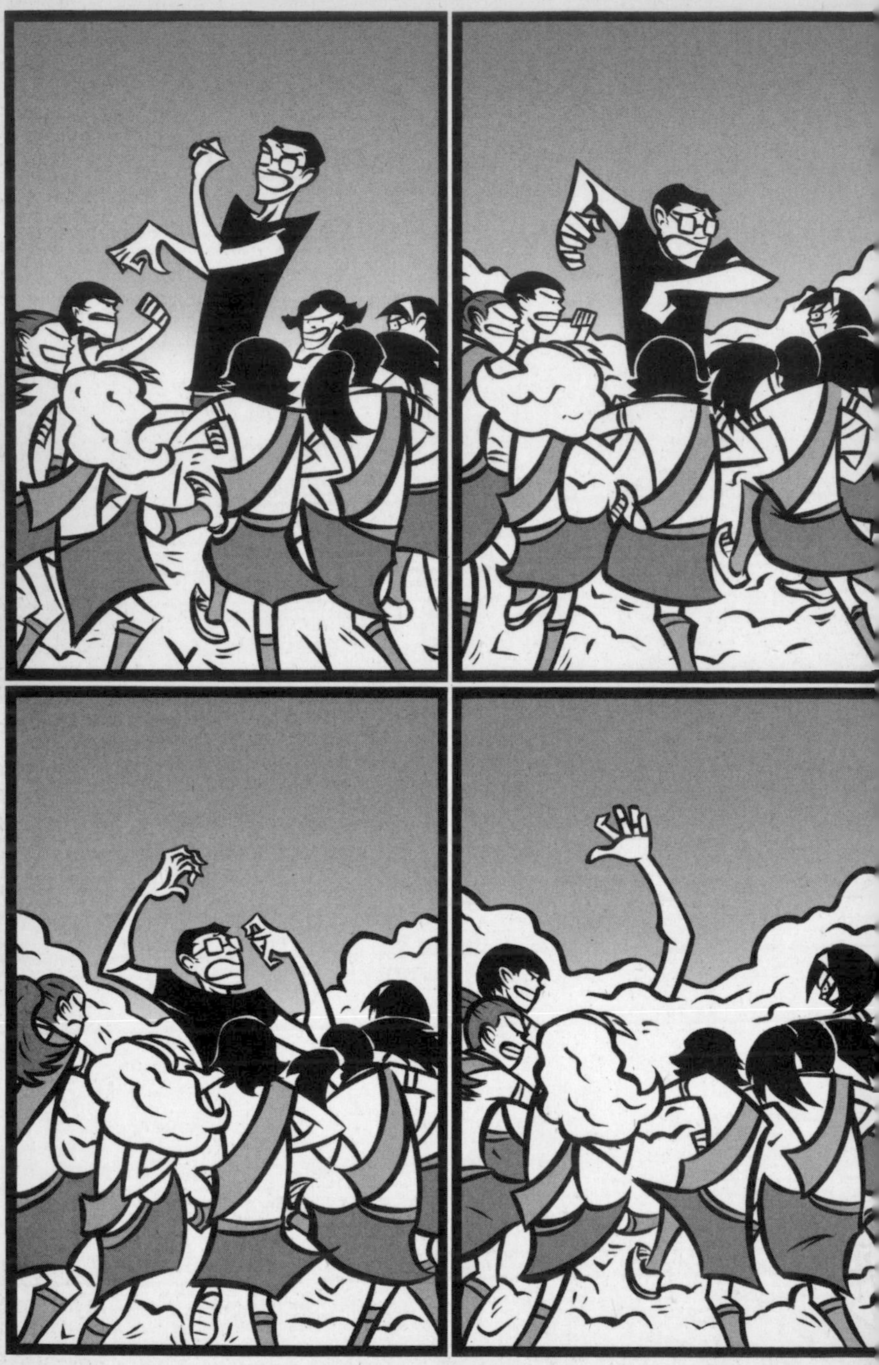

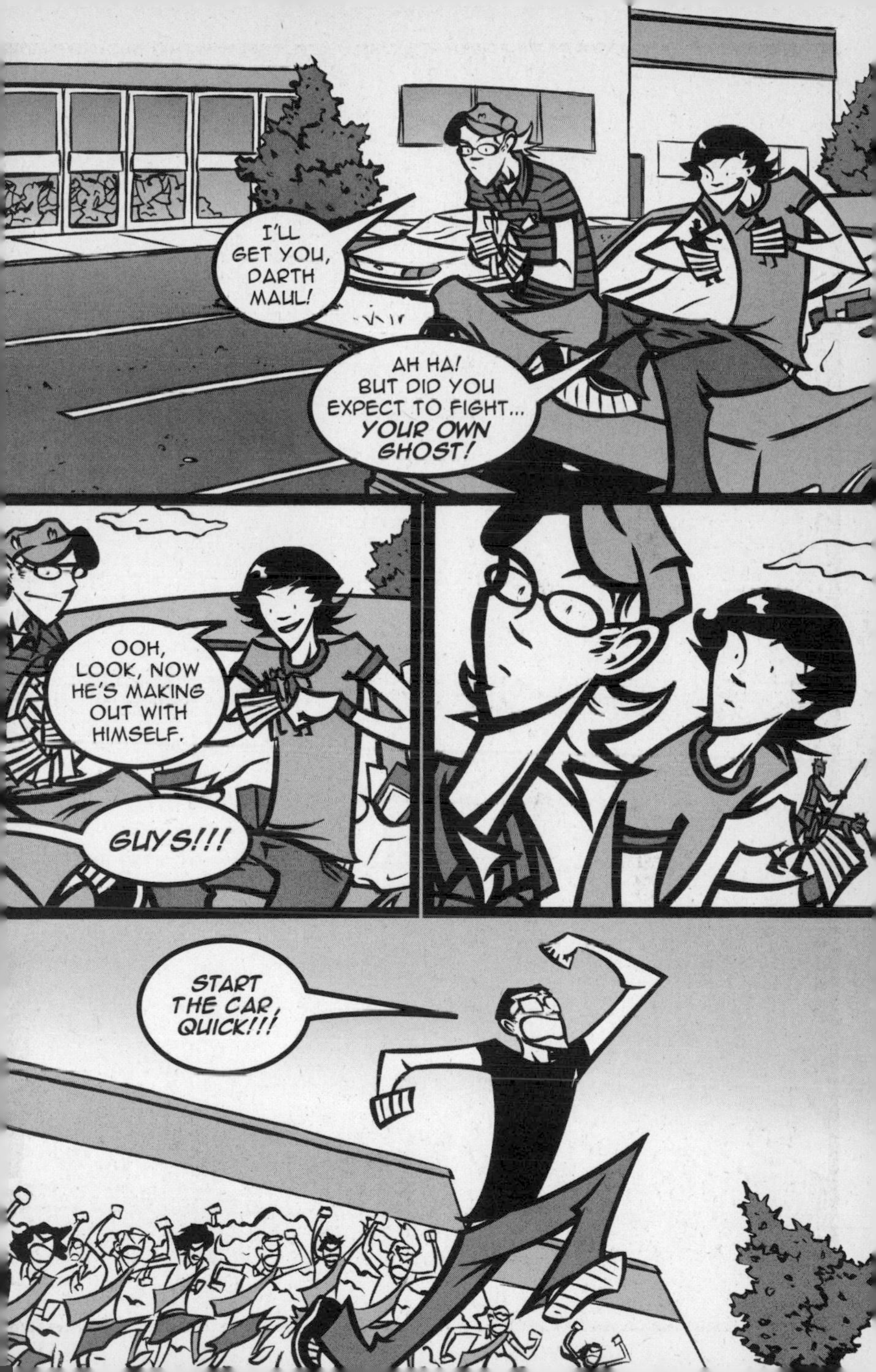

I'LL GET YOU, DARTH MAUL!
AH HA! BUT DID YOU EXPECT TO FIGHT... YOUR OWN GHOST!
OOH, LOOK, NOW HE'S MAKING OUT WITH HIMSELF.
GUYS!!!
START THE CAR, QUICK!!!

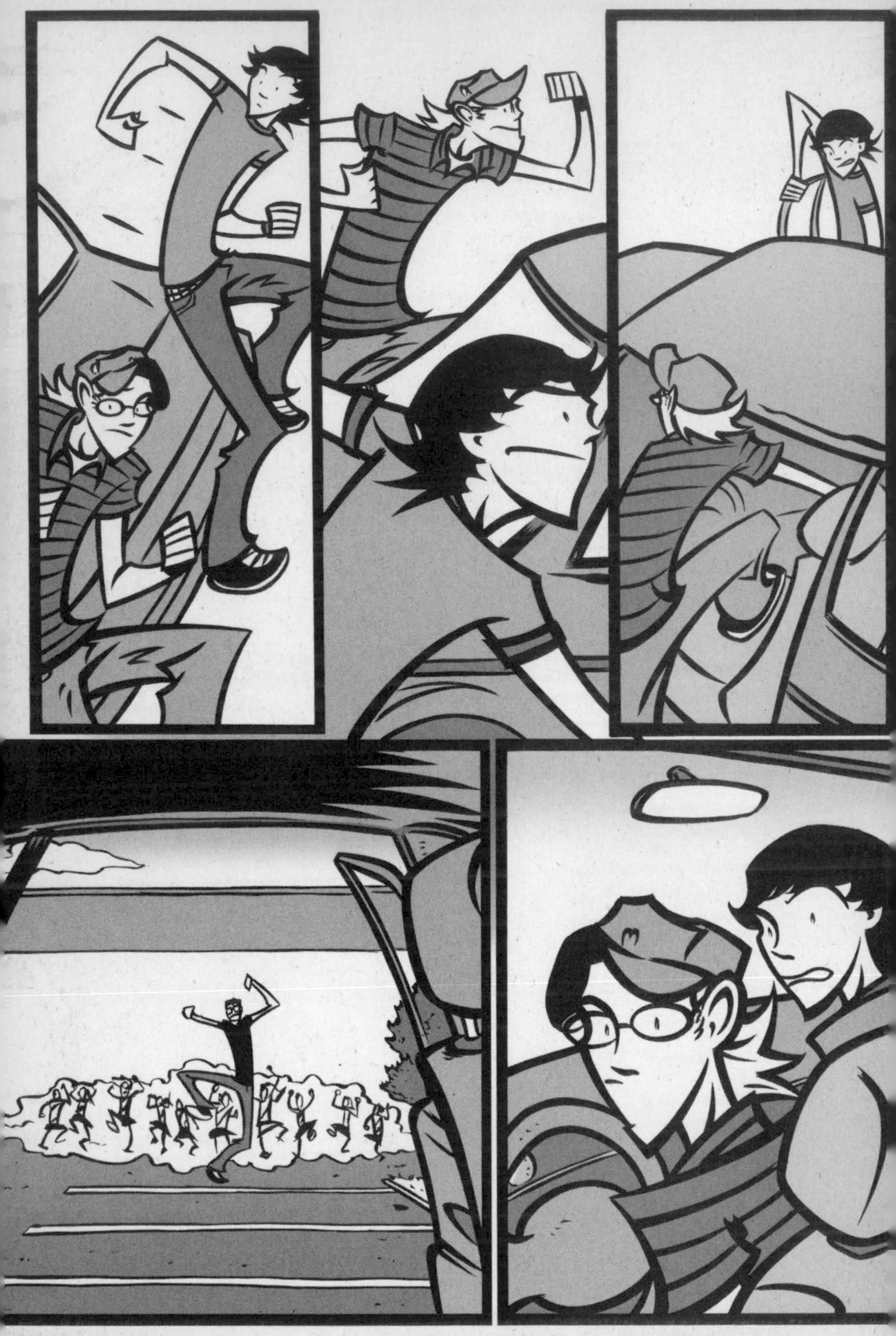

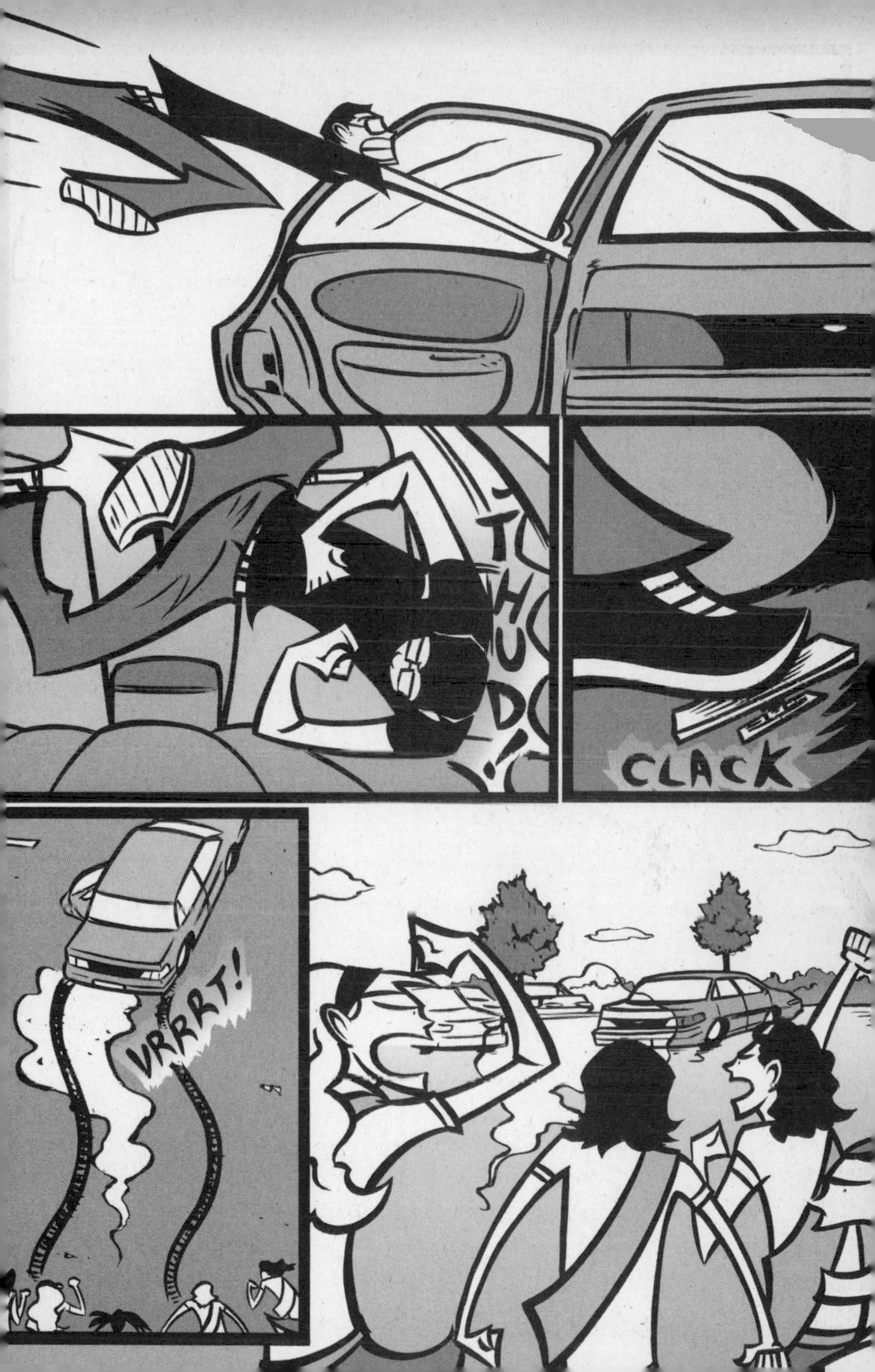
THUD!
CLACK
VRRRT!

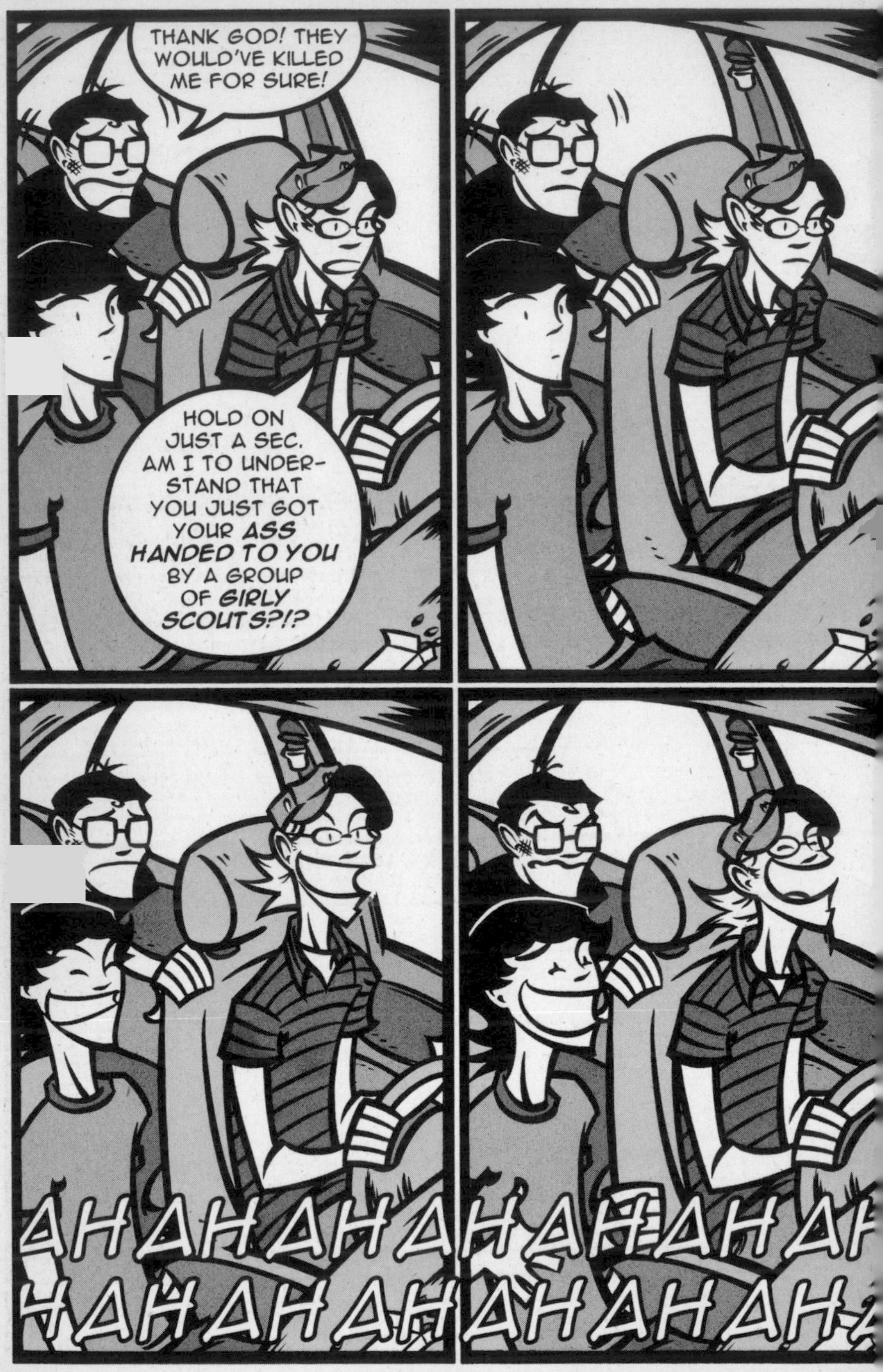

THANK GOD! THEY WOULD'VE KILLED ME FOR SURE!
HOLD ON JUST A SEC. AM I TO UNDER-STAND THAT YOU JUST GOT YOUR ASS HANDED TO YOU BY A GROUP OF GIRLY SCOUTS?!?
AHAHAHAHAHAHAHAHA
HAHAHAHAHAHAHAHAHA

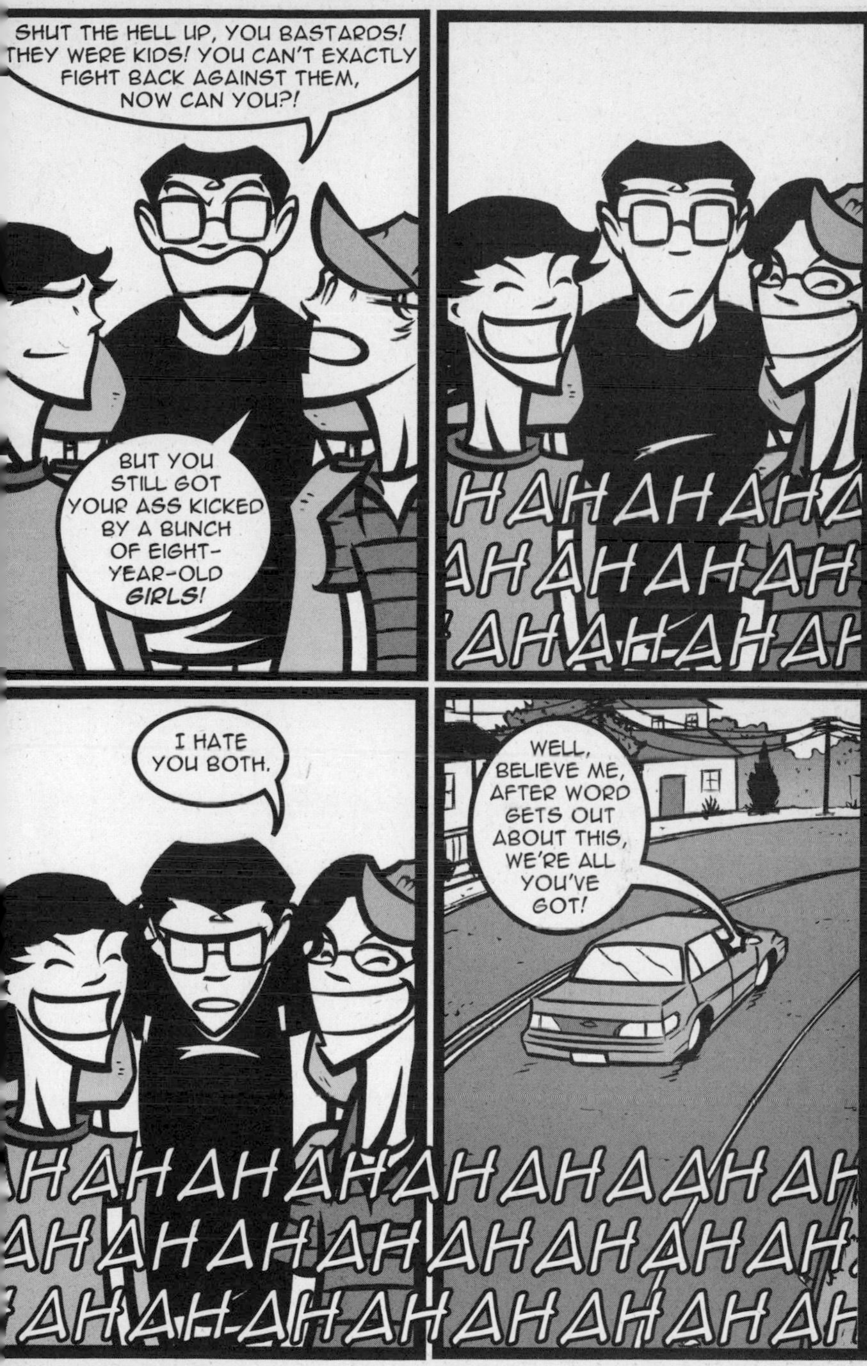
SHUT THE HELL UP, YOU BASTARDS! THEY WERE KIDS! YOU CAN'T EXACTLY FIGHT BACK AGAINST THEM, NOW CAN YOU?!
BUT YOU STILL GOT YOUR ASS KICKED BY A BUNCH OF EIGHT-YEAR-OLD GIRLS!
HAHAHAHAHA
AHAHAHAHAH
AHAHAHAHAH
I HATE YOU BOTH.
WELL, BELIEVE ME, AFTER WORD GETS OUT ABOUT THIS, WE'RE ALL YOU'VE GOT!
HAHAHAHAHAHAHAHAHAH
AHAHAHAHAHAHAHAHAH
AHAHAHAHAHAHAHAHAH

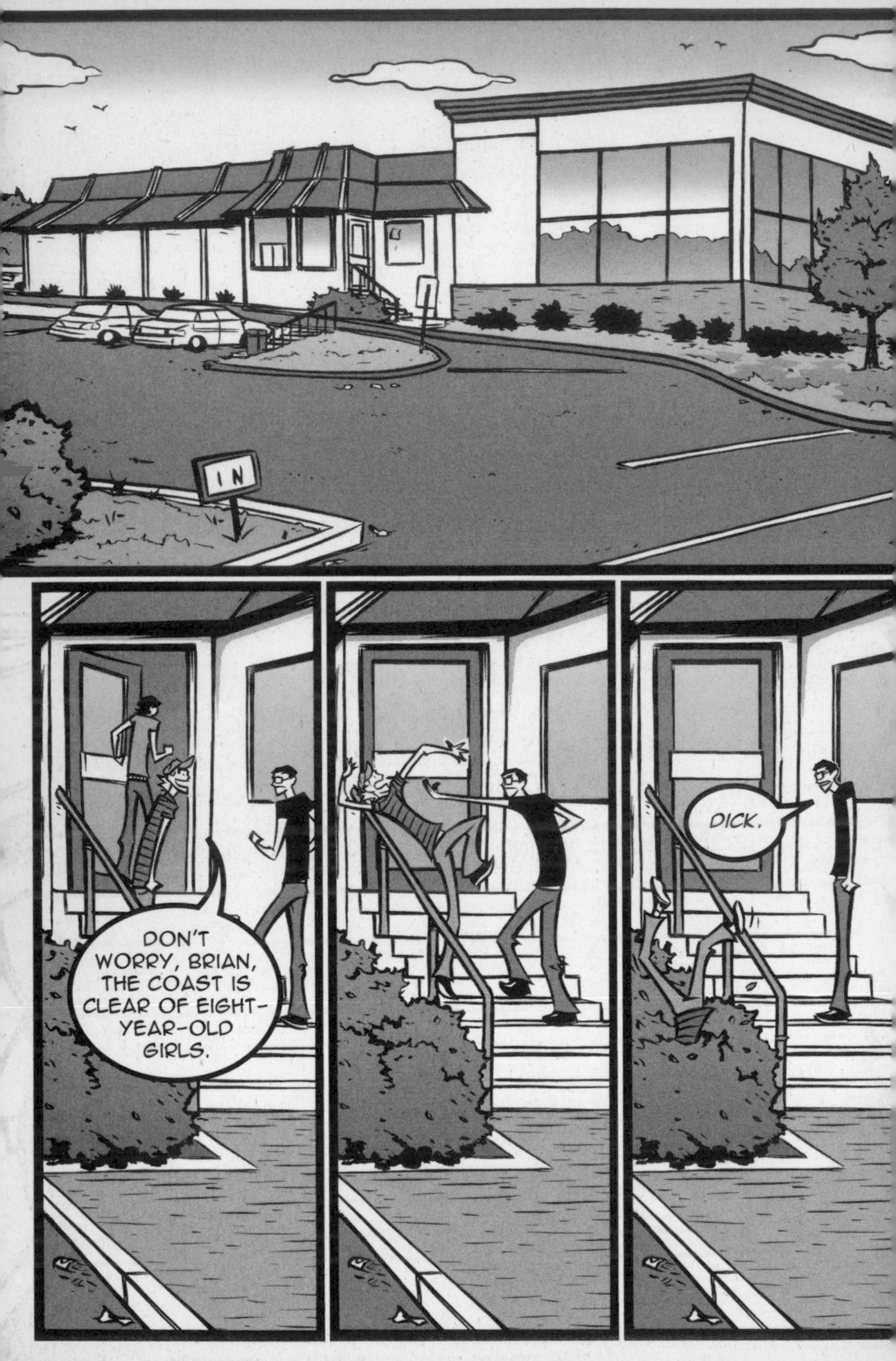
IN
DON'T WORRY, BRIAN, THE COAST IS CLEAR OF EIGHT-YEAR-OLD GIRLS.
DICK.

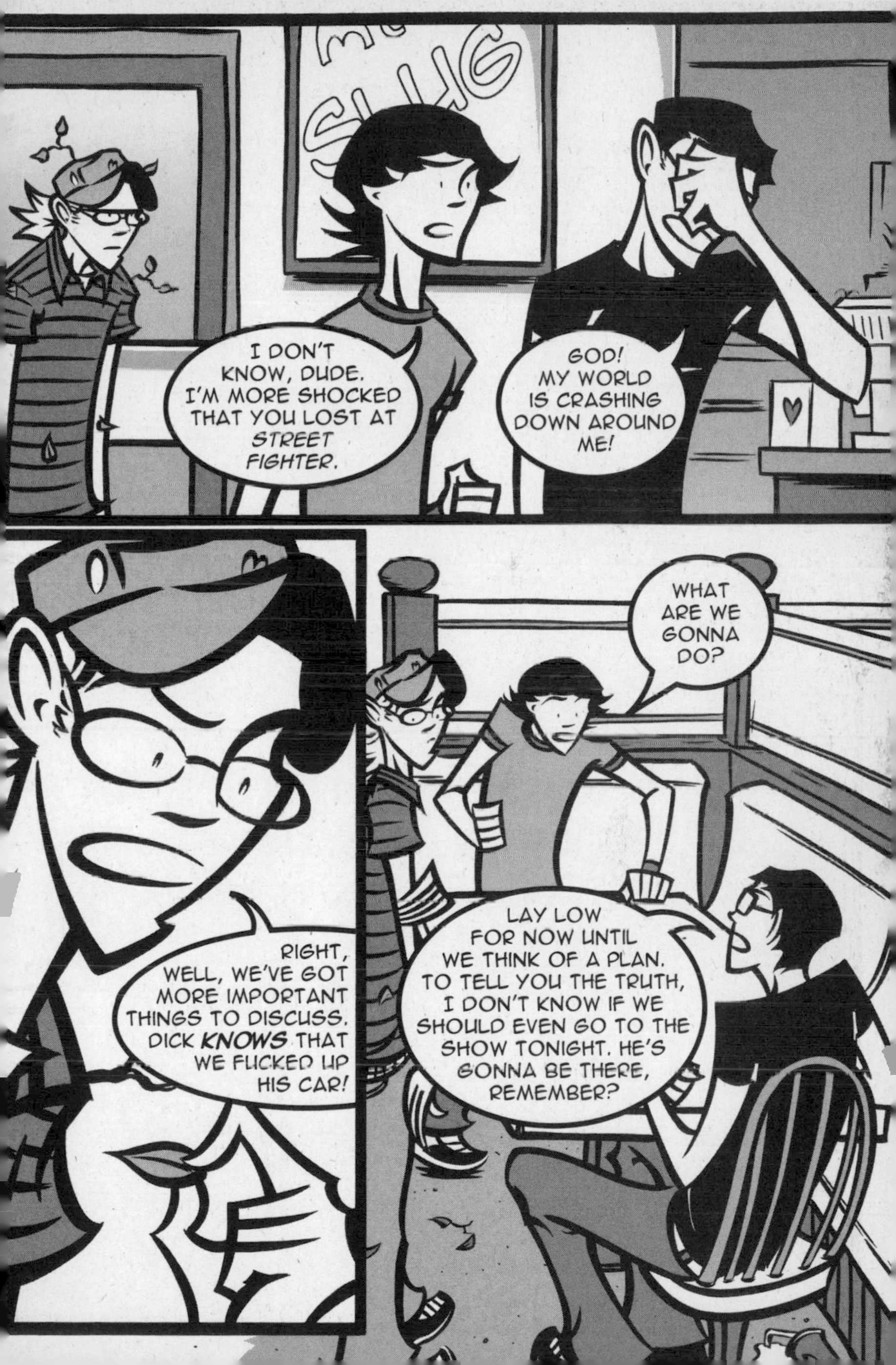
I DON'T KNOW, DUDE. I'M MORE SHOCKED THAT YOU LOST AT STREET FIGHTER.
GOD! MY WORLD IS CRASHING DOWN AROUND ME!
RIGHT, WELL, WE'VE GOT MORE IMPORTANT THINGS TO DISCUSS. DICK KNOWS THAT WE FUCKED UP HIS CAR!
WHAT ARE WE GONNA DO?
LAY LOW FOR NOW UNTIL WE THINK OF A PLAN. TO TELL YOU THE TRUTH, I DON'T KNOW IF WE SHOULD EVEN GO TO THE SHOW TONIGHT. HE'S GONNA BE THERE, REMEMBER?

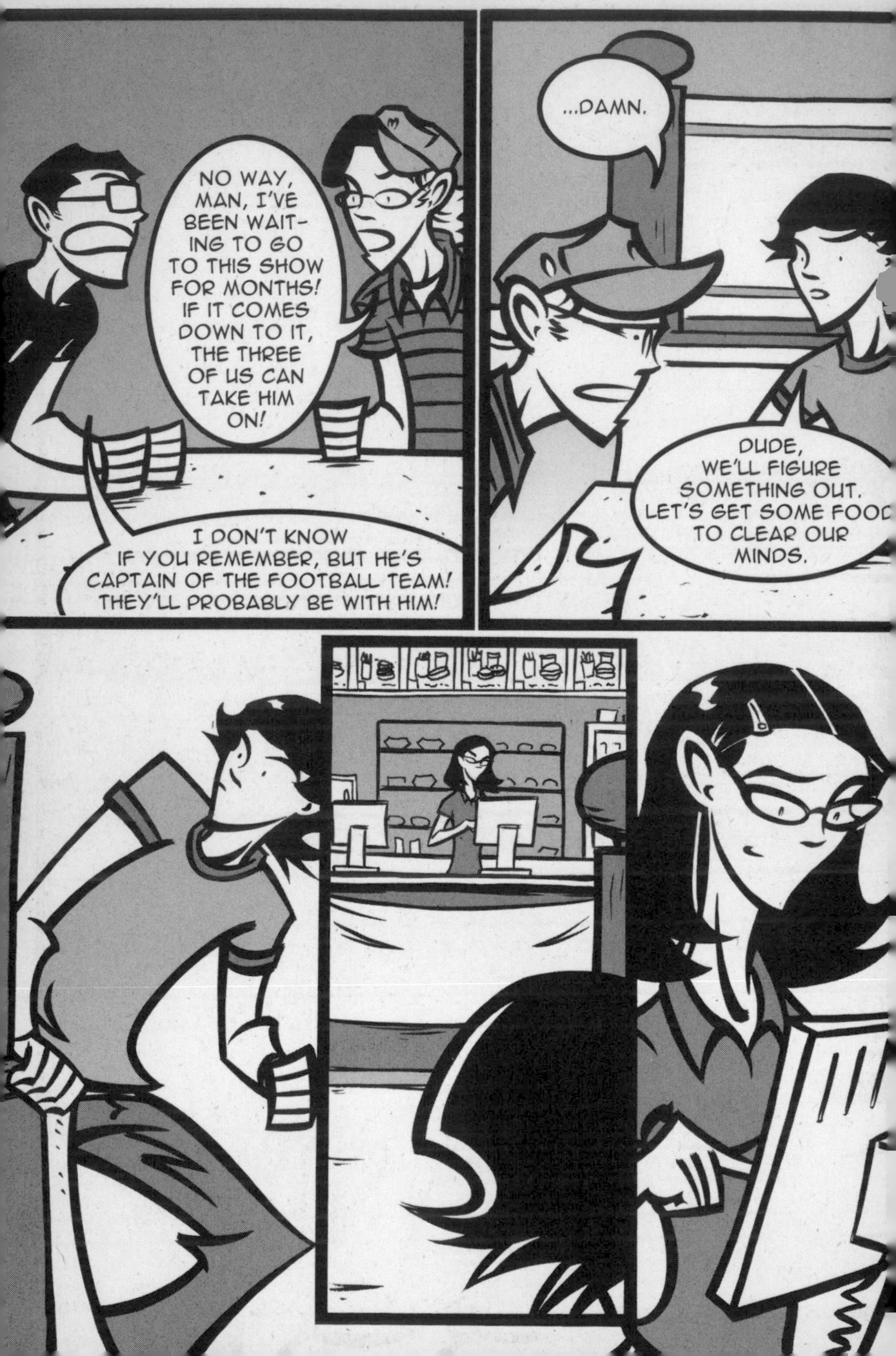
NO WAY, MAN, I'VE BEEN WAITING TO GO TO THIS SHOW FOR MONTHS! IF IT COMES DOWN TO IT, THE THREE OF US CAN TAKE HIM ON!
I DON'T KNOW IF YOU REMEMBER, BUT HE'S CAPTAIN OF THE FOOTBALL TEAM! THEY'LL PROBABLY BE WITH HIM!
...DAMN.
DUDE, WE'LL FIGURE SOMETHING OUT. LET'S GET SOME FOOD TO CLEAR OUR MINDS.

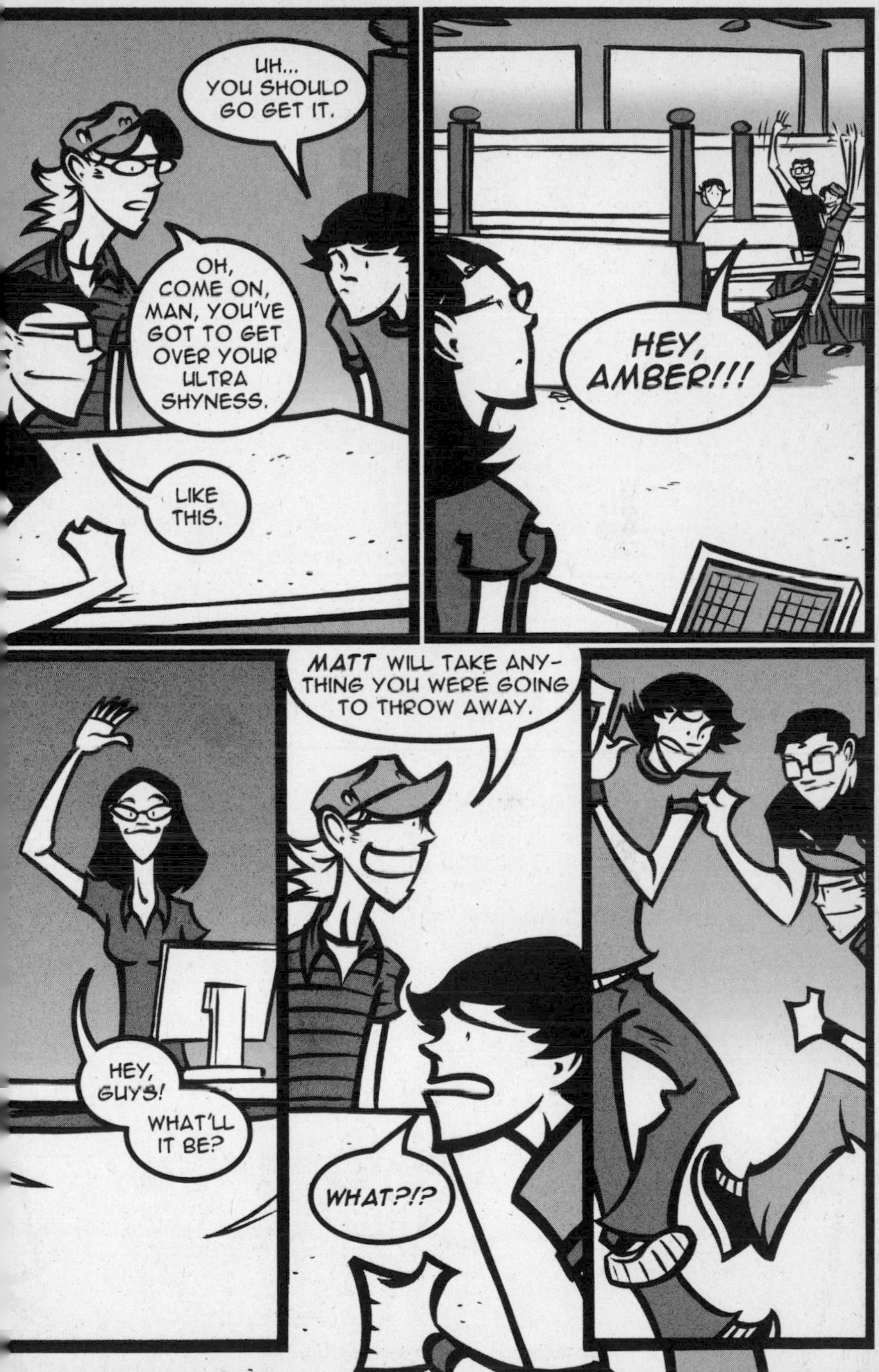
UH... YOU SHOULD GO GET IT.
OH, COME ON, MAN, YOU'VE GOT TO GET OVER YOUR ULTRA SHYNESS.
LIKE THIS.
HEY, AMBER!!!
HEY, GUYS!
WHAT'LL IT BE?
MATT WILL TAKE ANY-THING YOU WERE GOING TO THROW AWAY.
WHAT?!?

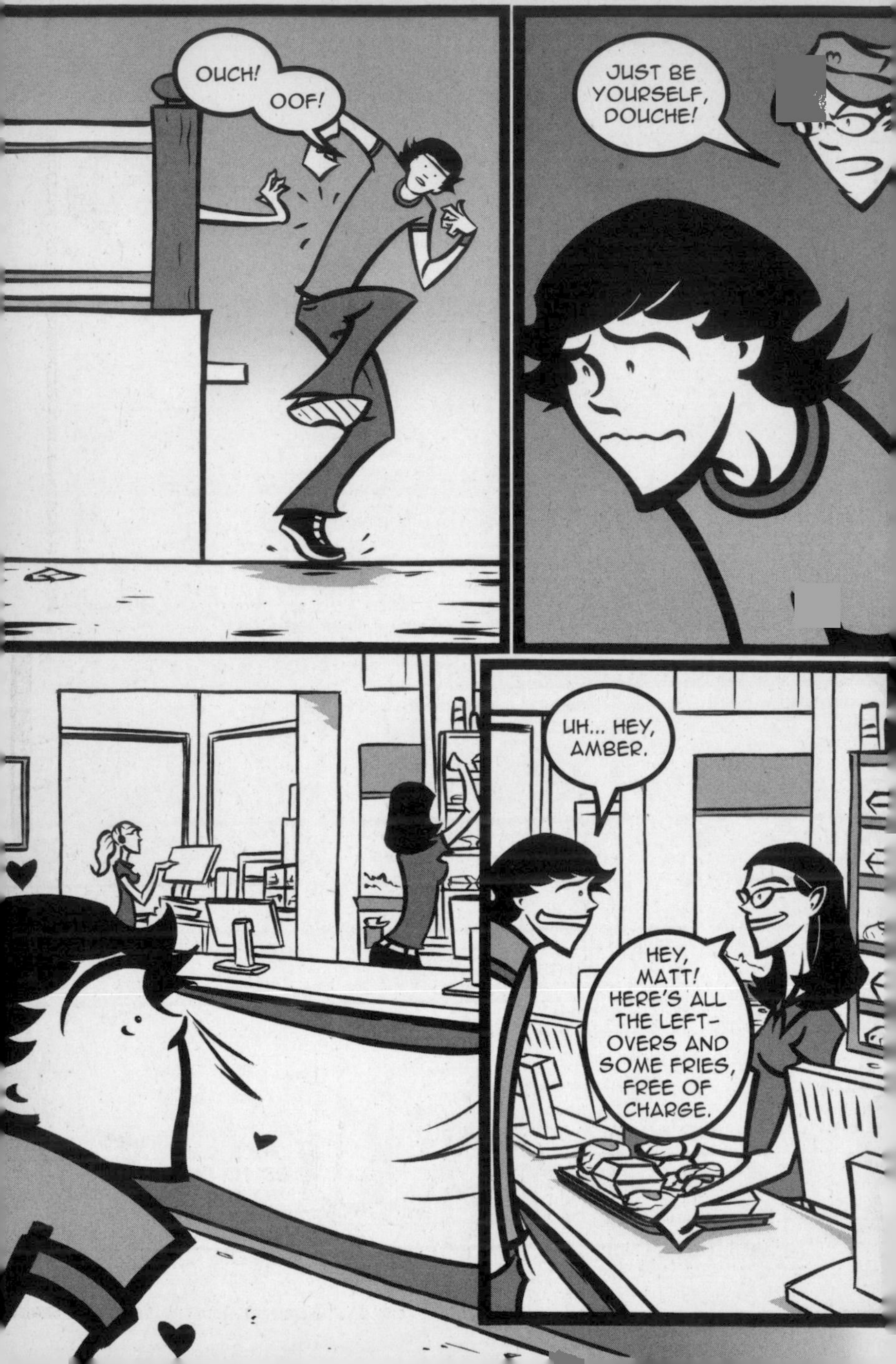
OUCH!
OOF!
JUST BE YOURSELF, DOUCHE!
UH... HEY, AMBER.
HEY, MATT! HERE'S ALL THE LEFT-OVERS AND SOME FRIES, FREE OF CHARGE.

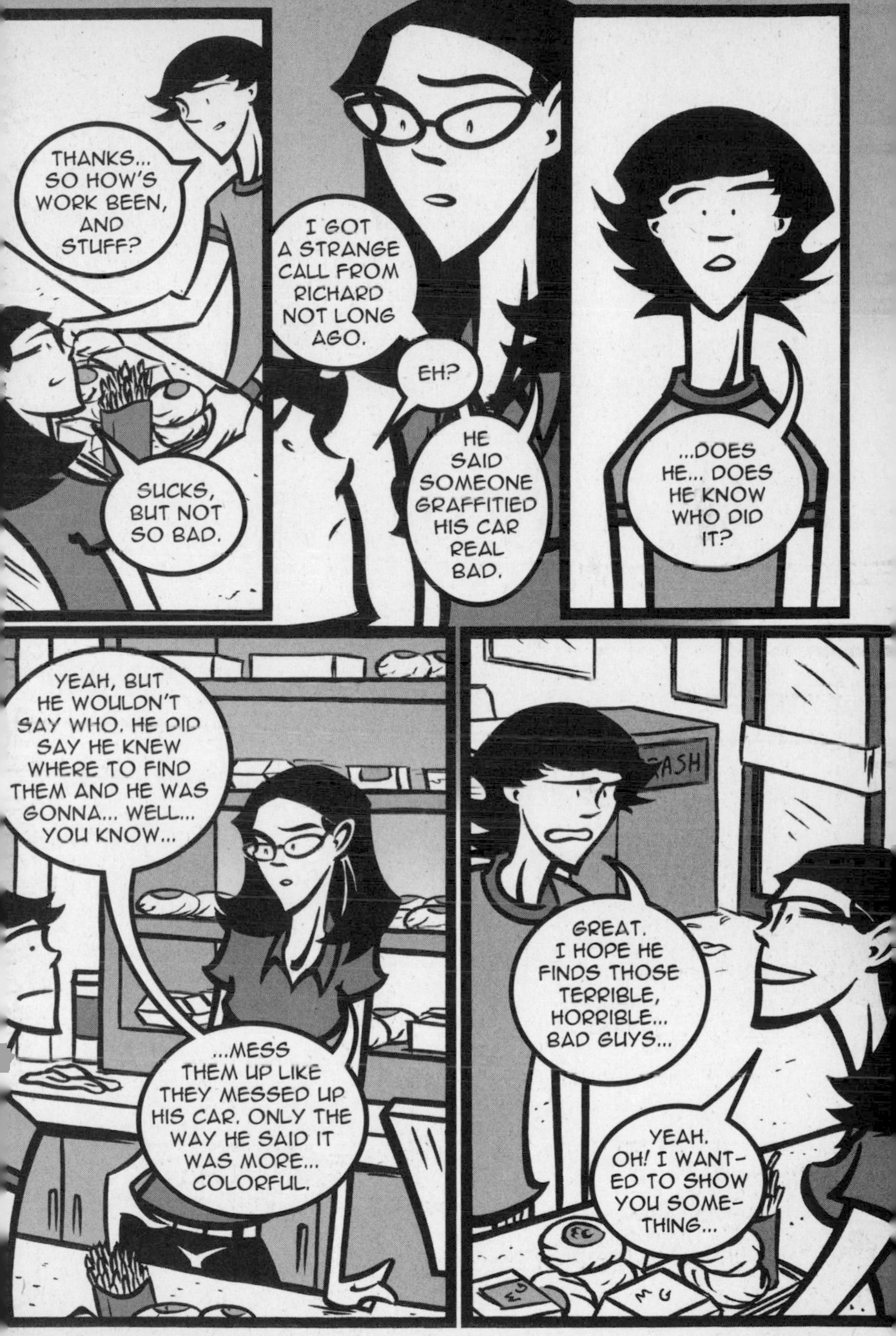
THANKS... SO HOW'S WORK BEEN, AND STUFF?
SUCKS, BUT NOT SO BAD.
I GOT A STRANGE CALL FROM RICHARD NOT LONG AGO.
EH?
HE SAID SOMEONE GRAFFITIED HIS CAR REAL BAD.
...DOES HE... DOES HE KNOW WHO DID IT?
YEAH, BUT HE WOULDN'T SAY WHO. HE DID SAY HE KNEW WHERE TO FIND THEM AND HE WAS GONNA... WELL... YOU KNOW...
...MESS THEM UP LIKE THEY MESSED UP HIS CAR. ONLY THE WAY HE SAID IT WAS MORE... COLORFUL.
TRASH
GREAT. I HOPE HE FINDS THOSE TERRIBLE, HORRIBLE... BAD GUYS...
YEAH. OH! I WANT-ED TO SHOW YOU SOME-THING...

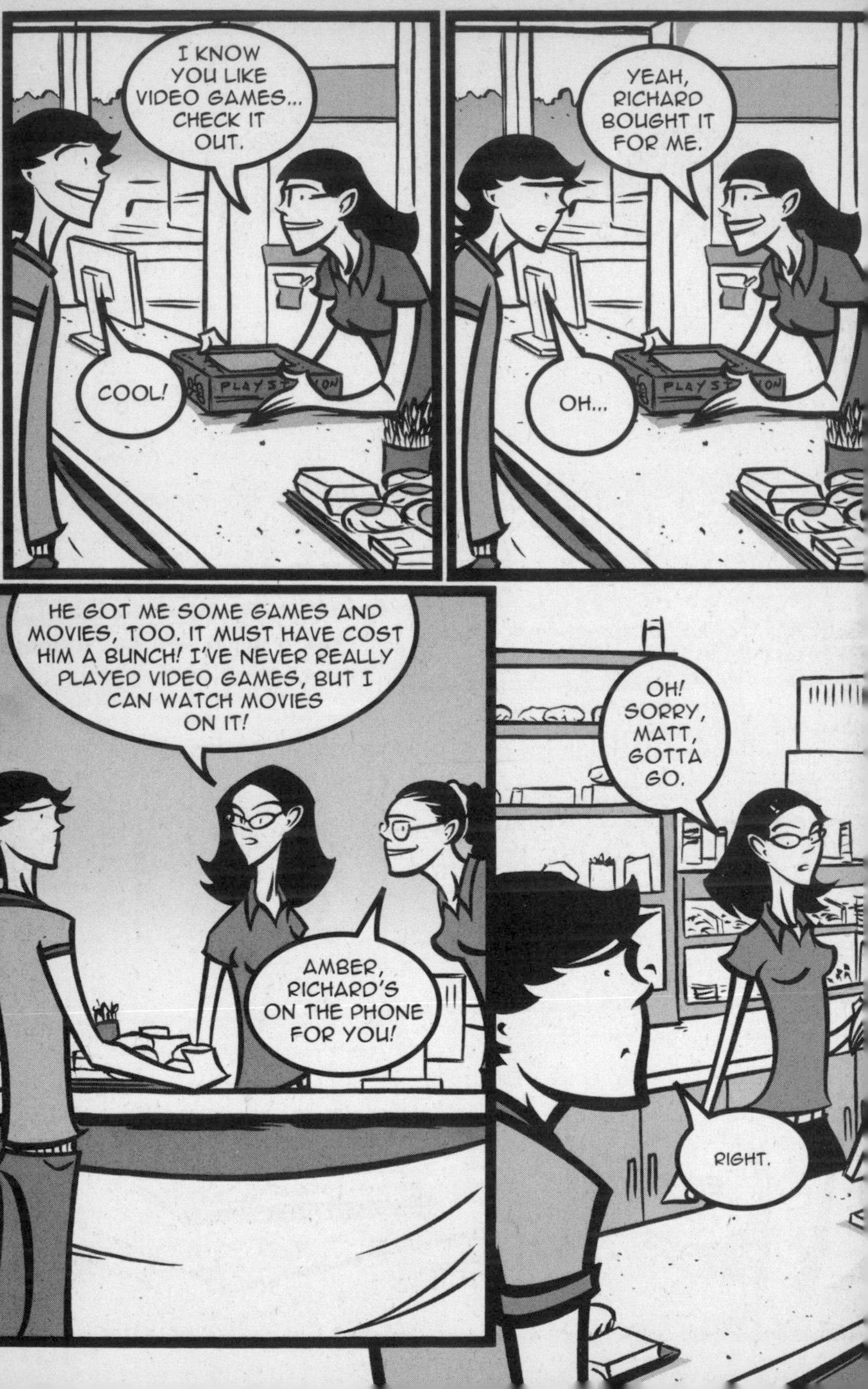
I KNOW YOU LIKE VIDEO GAMES... CHECK IT OUT.
COOL!
PLAYST ION
YEAH, RICHARD BOUGHT IT FOR ME.
OH...
PLAYST ION
HE GOT ME SOME GAMES AND MOVIES, TOO. IT MUST HAVE COST HIM A BUNCH! I'VE NEVER REALLY PLAYED VIDEO GAMES, BUT I CAN WATCH MOVIES ON IT!
AMBER, RICHARD'S ON THE PHONE FOR YOU!
OH! SORRY, MATT, GOTTA GO.
RIGHT.

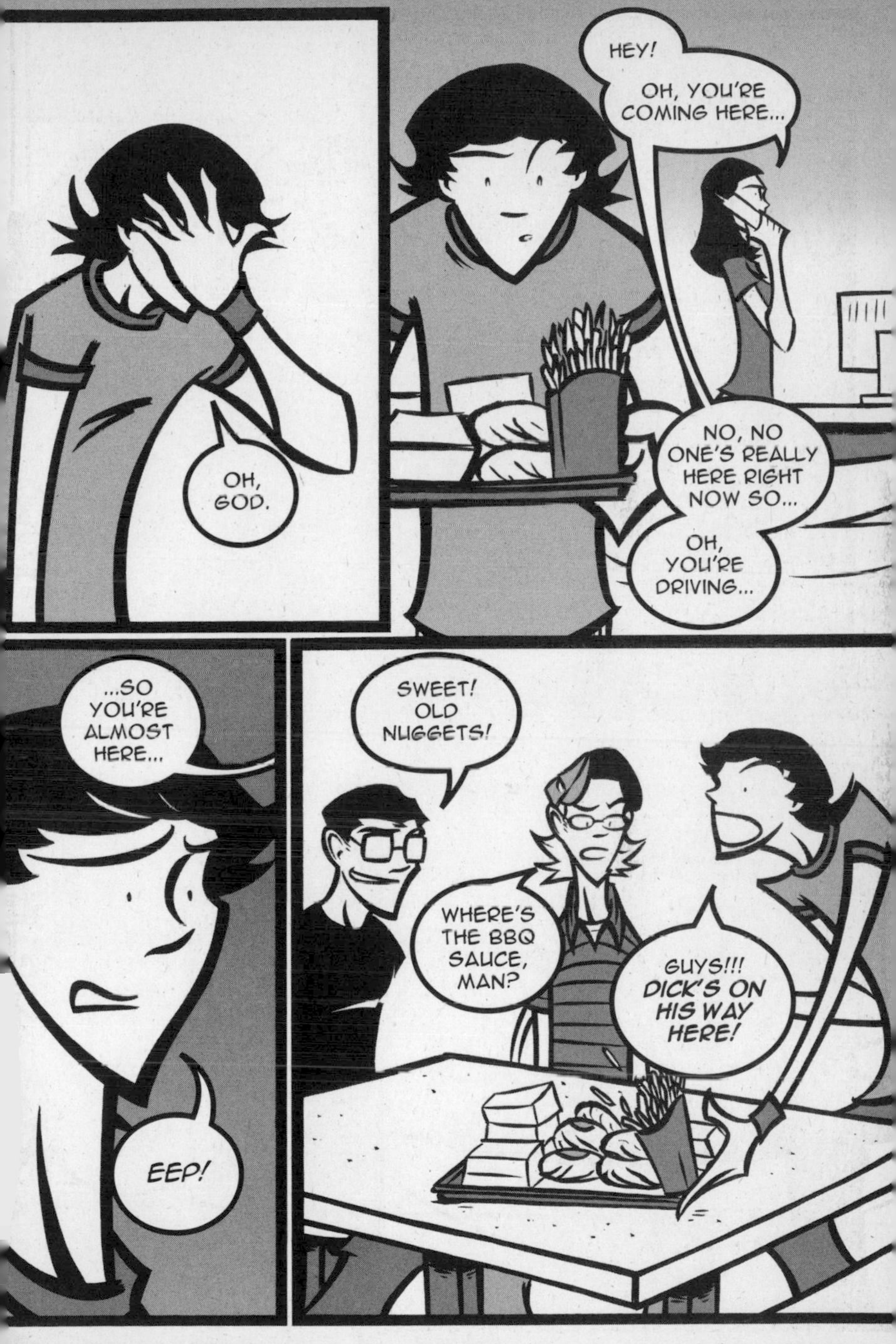
HEY!
OH, YOU'RE COMING HERE...
OH, GOD.
NO, NO ONE'S REALLY HERE RIGHT NOW SO...
OH, YOU'RE DRIVING...
...SO YOU'RE ALMOST HERE...
EEP!
SWEET! OLD NUGGETS!
WHERE'S THE BBQ SAUCE, MAN?
GUYS!!! DICK'S ON HIS WAY HERE!

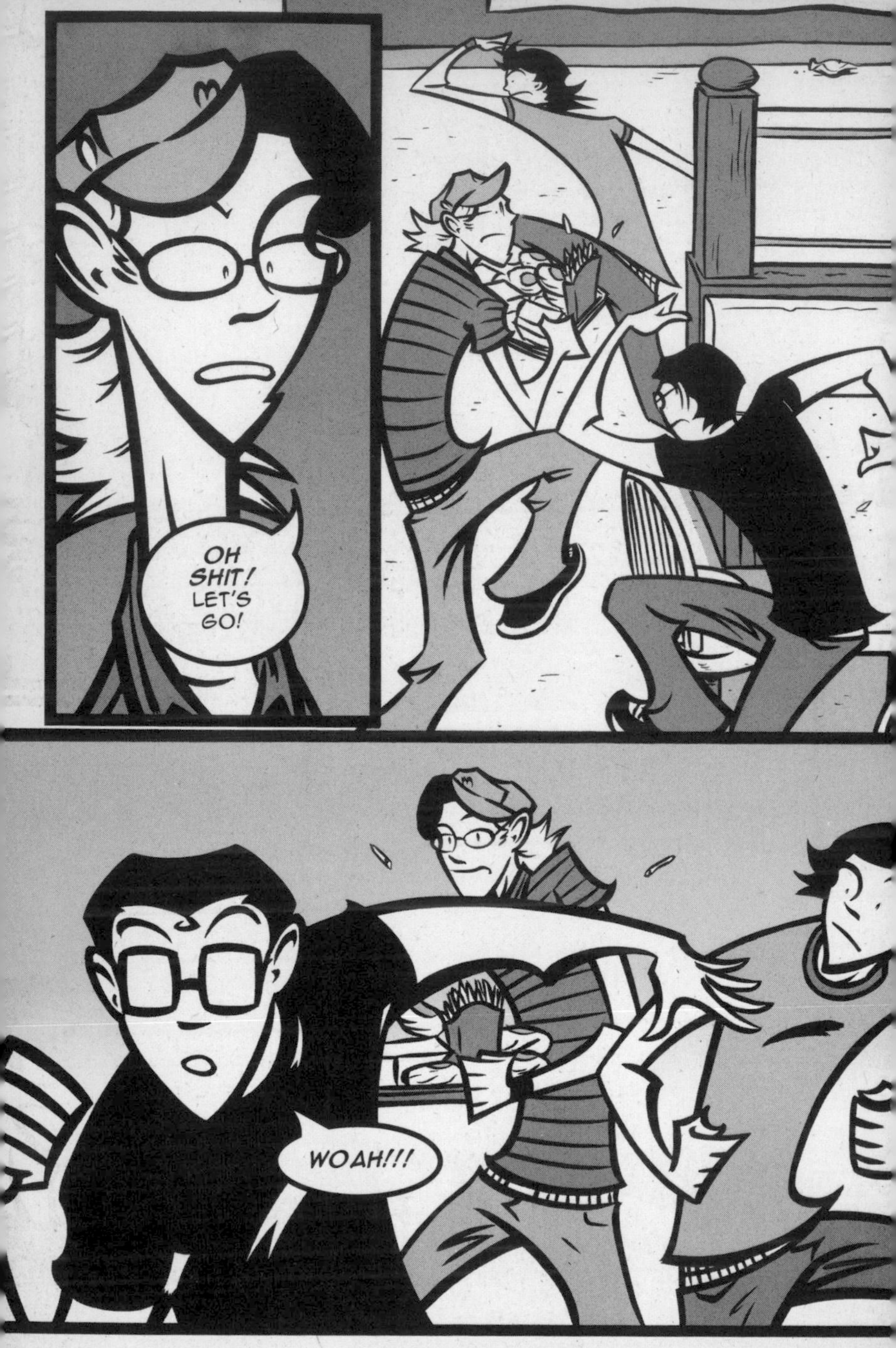
OH SHIT! LET'S GO!
WOAH!!!

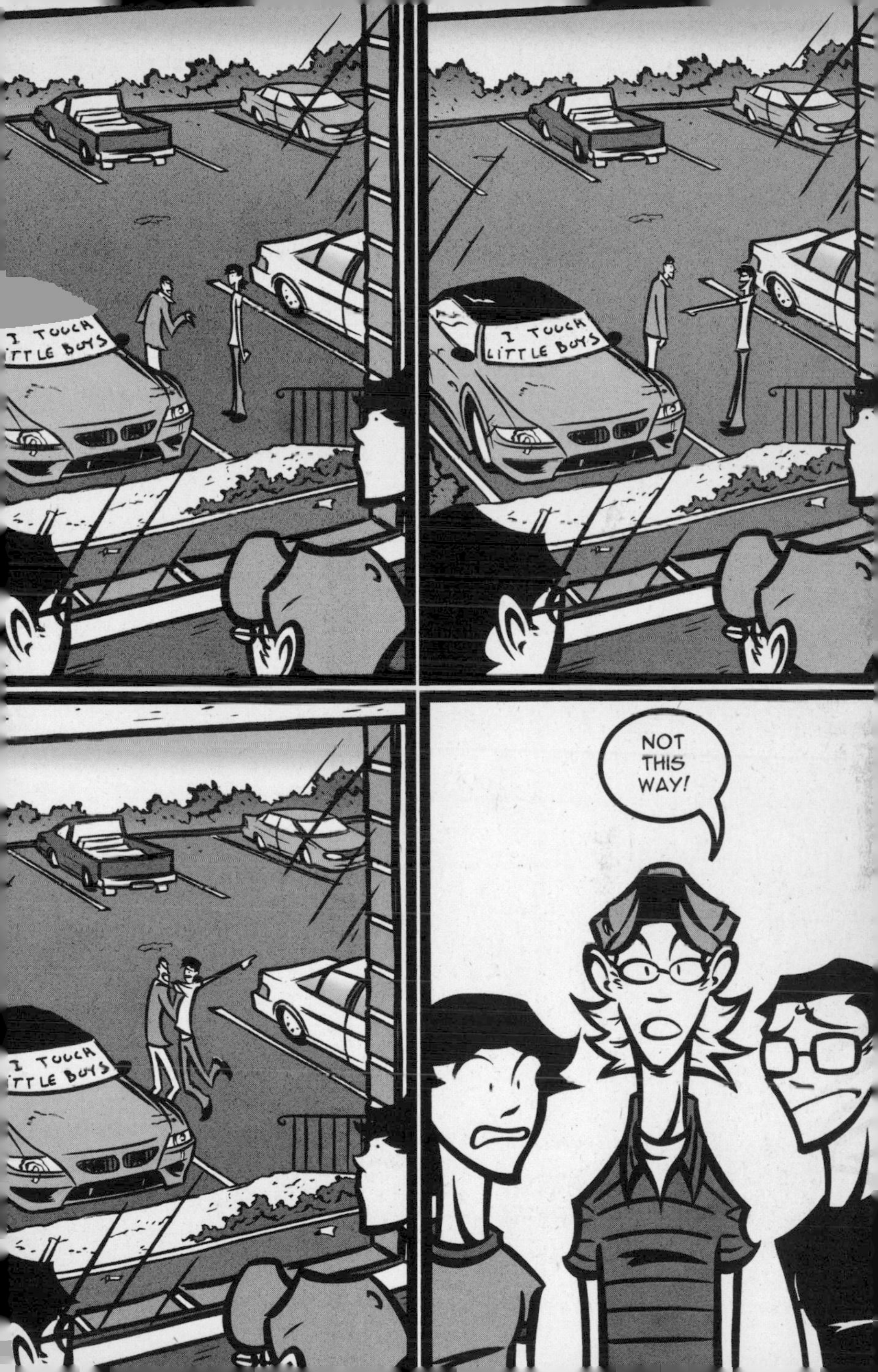
I TOUCH LITTLE BOYS
I TOUCH LITTLE BOYS
I TOUCH LITTLE BOYS
NOT THIS WAY!

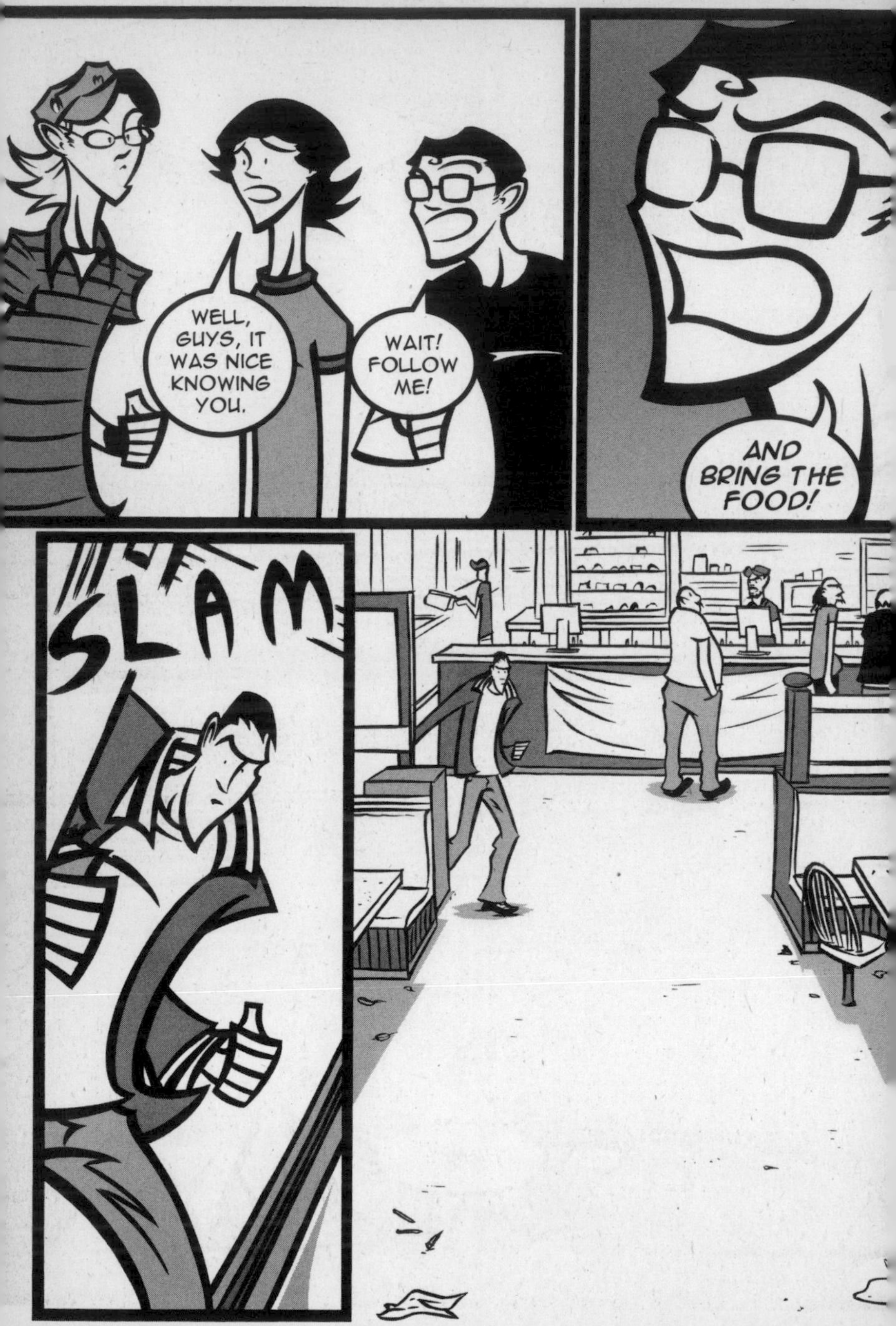
WELL, GUYS, IT WAS NICE KNOWING YOU.
WAIT! FOLLOW ME!
AND BRING THE FOOD!
SLAM

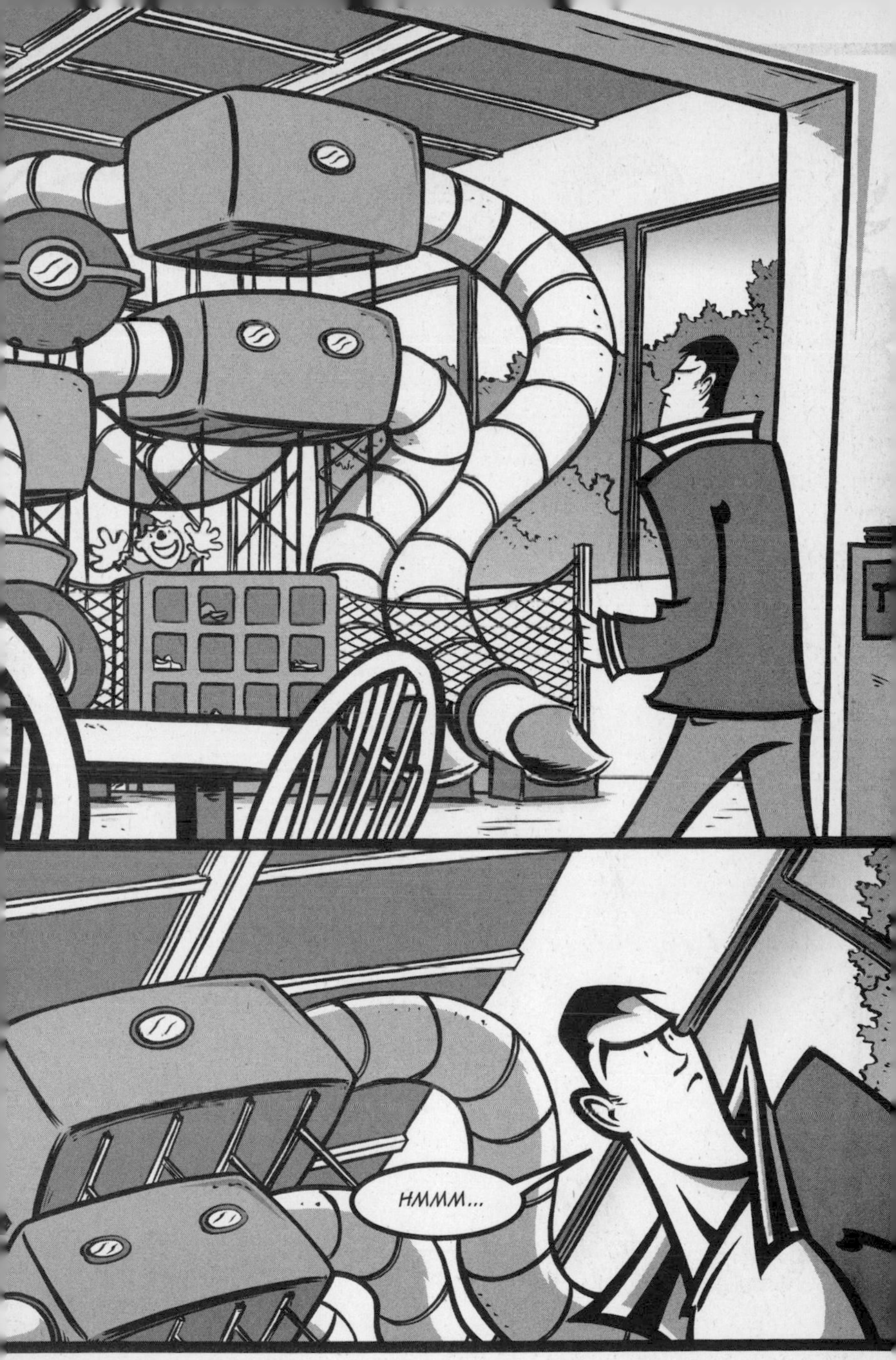
HMMM...

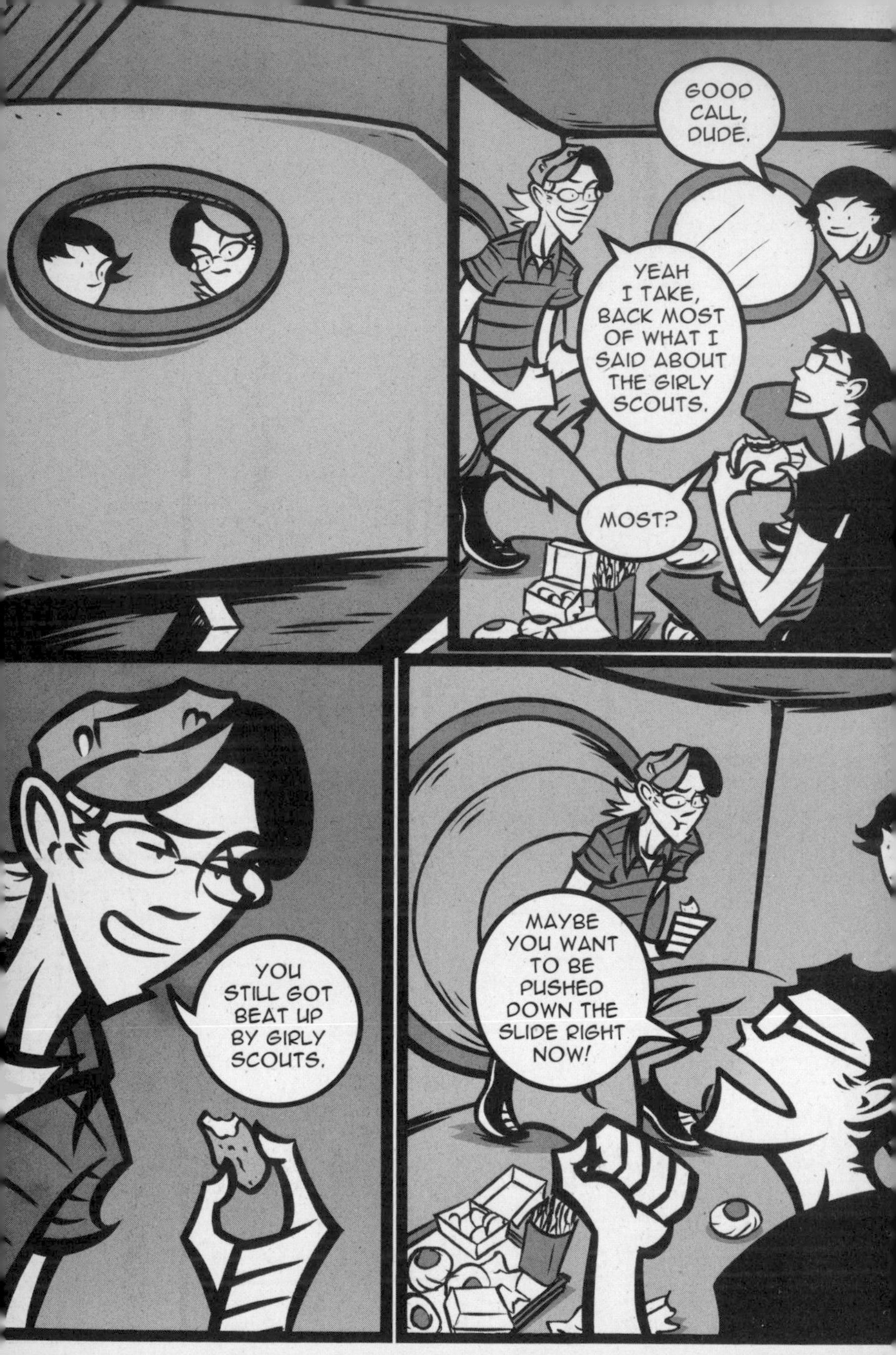
GOOD CALL, DUDE.
YEAH I TAKE, BACK MOST OF WHAT I SAID ABOUT THE GIRLY SCOUTS.
MOST?
YOU STILL GOT BEAT UP BY GIRLY SCOUTS.
MAYBE YOU WANT TO BE PUSHED DOWN THE SLIDE RIGHT NOW!

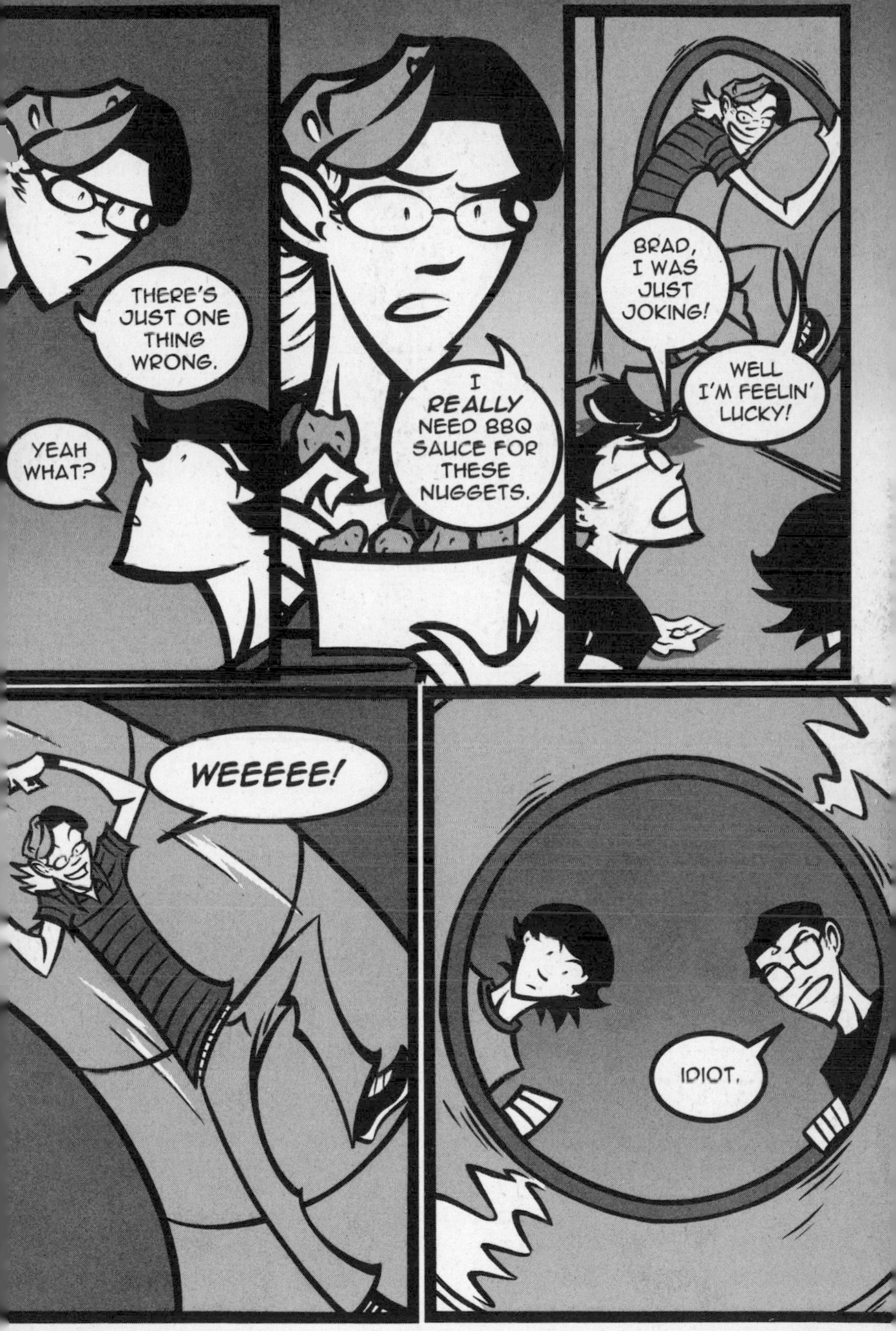
THERE'S JUST ONE THING WRONG.
YEAH WHAT?
I REALLY NEED BBQ SAUCE FOR THESE NUGGETS.
BRAD, I WAS JUST JOKING!
WELL I'M FEELIN' LUCKY!
WEEEEEE!
IDIOT.

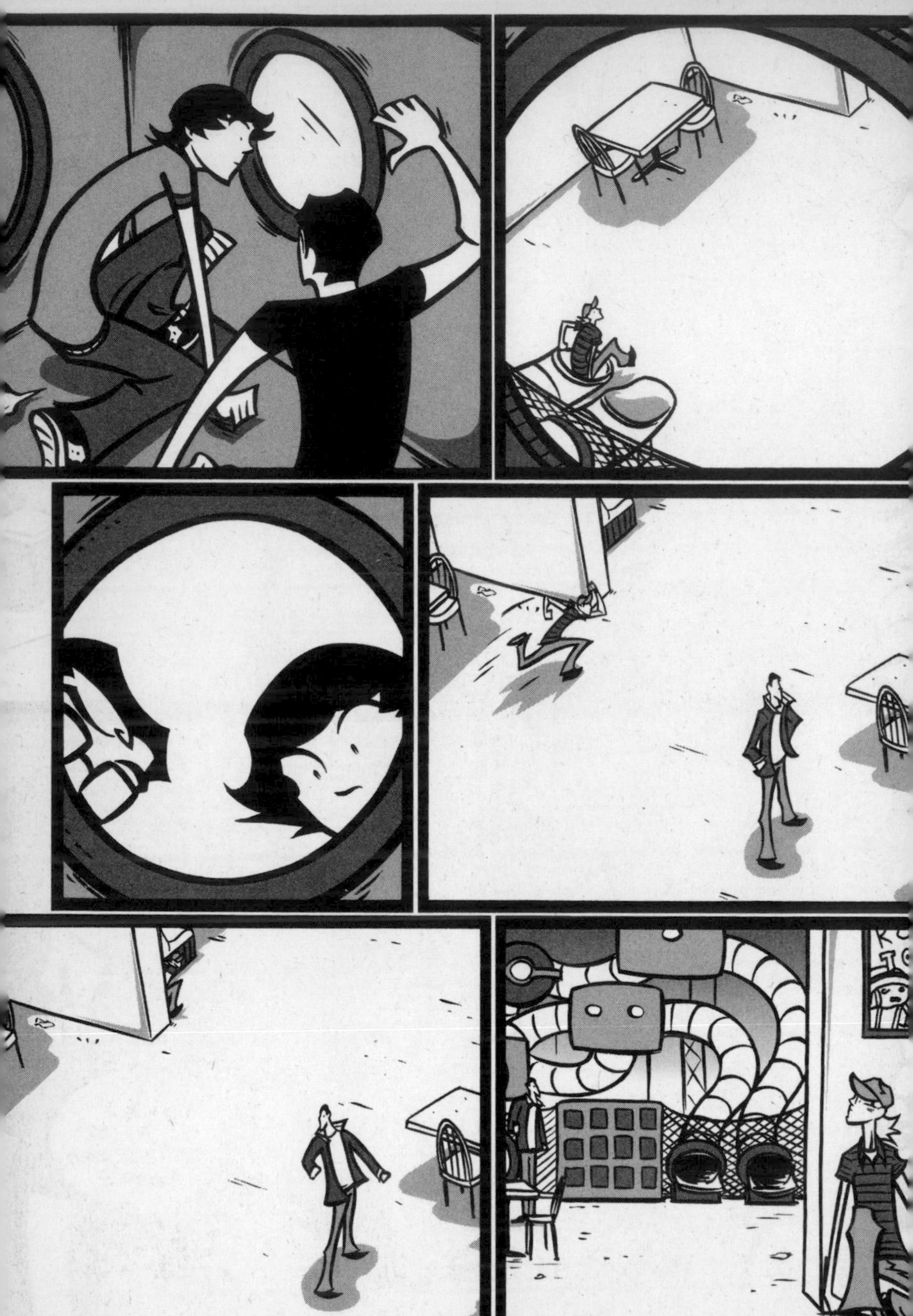

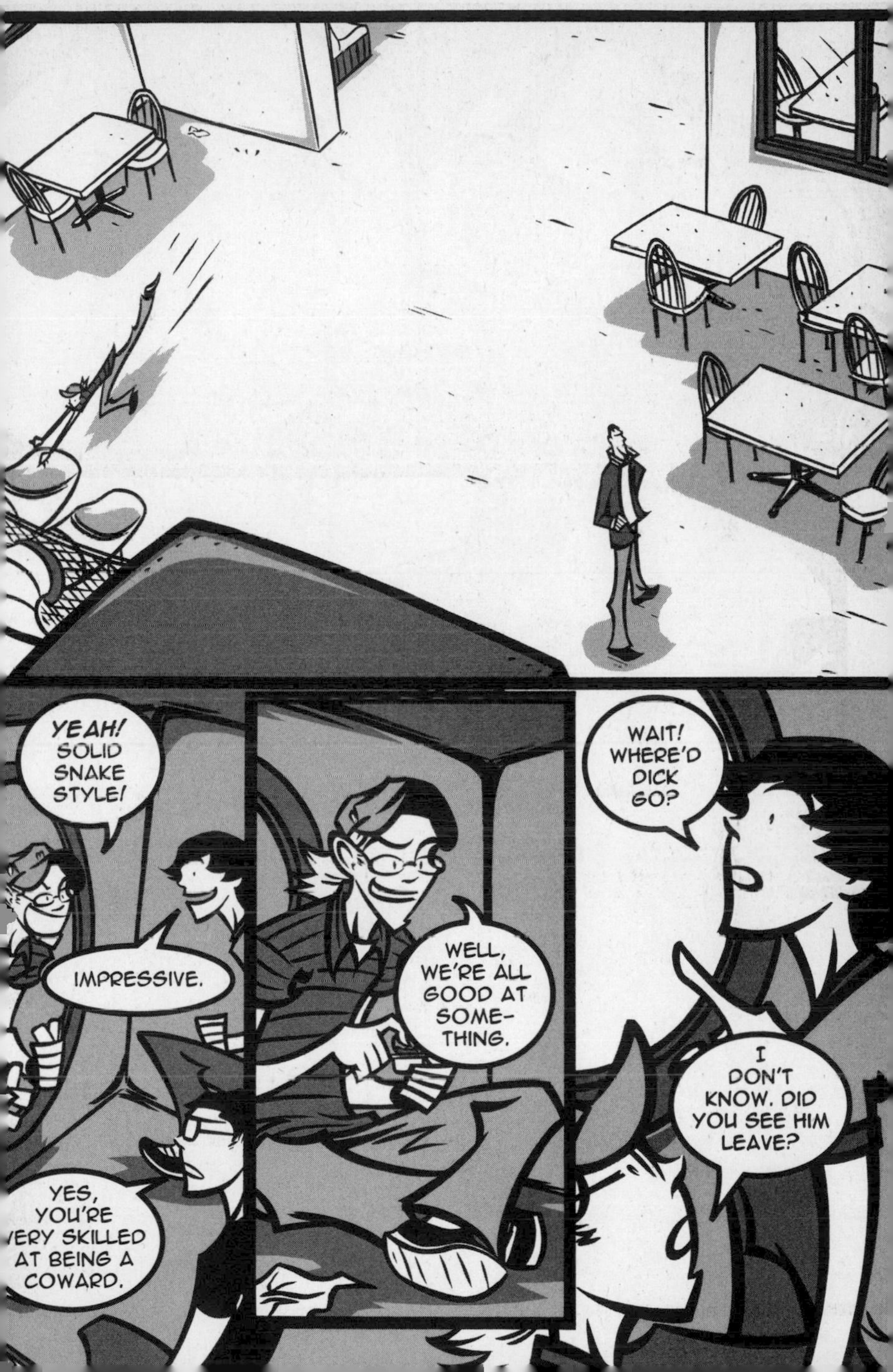
YEAH! SOLID SNAKE STYLE!
IMPRESSIVE.
YES, YOU'RE VERY SKILLED AT BEING A COWARD.
WELL, WE'RE ALL GOOD AT SOME-THING.
WAIT! WHERE'D DICK GO?
I DON'T KNOW. DID YOU SEE HIM LEAVE?

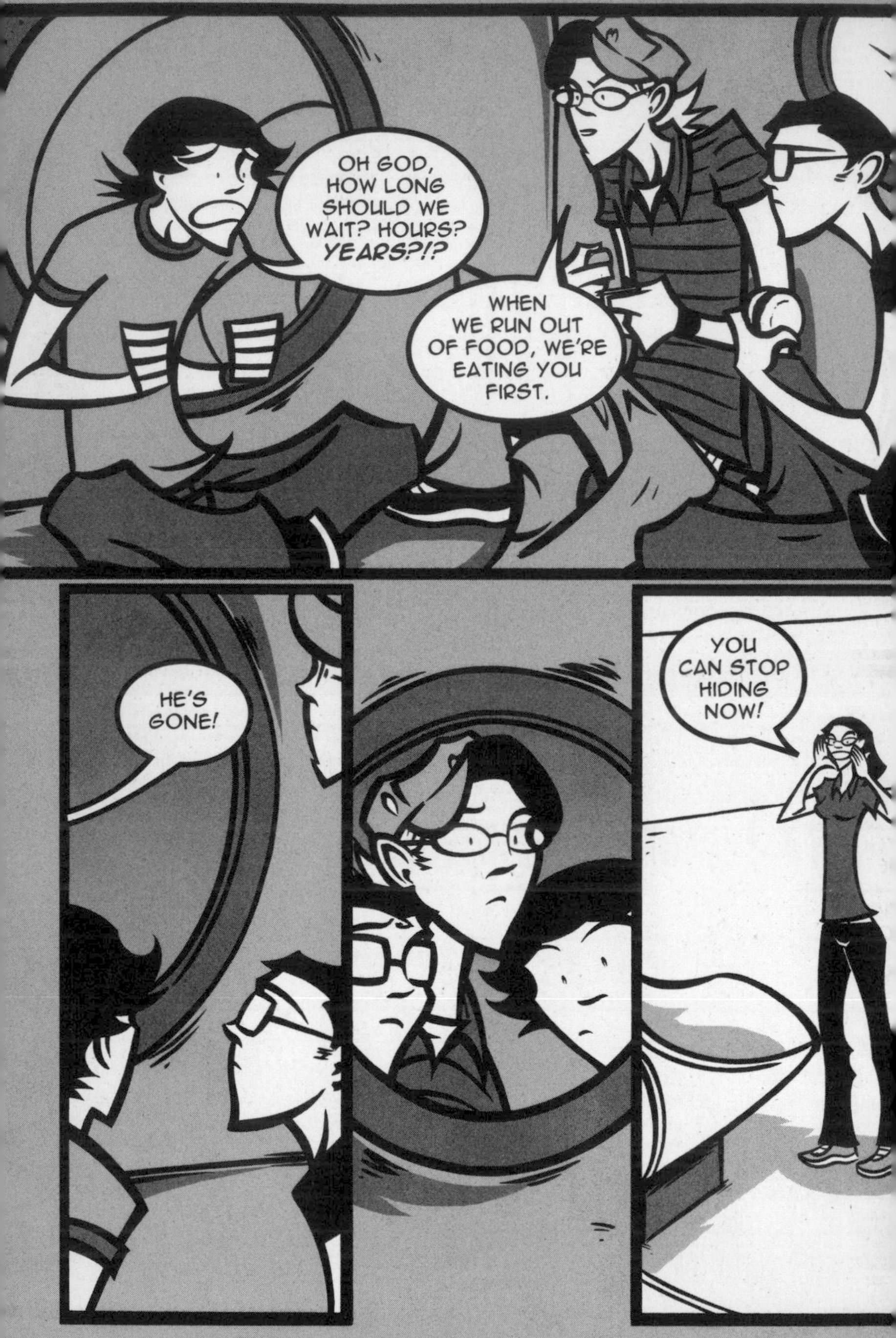
OH GOD, HOW LONG SHOULD WE WAIT? HOURS? *YEARS?!?*
WHEN WE RUN OUT OF FOOD, WE'RE EATING YOU FIRST.
HE'S GONE!
YOU CAN STOP HIDING NOW!

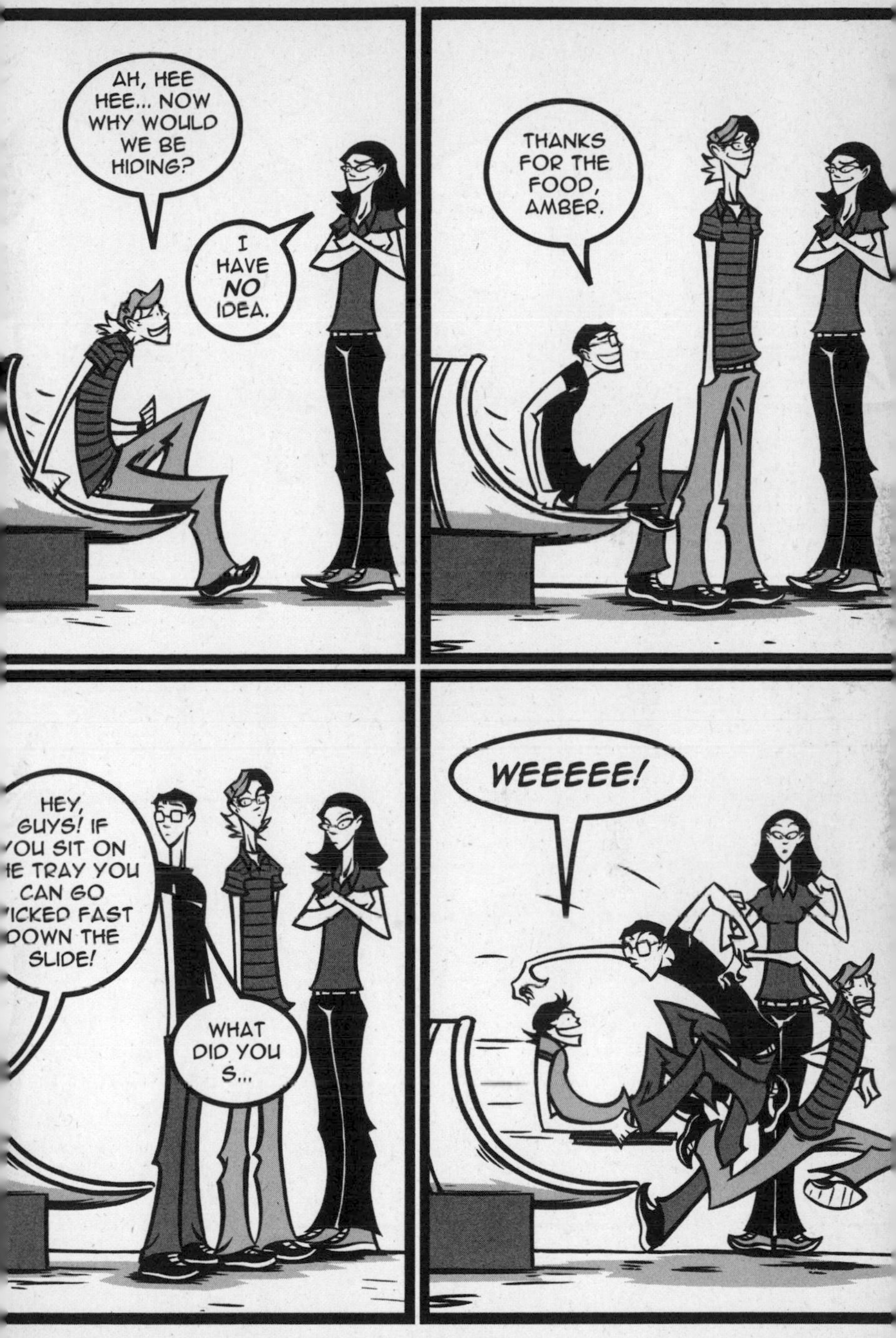
AH, HEE HEE... NOW WHY WOULD WE BE HIDING?
I HAVE NO IDEA.
THANKS FOR THE FOOD, AMBER.
HEY, GUYS! IF OU SIT ON E TRAY YOU CAN GO ICKED FAST DOWN THE SLIDE!
WHAT DID YOU S...
WEEEEEE!

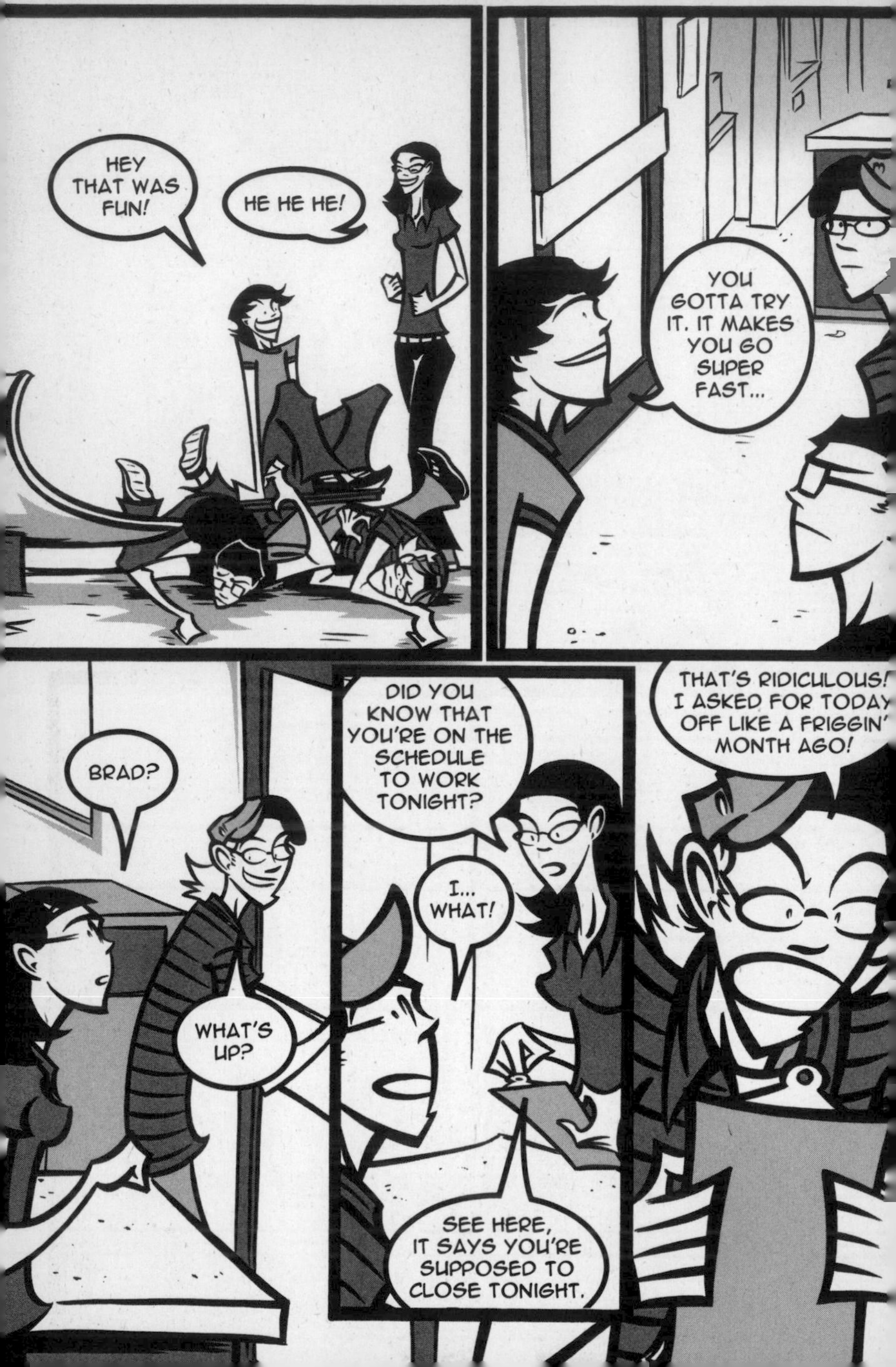
HEY THAT WAS FUN!
HE HE HE!
YOU GOTTA TRY IT. IT MAKES YOU GO SUPER FAST...
BRAD?
WHAT'S UP?
DID YOU KNOW THAT YOU'RE ON THE SCHEDULE TO WORK TONIGHT?
I... WHAT!
SEE HERE, IT SAYS YOU'RE SUPPOSED TO CLOSE TONIGHT.
THAT'S RIDICULOUS! I ASKED FOR TODAY OFF LIKE A FRIGGIN' MONTH AGO!

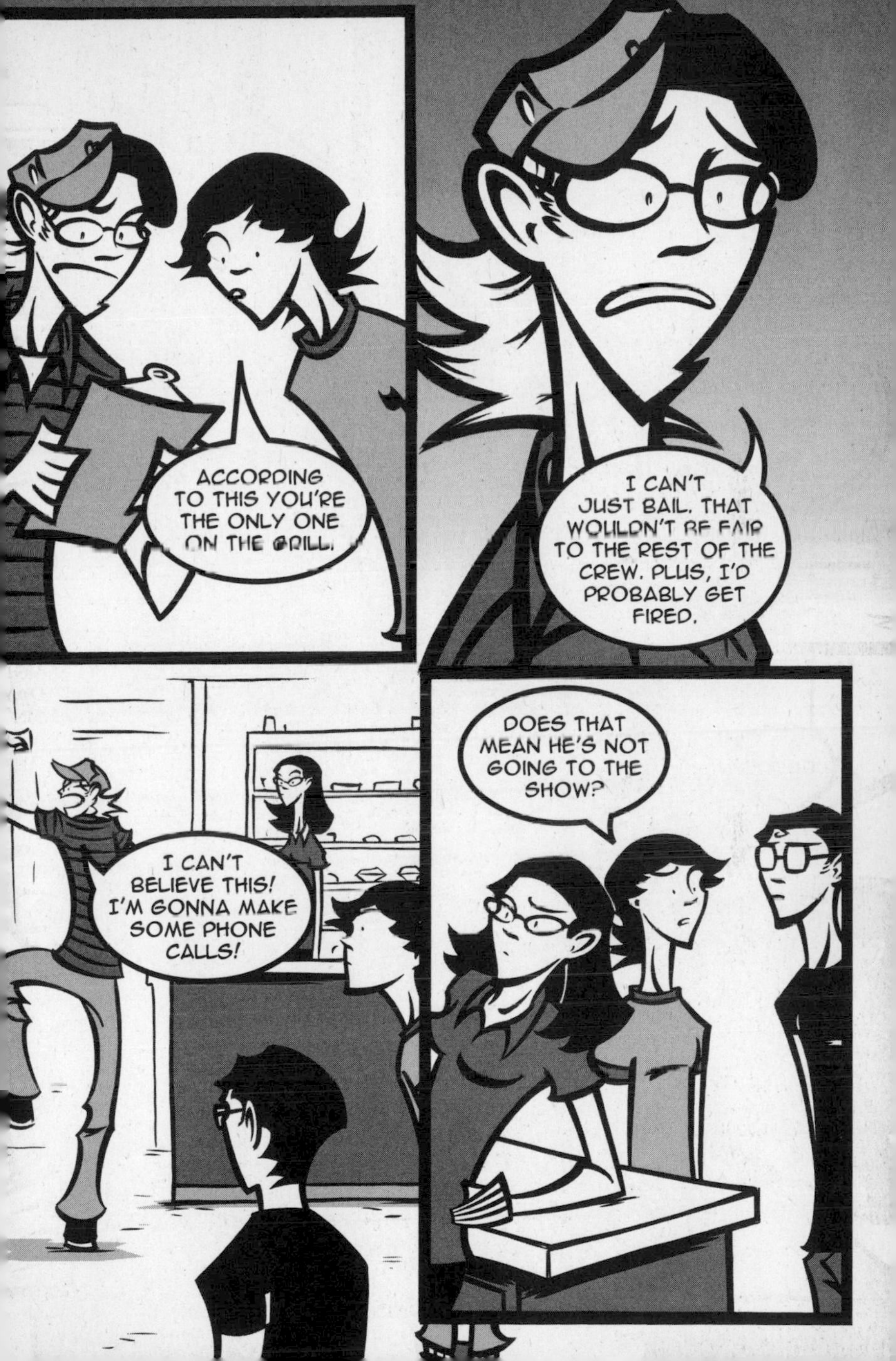
ACCORDING TO THIS YOU'RE THE ONLY ONE ON THE GRILL.
I CAN'T JUST BAIL. THAT WOULDN'T BE FAIR TO THE REST OF THE CREW. PLUS, I'D PROBABLY GET FIRED.
I CAN'T BELIEVE THIS! I'M GONNA MAKE SOME PHONE CALLS!
DOES THAT MEAN HE'S NOT GOING TO THE SHOW?

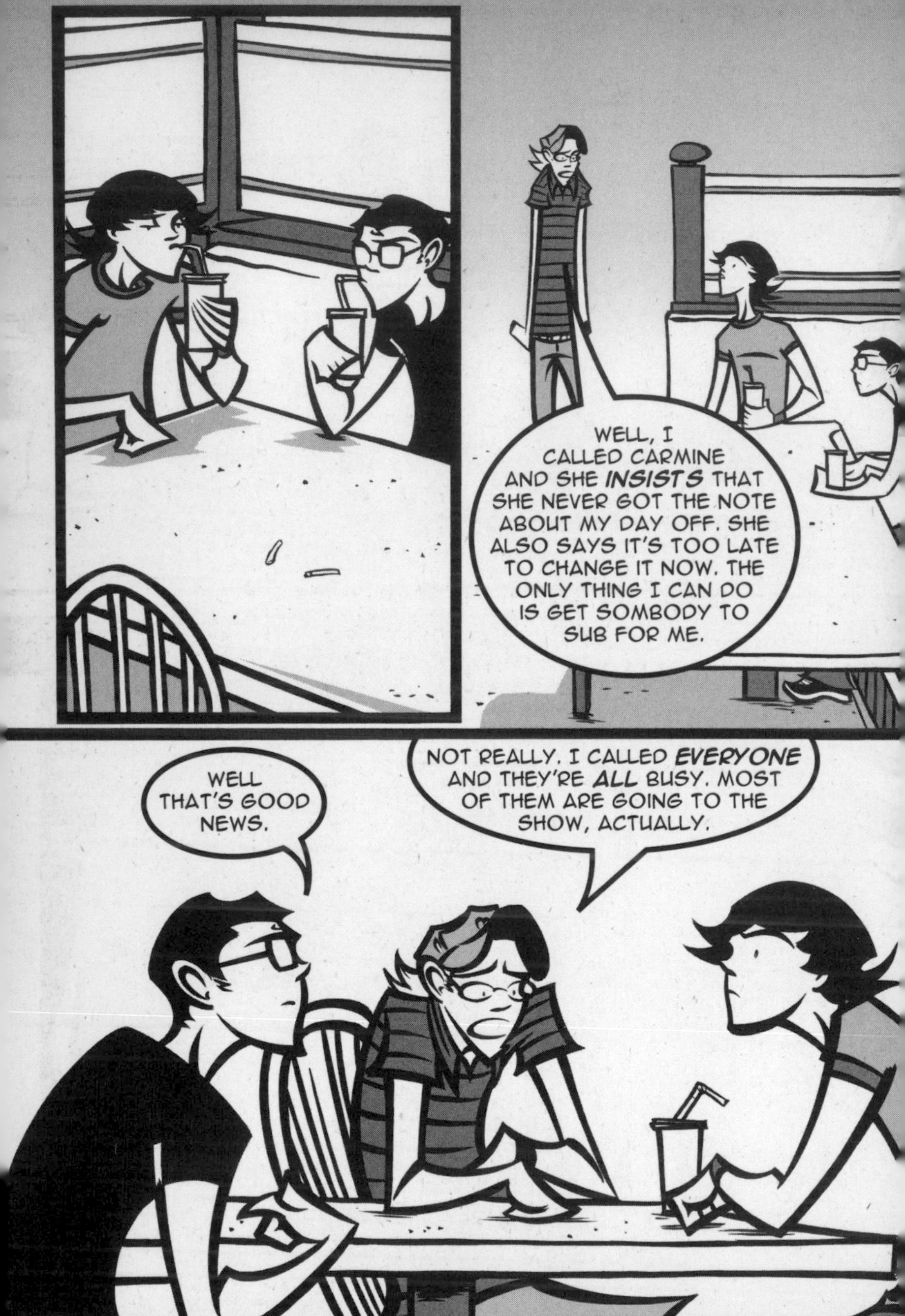
WELL, I CALLED CARMINE AND SHE INSISTS THAT SHE NEVER GOT THE NOTE ABOUT MY DAY OFF. SHE ALSO SAYS IT'S TOO LATE TO CHANGE IT NOW. THE ONLY THING I CAN DO IS GET SOMBODY TO SUB FOR ME.
WELL THAT'S GOOD NEWS.
NOT REALLY. I CALLED EVERYONE AND THEY'RE ALL BUSY. MOST OF THEM ARE GOING TO THE SHOW, ACTUALLY.

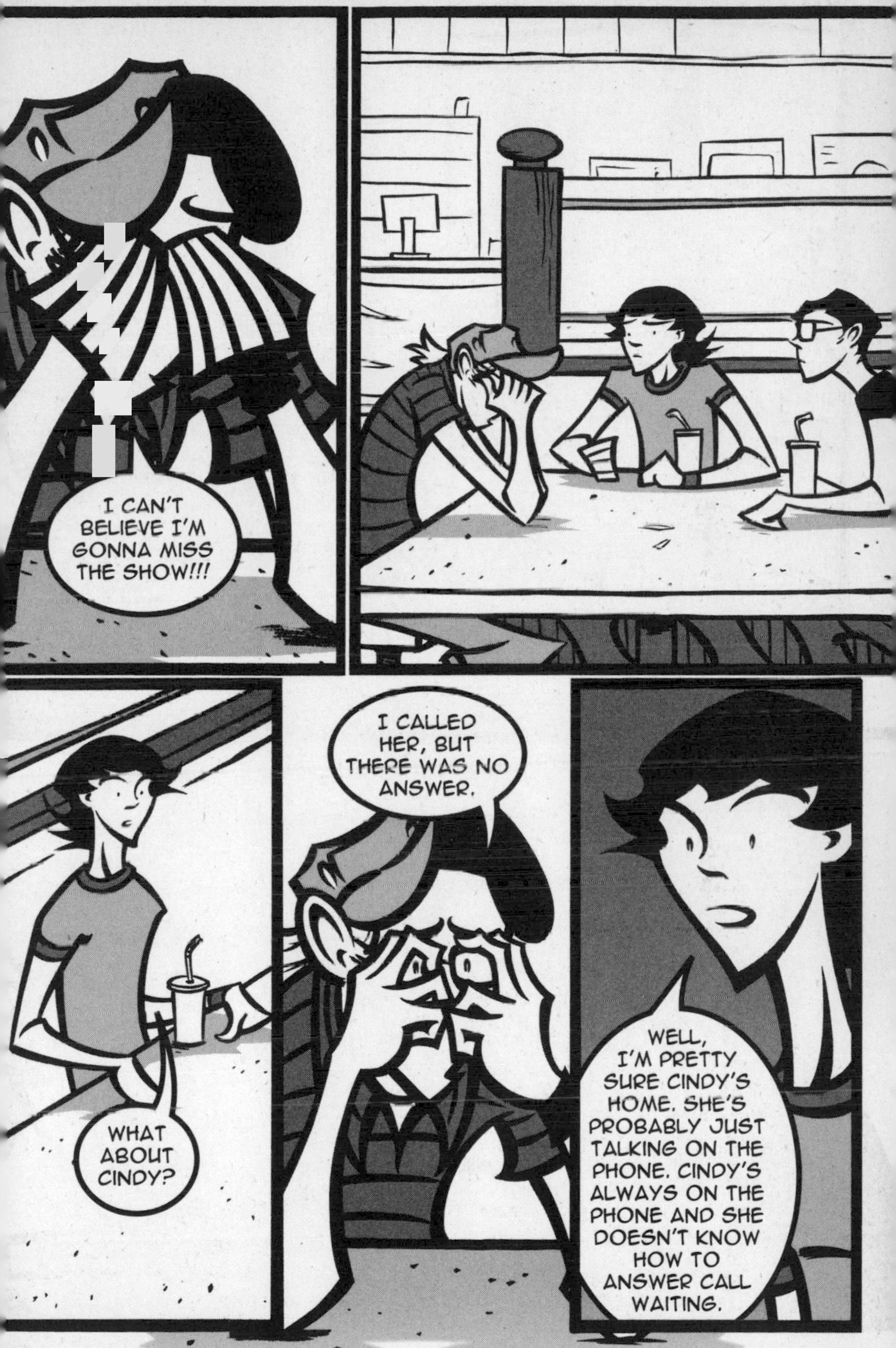
I CAN'T BELIEVE I'M GONNA MISS THE SHOW!!!
WHAT ABOUT CINDY?
I CALLED HER, BUT THERE WAS NO ANSWER.
WELL, I'M PRETTY SURE CINDY'S HOME. SHE'S PROBABLY JUST TALKING ON THE PHONE. CINDY'S ALWAYS ON THE PHONE AND SHE DOESN'T KNOW HOW TO ANSWER CALL WAITING.

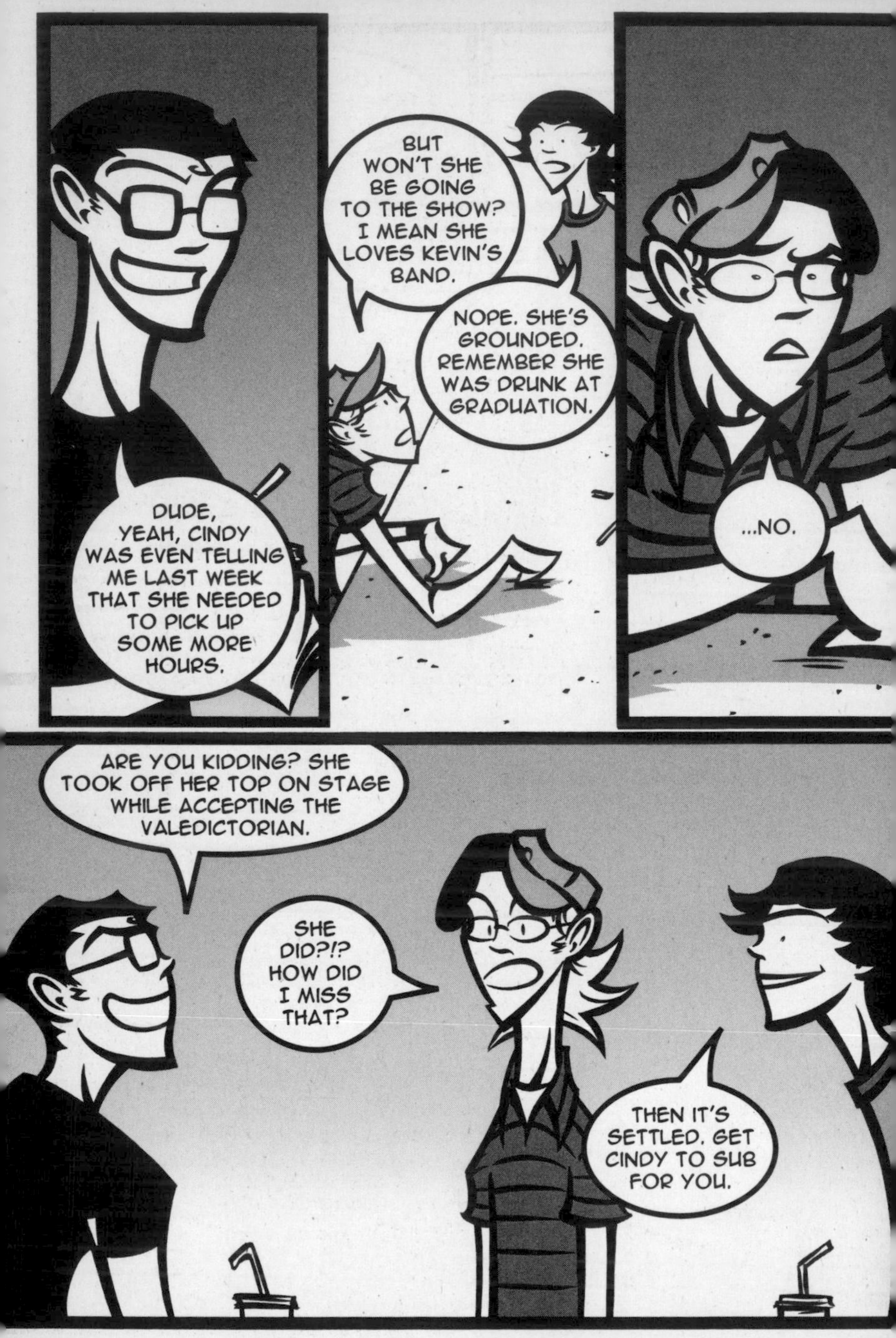
DUDE, YEAH, CINDY WAS EVEN TELLING ME LAST WEEK THAT SHE NEEDED TO PICK UP SOME MORE HOURS.
BUT WON'T SHE BE GOING TO THE SHOW? I MEAN SHE LOVES KEVIN'S BAND.
NOPE. SHE'S GROUNDED. REMEMBER SHE WAS DRUNK AT GRADUATION.
...NO.
ARE YOU KIDDING? SHE TOOK OFF HER TOP ON STAGE WHILE ACCEPTING THE VALEDICTORIAN.
SHE DID?!? HOW DID I MISS THAT?
THEN IT'S SETTLED. GET CINDY TO SUB FOR YOU.

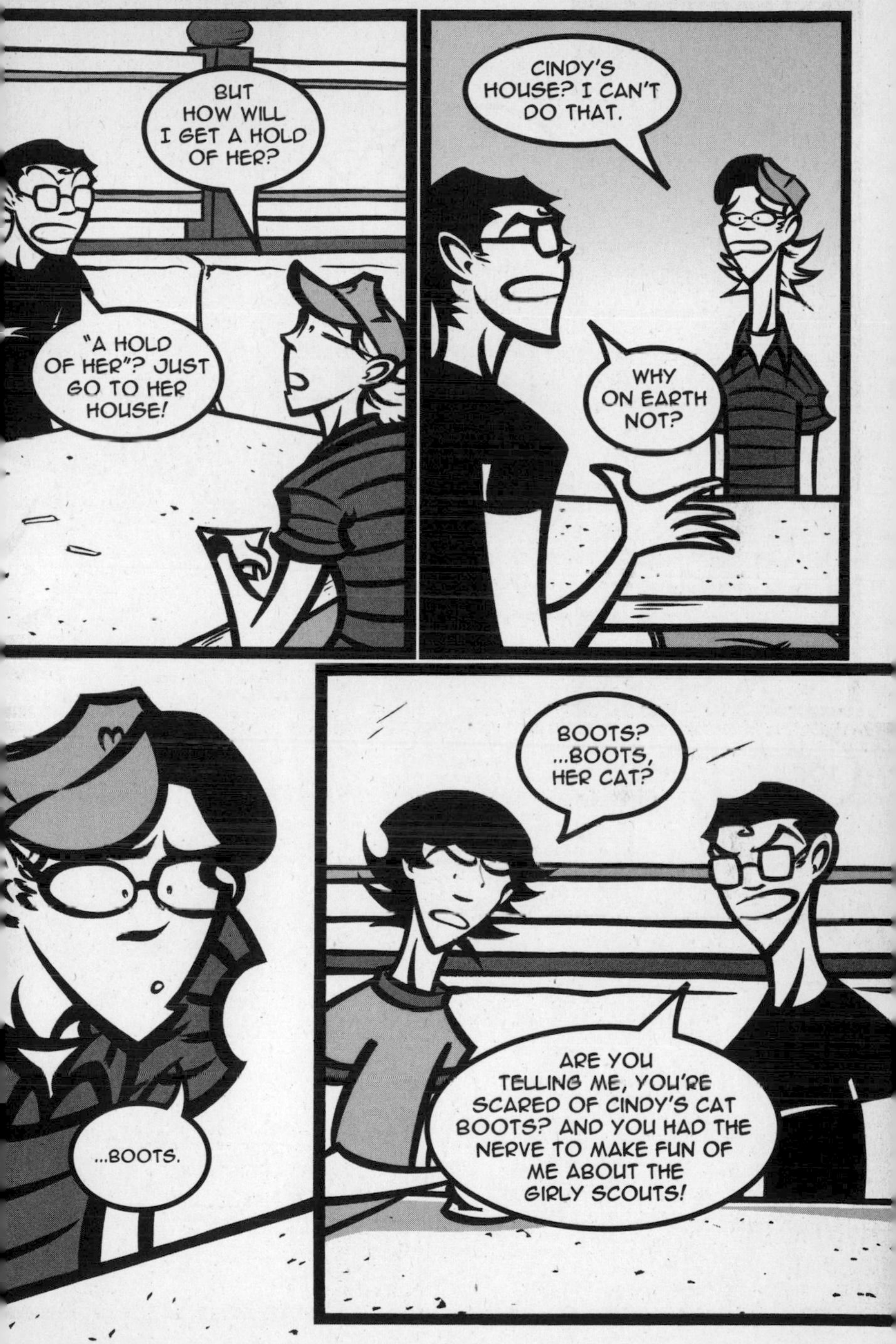
BUT HOW WILL I GET A HOLD OF HER?
"A HOLD OF HER"? JUST GO TO HER HOUSE!
CINDY'S HOUSE? I CAN'T DO THAT.
WHY ON EARTH NOT?
...BOOTS.
BOOTS? ...BOOTS, HER CAT?
ARE YOU TELLING ME, YOU'RE SCARED OF CINDY'S CAT BOOTS? AND YOU HAD THE NERVE TO MAKE FUN OF ME ABOUT THE GIRLY SCOUTS!

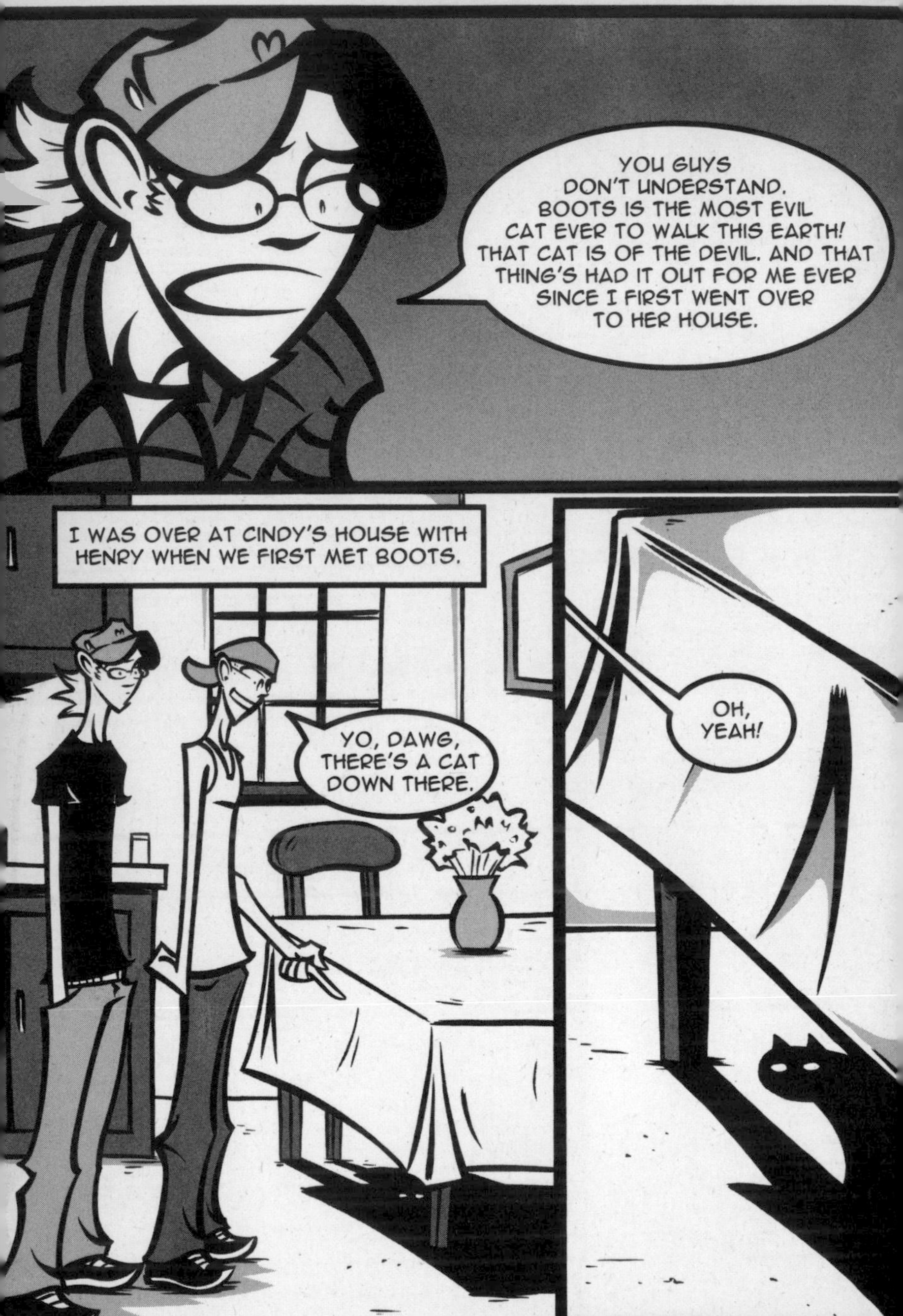
YOU GUYS DON'T UNDERSTAND. BOOTS IS THE MOST EVIL CAT EVER TO WALK THIS EARTH! THAT CAT IS OF THE DEVIL. AND THAT THING'S HAD IT OUT FOR ME EVER SINCE I FIRST WENT OVER TO HER HOUSE.
I WAS OVER AT CINDY'S HOUSE WITH HENRY WHEN WE FIRST MET BOOTS.
YO, DAWG, THERE'S A CAT DOWN THERE.
OH, YEAH!

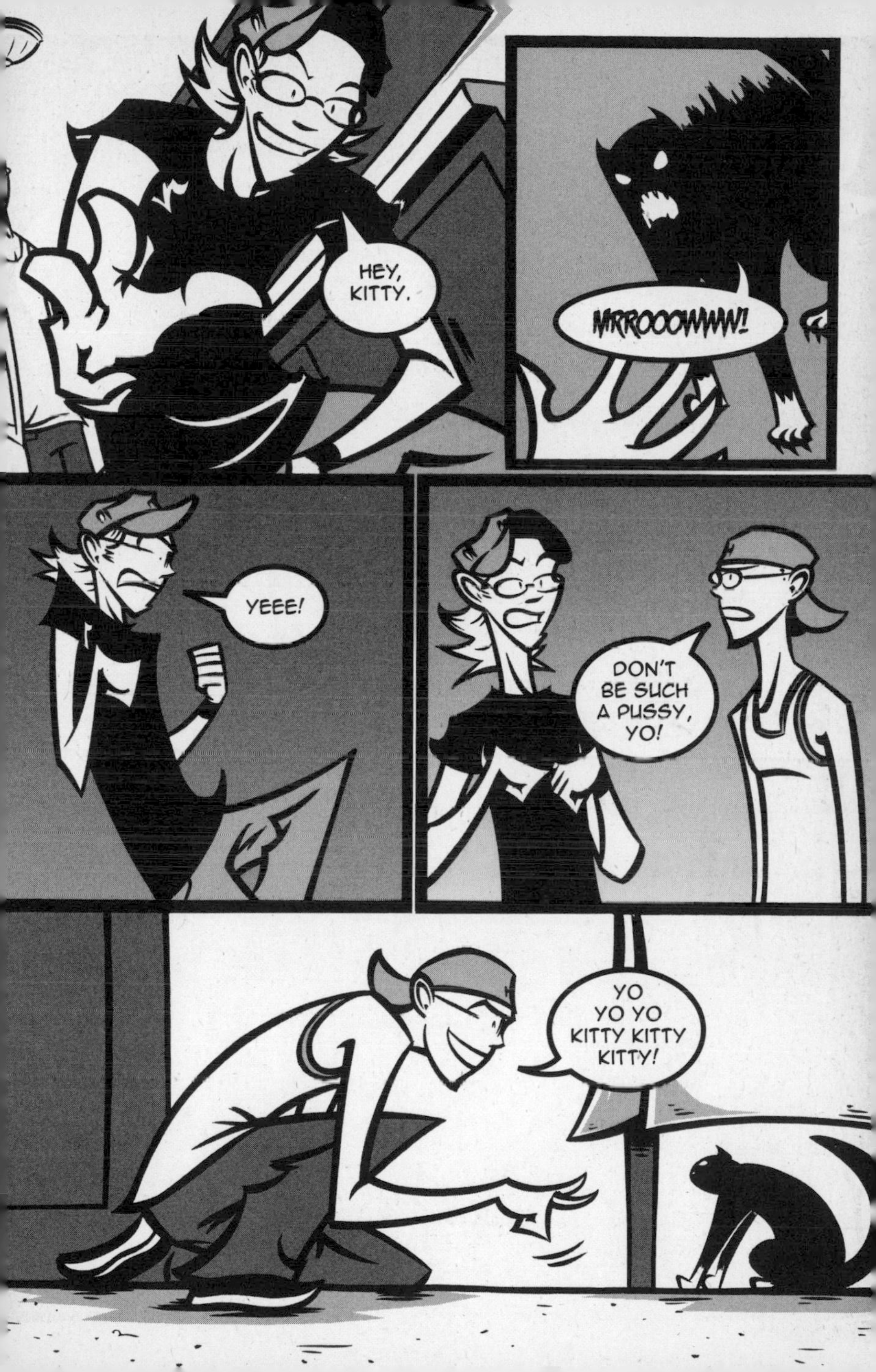
HEY, KITTY.
MRROOOWWW!
YEEE!
DON'T BE SUCH A PUSSY, YO!
YO YO YO KITTY KITTY KITTY!

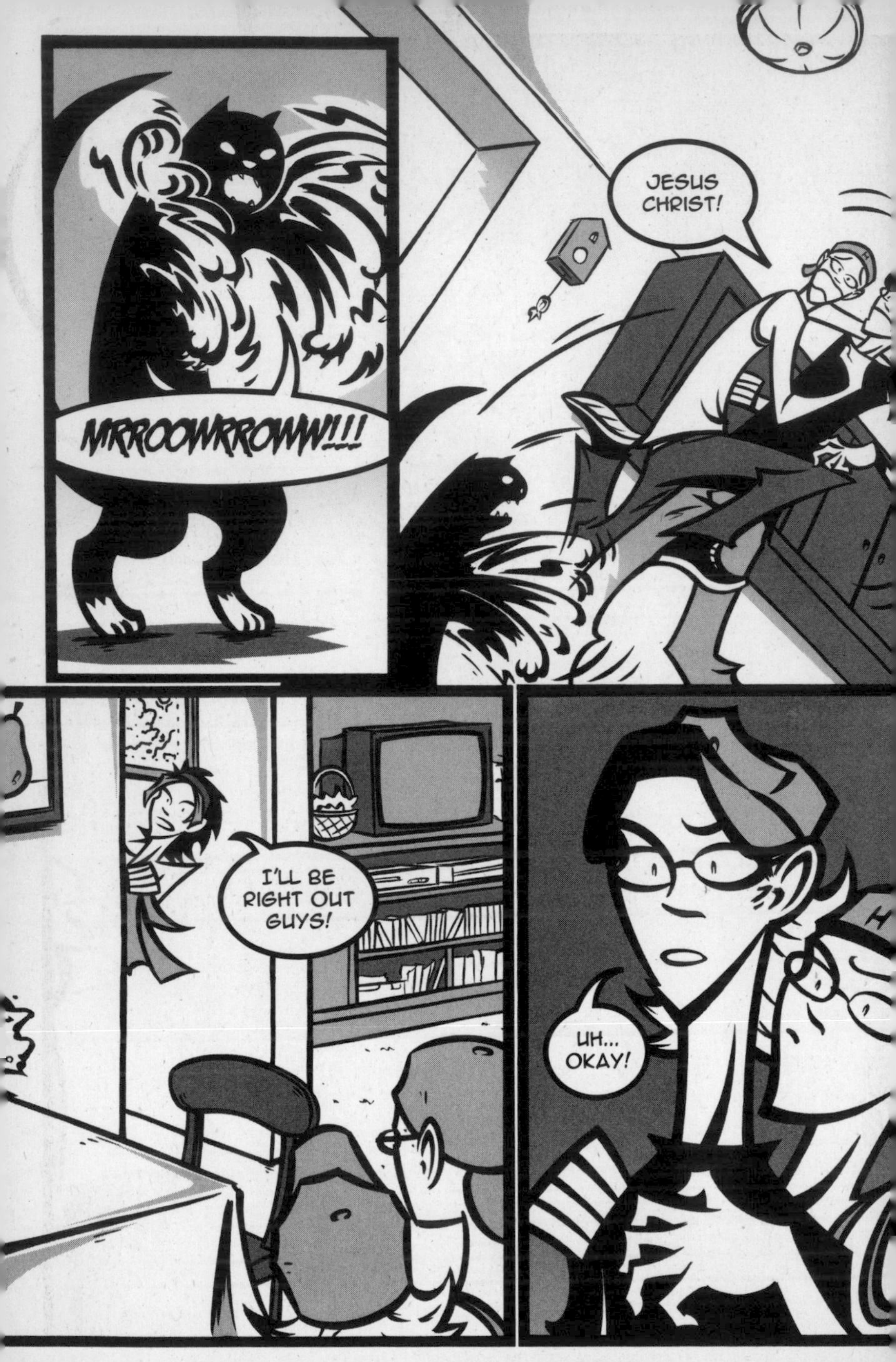
MRROOWRROWW!!!
JESUS CHRIST!
I'LL BE RIGHT OUT GUYS!
UH... OKAY!

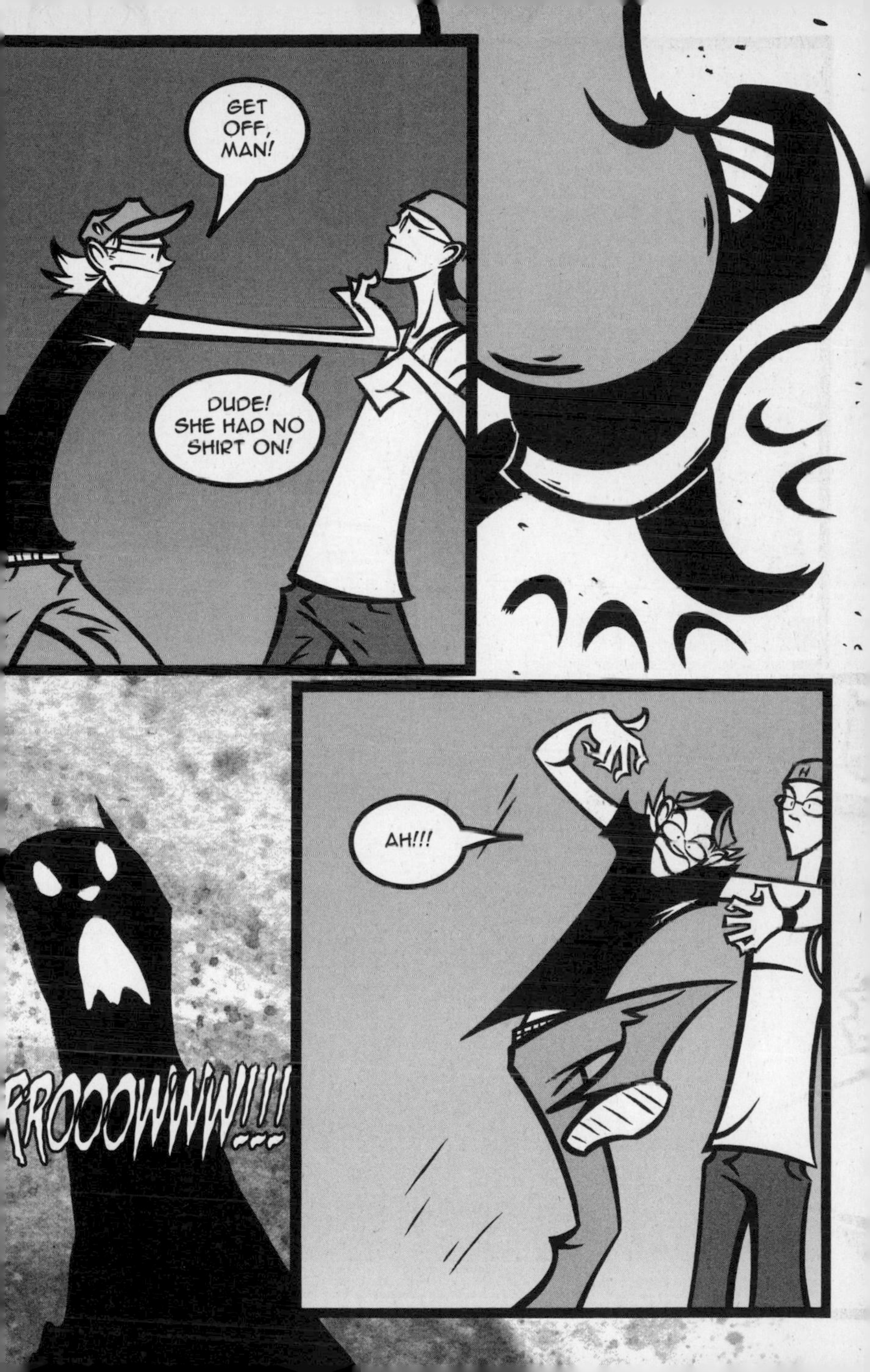
GET OFF, MAN!
DUDE! SHE HAD NO SHIRT ON!
AH!!!
RROOOWWW!!!

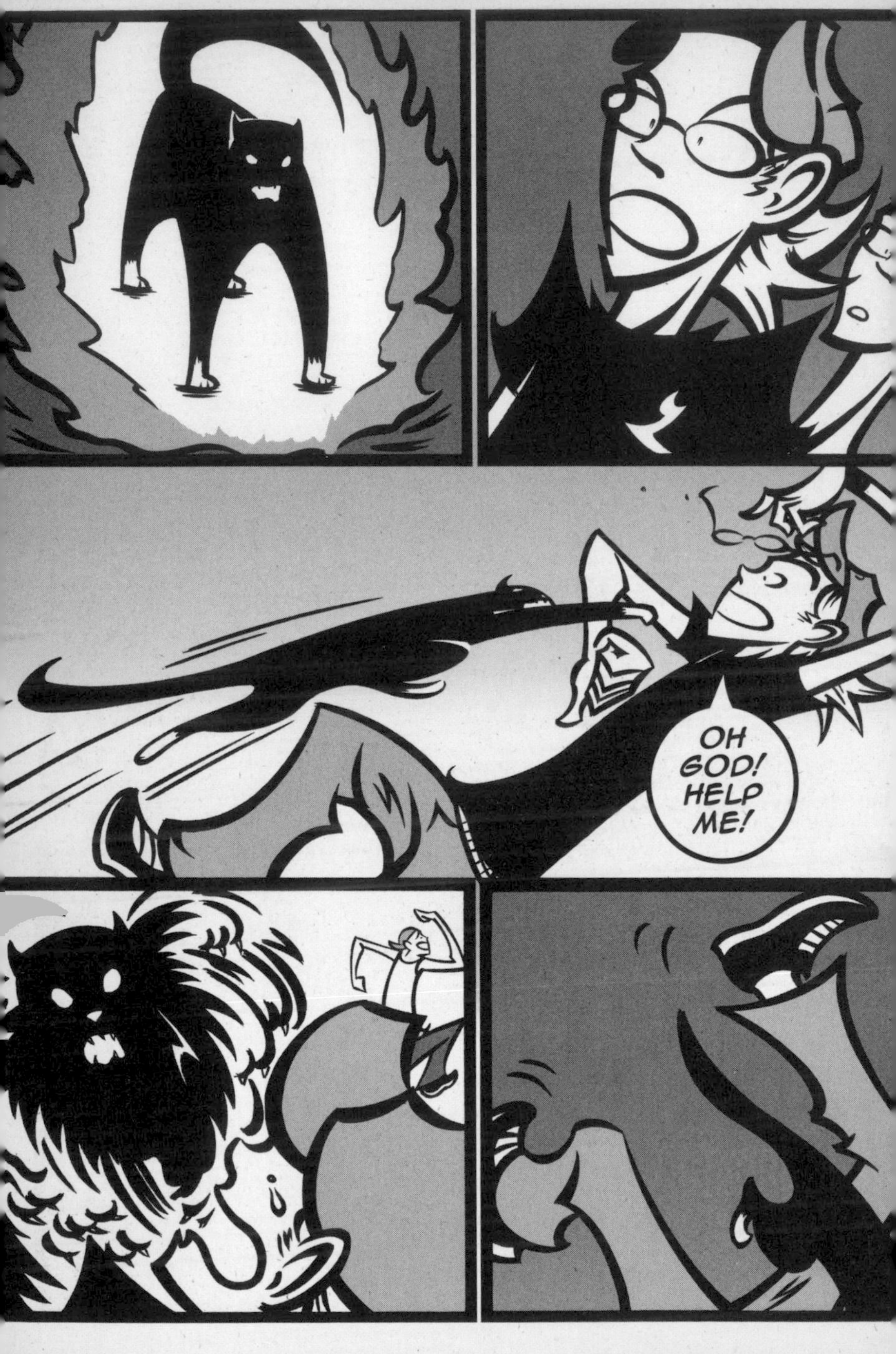
OH GOD! HELP ME!

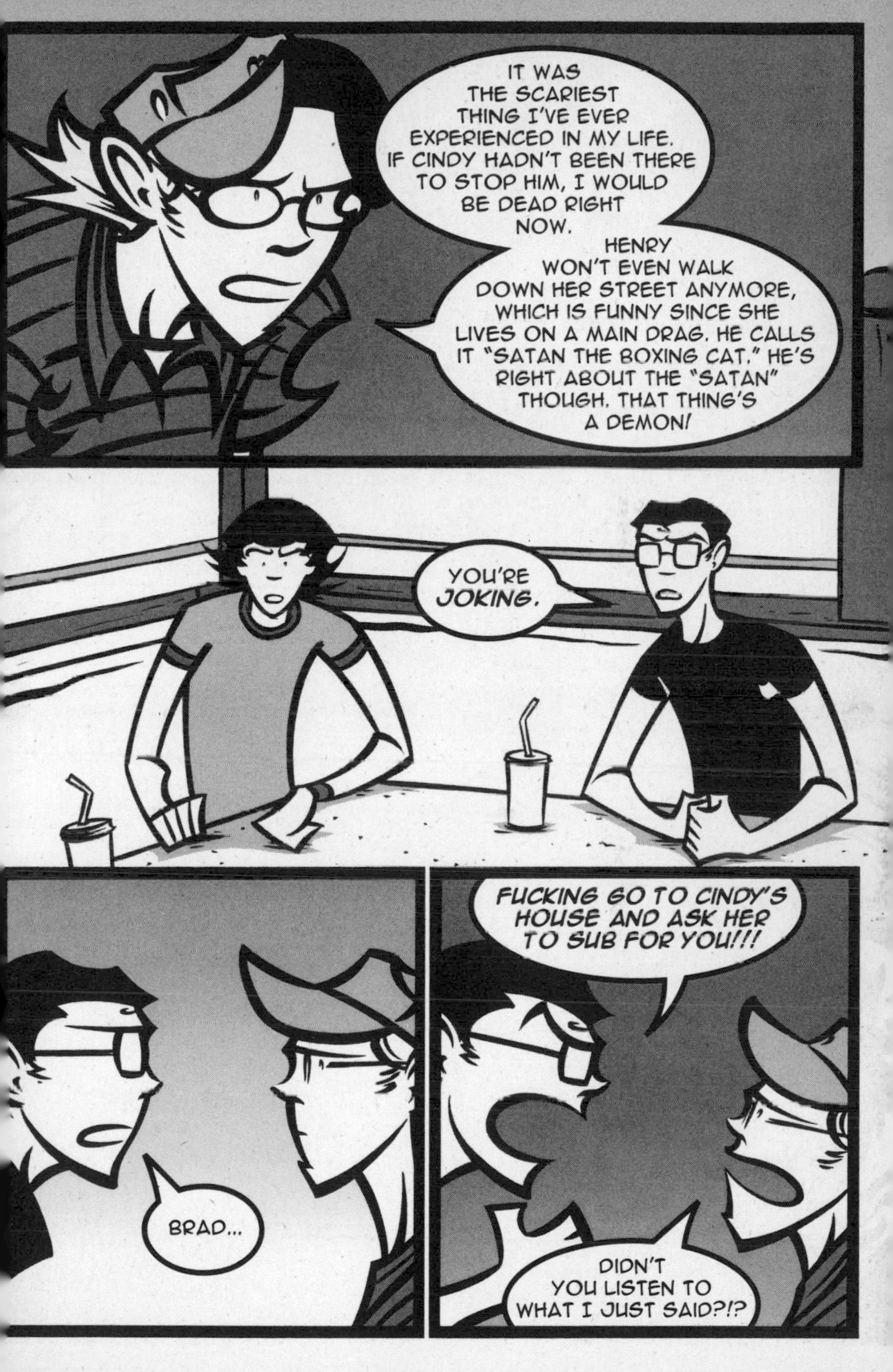
IT WAS THE SCARIEST THING I'VE EVER EXPERIENCED IN MY LIFE. IF CINDY HADN'T BEEN THERE TO STOP HIM, I WOULD BE DEAD RIGHT NOW.
HENRY WON'T EVEN WALK DOWN HER STREET ANYMORE, WHICH IS FUNNY SINCE SHE LIVES ON A MAIN DRAG. HE CALLS IT "SATAN THE BOXING CAT." HE'S RIGHT ABOUT THE "SATAN" THOUGH. THAT THING'S A DEMON!
YOU'RE JOKING.
BRAD...
FUCKING GO TO CINDY'S HOUSE AND ASK HER TO SUB FOR YOU!!!
DIDN'T YOU LISTEN TO WHAT I JUST SAID?!?

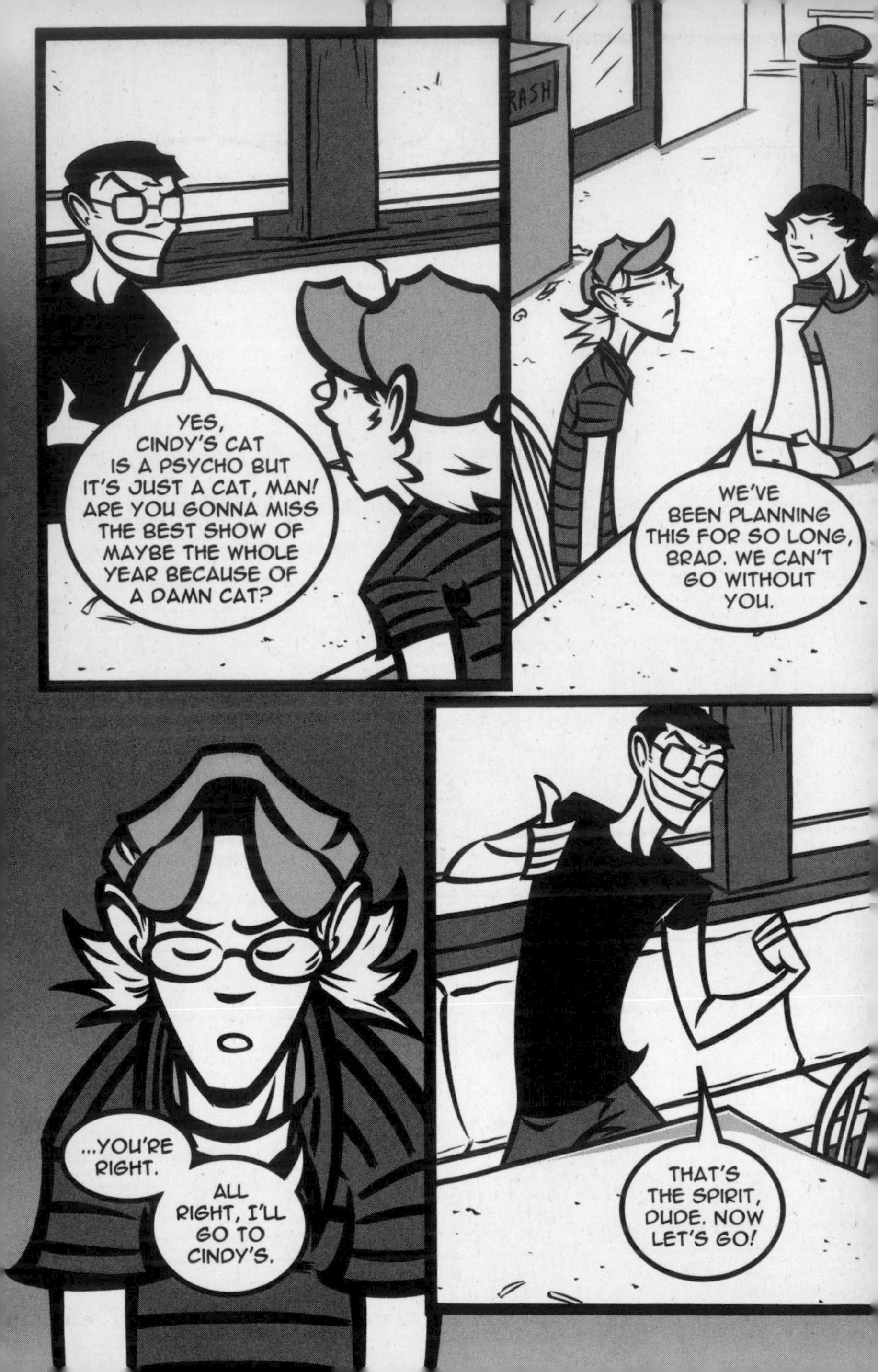
RASH
YES, CINDY'S CAT IS A PSYCHO BUT IT'S JUST A CAT, MAN! ARE YOU GONNA MISS THE BEST SHOW OF MAYBE THE WHOLE YEAR BECAUSE OF A DAMN CAT?
WE'VE BEEN PLANNING THIS FOR SO LONG, BRAD. WE CAN'T GO WITHOUT YOU.
...YOU'RE RIGHT.
ALL RIGHT, I'LL GO TO CINDY'S.
THAT'S THE SPIRIT, DUDE. NOW LET'S GO!

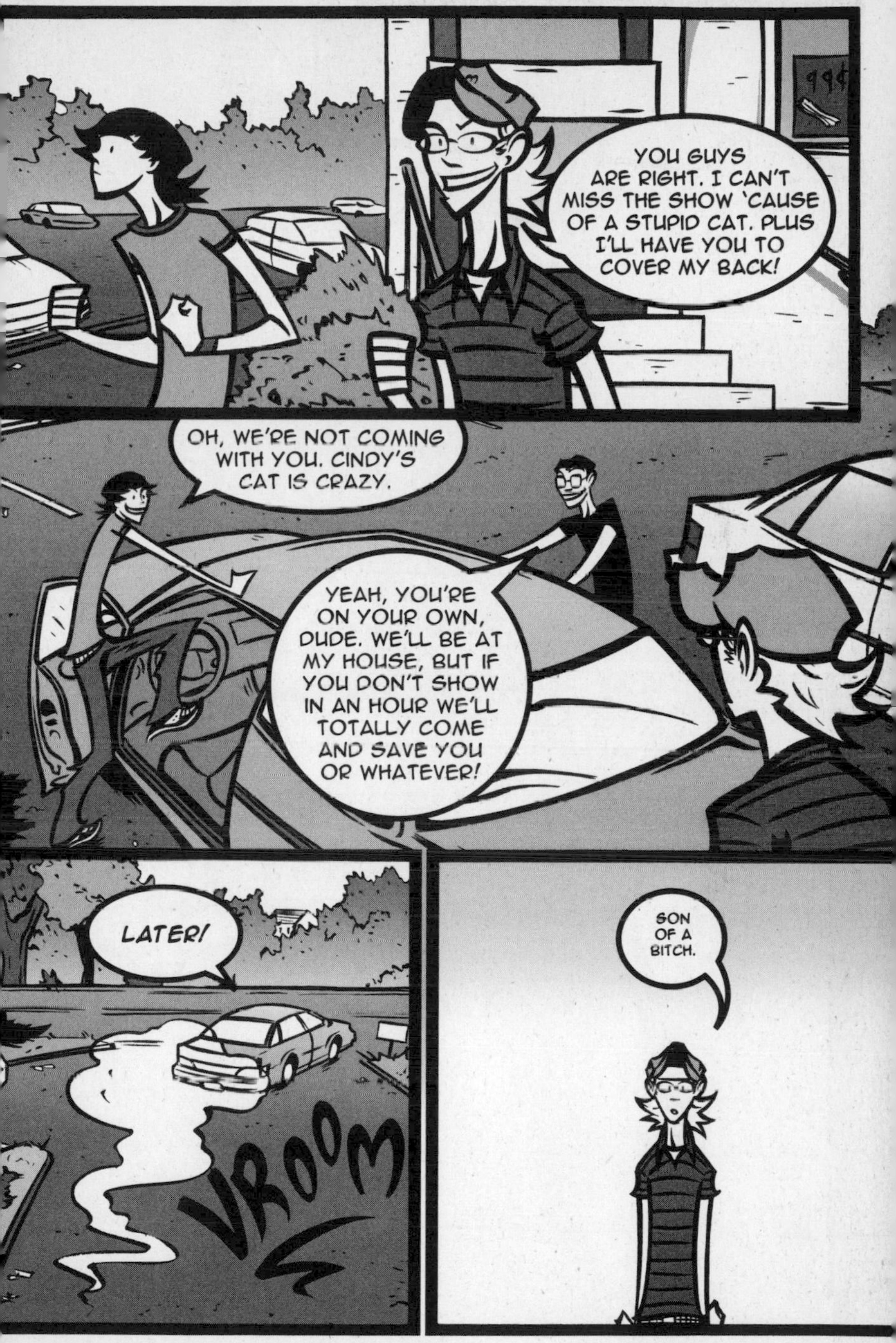
YOU GUYS ARE RIGHT. I CAN'T MISS THE SHOW 'CAUSE OF A STUPID CAT. PLUS I'LL HAVE YOU TO COVER MY BACK!
OH, WE'RE NOT COMING WITH YOU. CINDY'S CAT IS CRAZY.
YEAH, YOU'RE ON YOUR OWN, DUDE. WE'LL BE AT MY HOUSE, BUT IF YOU DON'T SHOW IN AN HOUR WE'LL TOTALLY COME AND SAVE YOU OR WHATEVER!
LATER!
VROOM
SON OF A BITCH.

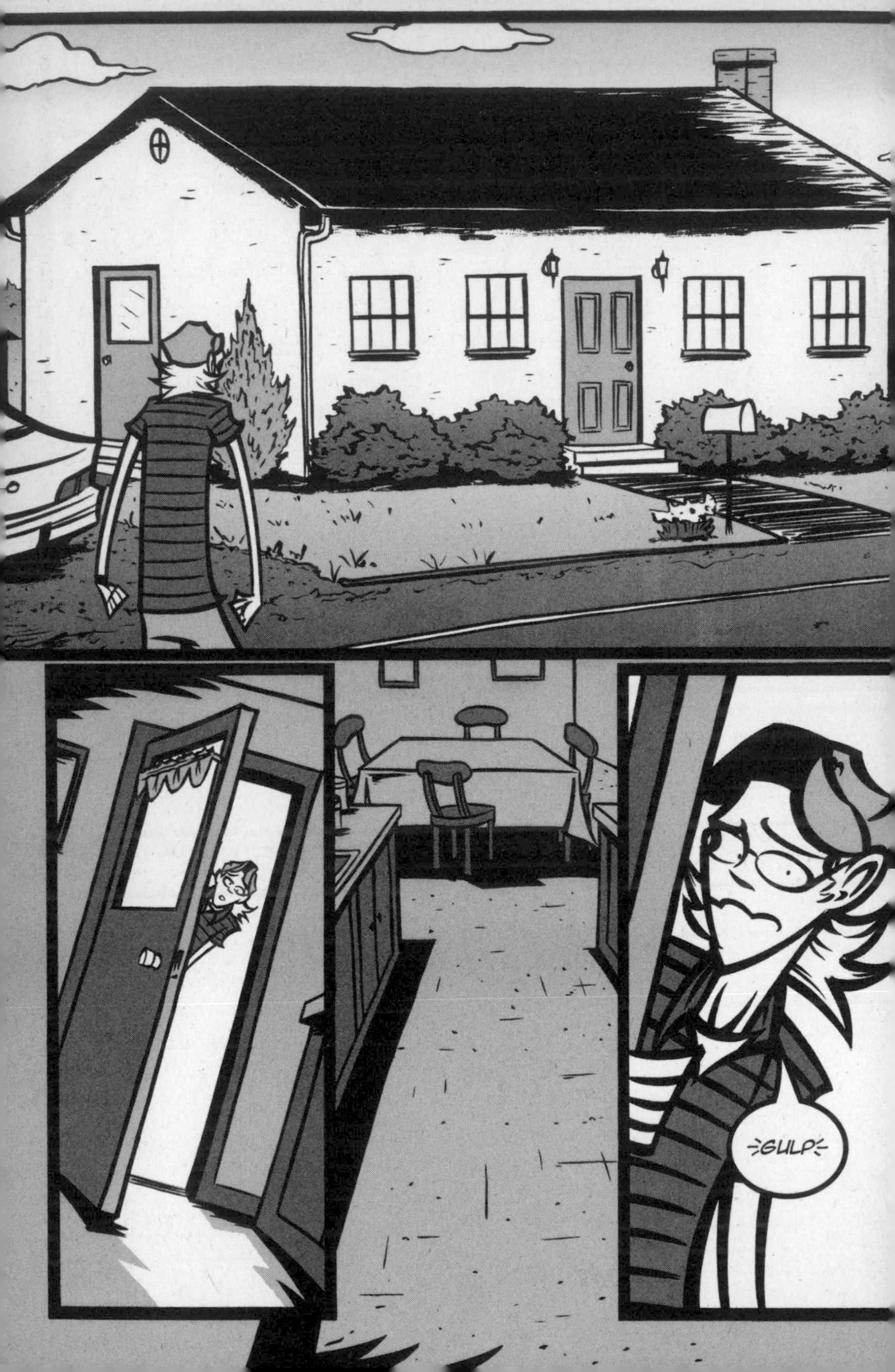
GULP

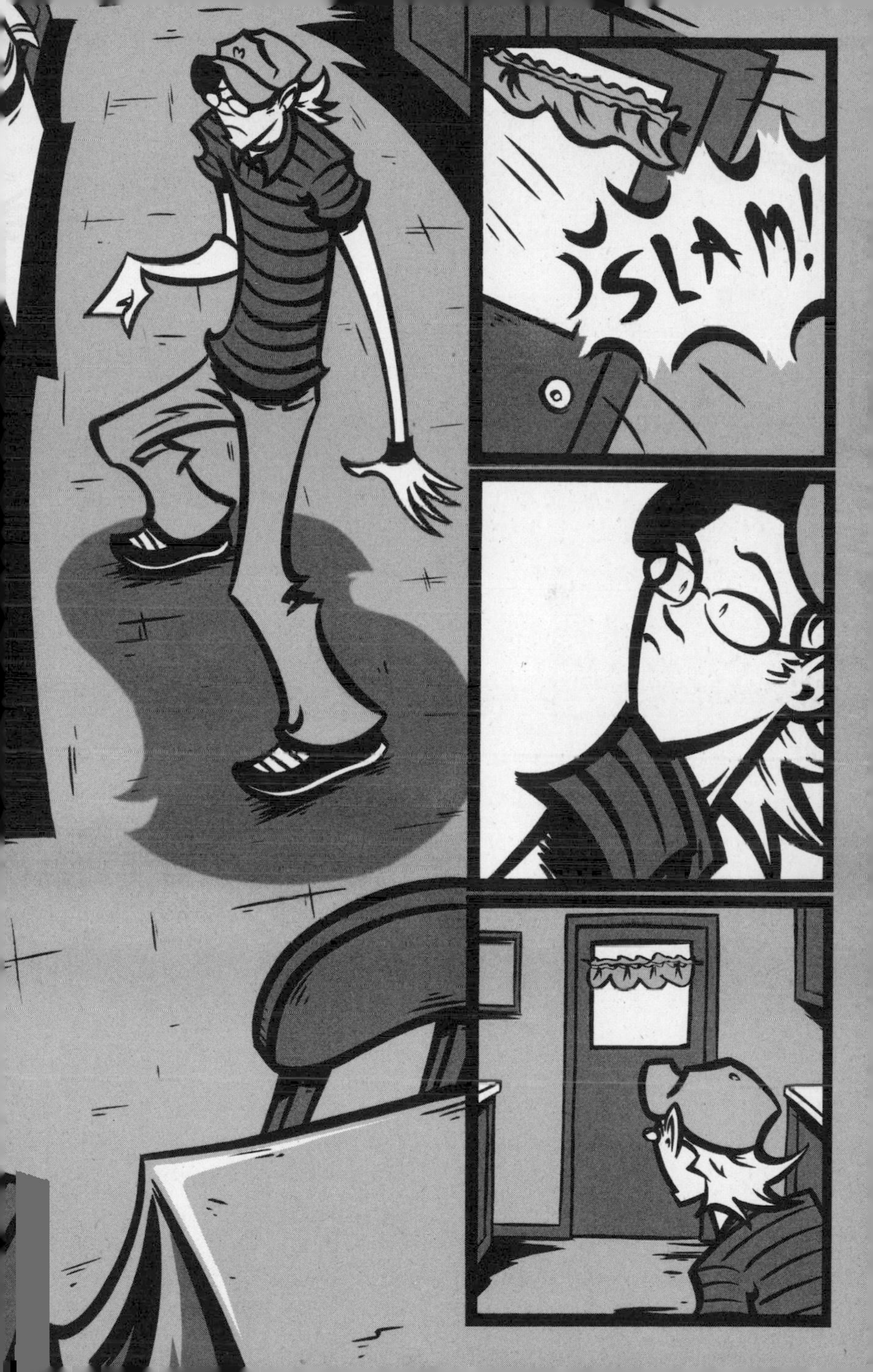
SLAM!

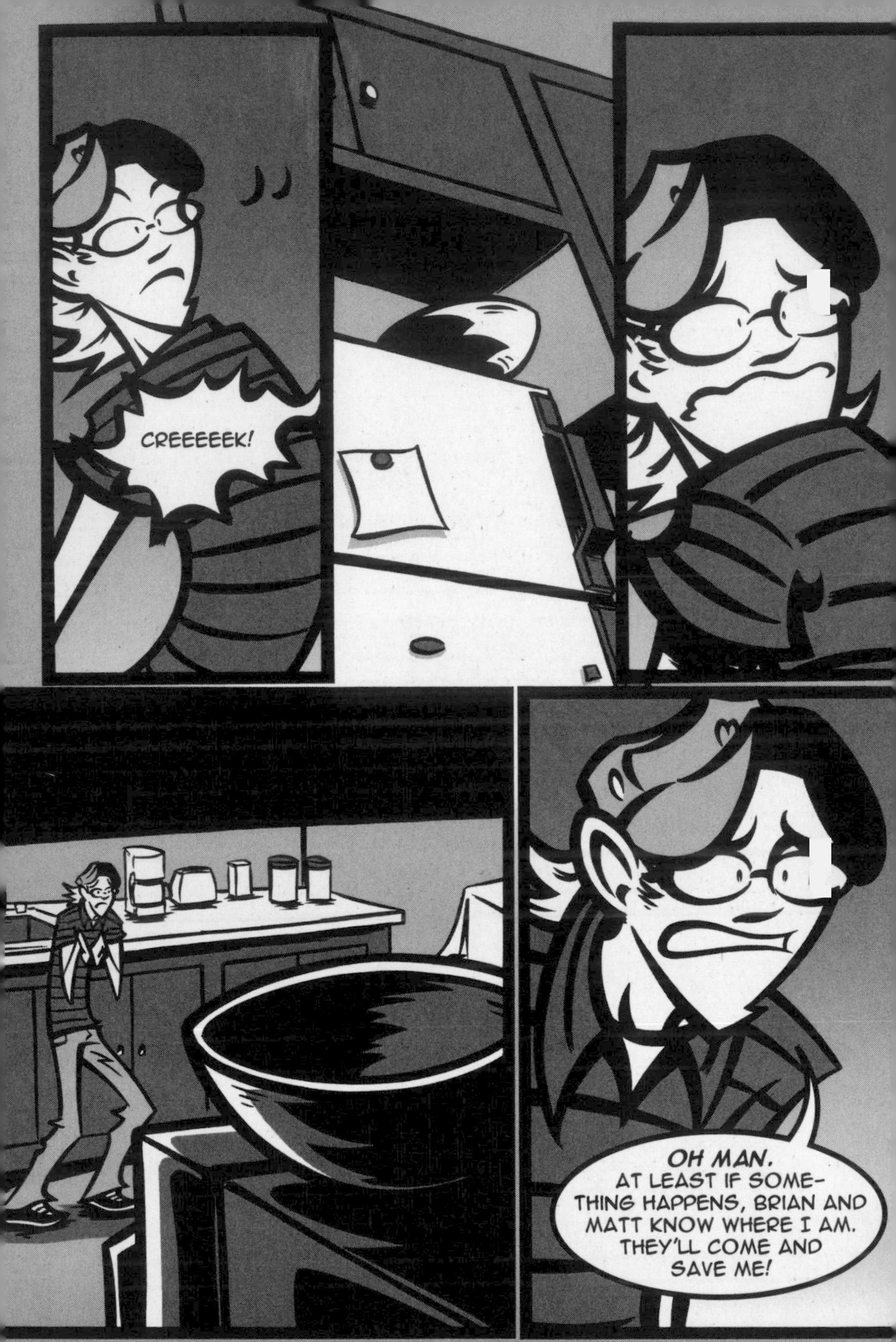
CREEEEEK!
OH MAN.
AT LEAST IF SOME-THING HAPPENS, BRIAN AND MATT KNOW WHERE I AM. THEY'LL COME AND SAVE ME!

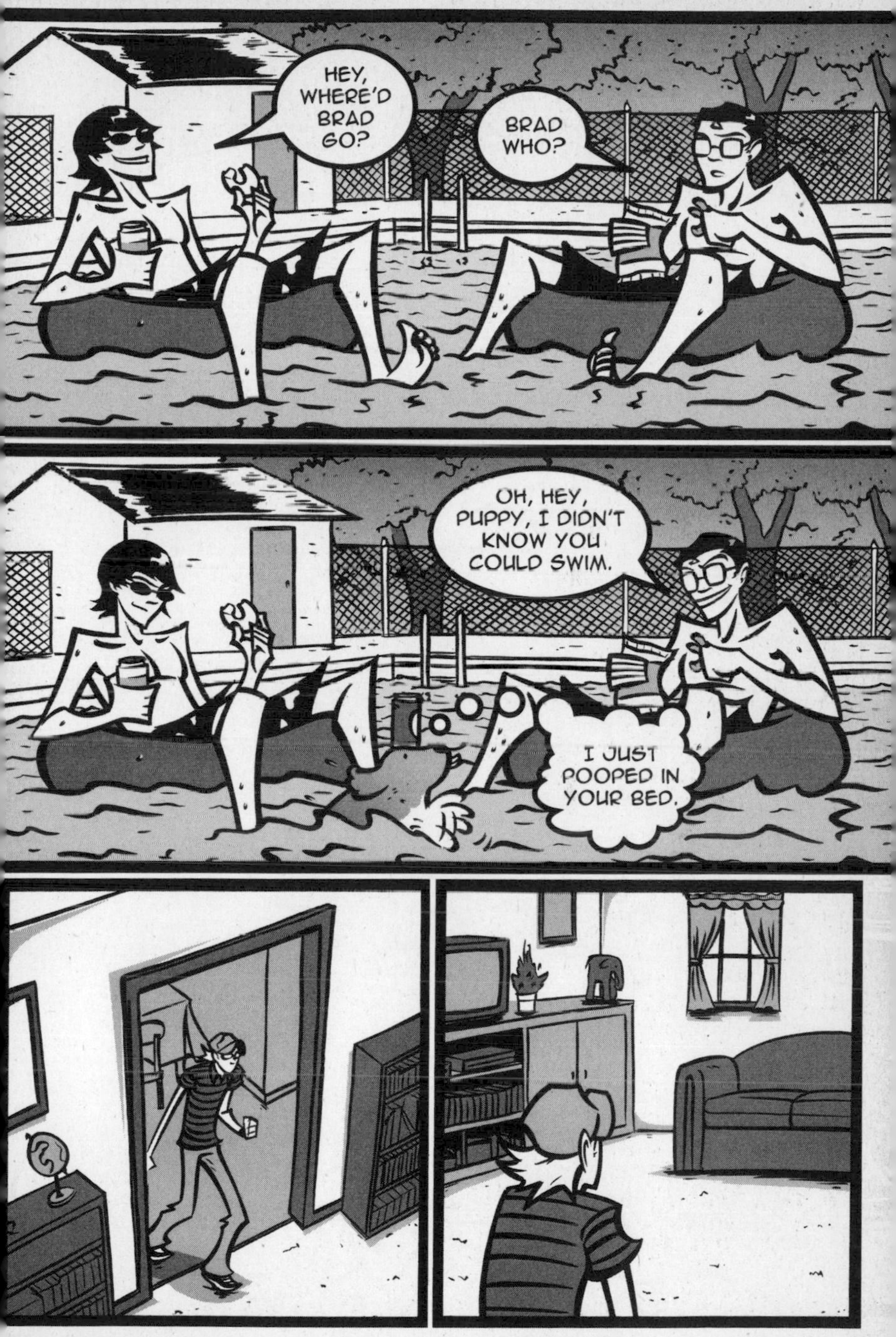
HEY, WHERE'D BRAD GO?
BRAD WHO?
OH, HEY, PUPPY, I DIDN'T KNOW YOU COULD SWIM.
I JUST POOPED IN YOUR BED.

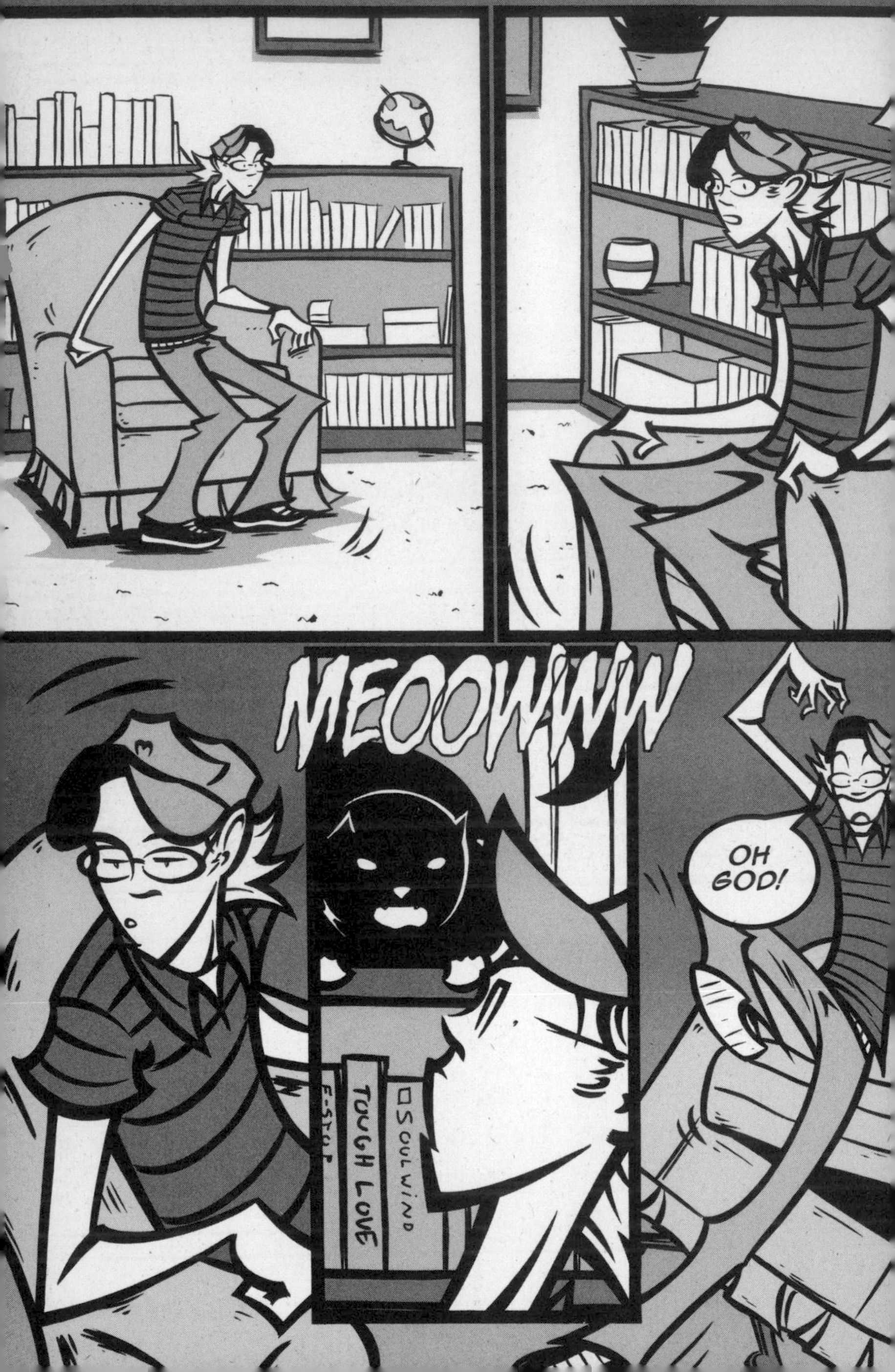
MEOOWWW
OH GOD!
SOULWIND
TOUGH LOVE
F-STOP

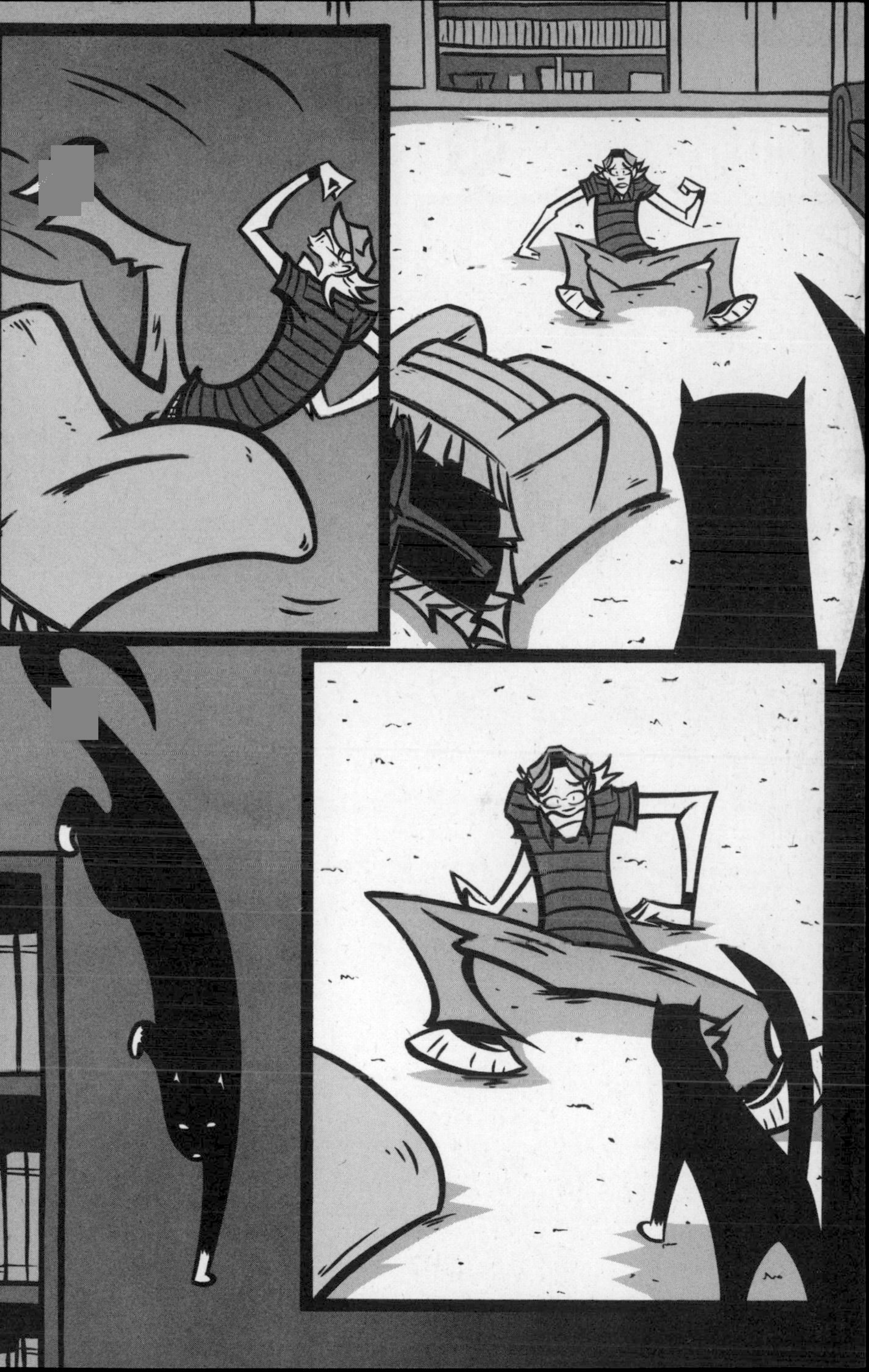

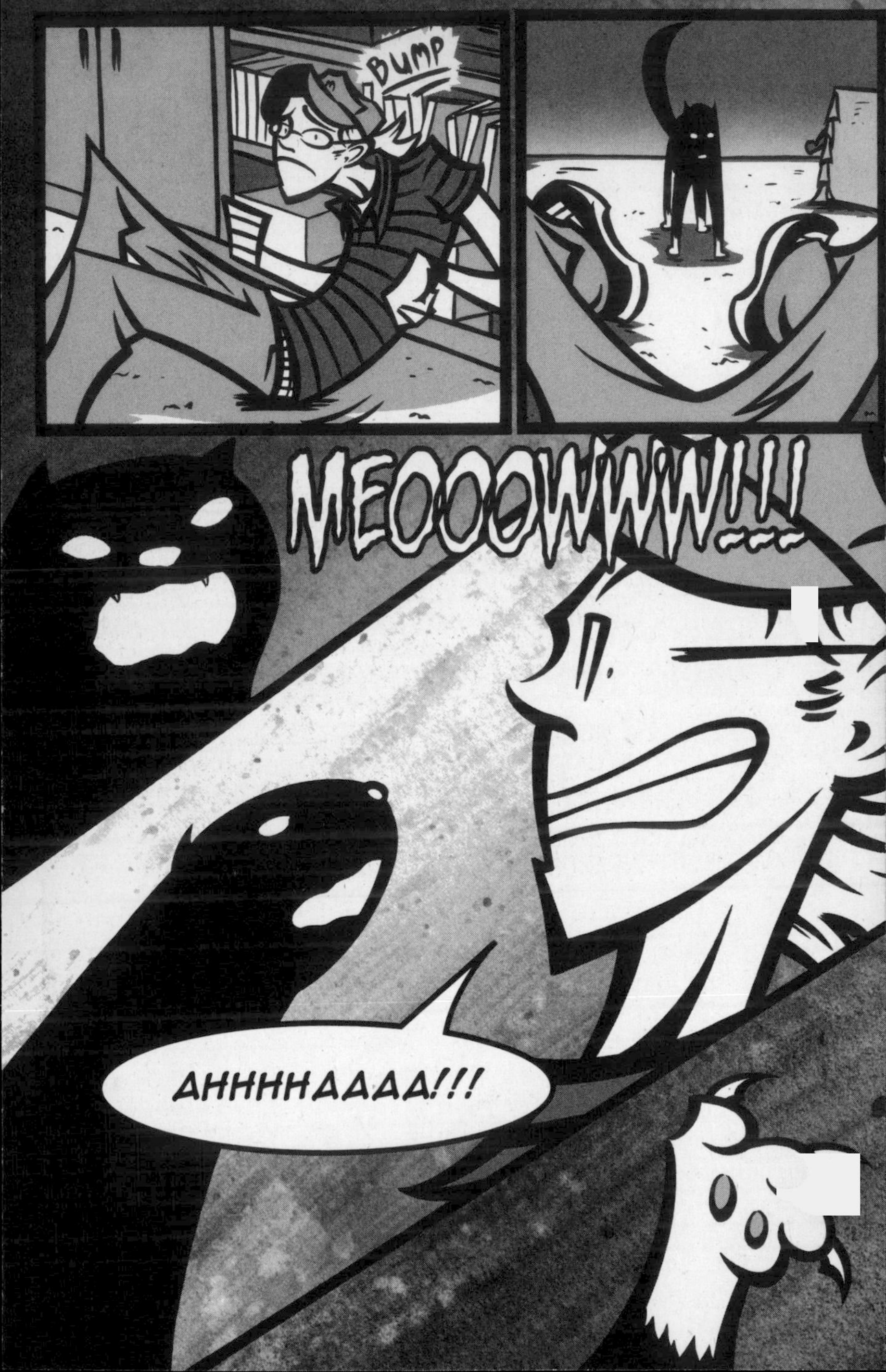
BUMP
MEOOOWWW!!!
AHHHHAAAA!!!

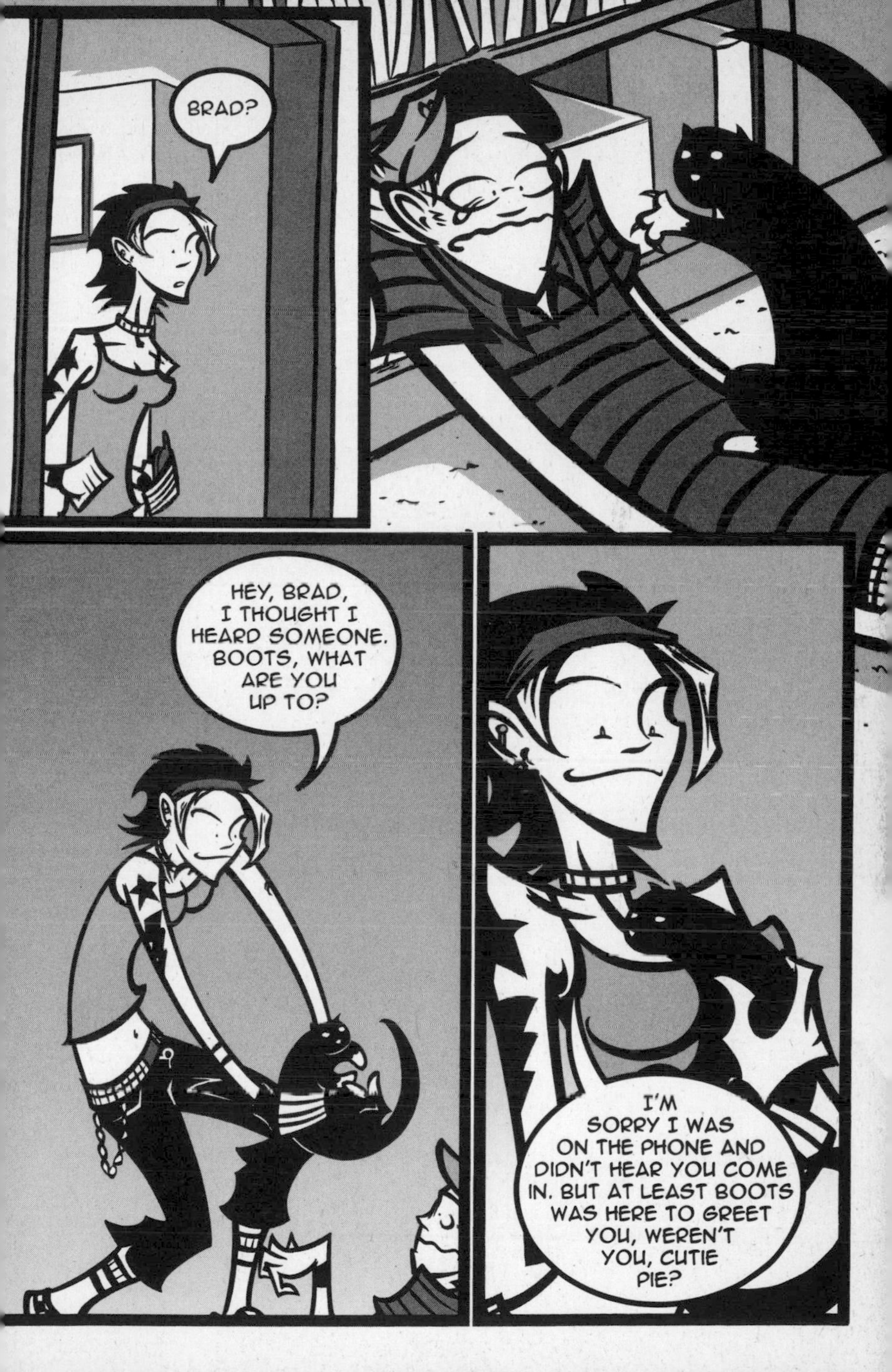
BRAD?
HEY, BRAD, I THOUGHT I HEARD SOMEONE. BOOTS, WHAT ARE YOU UP TO?
I'M SORRY I WAS ON THE PHONE AND DIDN'T HEAR YOU COME IN. BUT AT LEAST BOOTS WAS HERE TO GREET YOU, WEREN'T YOU, CUTIE PIE?

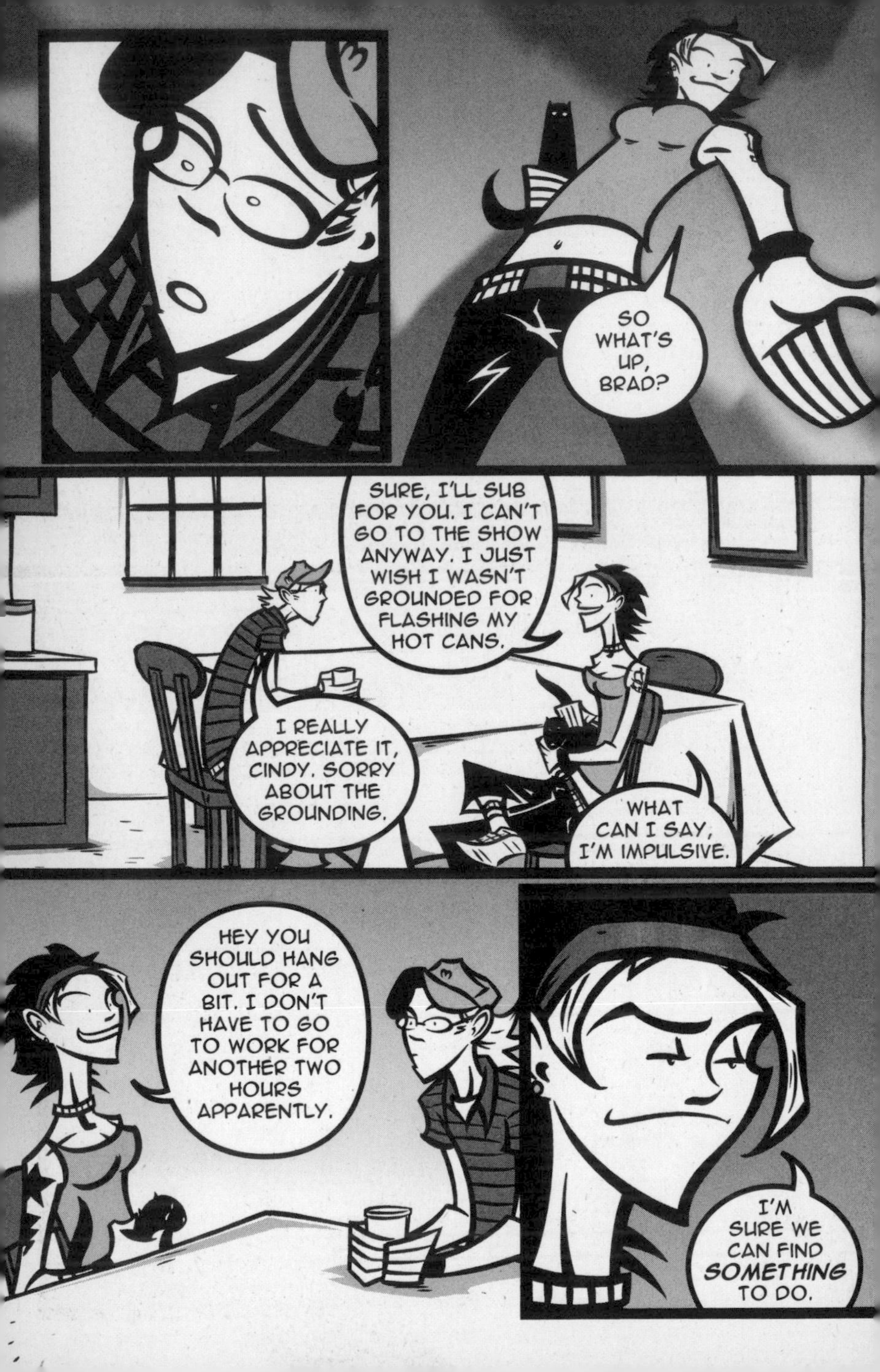
SO WHAT'S UP, BRAD?
SURE, I'LL SUB FOR YOU. I CAN'T GO TO THE SHOW ANYWAY. I JUST WISH I WASN'T GROUNDED FOR FLASHING MY HOT CANS.
I REALLY APPRECIATE IT, CINDY. SORRY ABOUT THE GROUNDING.
WHAT CAN I SAY, I'M IMPULSIVE.
HEY YOU SHOULD HANG OUT FOR A BIT. I DON'T HAVE TO GO TO WORK FOR ANOTHER TWO HOURS APPARENTLY.
I'M SURE WE CAN FIND *SOMETHING* TO DO.

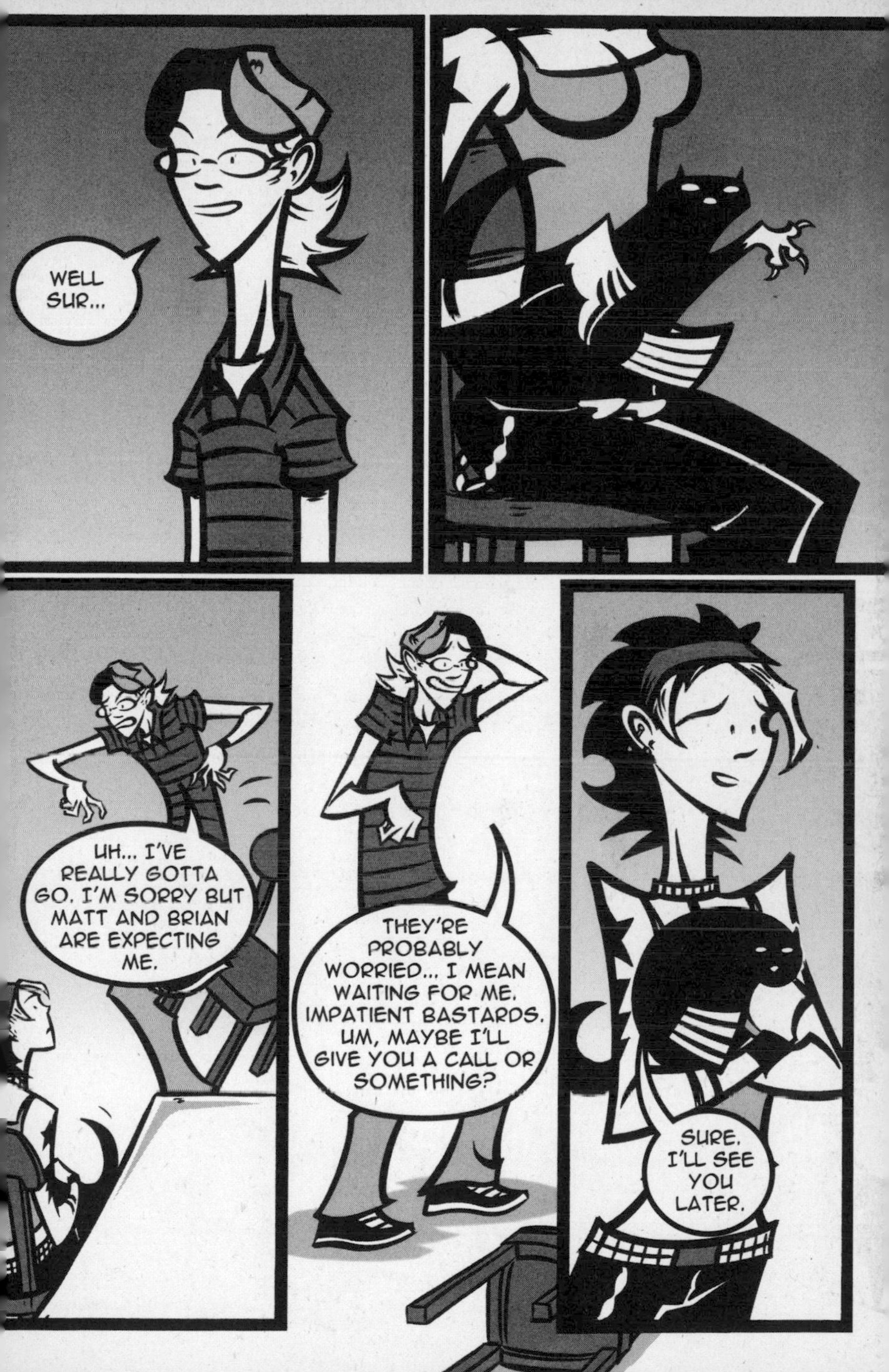
WELL SUR...
UH... I'VE REALLY GOTTA GO. I'M SORRY BUT MATT AND BRIAN ARE EXPECTING ME.
THEY'RE PROBABLY WORRIED... I MEAN WAITING FOR ME. IMPATIENT BASTARDS. UM, MAYBE I'LL GIVE YOU A CALL OR SOMETHING?
SURE. I'LL SEE YOU LATER.

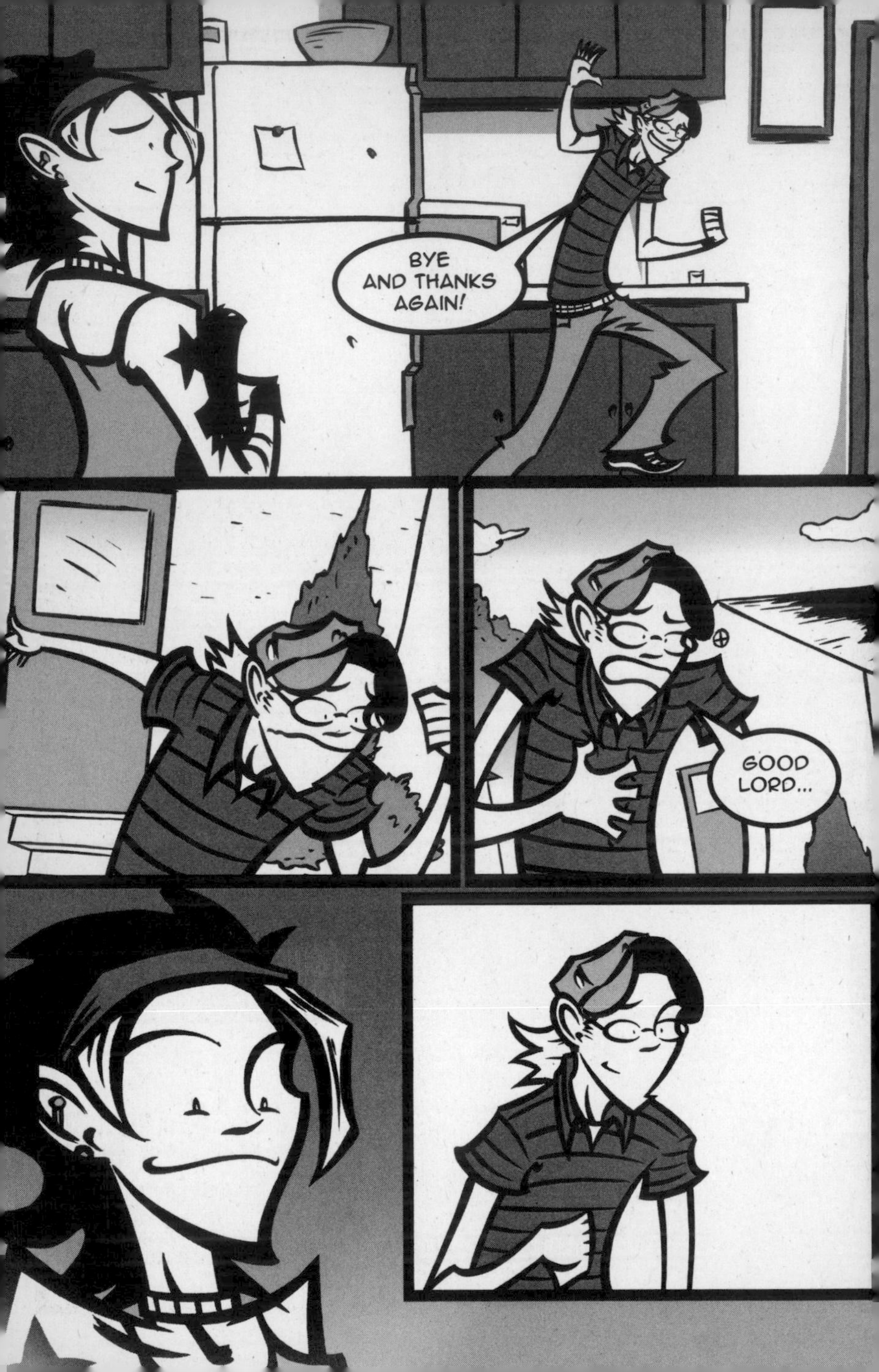
BYE
AND THANKS
AGAIN!
GOOD
LORD...

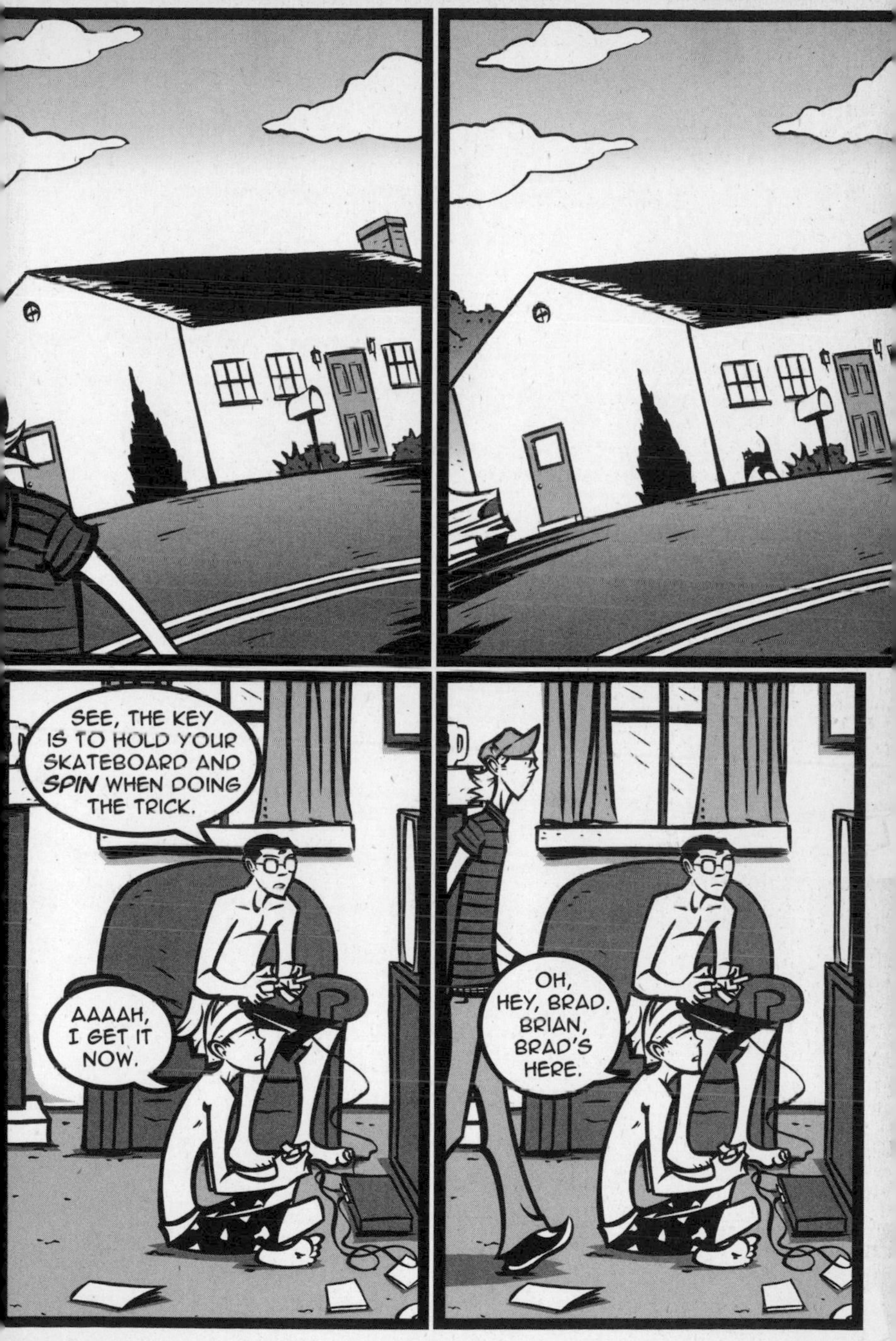

SEE, THE KEY IS TO HOLD YOUR SKATEBOARD AND *SPIN* WHEN DOING THE TRICK.
AAAAH, I GET IT NOW.
OH, HEY, BRAD. BRIAN, BRAD'S HERE.

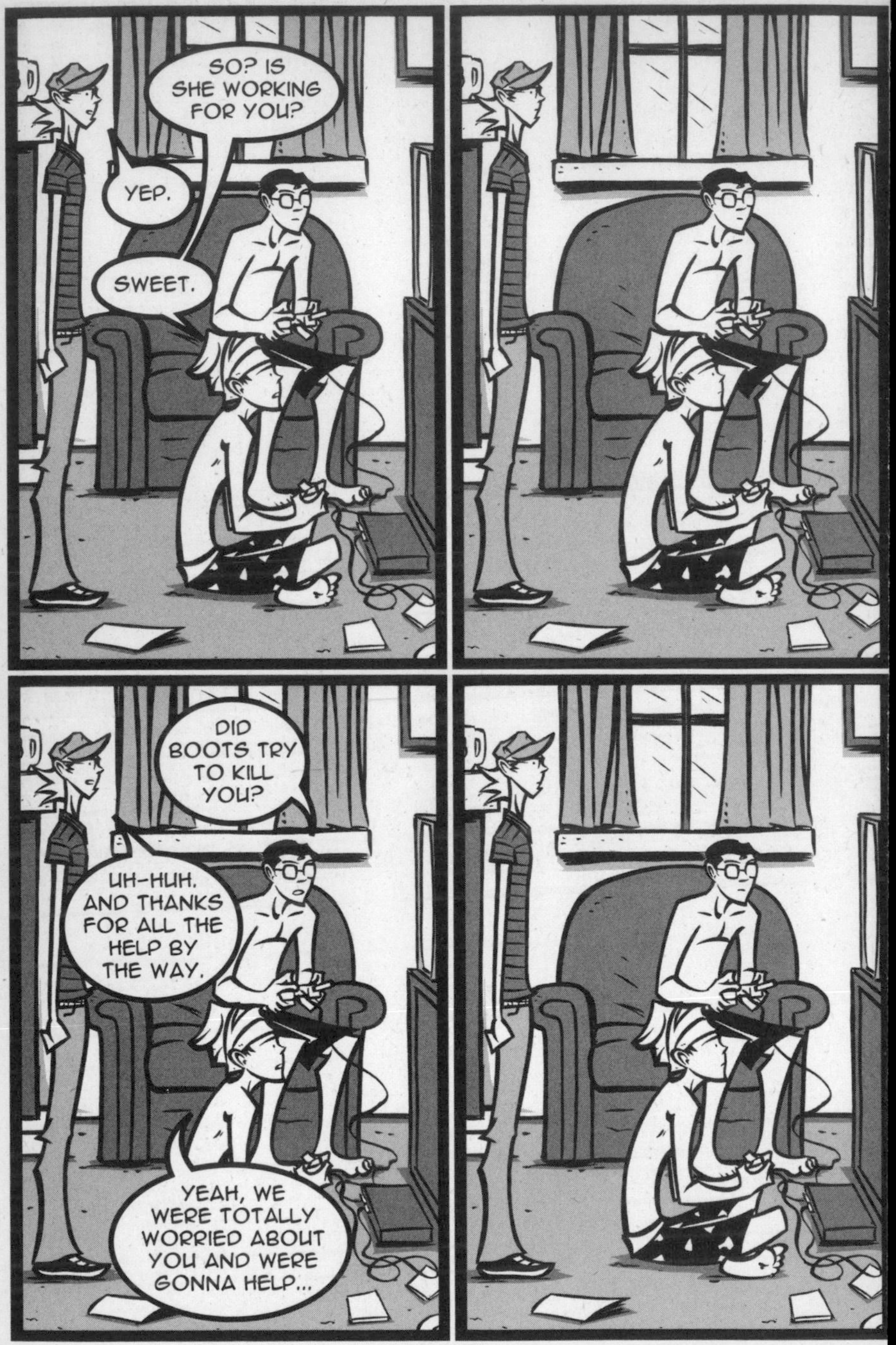
SO? IS SHE WORKING FOR YOU?
YEP.
SWEET.
DID BOOTS TRY TO KILL YOU?
UH-HUH. AND THANKS FOR ALL THE HELP BY THE WAY.
YEAH, WE WERE TOTALLY WORRIED ABOUT YOU AND WERE GONNA HELP...

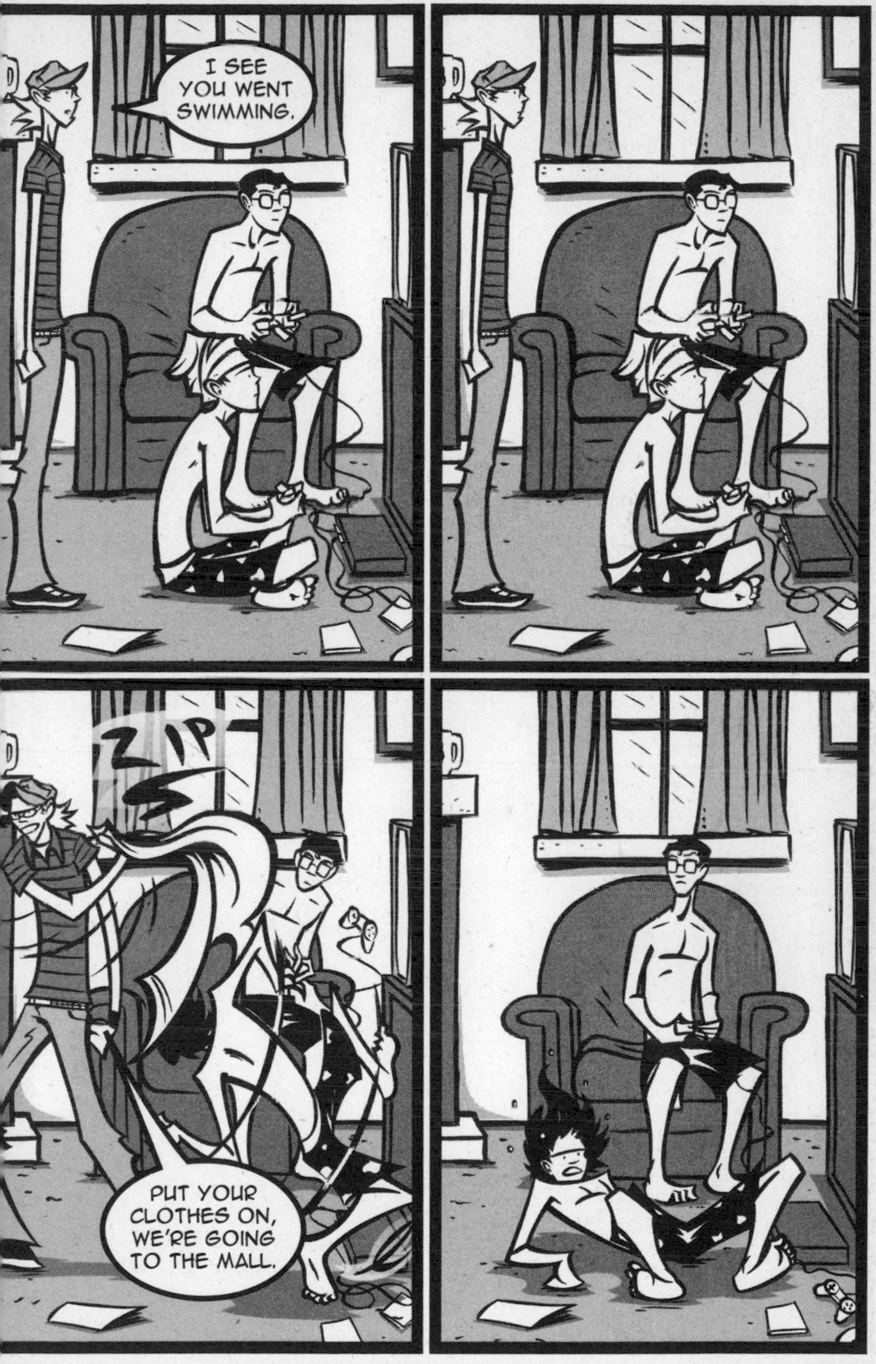
I SEE YOU WENT SWIMMING.
ZIP
PUT YOUR CLOTHES ON, WE'RE GOING TO THE MALL.

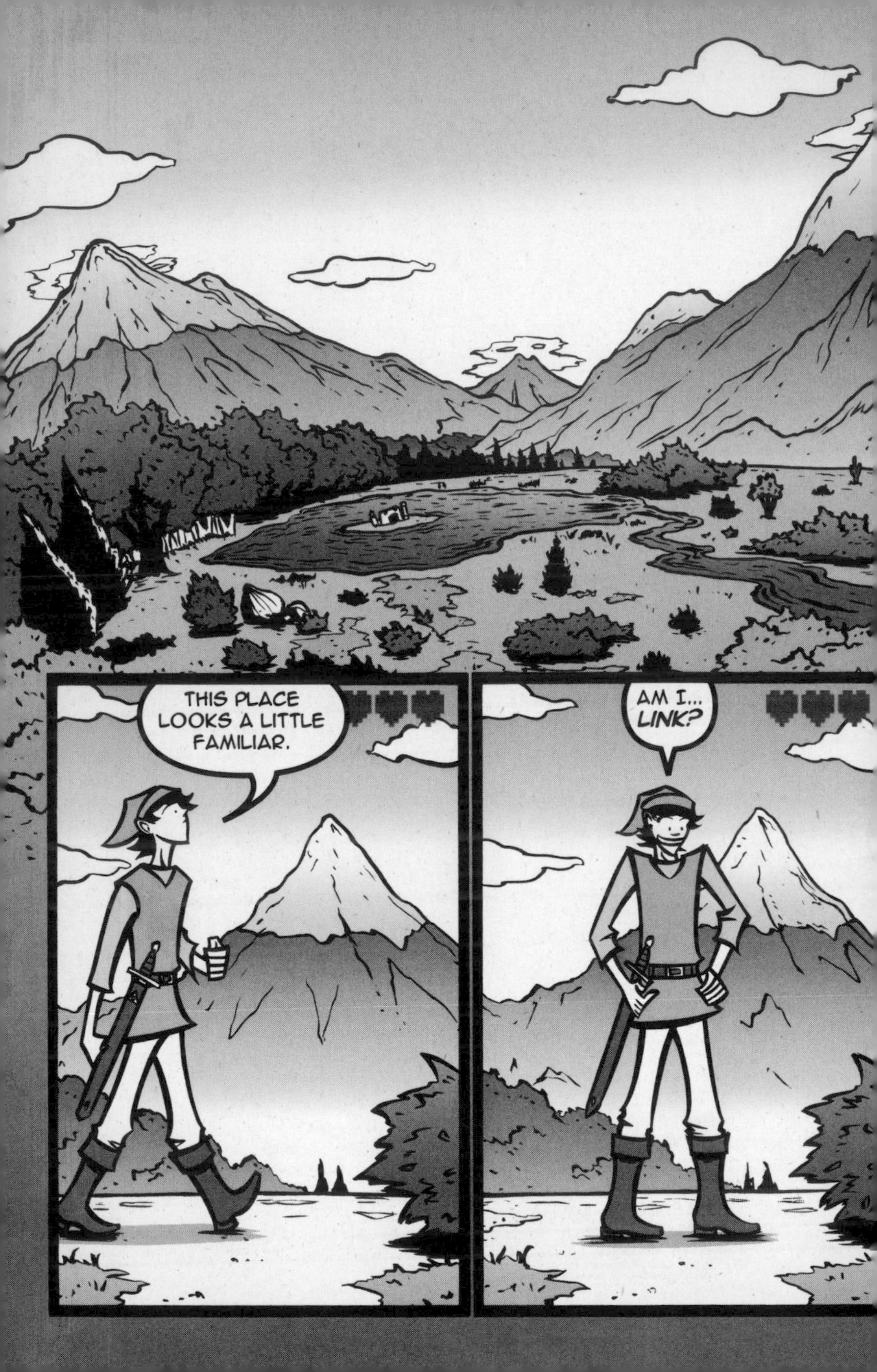
THIS PLACE LOOKS A LITTLE FAMILIAR.
AM I... LINK?

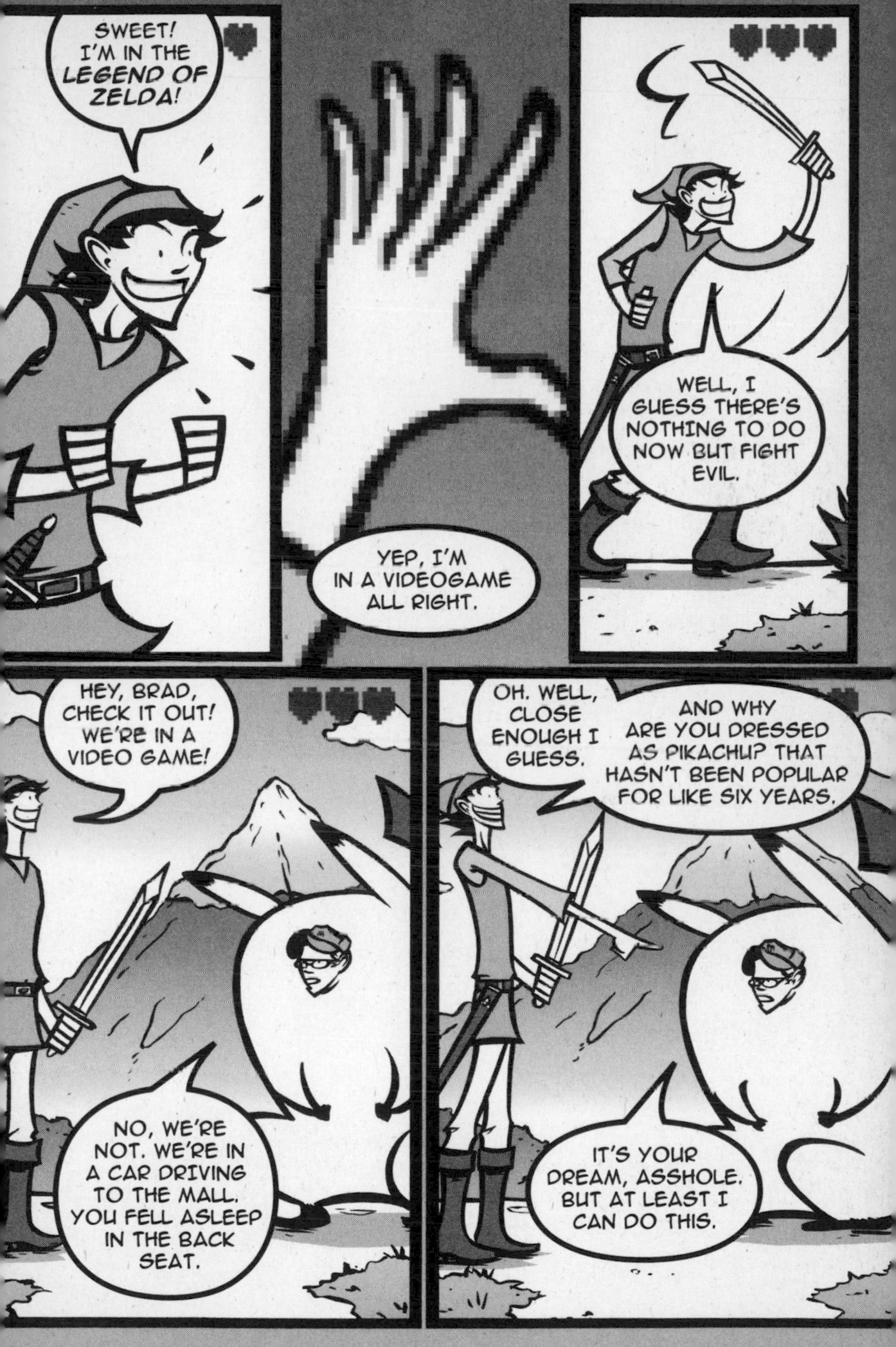
SWEET! I'M IN THE LEGEND OF ZELDA!
YEP, I'M IN A VIDEOGAME ALL RIGHT.
WELL, I GUESS THERE'S NOTHING TO DO NOW BUT FIGHT EVIL.
HEY, BRAD, CHECK IT OUT! WE'RE IN A VIDEO GAME!
NO, WE'RE NOT. WE'RE IN A CAR DRIVING TO THE MALL. YOU FELL ASLEEP IN THE BACK SEAT.
OH. WELL, CLOSE ENOUGH I GUESS.
AND WHY ARE YOU DRESSED AS PIKACHU? THAT HASN'T BEEN POPULAR FOR LIKE SIX YEARS.
IT'S YOUR DREAM, ASSHOLE. BUT AT LEAST I CAN DO THIS.

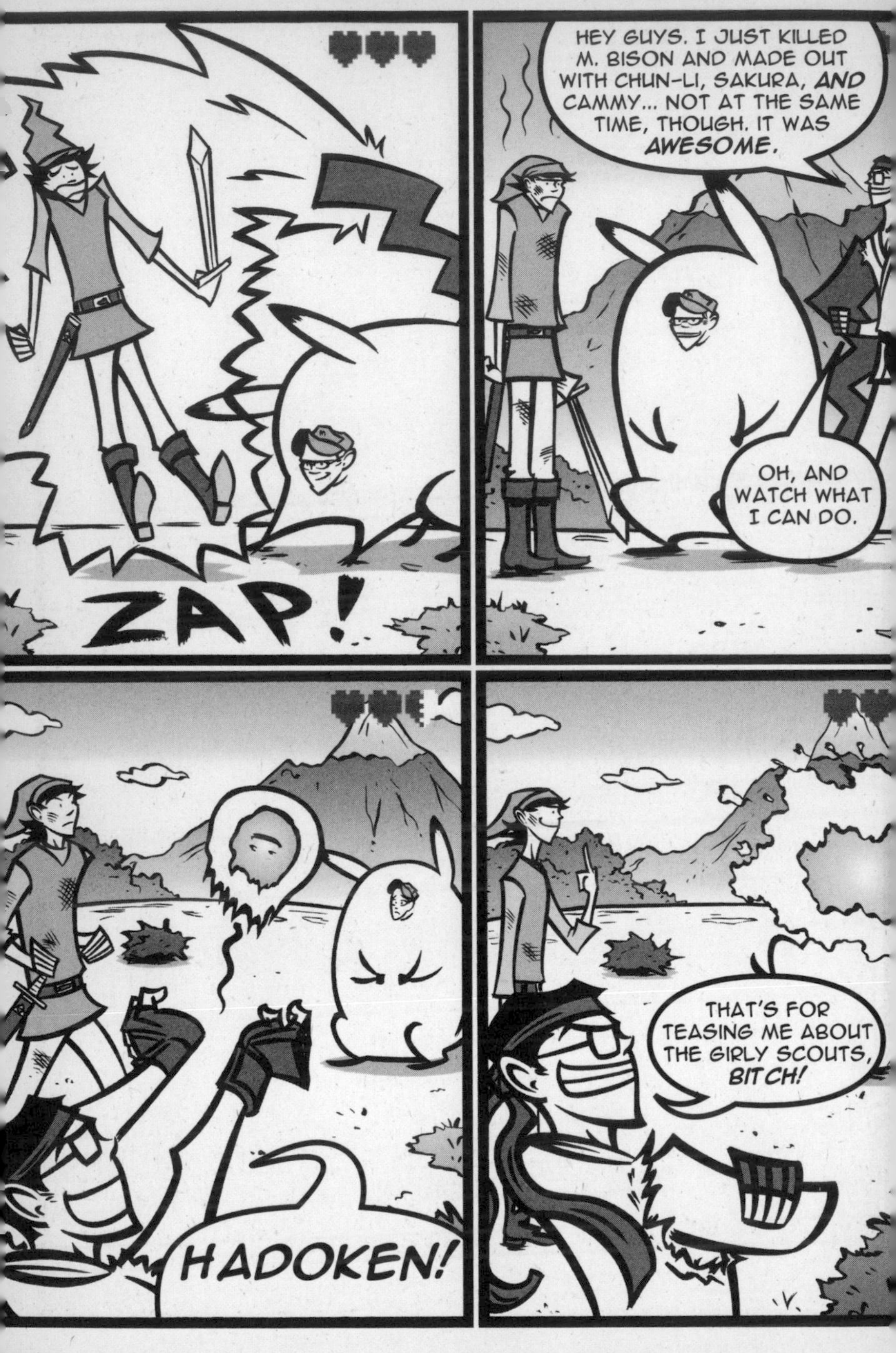
ZAP!
HEY GUYS. I JUST KILLED M. BISON AND MADE OUT WITH CHUN-LI, SAKURA, AND CAMMY... NOT AT THE SAME TIME, THOUGH. IT WAS AWESOME.
OH, AND WATCH WHAT I CAN DO.
HADOKEN!
THAT'S FOR TEASING ME ABOUT THE GIRLY SCOUTS, BITCH!

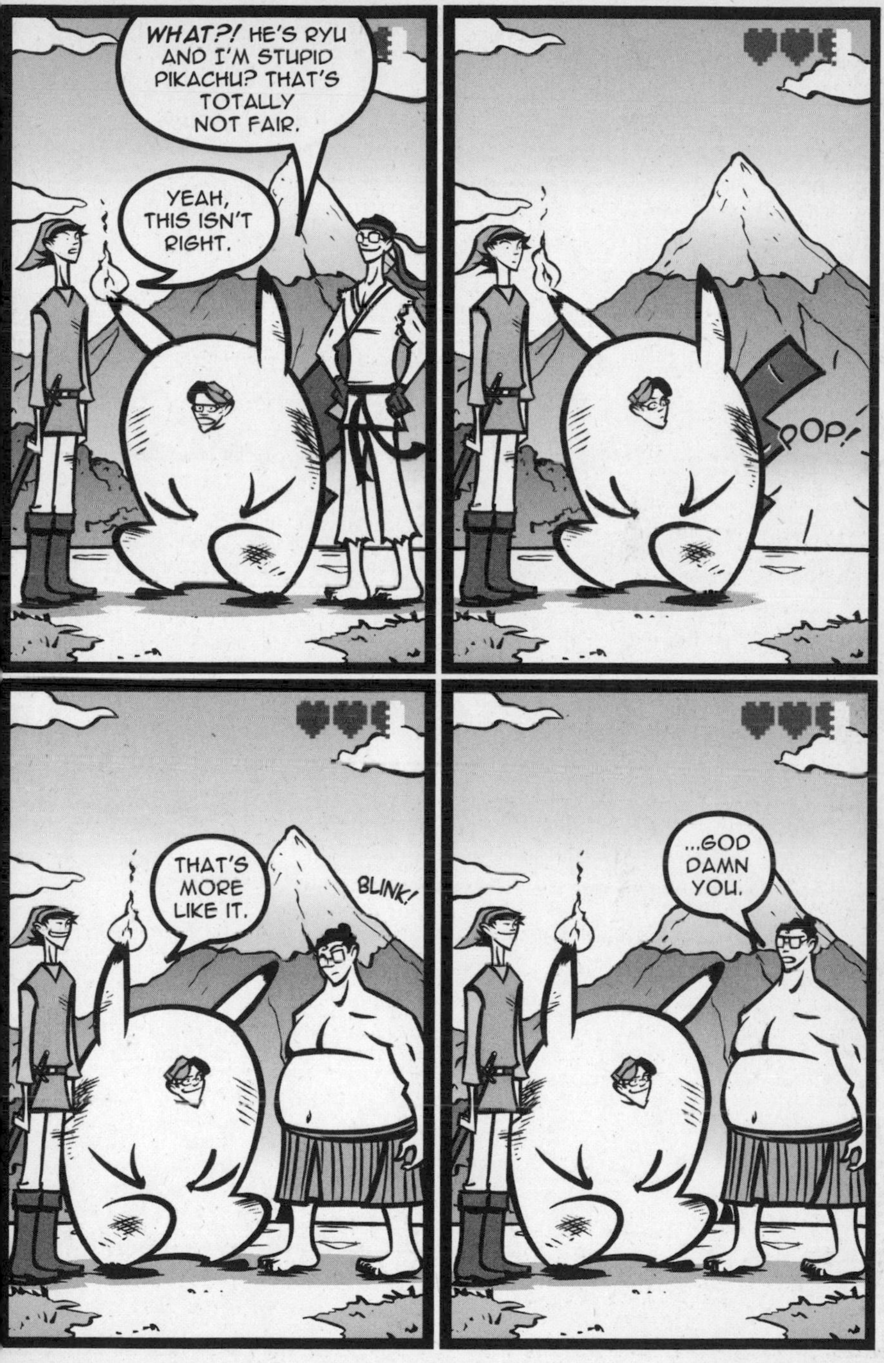

WHAT?! HE'S RYU AND I'M STUPID PIKACHU? THAT'S TOTALLY NOT FAIR.
YEAH, THIS ISN'T RIGHT.
POP!
THAT'S MORE LIKE IT.
BLINK!
...GOD DAMN YOU.

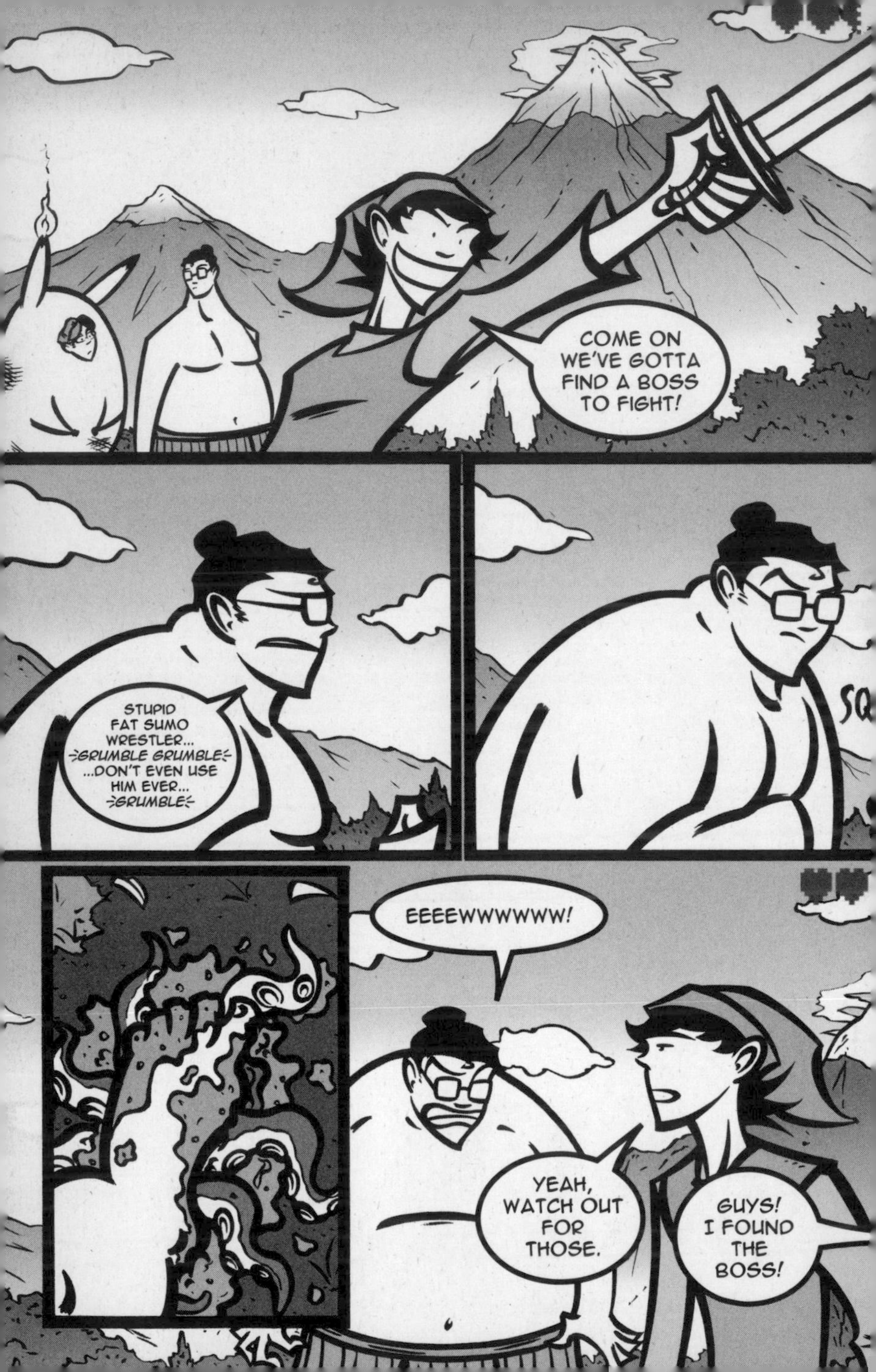
COME ON WE'VE GOTTA FIND A BOSS TO FIGHT!
STUPID FAT SUMO WRESTLER... -GRUMBLE GRUMBLE- ...DON'T EVEN USE HIM EVER... -GRUMBLE-
EEEEWWWWWW!
YEAH, WATCH OUT FOR THOSE.
GUYS! I FOUND THE BOSS!

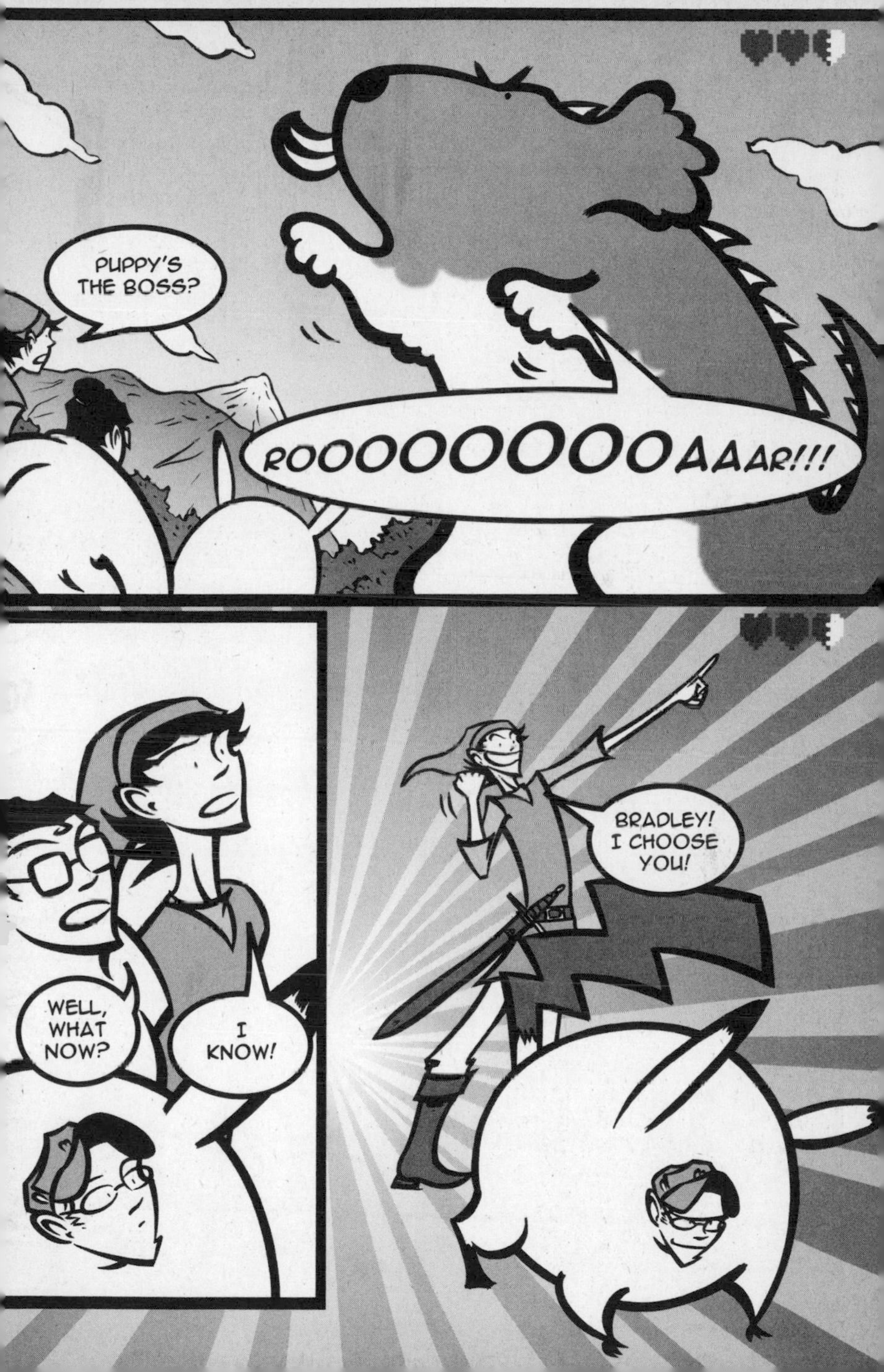
PUPPY'S THE BOSS?
ROOOOOOOOOAAAR!!!
WELL, WHAT NOW?
I KNOW!
BRADLEY! I CHOOSE YOU!

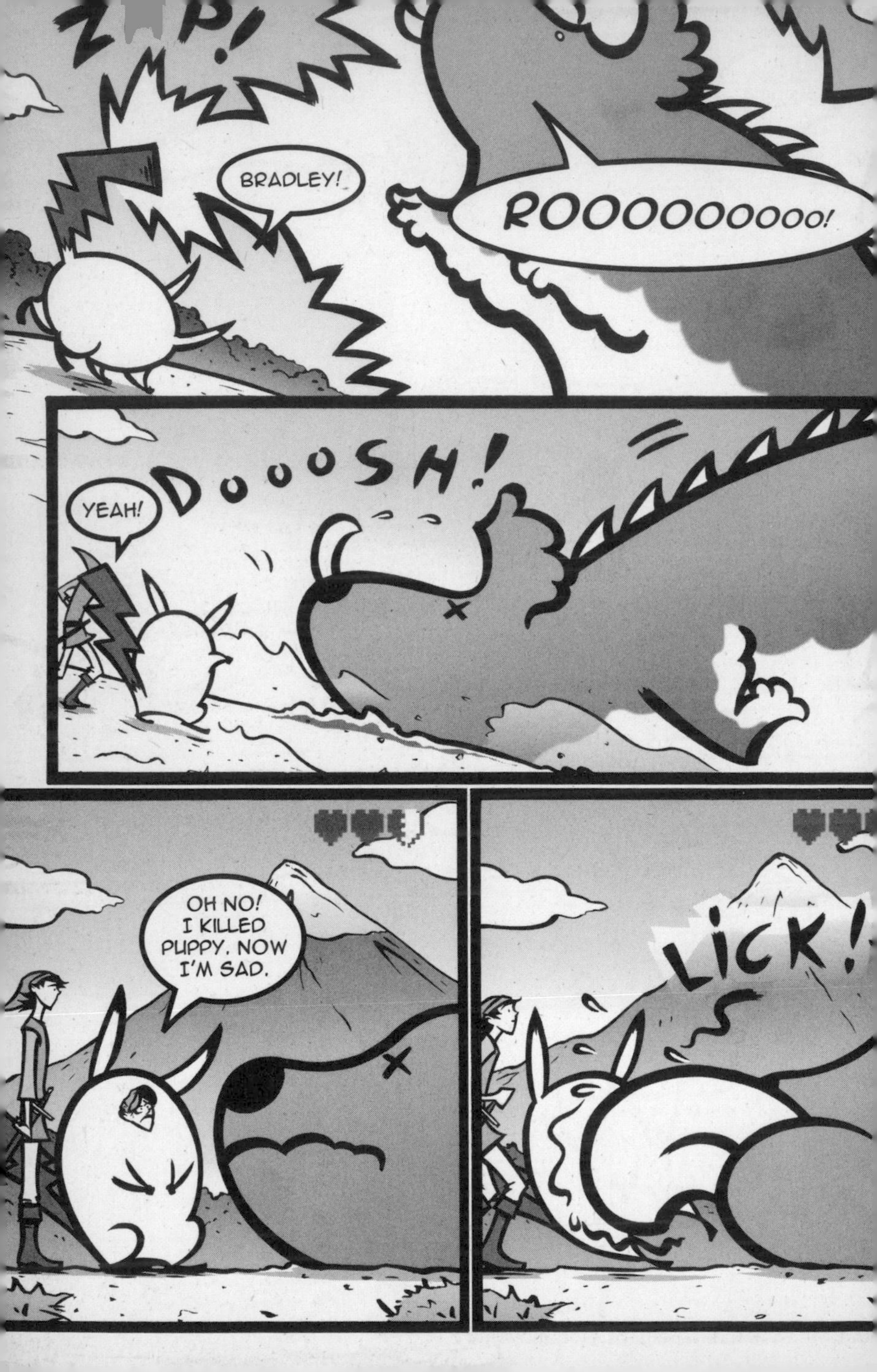
ZAP!
BRADLEY!
ROOOOOOOOOO!
YEAH!
DOOOSH!
OH NO! I KILLED PUPPY. NOW I'M SAD.
LICK!

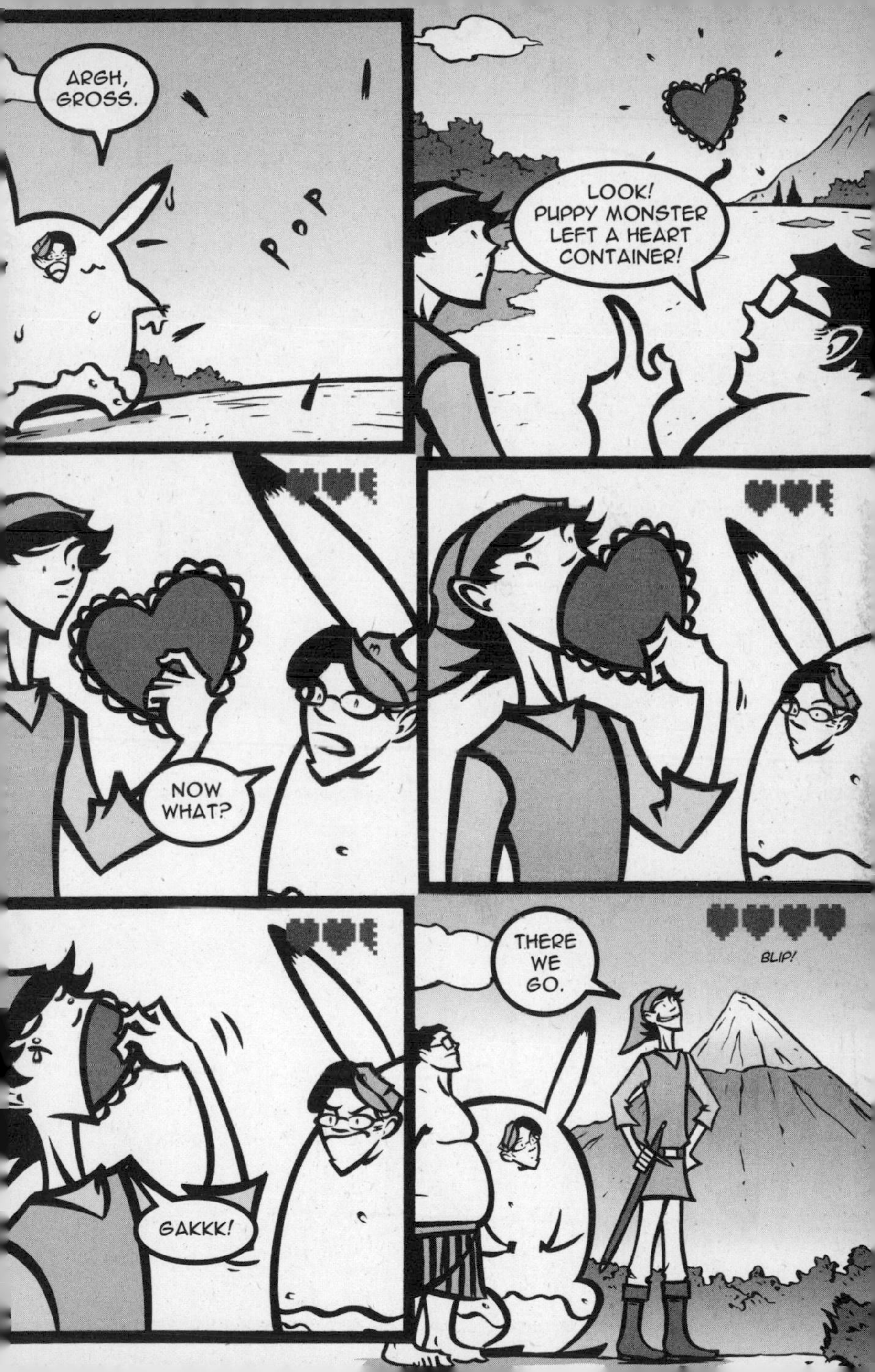
ARGH, GROSS.
POP
LOOK! PUPPY MONSTER LEFT A HEART CONTAINER!
NOW WHAT?
GAKKK!
THERE WE GO.
BLIP!

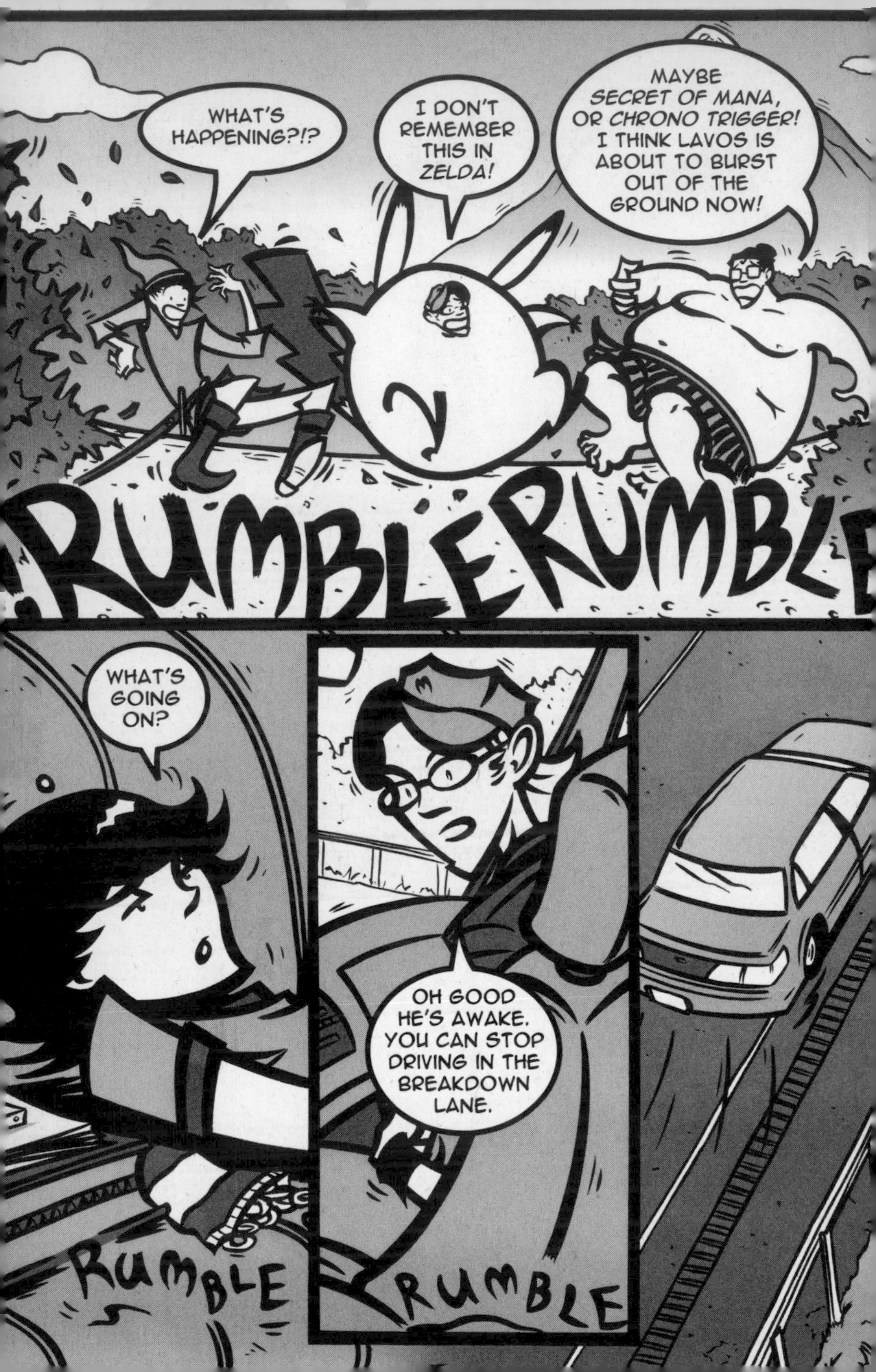
WHAT'S HAPPENING?!?
I DON'T REMEMBER THIS IN ZELDA!
MAYBE SECRET OF MANA, OR CHRONO TRIGGER! I THINK LAVOS IS ABOUT TO BURST OUT OF THE GROUND NOW!
RUMBLERUMBLE
WHAT'S GOING ON?
OH GOOD HE'S AWAKE. YOU CAN STOP DRIVING IN THE BREAKDOWN LANE.
RUMBLE
RUMBLE

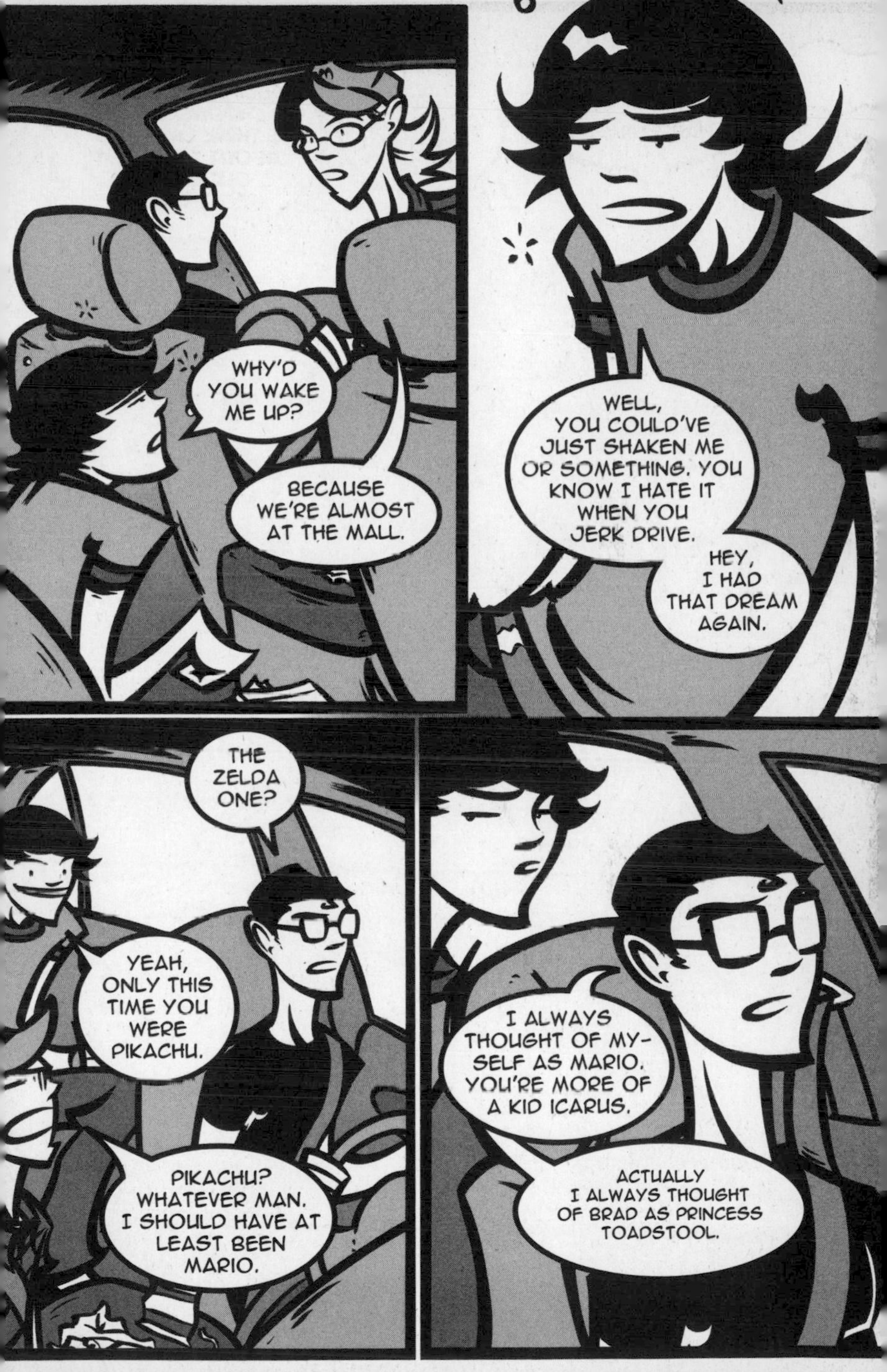
WHY'D YOU WAKE ME UP?
BECAUSE WE'RE ALMOST AT THE MALL.
WELL, YOU COULD'VE JUST SHAKEN ME OR SOMETHING. YOU KNOW I HATE IT WHEN YOU JERK DRIVE.
HEY, I HAD THAT DREAM AGAIN.
THE ZELDA ONE?
YEAH, ONLY THIS TIME YOU WERE PIKACHU.
PIKACHU? WHATEVER MAN. I SHOULD HAVE AT LEAST BEEN MARIO.
I ALWAYS THOUGHT OF MY-SELF AS MARIO. YOU'RE MORE OF A KID ICARUS.
ACTUALLY I ALWAYS THOUGHT OF BRAD AS PRINCESS TOADSTOOL.

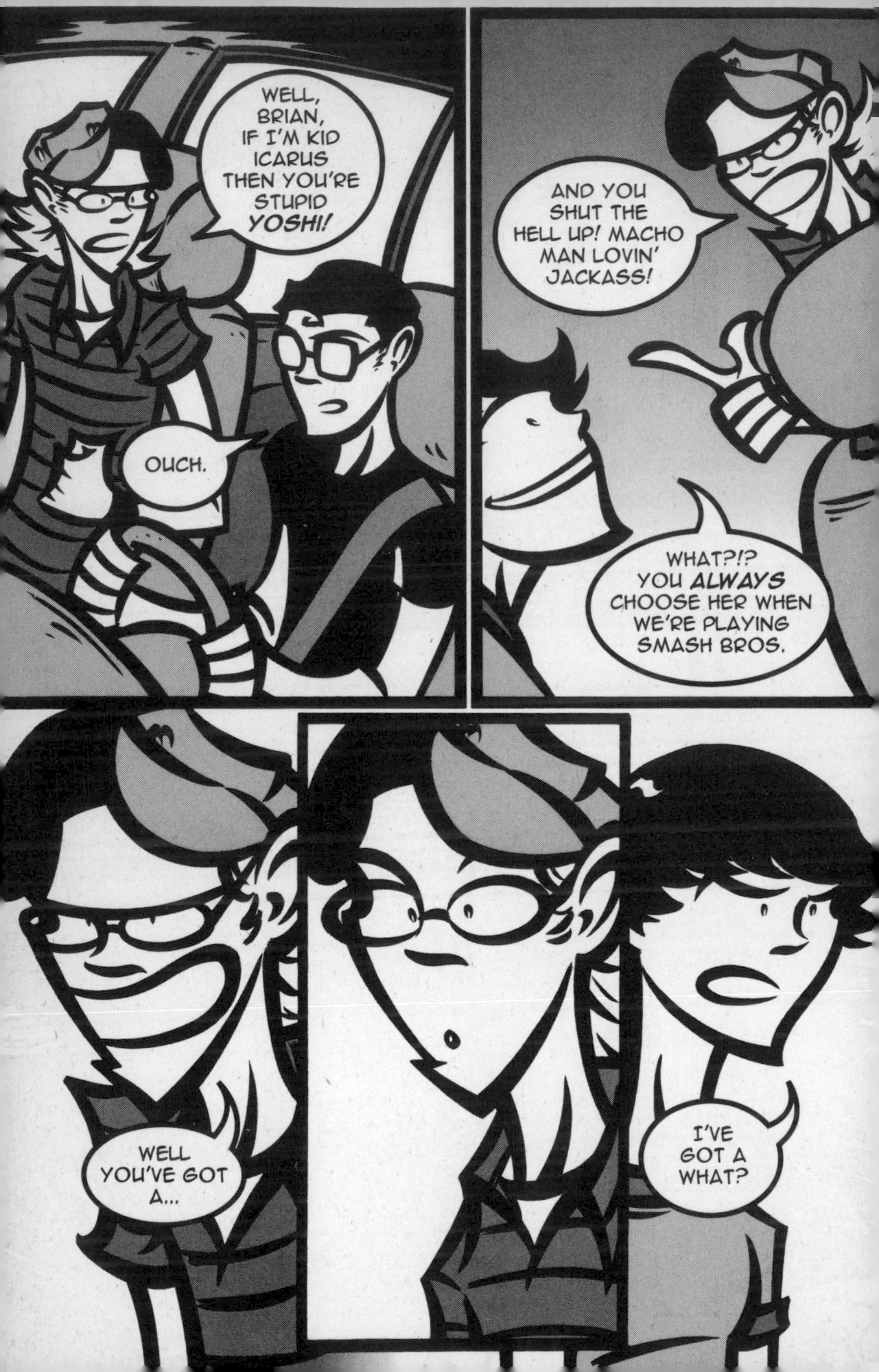
WELL, BRIAN, IF I'M KID ICARUS THEN YOU'RE STUPID *YOSHI!*
OUCH.
AND YOU SHUT THE HELL UP! MACHO MAN LOVIN' JACKASS!
WHAT?!? YOU **ALWAYS** CHOOSE HER WHEN WE'RE PLAYING SMASH BROS.
WELL YOU'VE GOT A...
I'VE GOT A WHAT?

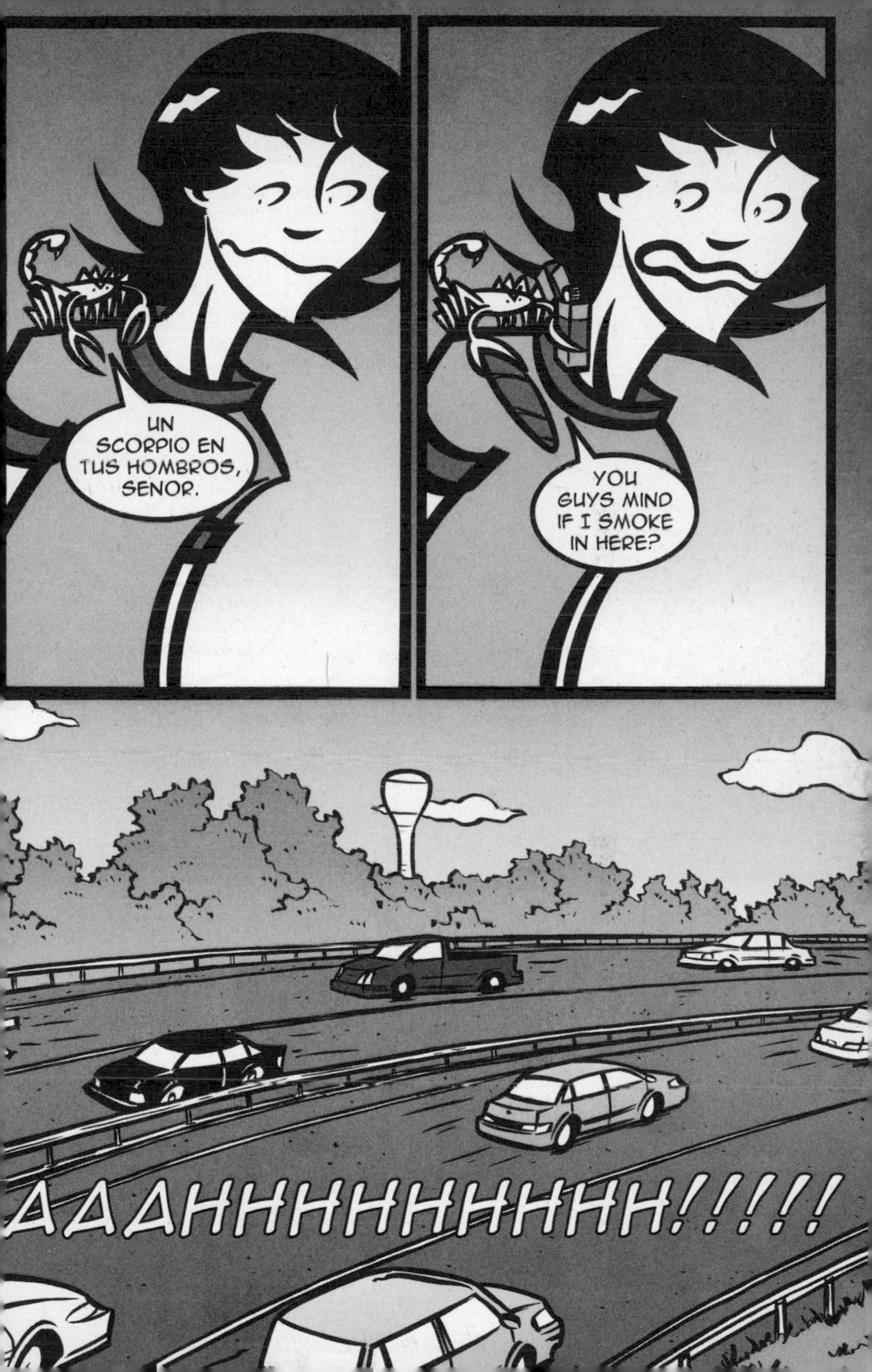
UN SCORPIO EN TUS HOMBROS, SENOR.
YOU GUYS MIND IF I SMOKE IN HERE?
AAAHHHHHHHHH!!!!!

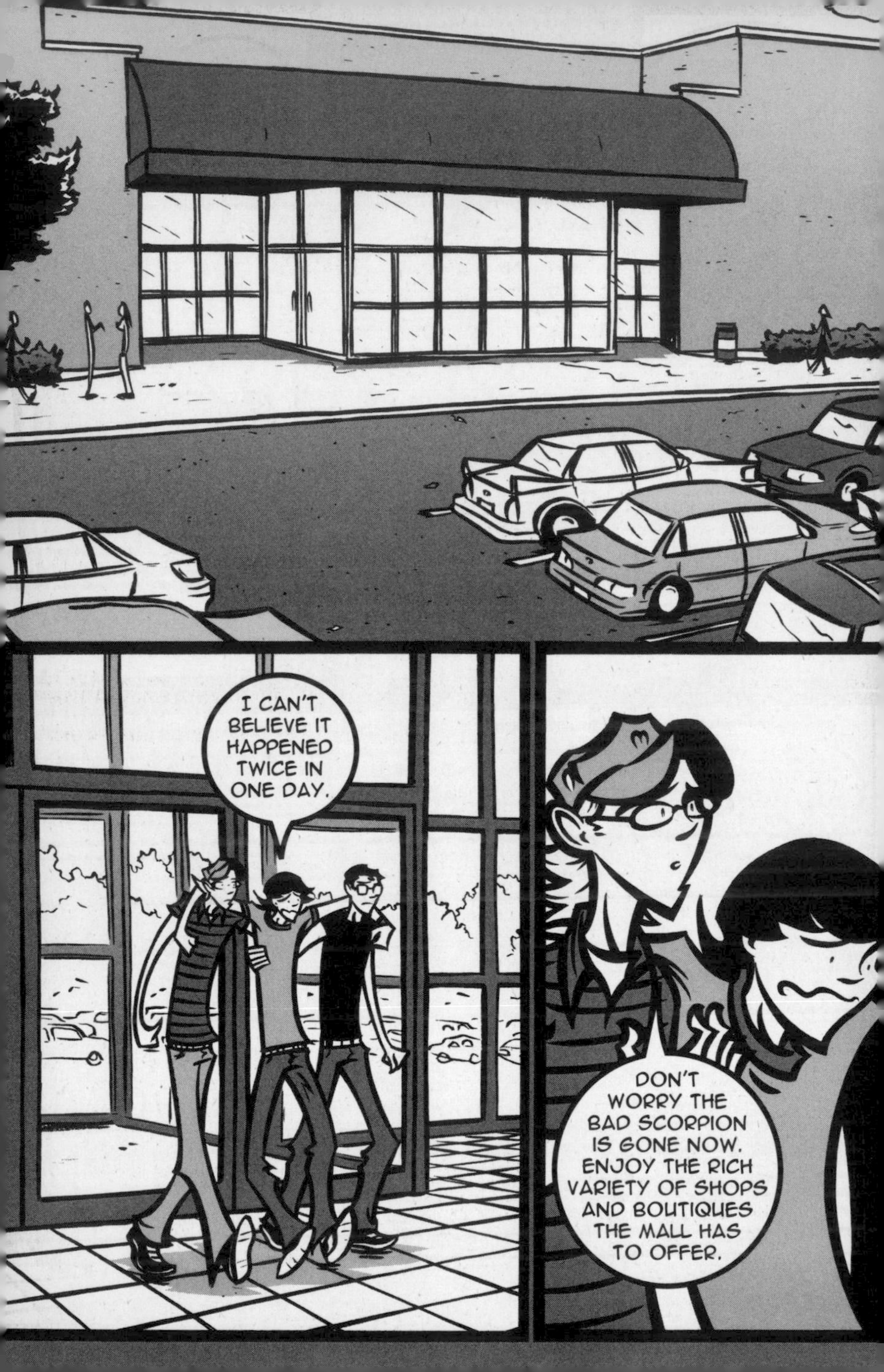
I CAN'T BELIEVE IT HAPPENED TWICE IN ONE DAY.
DON'T WORRY THE BAD SCORPION IS GONE NOW. ENJOY THE RICH VARIETY OF SHOPS AND BOUTIQUES THE MALL HAS TO OFFER.

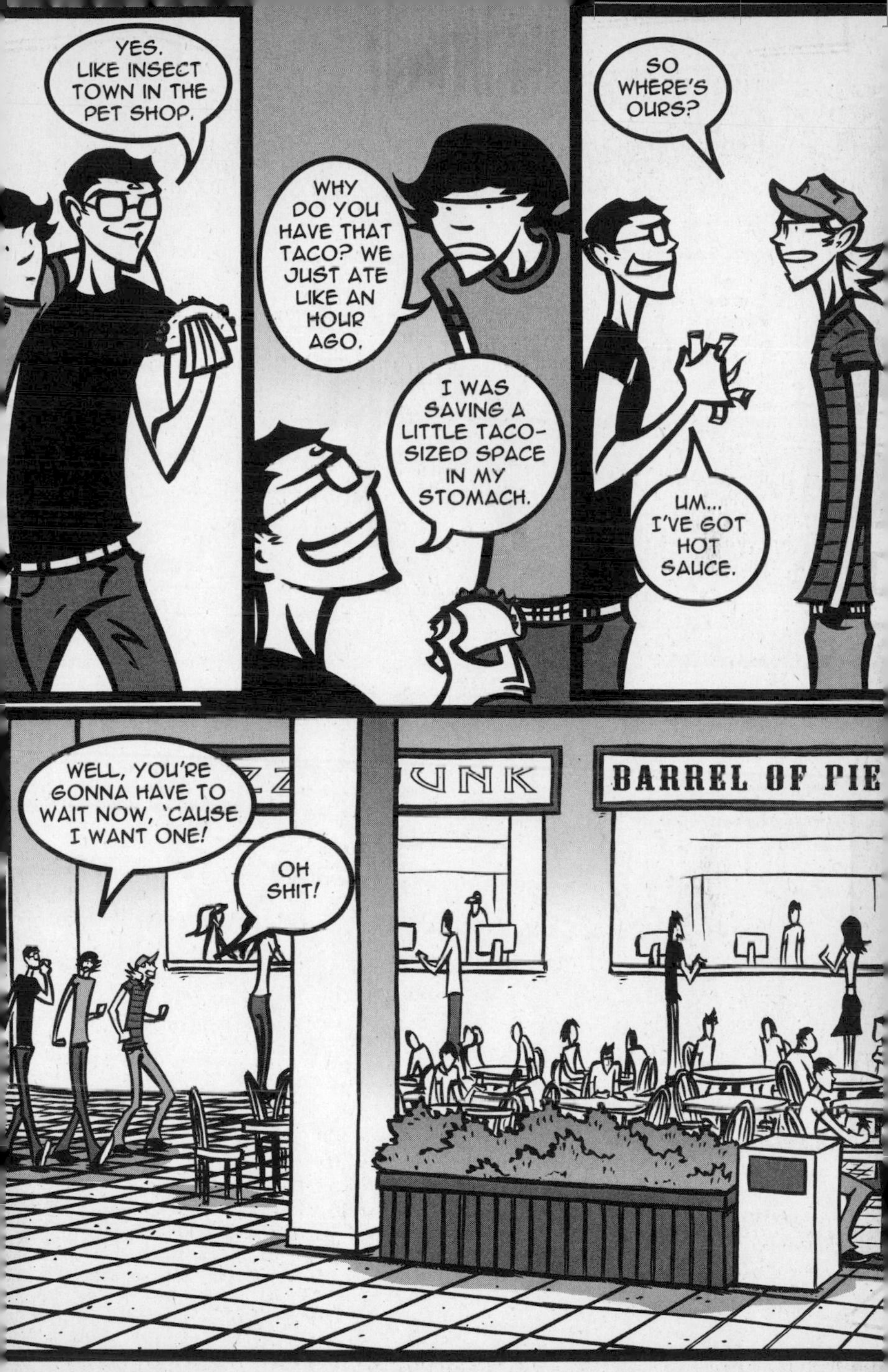
YES. LIKE INSECT TOWN IN THE PET SHOP.
WHY DO YOU HAVE THAT TACO? WE JUST ATE LIKE AN HOUR AGO.
I WAS SAVING A LITTLE TACO-SIZED SPACE IN MY STOMACH.
SO WHERE'S OURS?
UM... I'VE GOT HOT SAUCE.
UNK
BARREL OF PIE
WELL, YOU'RE GONNA HAVE TO WAIT NOW, 'CAUSE I WANT ONE!
OH SHIT!

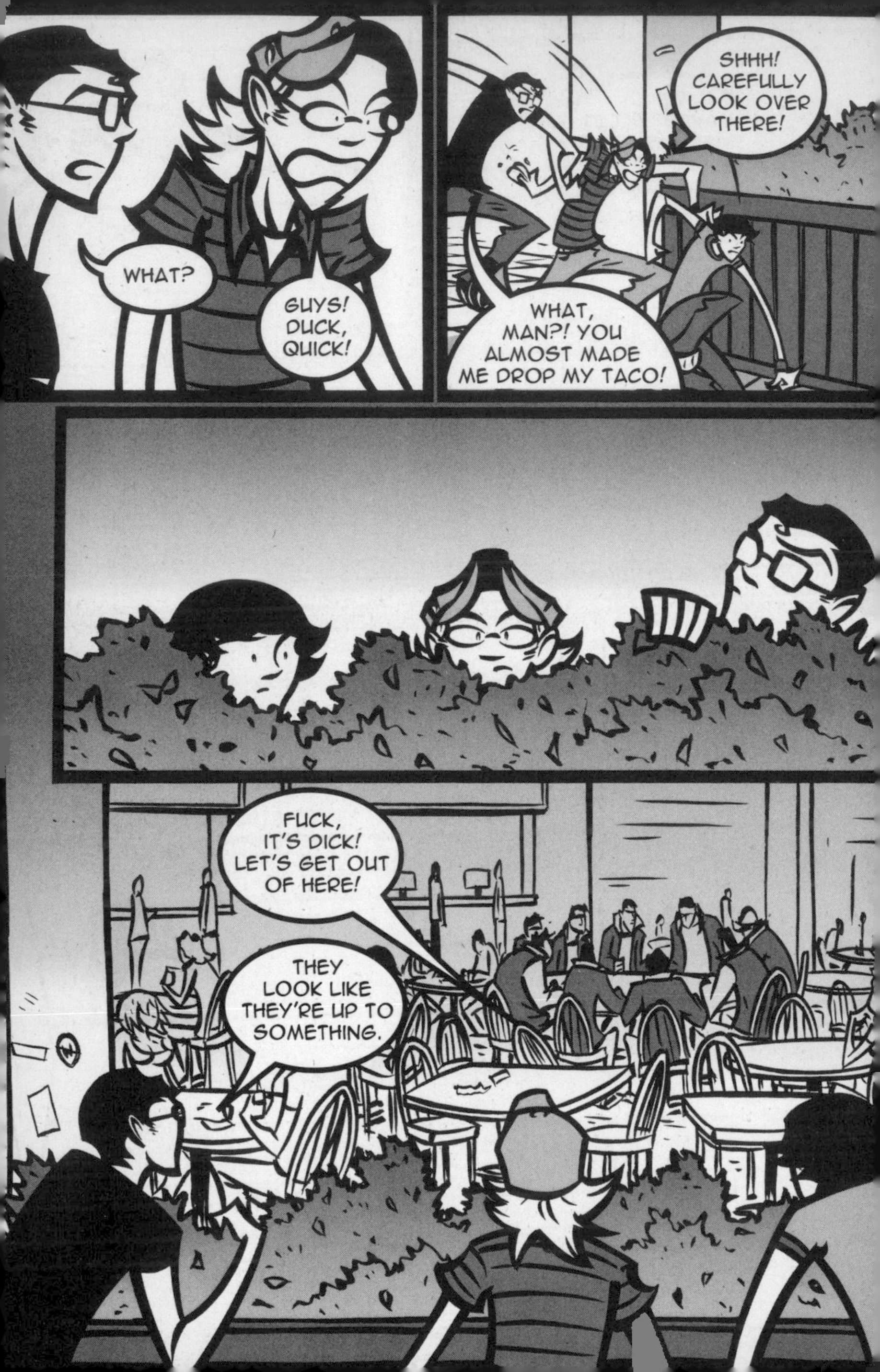
WHAT?
GUYS! DUCK, QUICK!
SHHH! CAREFULLY LOOK OVER THERE!
WHAT, MAN?! YOU ALMOST MADE ME DROP MY TACO!
FUCK, IT'S DICK! LET'S GET OUT OF HERE!
THEY LOOK LIKE THEY'RE UP TO SOMETHING.

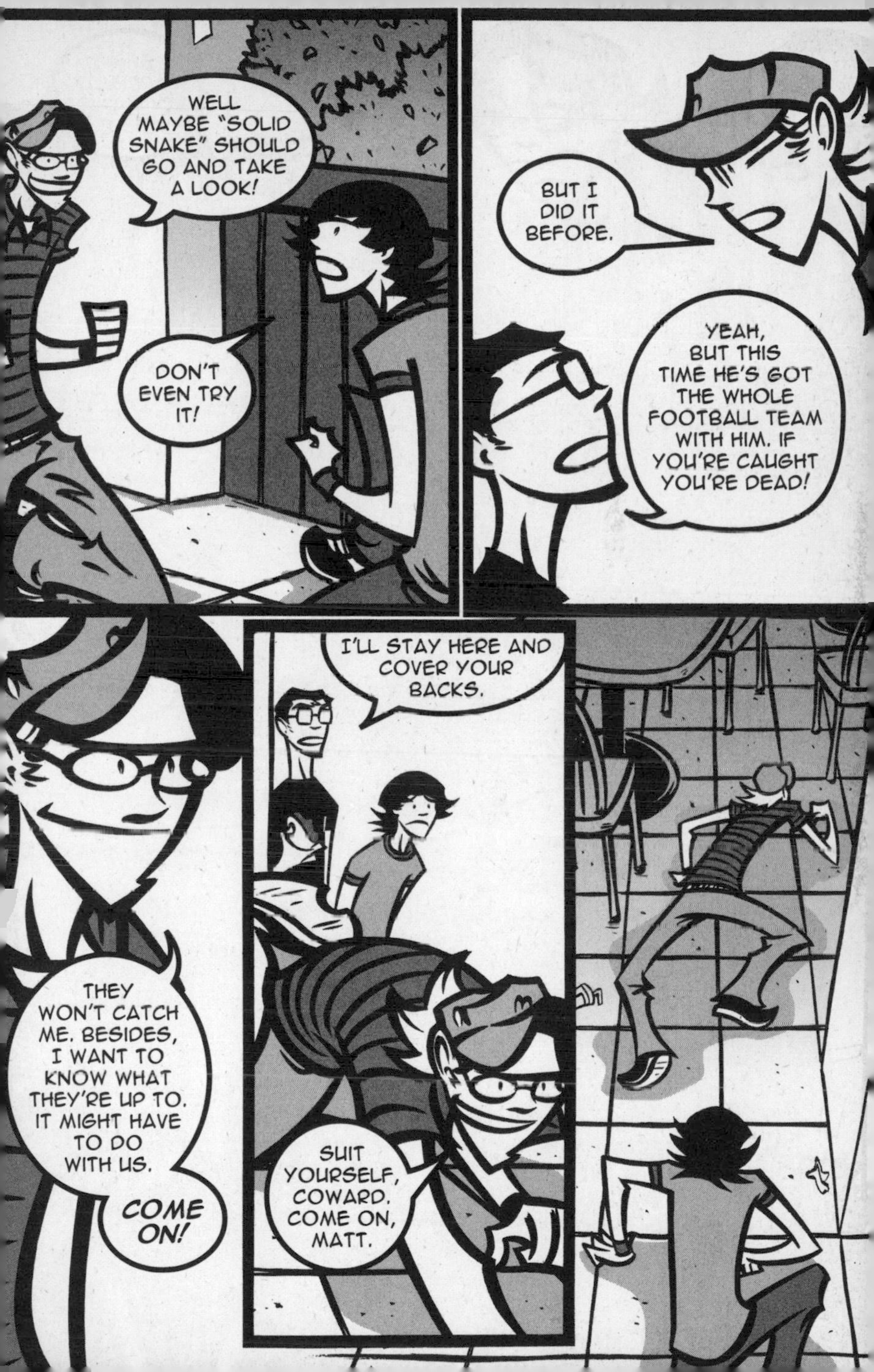

WELL MAYBE "SOLID SNAKE" SHOULD GO AND TAKE A LOOK!
DON'T EVEN TRY IT!
BUT I DID IT BEFORE.
YEAH, BUT THIS TIME HE'S GOT THE WHOLE FOOTBALL TEAM WITH HIM. IF YOU'RE CAUGHT YOU'RE DEAD!
THEY WON'T CATCH ME. BESIDES, I WANT TO KNOW WHAT THEY'RE UP TO. IT MIGHT HAVE TO DO WITH US.
COME ON!
I'LL STAY HERE AND COVER YOUR BACKS.
SUIT YOURSELF, COWARD. COME ON, MATT.

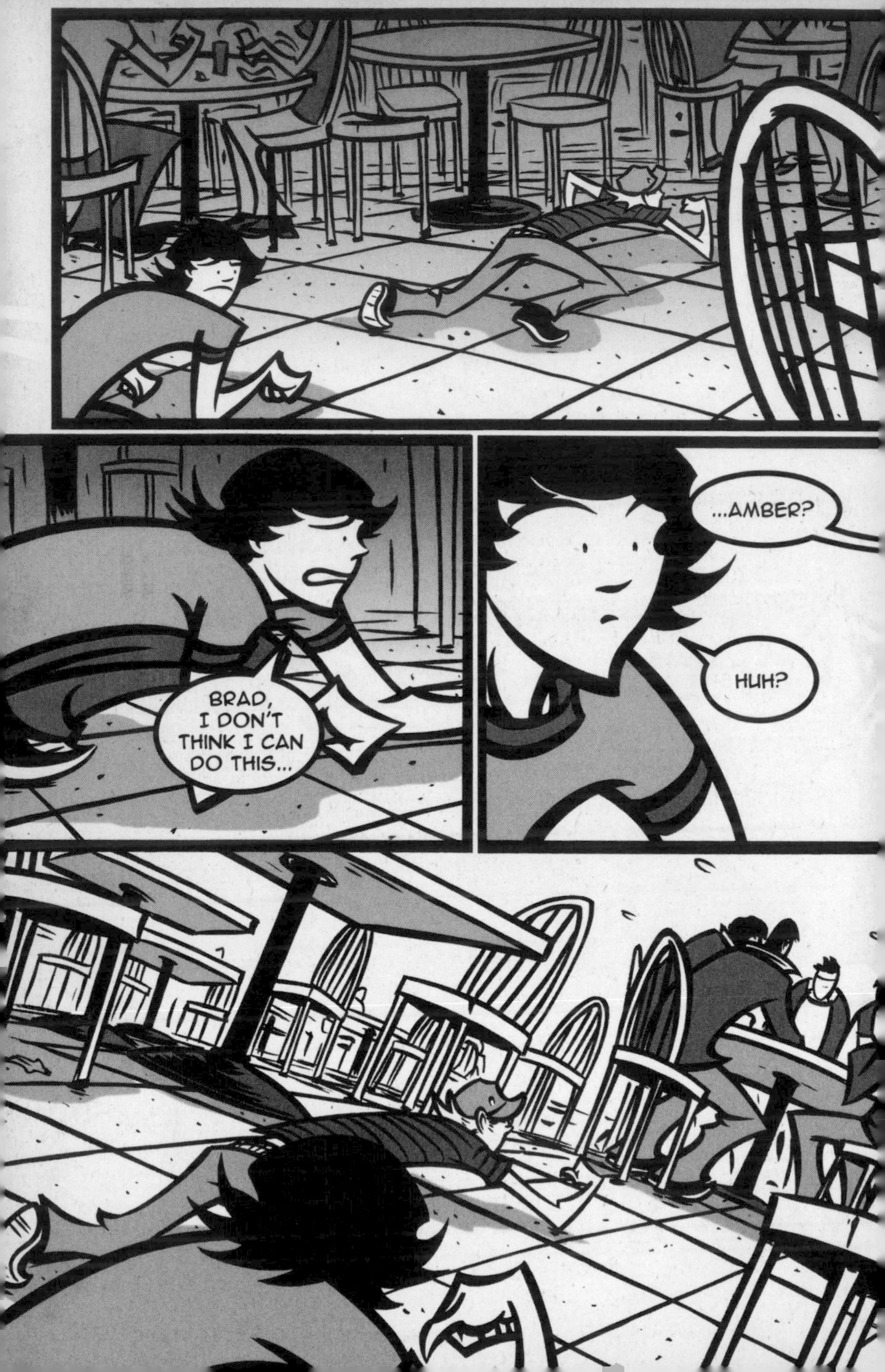
BRAD, I DON'T THINK I CAN DO THIS...
...AMBER?
HUH?

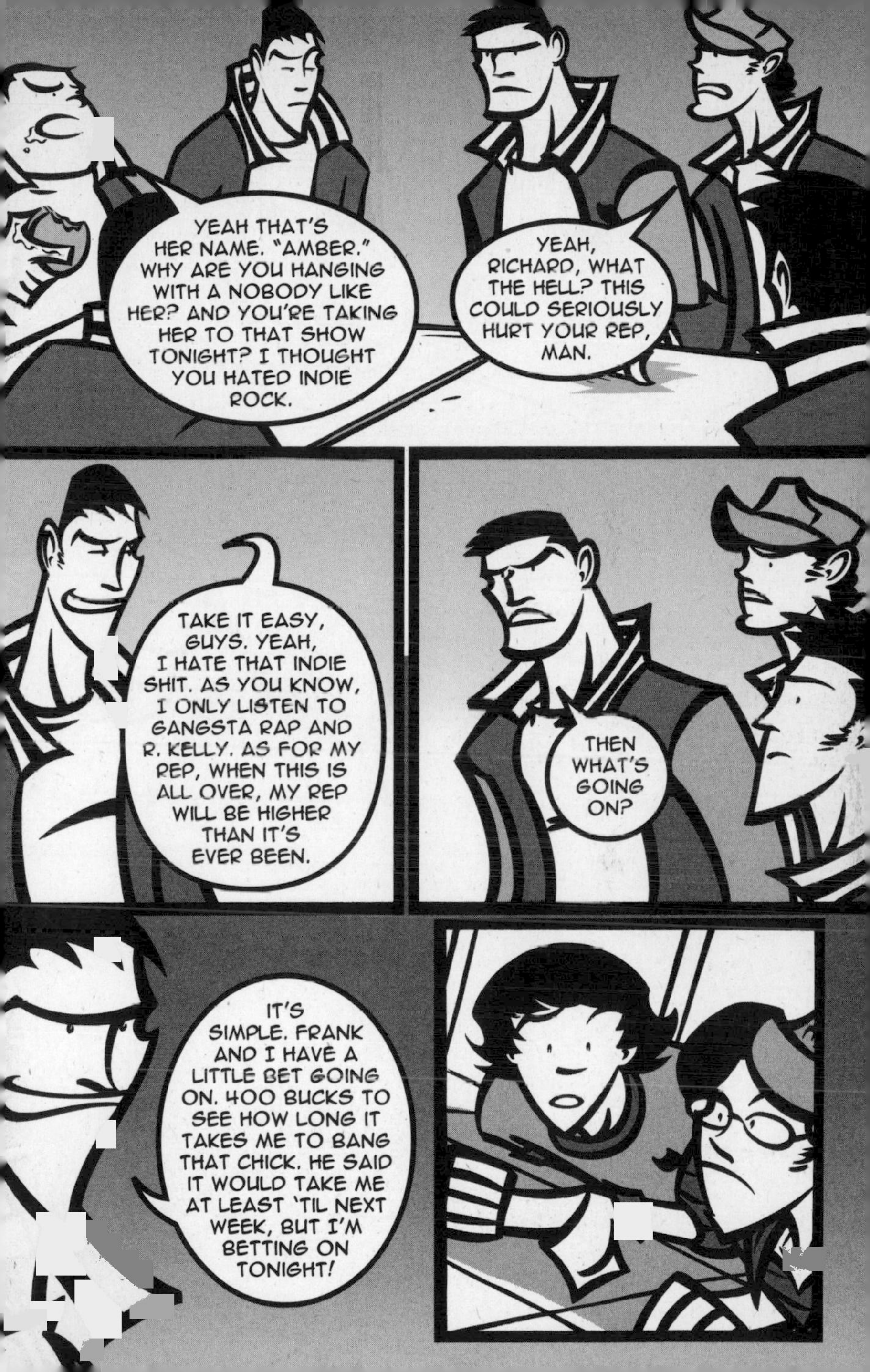
YEAH THAT'S HER NAME. "AMBER." WHY ARE YOU HANGING WITH A NOBODY LIKE HER? AND YOU'RE TAKING HER TO THAT SHOW TONIGHT? I THOUGHT YOU HATED INDIE ROCK.
YEAH, RICHARD, WHAT THE HELL? THIS COULD SERIOUSLY HURT YOUR REP, MAN.
TAKE IT EASY, GUYS. YEAH, I HATE THAT INDIE SHIT. AS YOU KNOW, I ONLY LISTEN TO GANGSTA RAP AND R. KELLY. AS FOR MY REP, WHEN THIS IS ALL OVER, MY REP WILL BE HIGHER THAN IT'S EVER BEEN.
THEN WHAT'S GOING ON?
IT'S SIMPLE. FRANK AND I HAVE A LITTLE BET GOING ON. 400 BUCKS TO SEE HOW LONG IT TAKES ME TO BANG THAT CHICK. HE SAID IT WOULD TAKE ME AT LEAST 'TIL NEXT WEEK, BUT I'M BETTING ON TONIGHT!

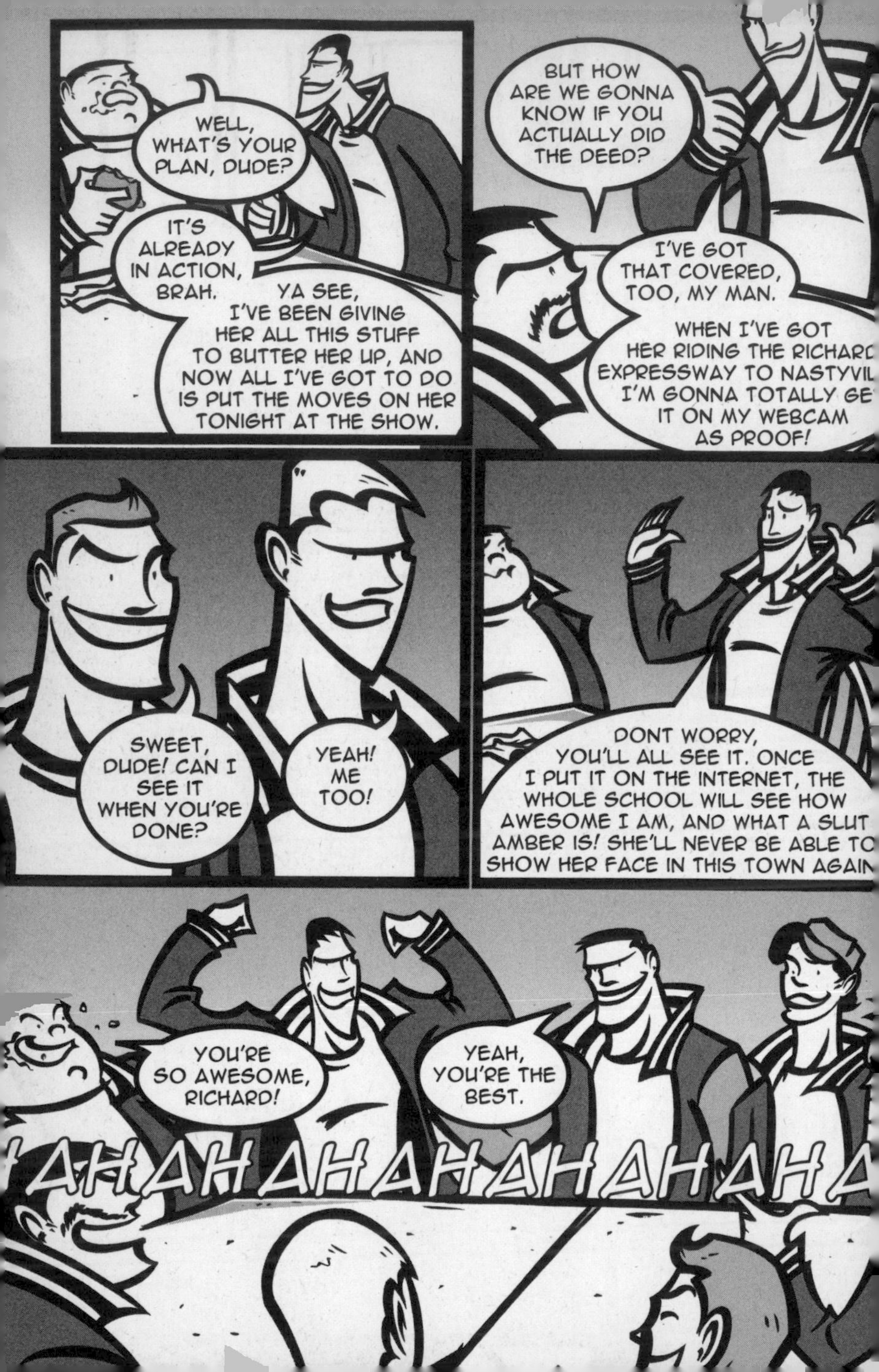
WELL, WHAT'S YOUR PLAN, DUDE?
IT'S ALREADY IN ACTION, BRAH.
YA SEE, I'VE BEEN GIVING HER ALL THIS STUFF TO BUTTER HER UP, AND NOW ALL I'VE GOT TO DO IS PUT THE MOVES ON HER TONIGHT AT THE SHOW.
BUT HOW ARE WE GONNA KNOW IF YOU ACTUALLY DID THE DEED?
I'VE GOT THAT COVERED, TOO, MY MAN.
WHEN I'VE GOT HER RIDING THE RICHARD EXPRESSWAY TO NASTYVIL I'M GONNA TOTALLY GE IT ON MY WEBCAM AS PROOF!
SWEET, DUDE! CAN I SEE IT WHEN YOU'RE DONE?
YEAH! ME TOO!
DONT WORRY, YOU'LL ALL SEE IT. ONCE I PUT IT ON THE INTERNET, THE WHOLE SCHOOL WILL SEE HOW AWESOME I AM, AND WHAT A SLUT AMBER IS! SHE'LL NEVER BE ABLE TO SHOW HER FACE IN THIS TOWN AGAIN
YOU'RE SO AWESOME, RICHARD!
YEAH, YOU'RE THE BEST.
AHAHAHAHAHAHAHAHA

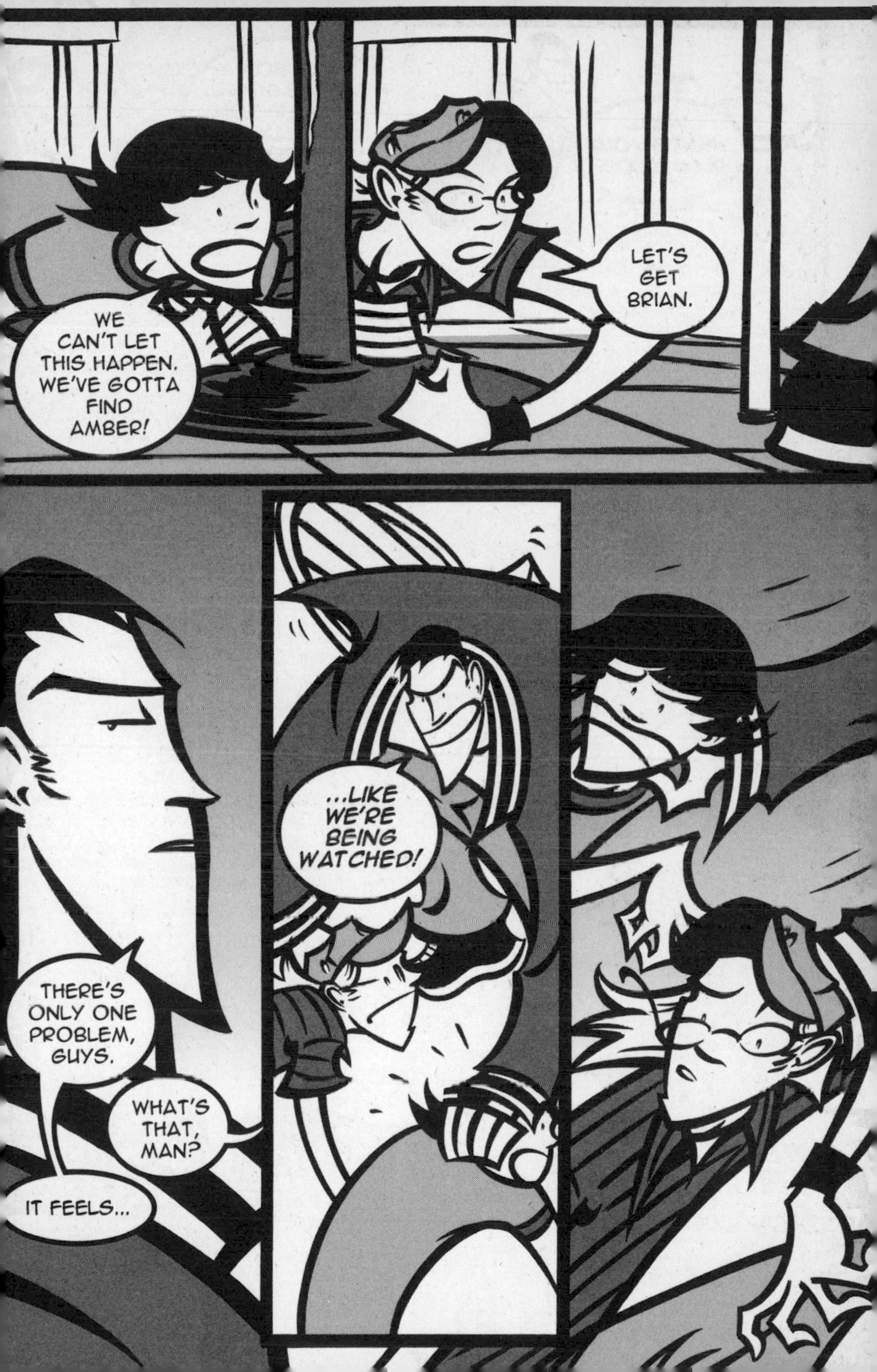
WE CAN'T LET THIS HAPPEN. WE'VE GOTTA FIND AMBER!
LET'S GET BRIAN.
THERE'S ONLY ONE PROBLEM, GUYS.
WHAT'S THAT, MAN?
IT FEELS...
...LIKE WE'RE BEING WATCHED!

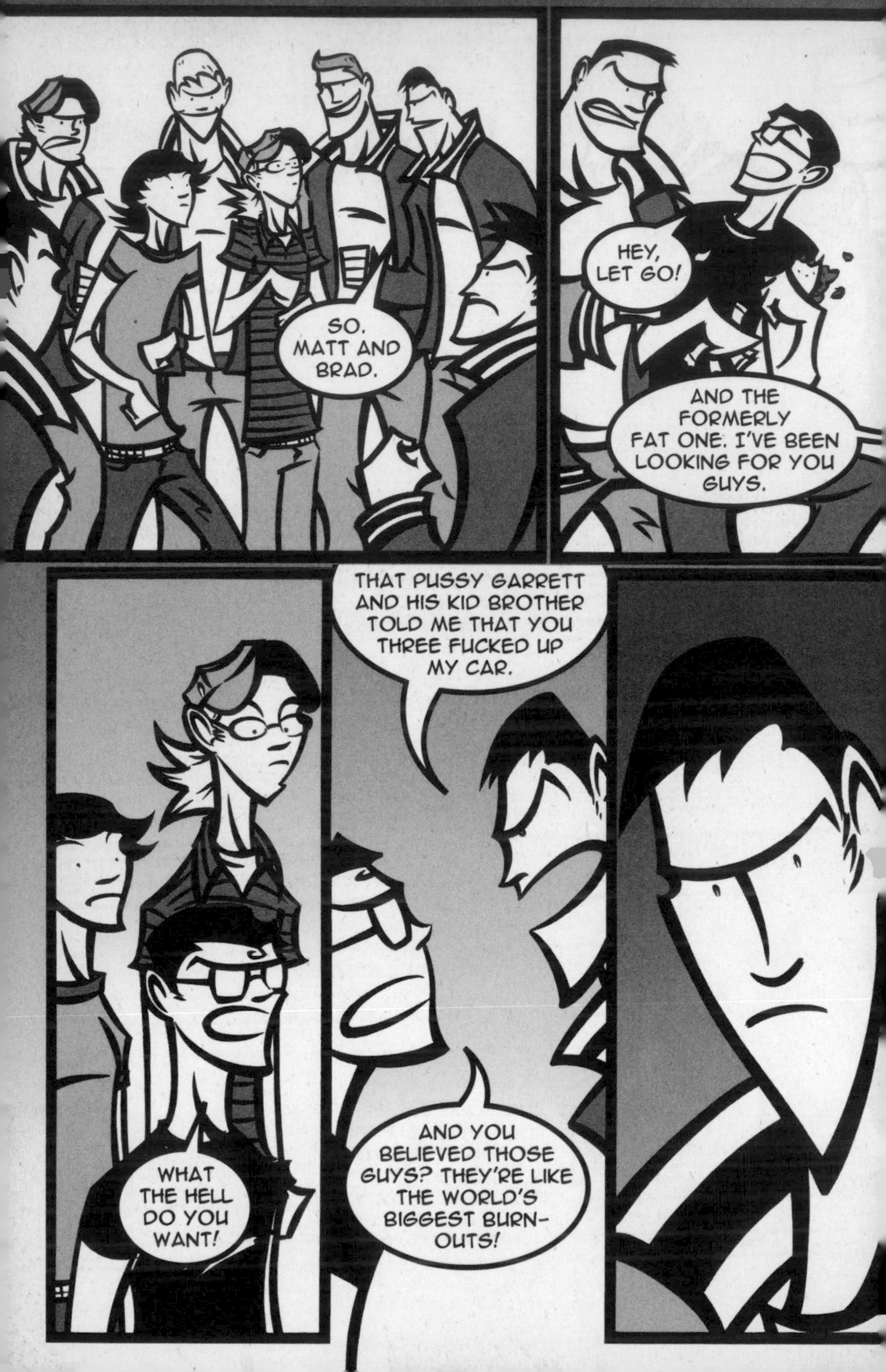
SO. MATT AND BRAD.
HEY, LET GO!
AND THE FORMERLY FAT ONE. I'VE BEEN LOOKING FOR YOU GUYS.
THAT PUSSY GARRETT AND HIS KID BROTHER TOLD ME THAT YOU THREE FUCKED UP MY CAR.
WHAT THE HELL DO YOU WANT!
AND YOU BELIEVED THOSE GUYS? THEY'RE LIKE THE WORLD'S BIGGEST BURN-OUTS!

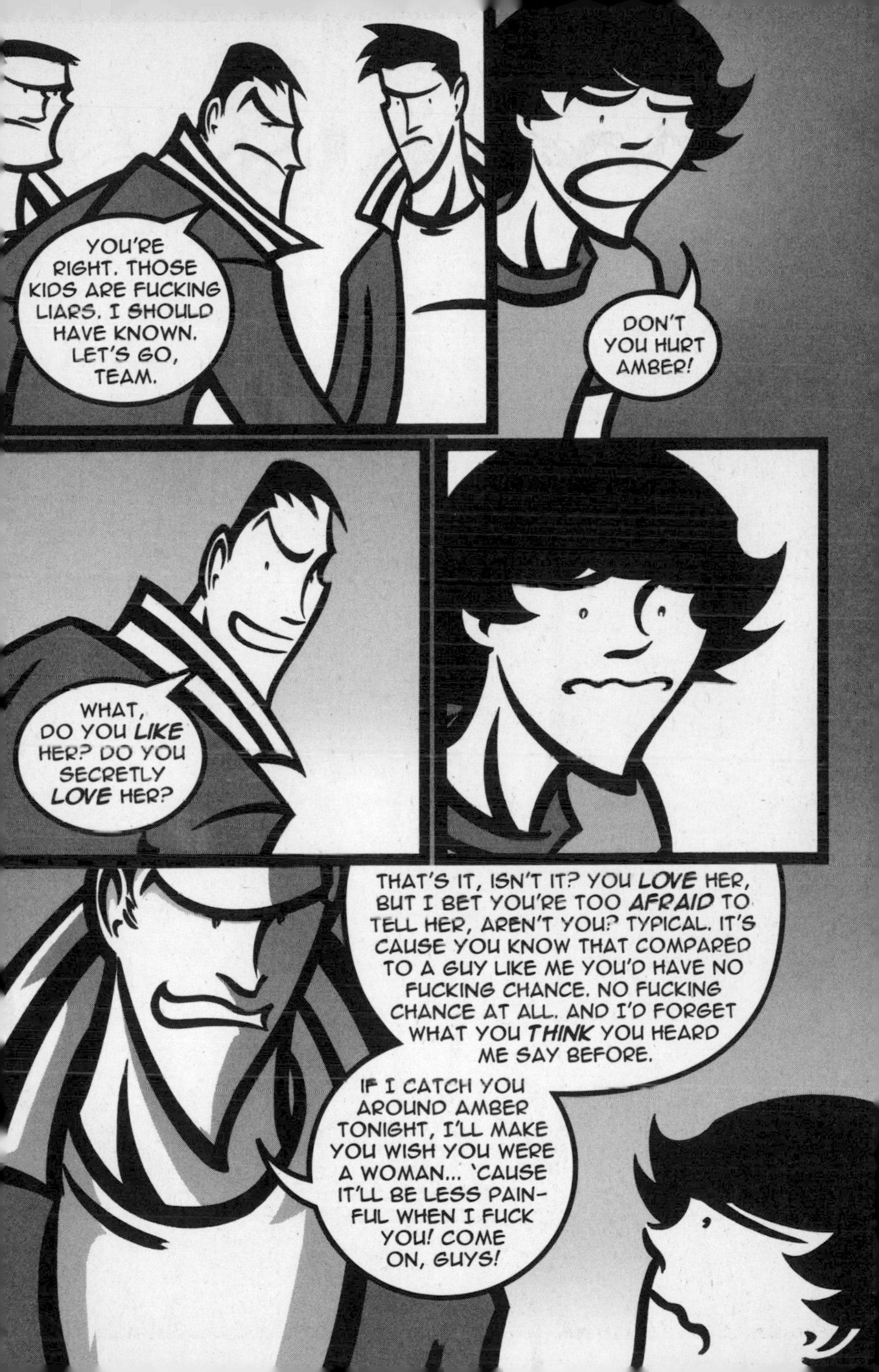

YOU'RE RIGHT. THOSE KIDS ARE FUCKING LIARS. I SHOULD HAVE KNOWN. LET'S GO, TEAM.
DON'T YOU HURT AMBER!
WHAT, DO YOU *LIKE* HER? DO YOU SECRETLY *LOVE* HER?
THAT'S IT, ISN'T IT? YOU *LOVE* HER, BUT I BET YOU'RE TOO *AFRAID* TO TELL HER, AREN'T YOU? TYPICAL. IT'S CAUSE YOU KNOW THAT COMPARED TO A GUY LIKE ME YOU'D HAVE NO FUCKING CHANCE. NO FUCKING CHANCE AT ALL. AND I'D FORGET WHAT YOU *THINK* YOU HEARD ME SAY BEFORE.
IF I CATCH YOU AROUND AMBER TONIGHT, I'LL MAKE YOU WISH YOU WERE A WOMAN... 'CAUSE IT'LL BE LESS PAIN-FUL WHEN I FUCK YOU! COME ON, GUYS!

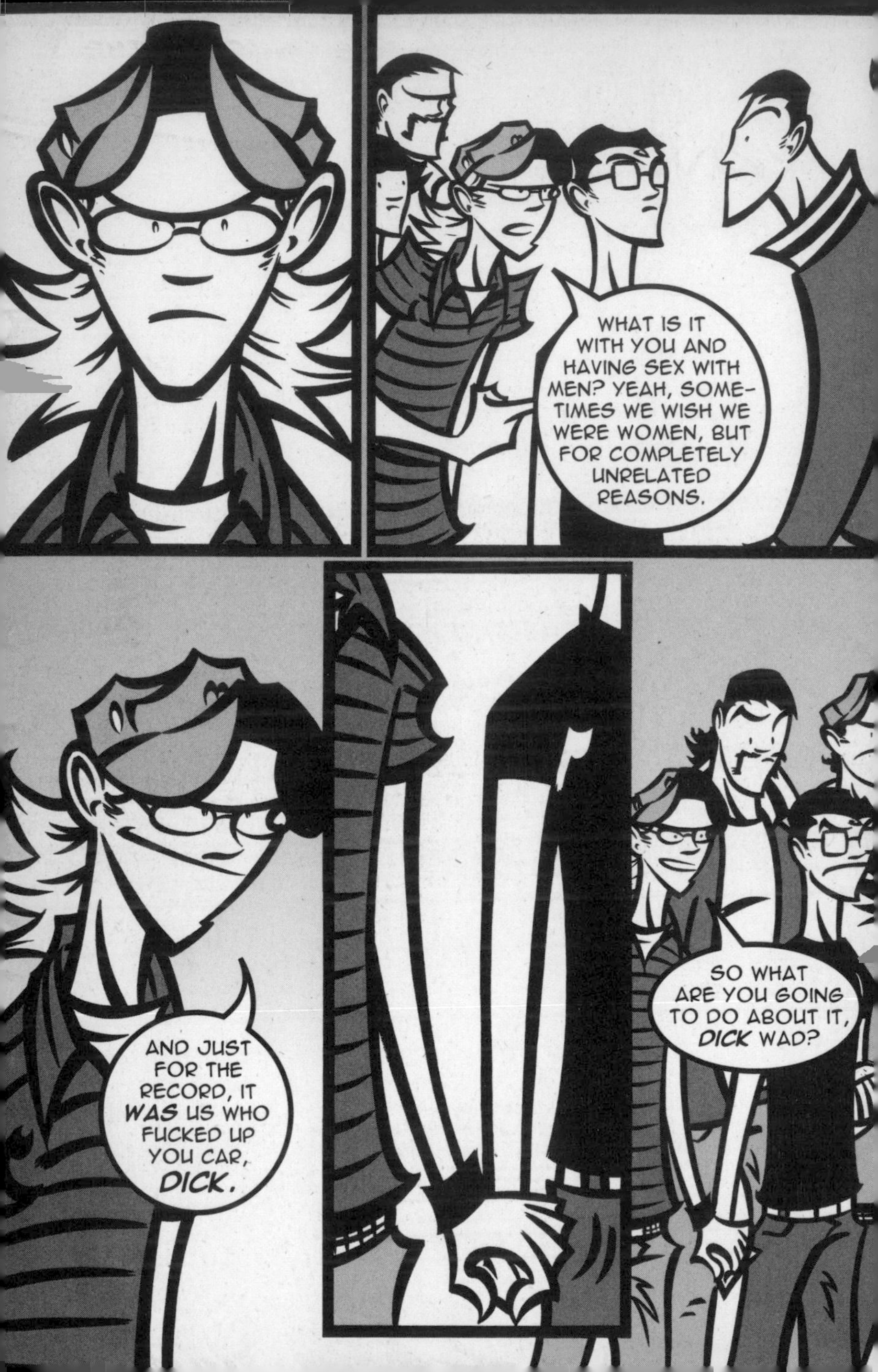
WHAT IS IT WITH YOU AND HAVING SEX WITH MEN? YEAH, SOME-TIMES WE WISH WE WERE WOMEN, BUT FOR COMPLETELY UNRELATED REASONS.
AND JUST FOR THE RECORD, IT WAS US WHO FUCKED UP YOU CAR, DICK.
SO WHAT ARE YOU GOING TO DO ABOUT IT, DICK WAD?

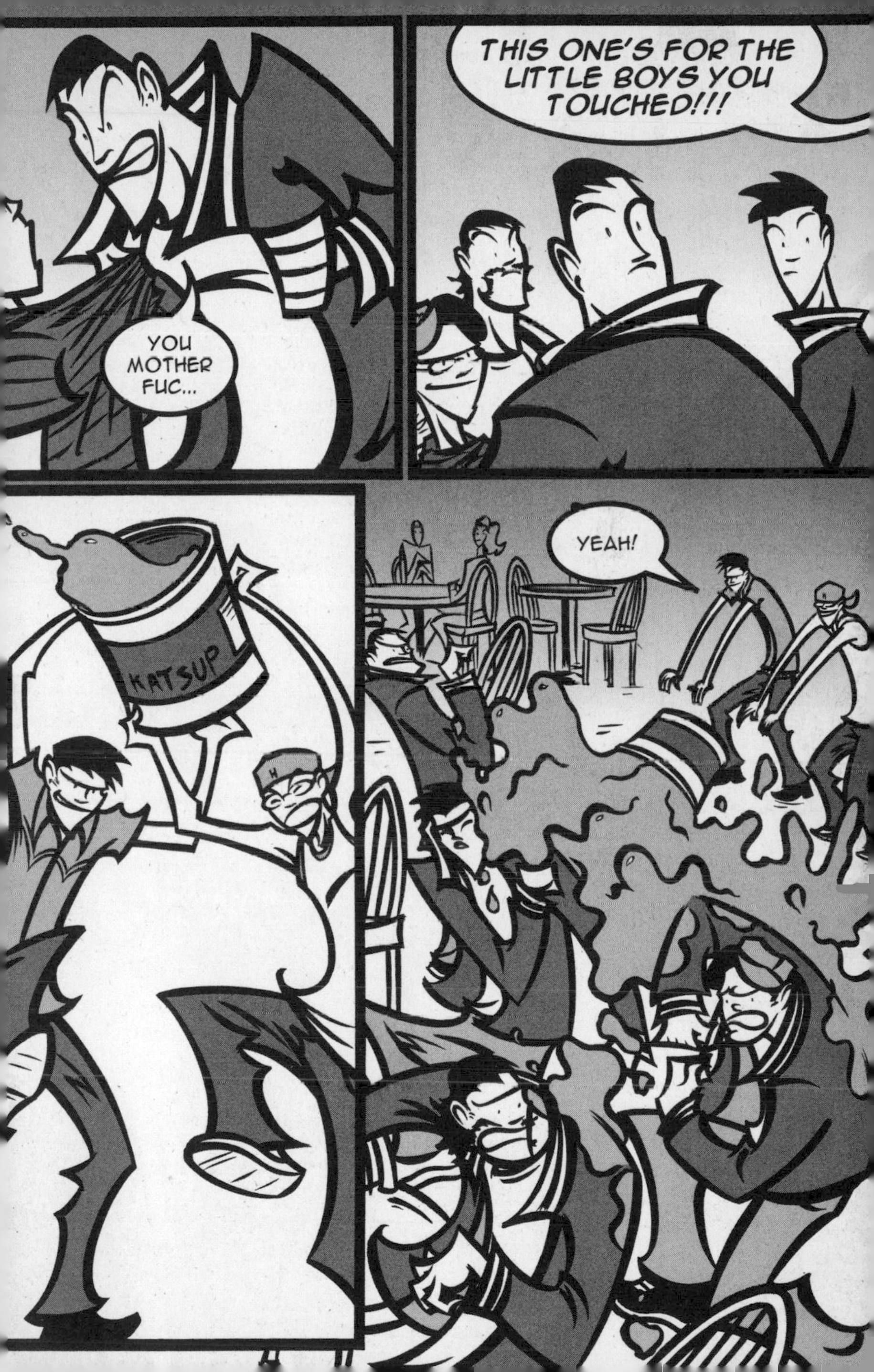
YOU MOTHER FUC...
THIS ONE'S FOR THE LITTLE BOYS YOU TOUCHED!!!
KATSUP
YEAH!

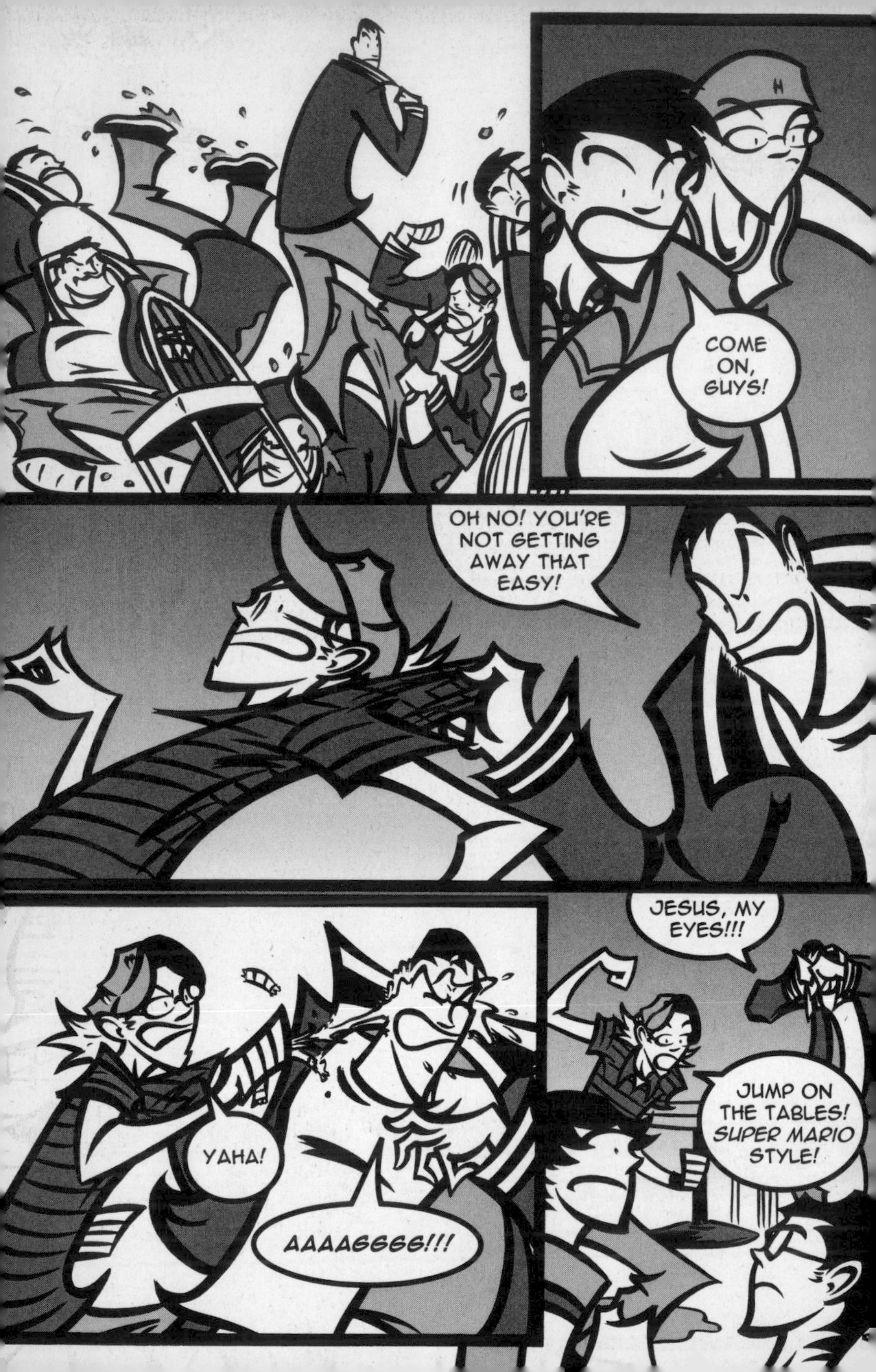
COME ON, GUYS!
OH NO! YOU'RE NOT GETTING AWAY THAT EASY!
YAHA!
AAAAGGGG!!!
JESUS, MY EYES!!!
JUMP ON THE TABLES! SUPER MARIO STYLE!

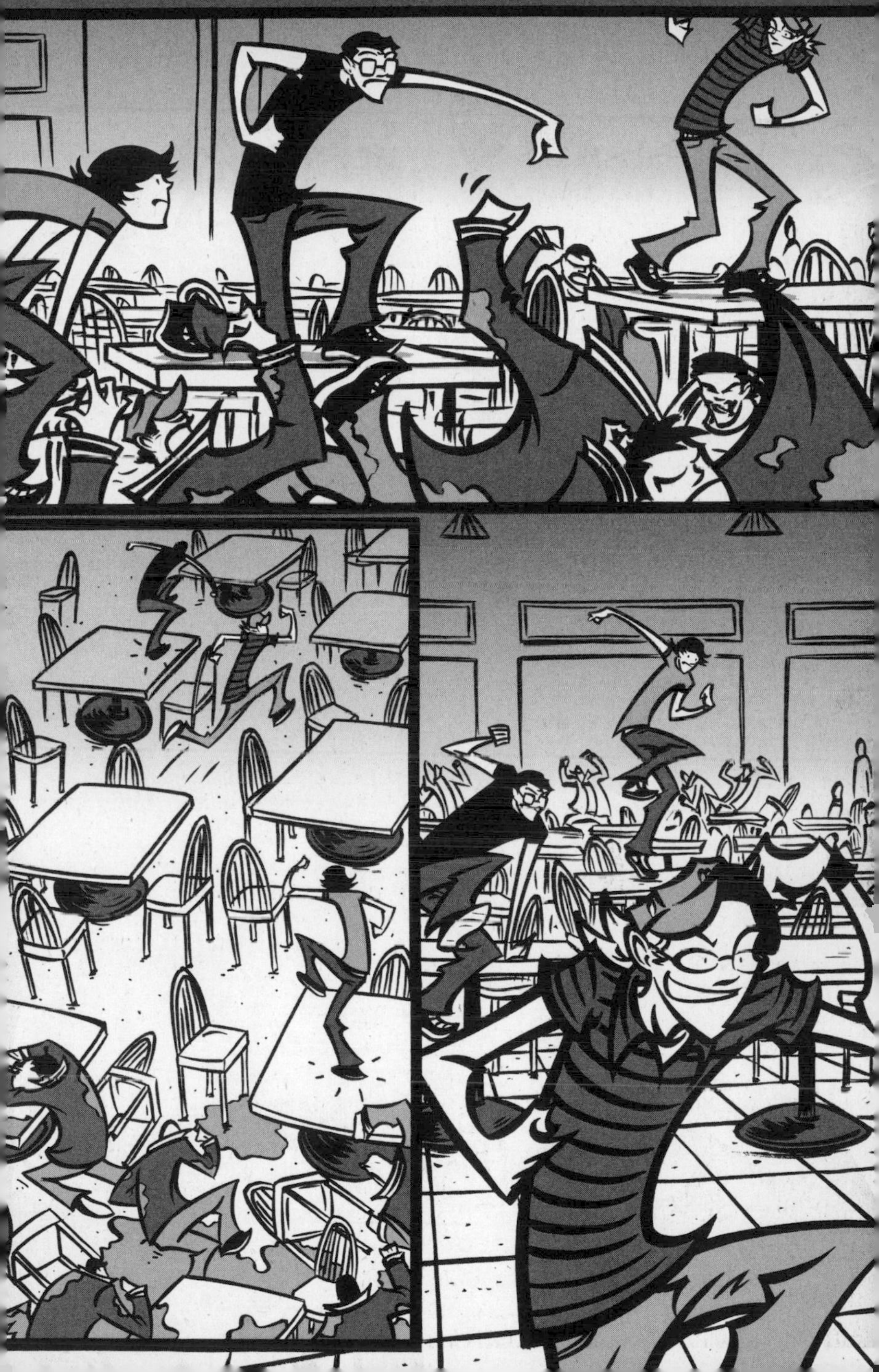

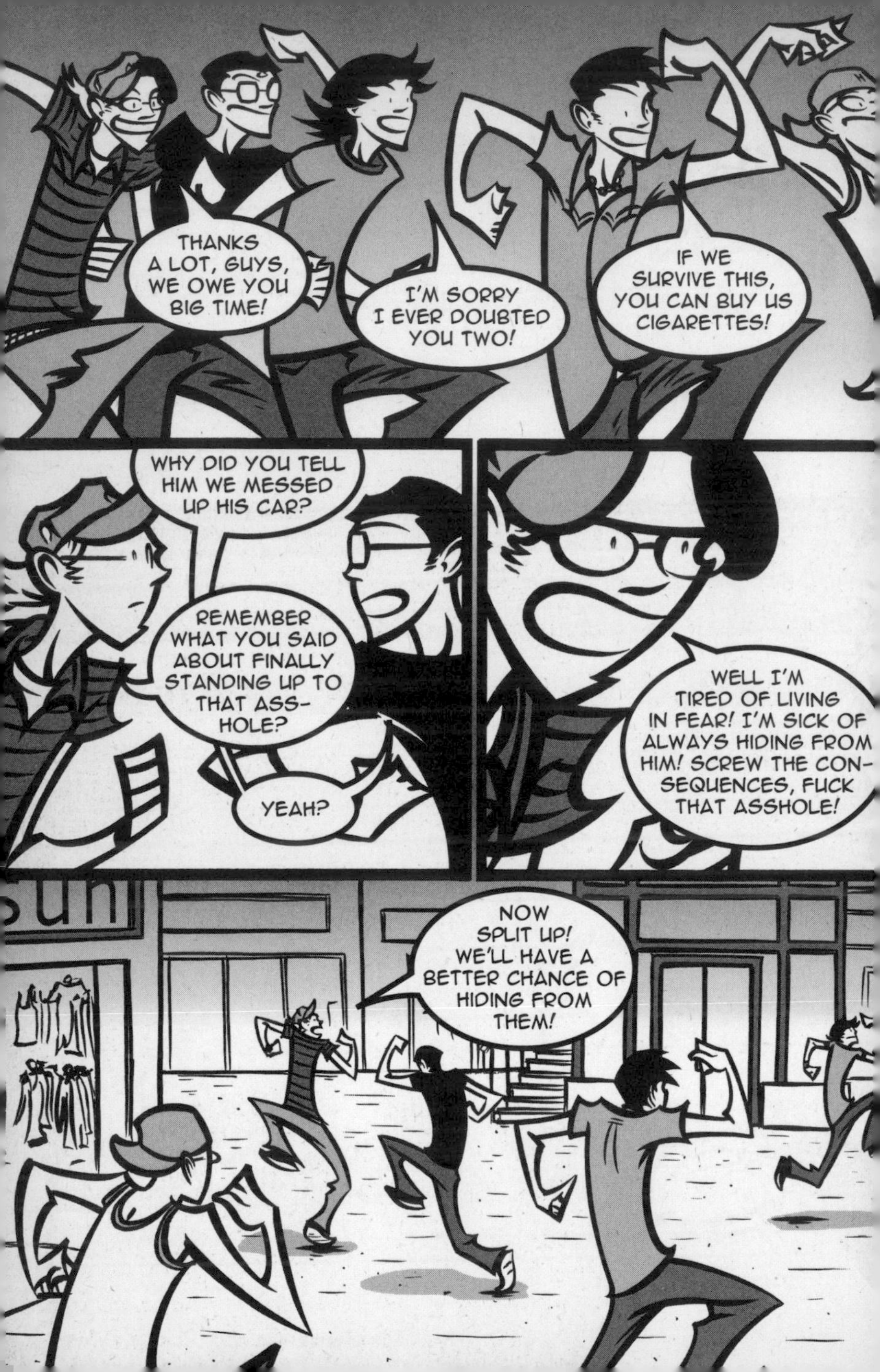
THANKS A LOT, GUYS, WE OWE YOU BIG TIME!
I'M SORRY I EVER DOUBTED YOU TWO!
IF WE SURVIVE THIS, YOU CAN BUY US CIGARETTES!
WHY DID YOU TELL HIM WE MESSED UP HIS CAR?
REMEMBER WHAT YOU SAID ABOUT FINALLY STANDING UP TO THAT ASS-HOLE?
YEAH?
WELL I'M TIRED OF LIVING IN FEAR! I'M SICK OF ALWAYS HIDING FROM HIM! SCREW THE CON-SEQUENCES, FUCK THAT ASSHOLE!
NOW SPLIT UP! WE'LL HAVE A BETTER CHANCE OF HIDING FROM THEM!

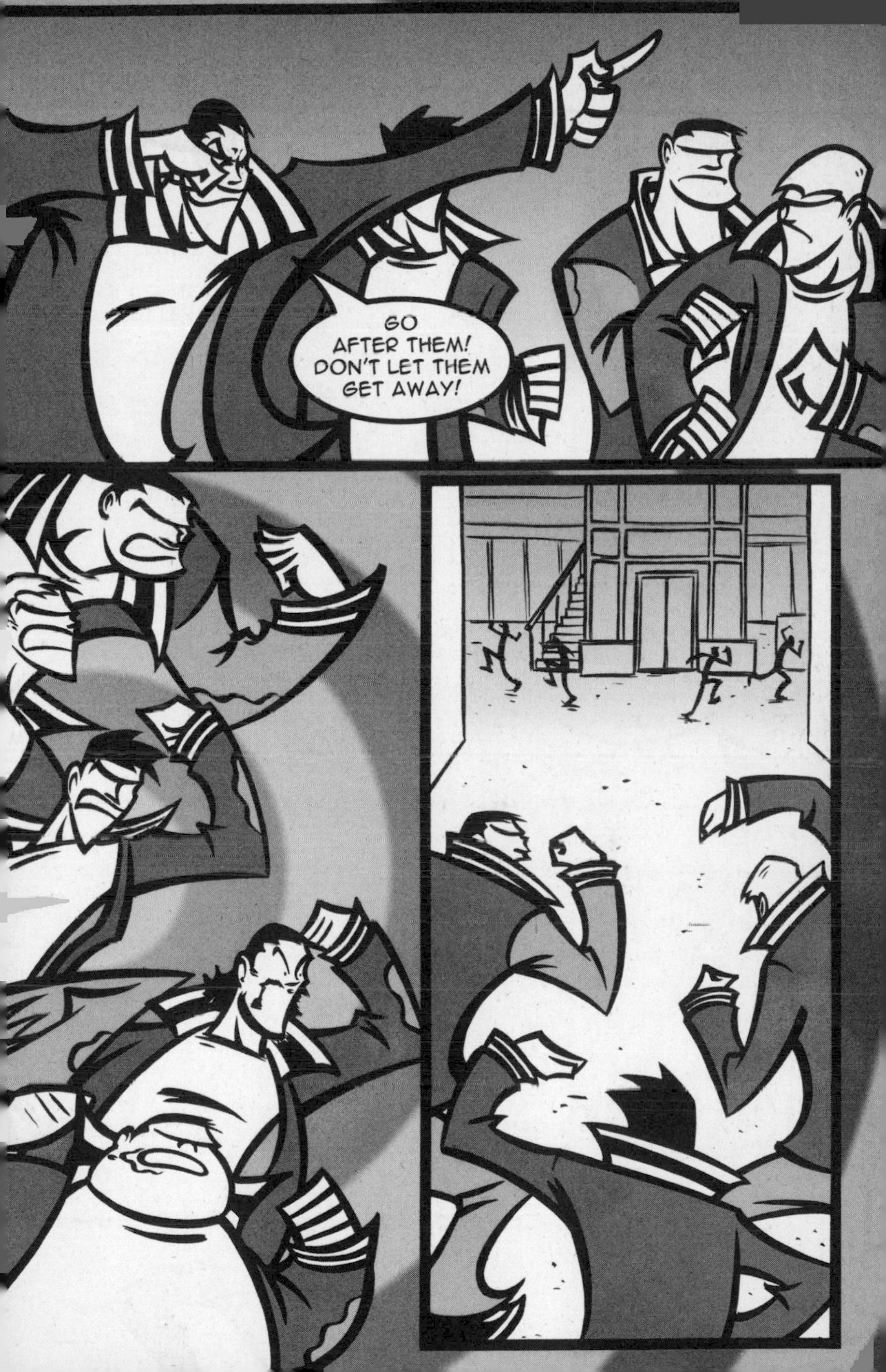
GO AFTER THEM! DON'T LET THEM GET AWAY!

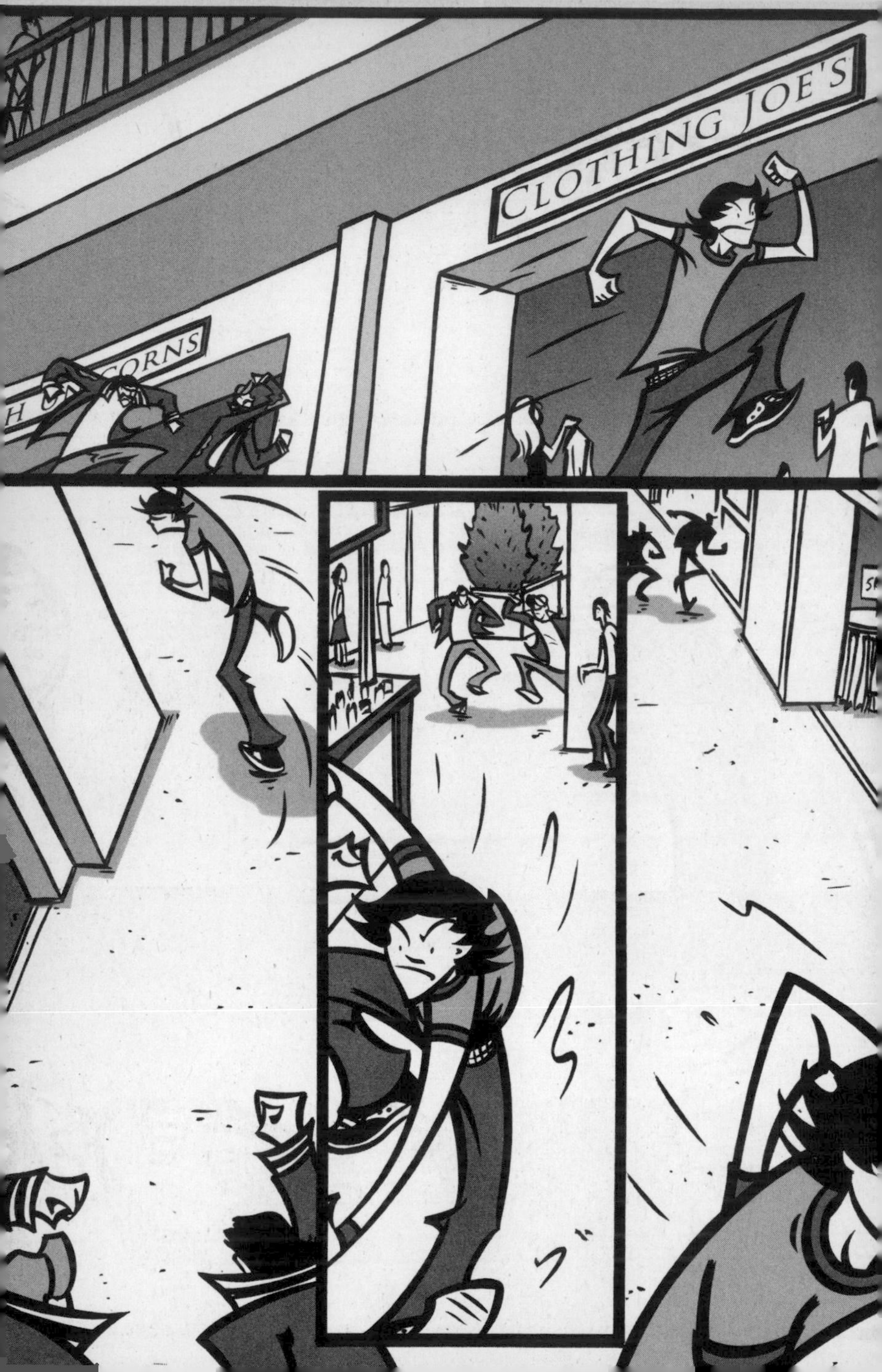
CLOTHING JOE'S

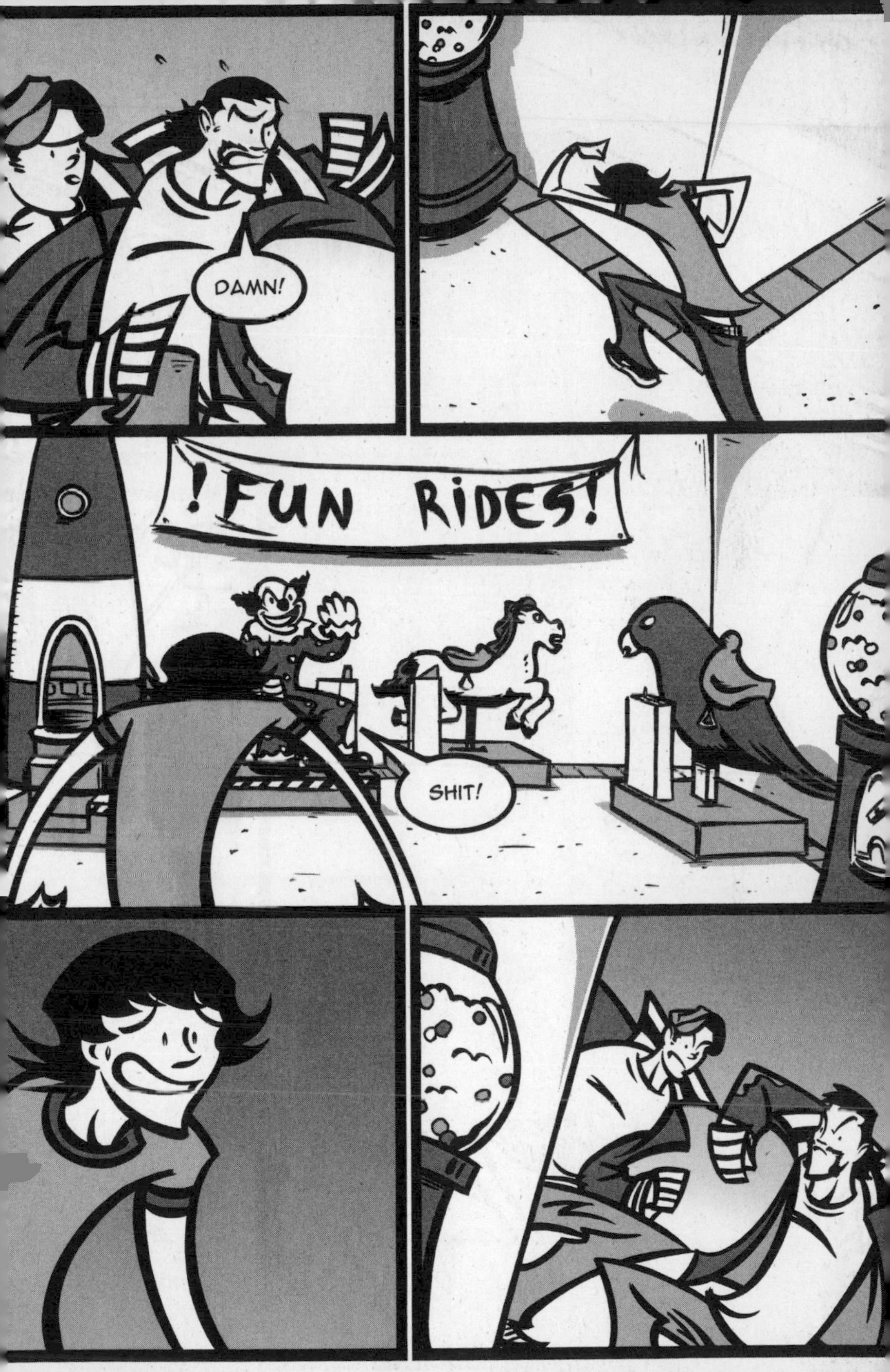
DAMN!
!FUN RIDES!
SHIT!

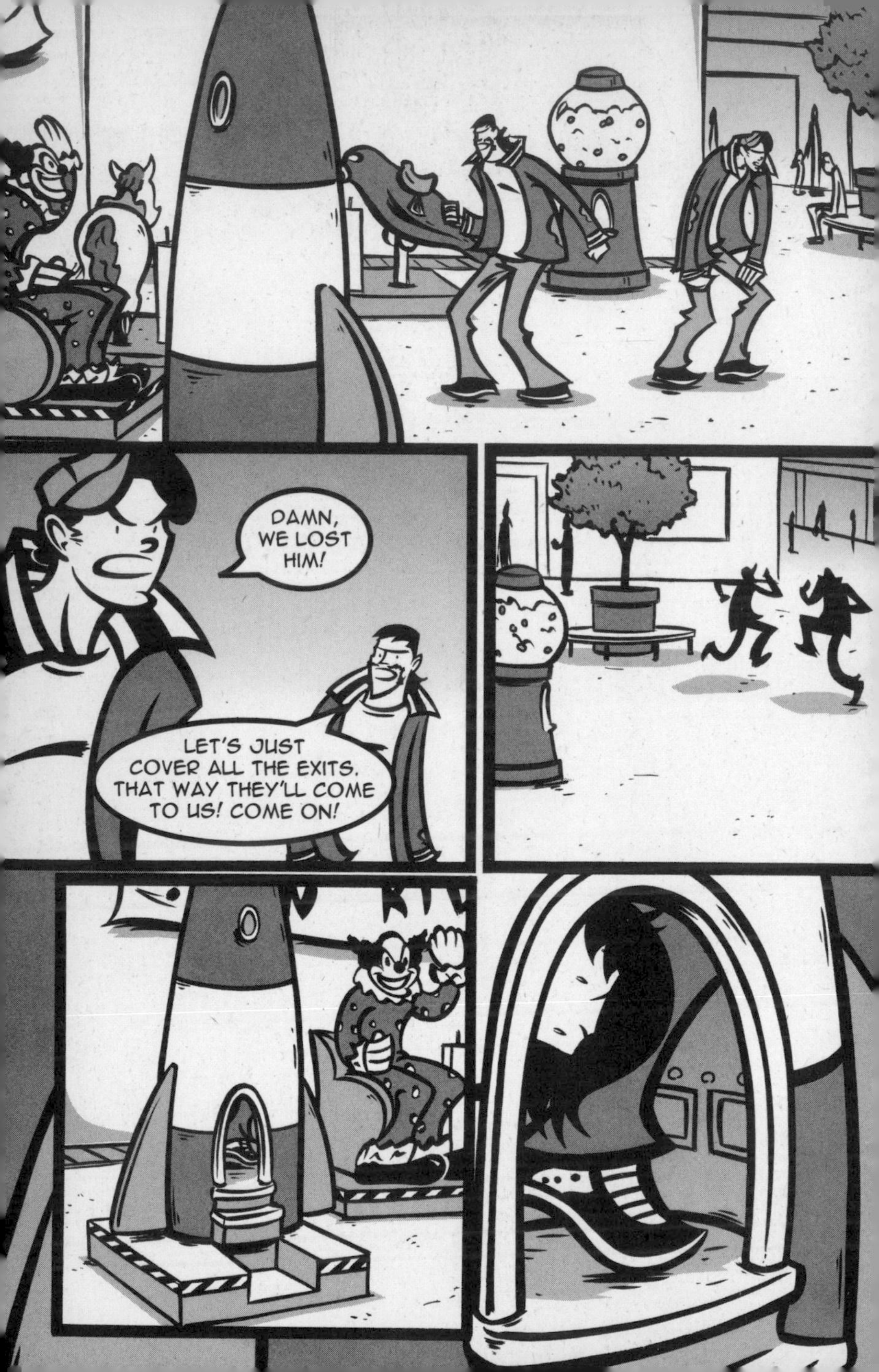
DAMN, WE LOST HIM!
LET'S JUST COVER ALL THE EXITS. THAT WAY THEY'LL COME TO US! COME ON!

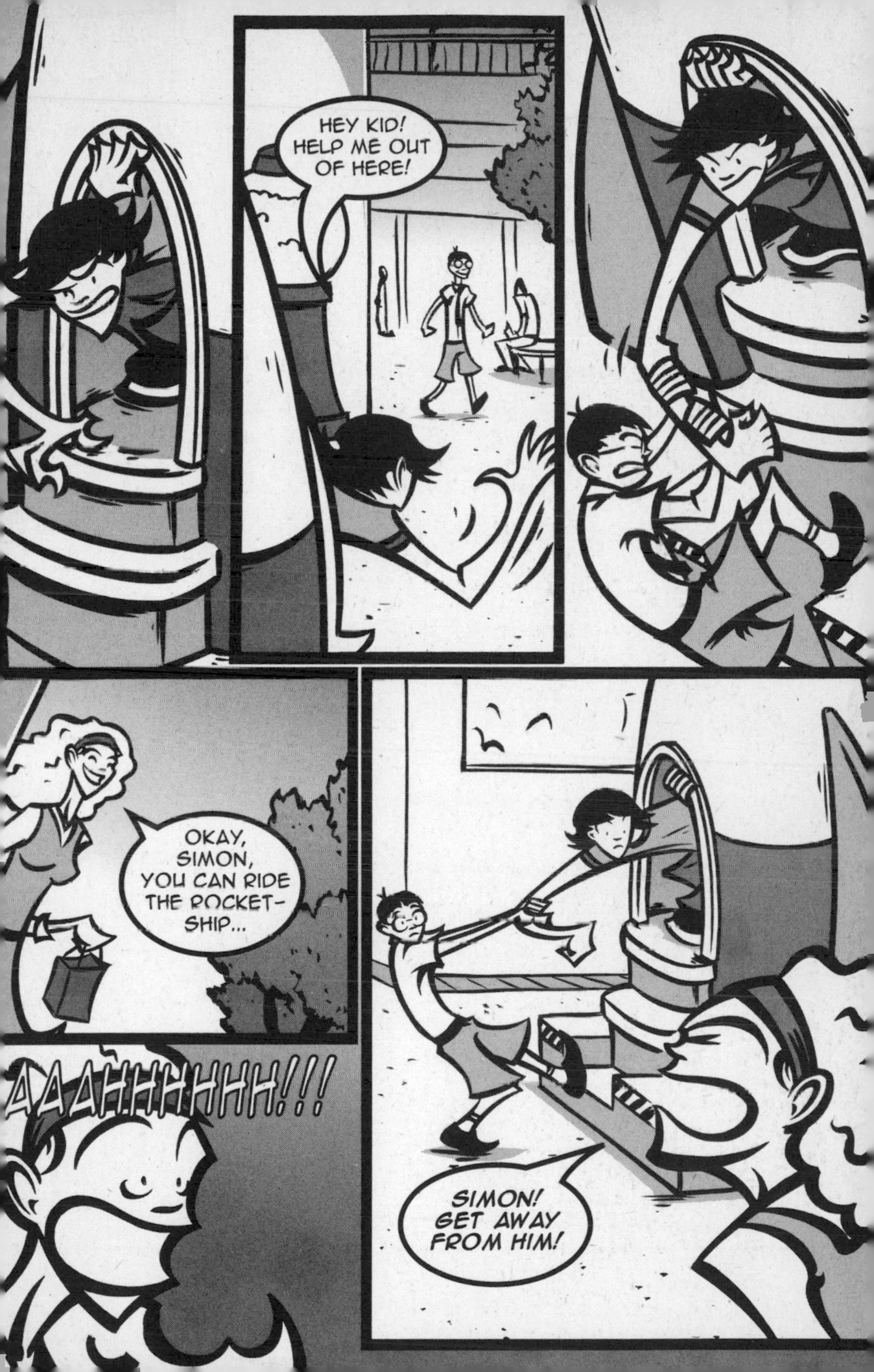
HEY KID! HELP ME OUT OF HERE!
OKAY, SIMON, YOU CAN RIDE THE ROCKET-SHIP...
AAAHHHHHH!!!
SIMON! GET AWAY FROM HIM!

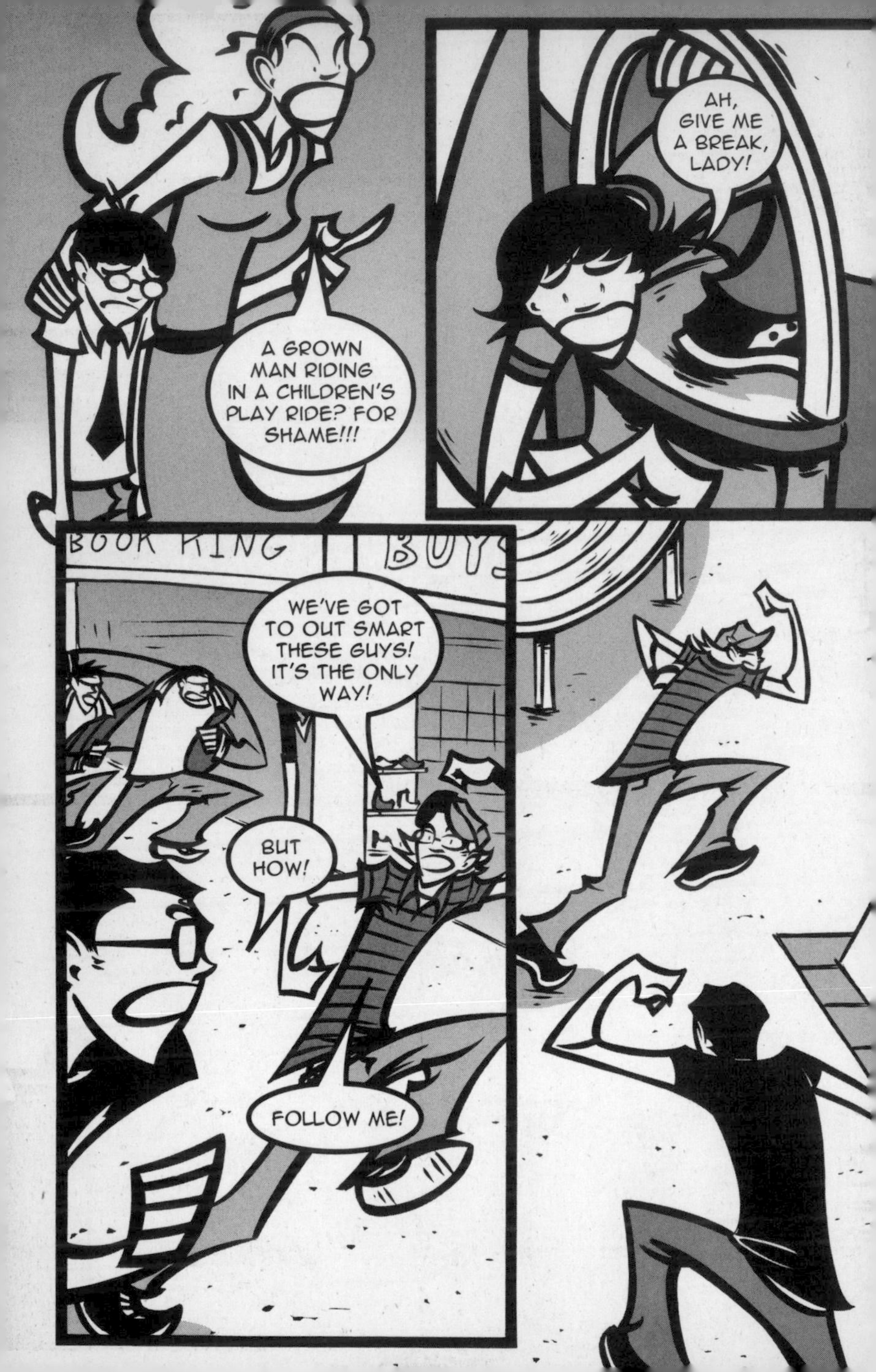
A GROWN MAN RIDING IN A CHILDREN'S PLAY RIDE? FOR SHAME!!!
AH, GIVE ME A BREAK, LADY!
BOOK KING
BUYS
WE'VE GOT TO OUT SMART THESE GUYS! IT'S THE ONLY WAY!
BUT HOW!
FOLLOW ME!

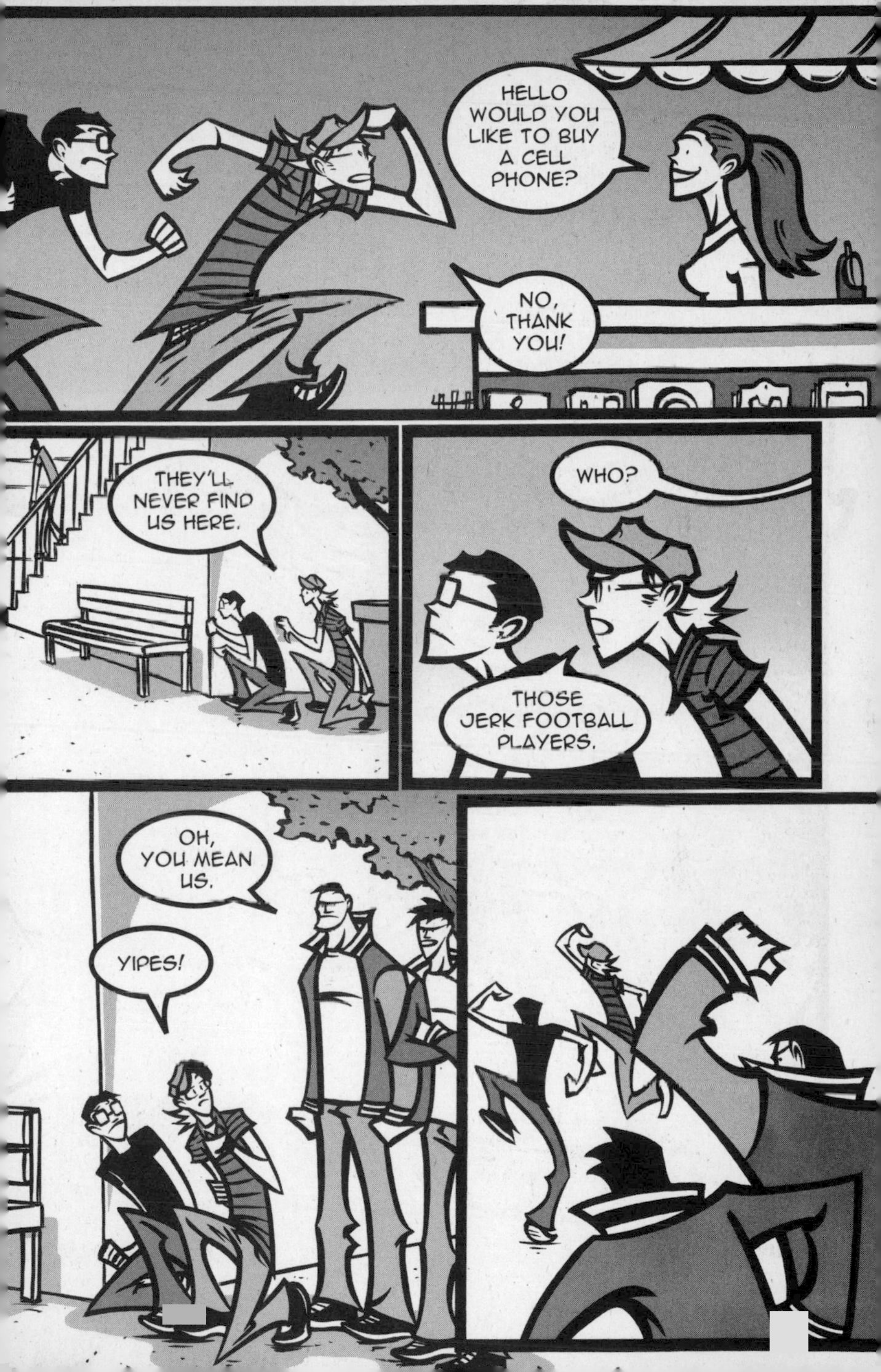
HELLO WOULD YOU LIKE TO BUY A CELL PHONE?
NO, THANK YOU!
THEY'LL NEVER FIND US HERE.
WHO?
THOSE JERK FOOTBALL PLAYERS.
OH, YOU MEAN US.
YIPES!

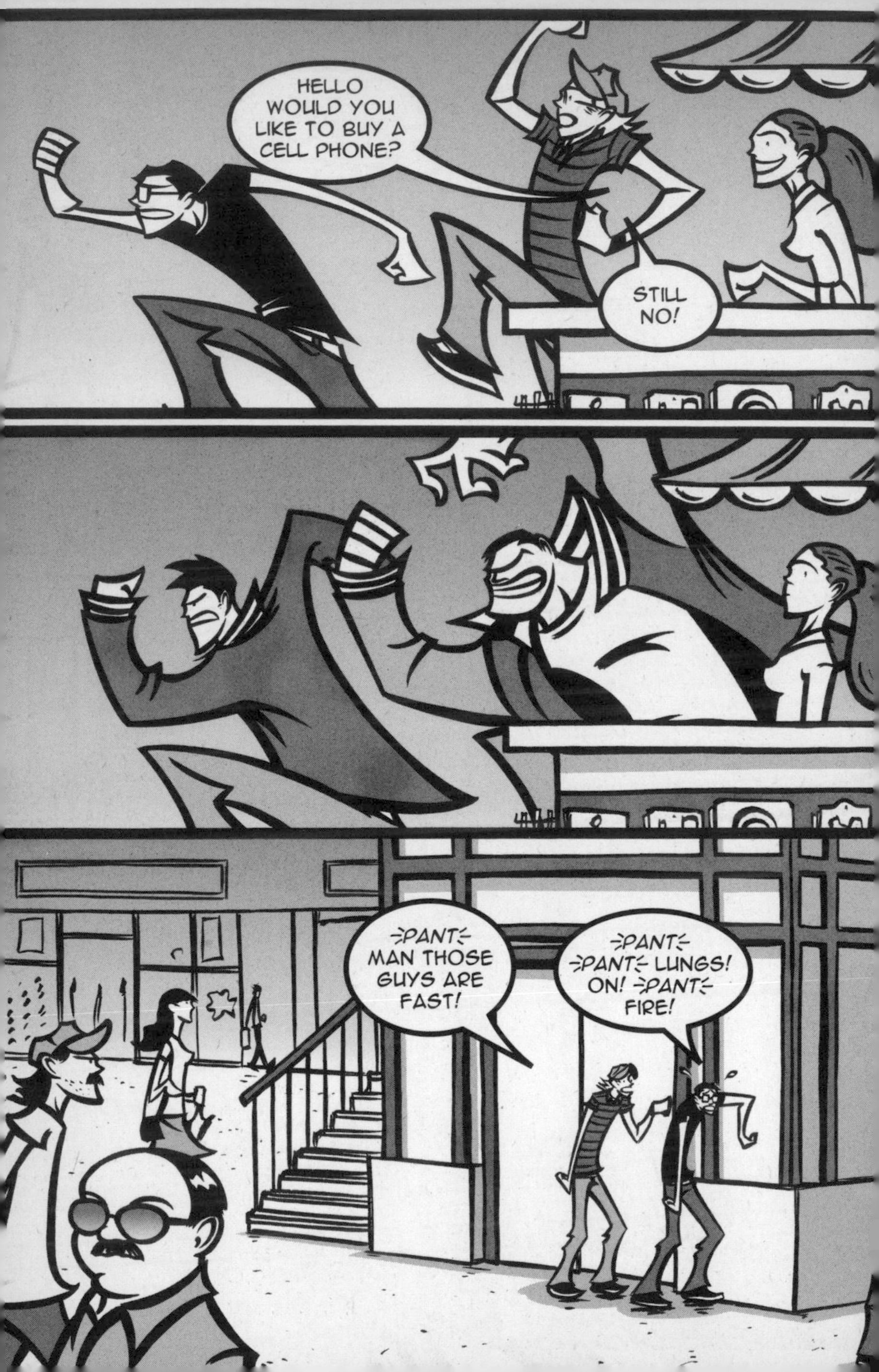
HELLO WOULD YOU LIKE TO BUY A CELL PHONE?
STILL NO!
=PANT= MAN THOSE GUYS ARE FAST!
=PANT= =PANT= LUNGS! ON! =PANT= FIRE!

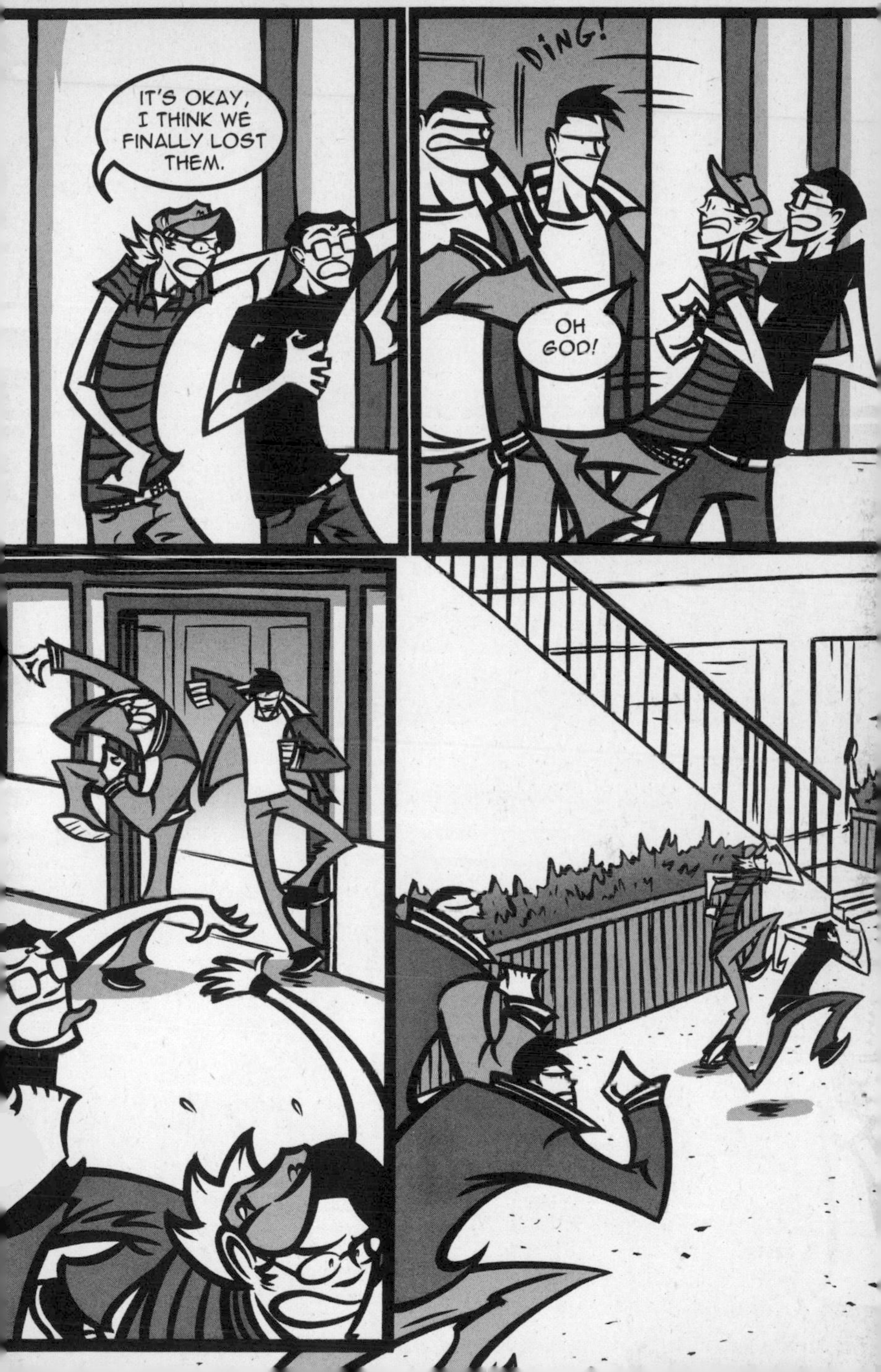
IT'S OKAY, I THINK WE FINALLY LOST THEM.
DING!
OH GOD!

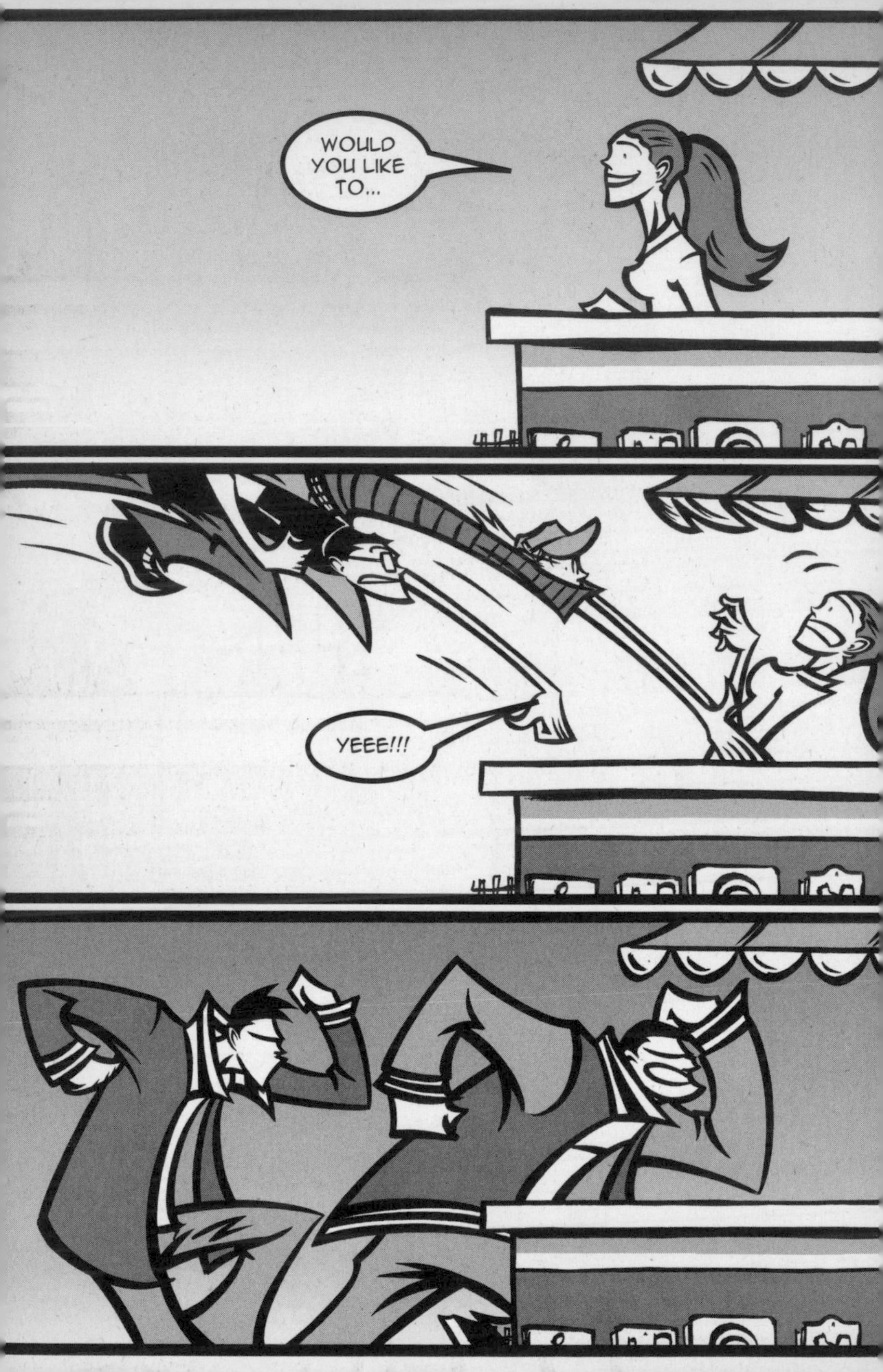
WOULD YOU LIKE TO...
YEEE!!!

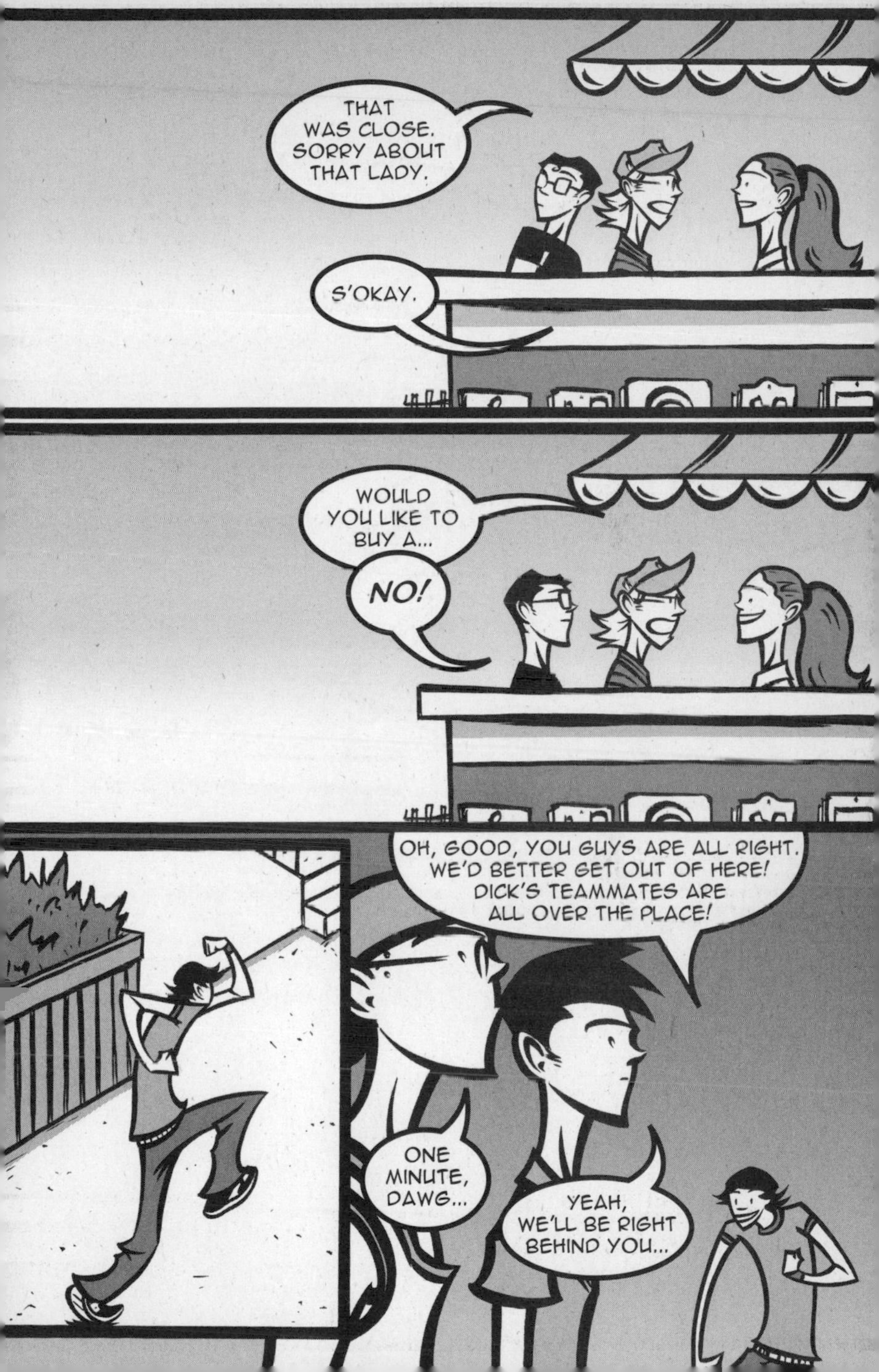
THAT WAS CLOSE. SORRY ABOUT THAT LADY.
S'OKAY.
WOULD YOU LIKE TO BUY A...
NO!
OH, GOOD, YOU GUYS ARE ALL RIGHT. WE'D BETTER GET OUT OF HERE! DICK'S TEAMMATES ARE ALL OVER THE PLACE!
ONE MINUTE, DAWG...
YEAH, WE'LL BE RIGHT BEHIND YOU...

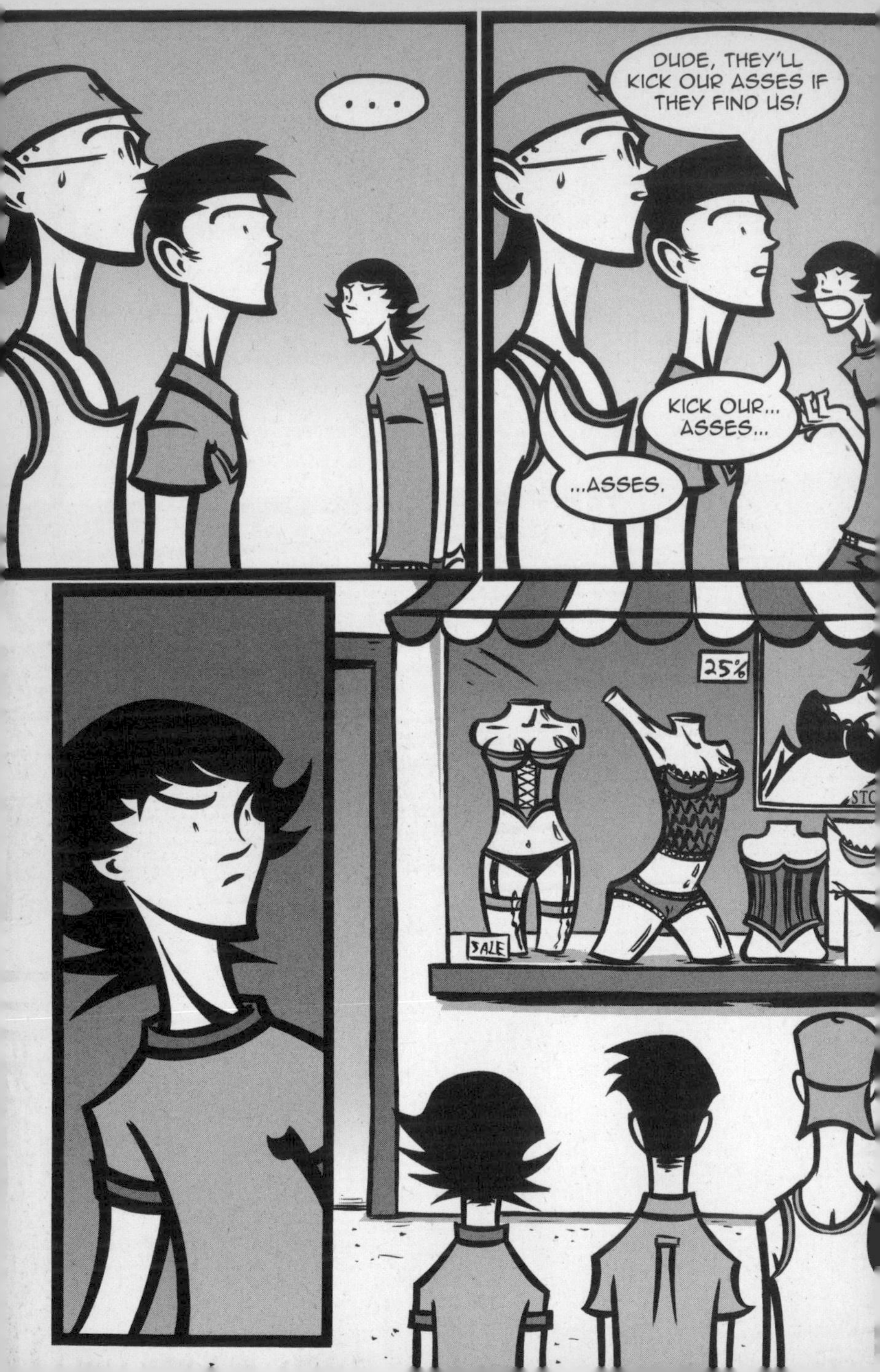
...
DUDE, THEY'LL KICK OUR ASSES IF THEY FIND US!
KICK OUR... ASSES...
...ASSES.
25%
SALE

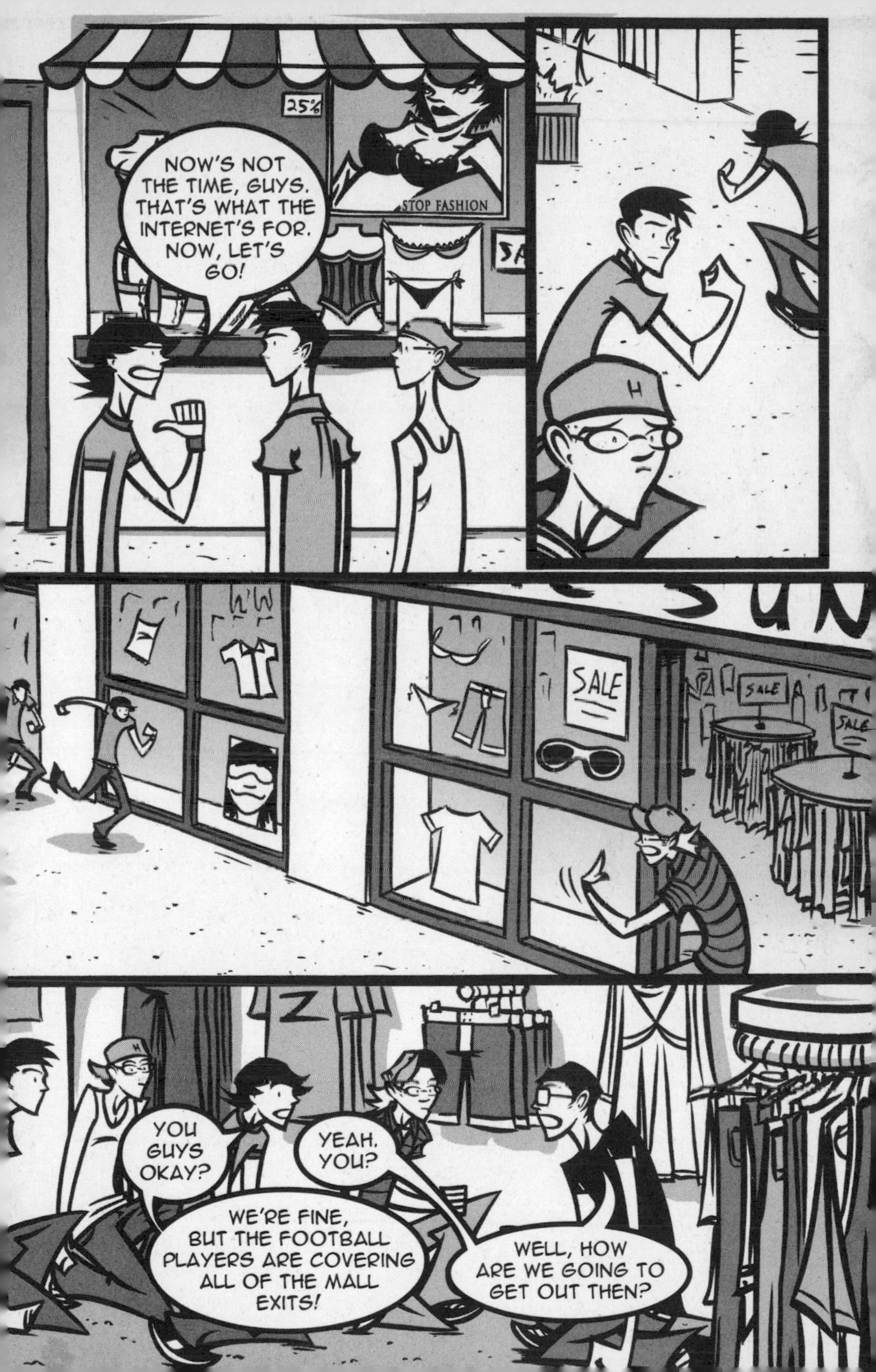
25%
STOP FASHION
NOW'S NOT THE TIME, GUYS. THAT'S WHAT THE INTERNET'S FOR. NOW, LET'S GO!
SALE
SALE
SALE
YOU GUYS OKAY?
YEAH. YOU?
WE'RE FINE, BUT THE FOOTBALL PLAYERS ARE COVERING ALL OF THE MALL EXITS!
WELL, HOW ARE WE GOING TO GET OUT THEN?

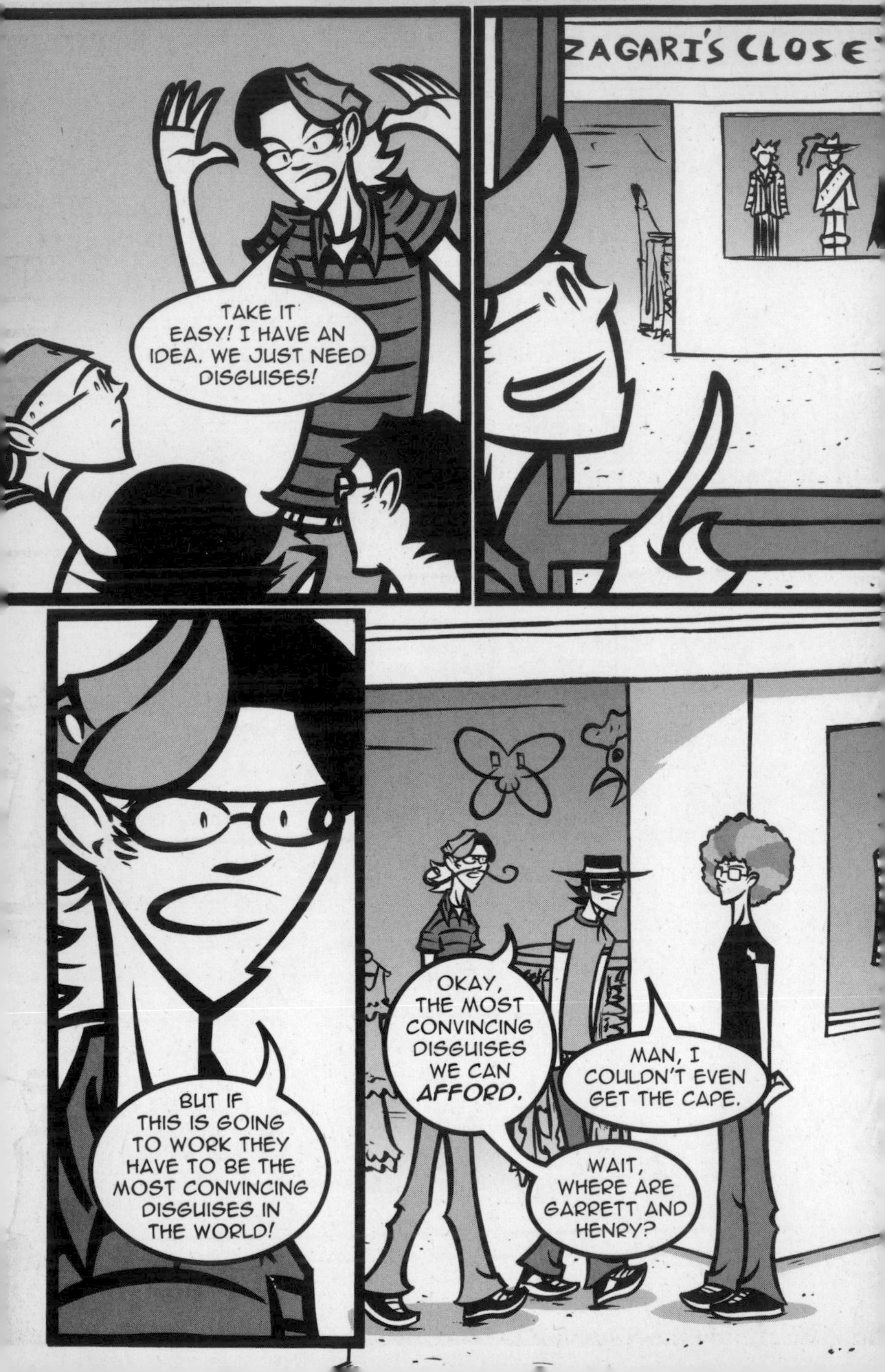

TAKE IT EASY! I HAVE AN IDEA. WE JUST NEED DISGUISES!
ZAGARI'S CLOSET
BUT IF THIS IS GOING TO WORK THEY HAVE TO BE THE MOST CONVINCING DISGUISES IN THE WORLD!
OKAY, THE MOST CONVINCING DISGUISES WE CAN *AFFORD*.
MAN, I COULDN'T EVEN GET THE CAPE.
WAIT, WHERE ARE GARRETT AND HENRY?

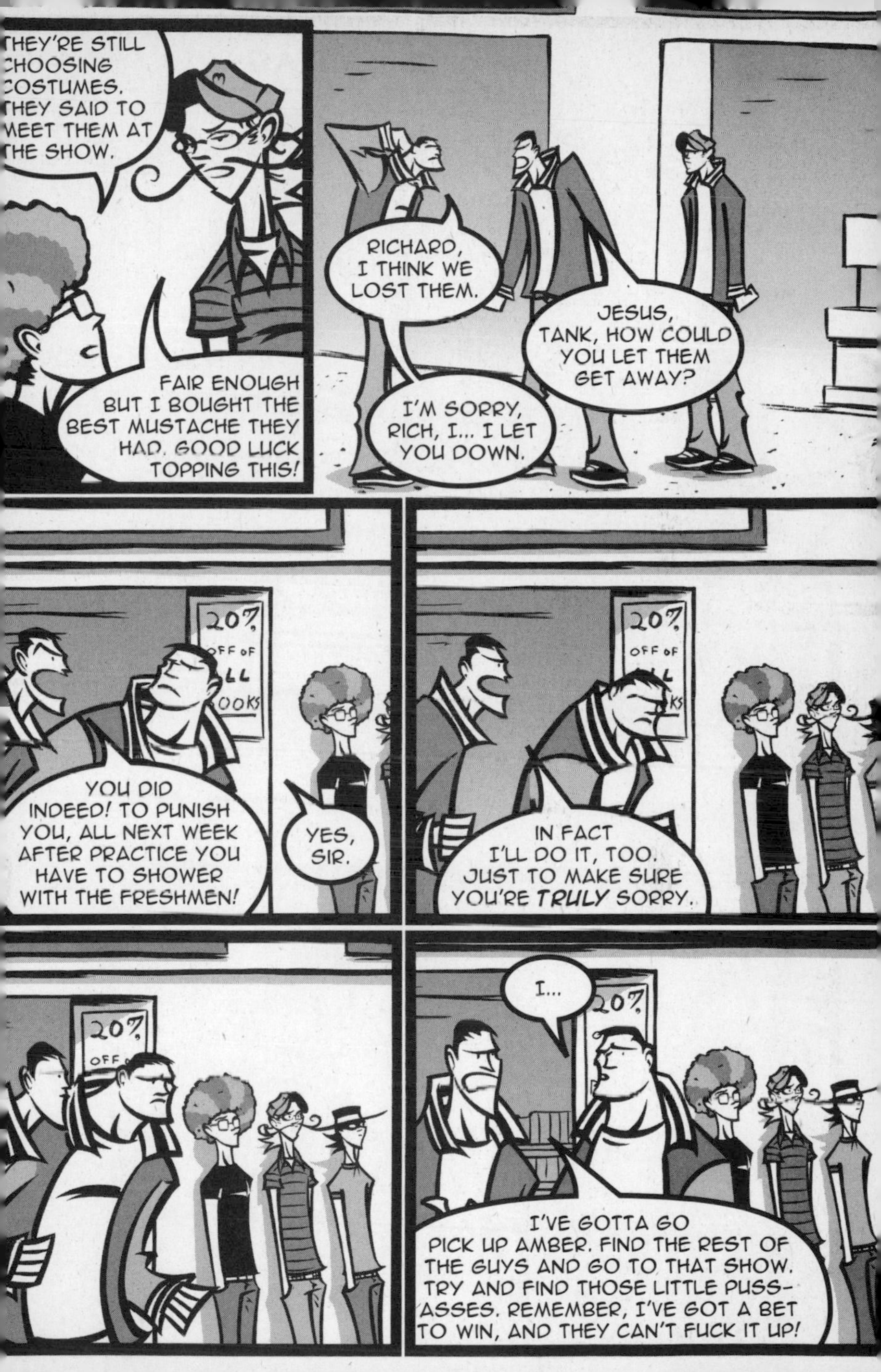
THEY'RE STILL CHOOSING COSTUMES. THEY SAID TO MEET THEM AT THE SHOW.
FAIR ENOUGH BUT I BOUGHT THE BEST MUSTACHE THEY HAD. GOOD LUCK TOPPING THIS!
RICHARD, I THINK WE LOST THEM.
JESUS, TANK, HOW COULD YOU LET THEM GET AWAY?
I'M SORRY, RICH, I... I LET YOU DOWN.
20% OFF OF
YOU DID INDEED! TO PUNISH YOU, ALL NEXT WEEK AFTER PRACTICE YOU HAVE TO SHOWER WITH THE FRESHMEN!
YES, SIR.
20% OFF OF
IN FACT I'LL DO IT, TOO. JUST TO MAKE SURE YOU'RE *TRULY* SORRY.
20% OFF
I...
20%
I'VE GOTTA GO PICK UP AMBER. FIND THE REST OF THE GUYS AND GO TO THAT SHOW. TRY AND FIND THOSE LITTLE PUSS-ASSES. REMEMBER, I'VE GOT A BET TO WIN, AND THEY CAN'T FUCK IT UP!

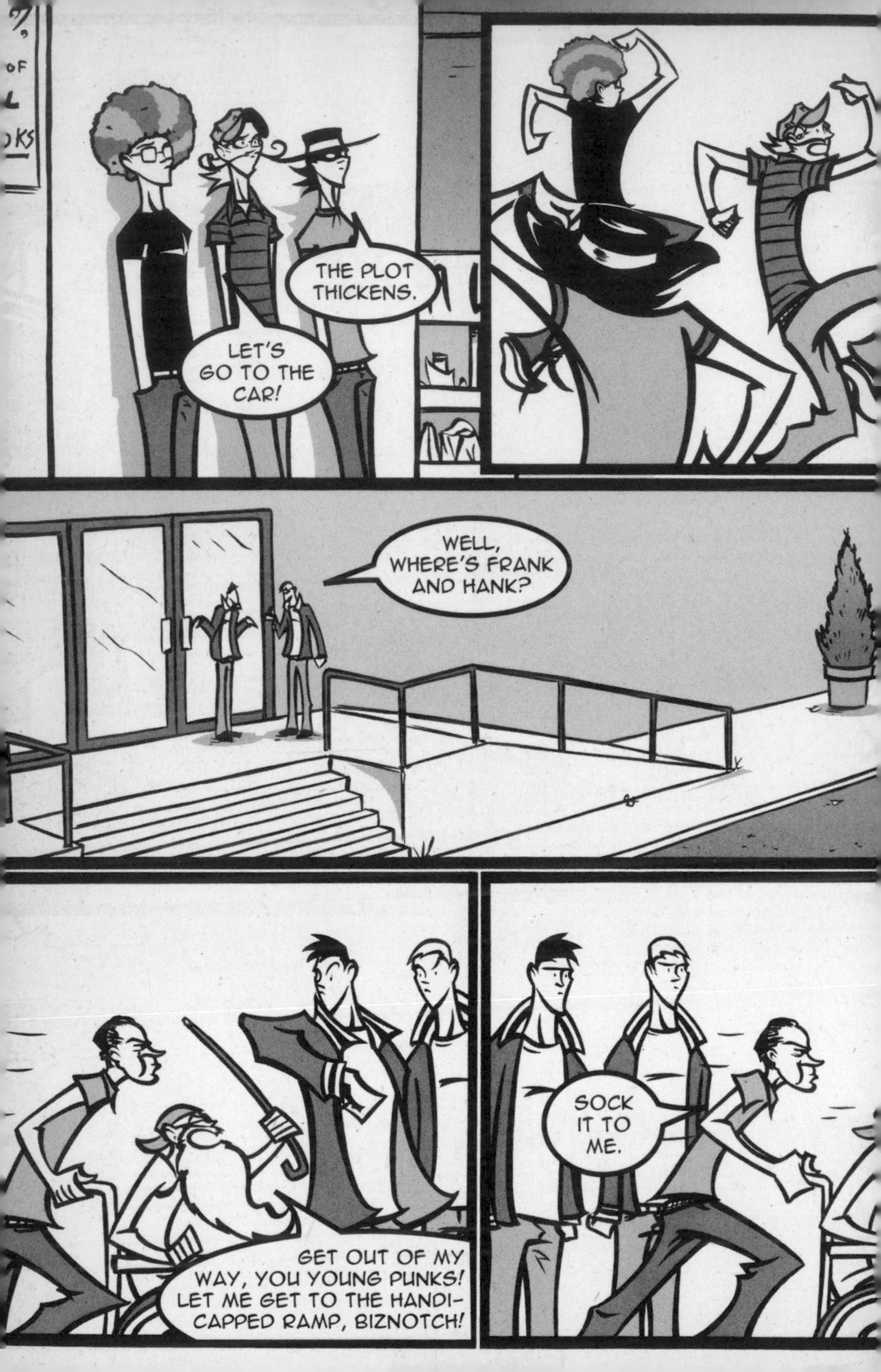
THE PLOT THICKENS.
LET'S GO TO THE CAR!
WELL, WHERE'S FRANK AND HANK?
GET OUT OF MY WAY, YOU YOUNG PUNKS! LET ME GET TO THE HANDI-CAPPED RAMP, BIZNOTCH!
SOCK IT TO ME.

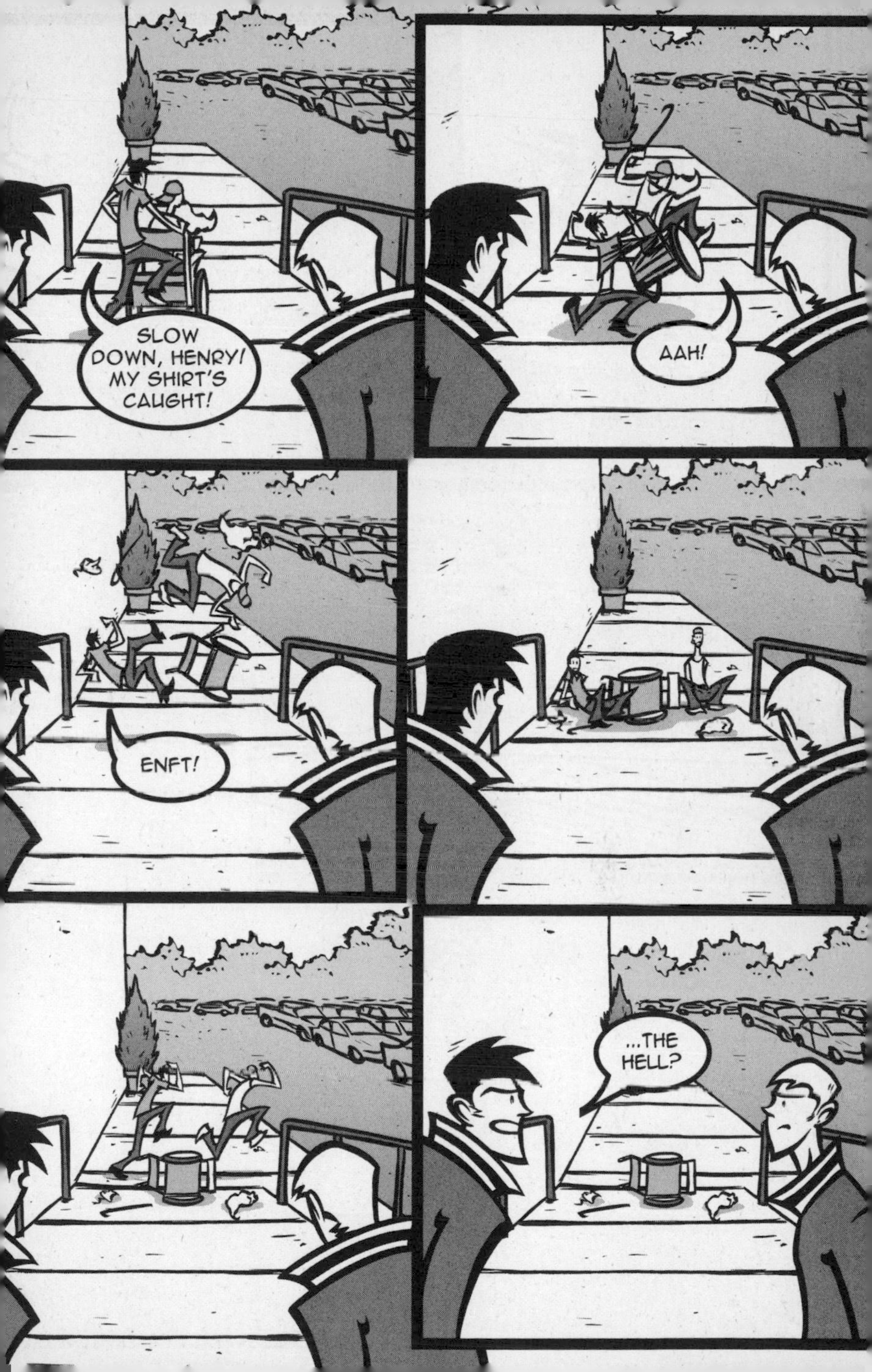
SLOW DOWN, HENRY! MY SHIRT'S CAUGHT!
AAH!
ENFT!
...THE HELL?

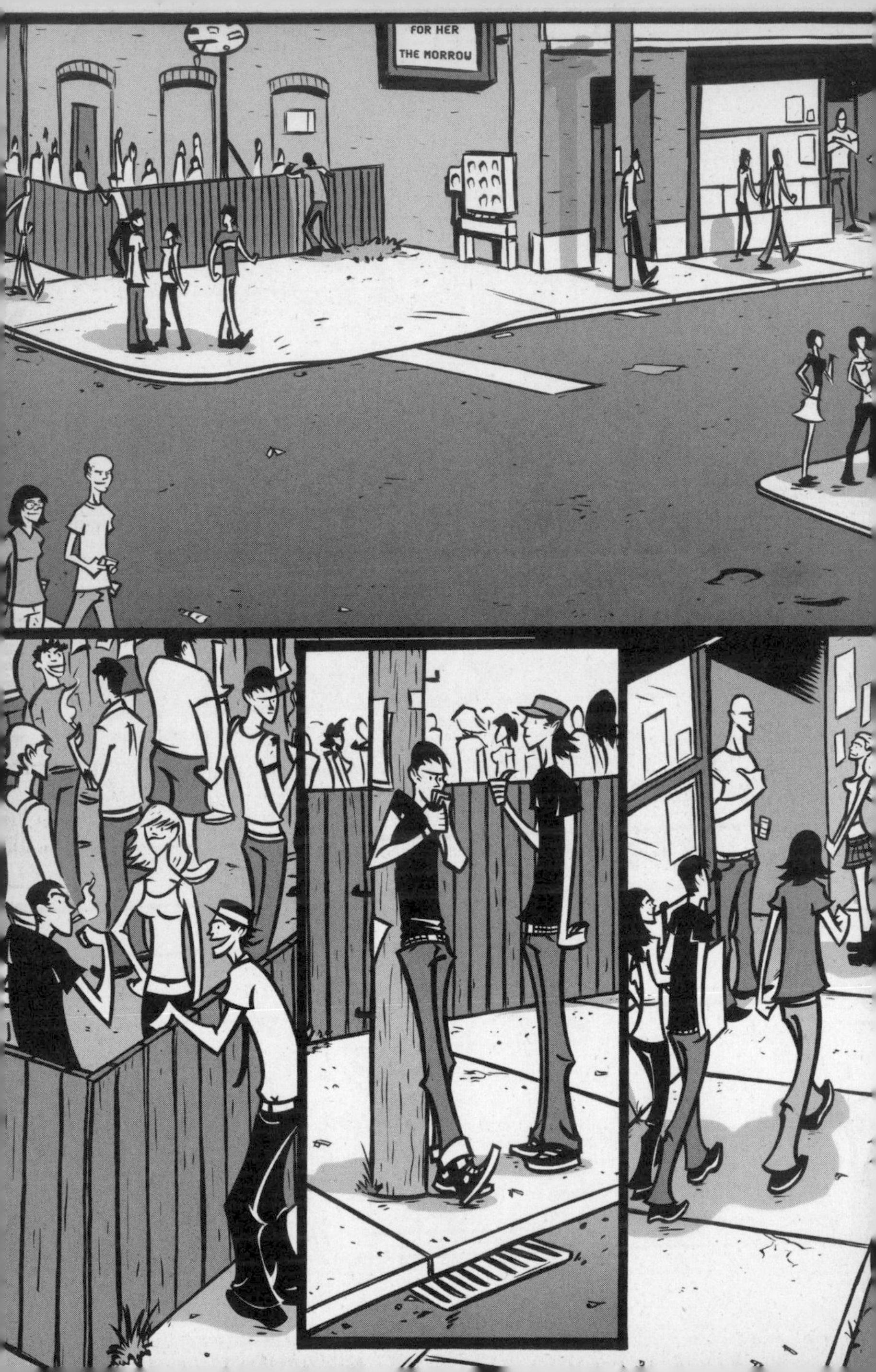
FOR HER
THE MORROW

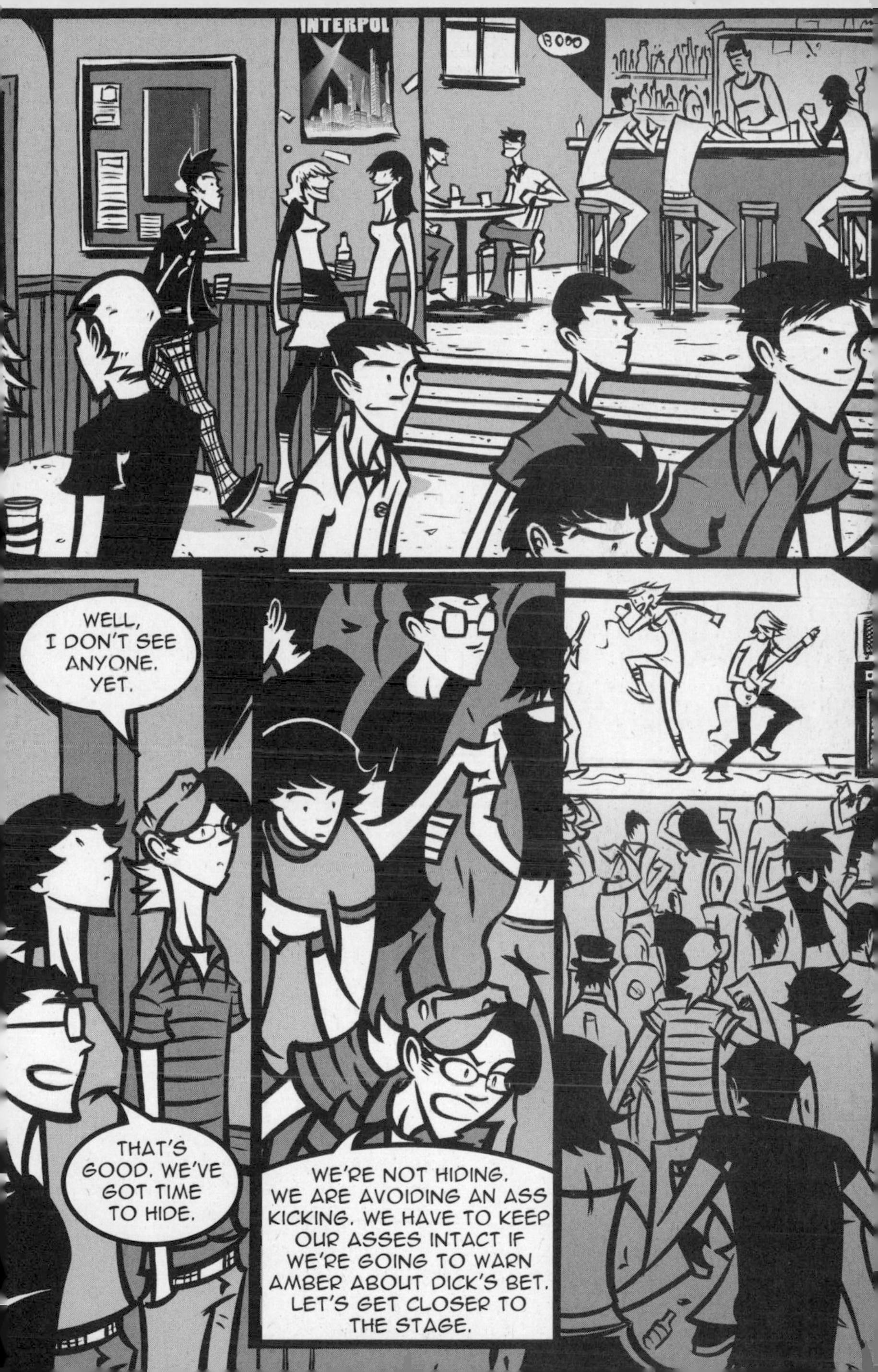
INTERPOL
BOOO
WELL, I DON'T SEE ANYONE. YET.
THAT'S GOOD. WE'VE GOT TIME TO HIDE.
WE'RE NOT HIDING. WE ARE AVOIDING AN ASS KICKING. WE HAVE TO KEEP OUR ASSES INTACT IF WE'RE GOING TO WARN AMBER ABOUT DICK'S BET. LET'S GET CLOSER TO THE STAGE.

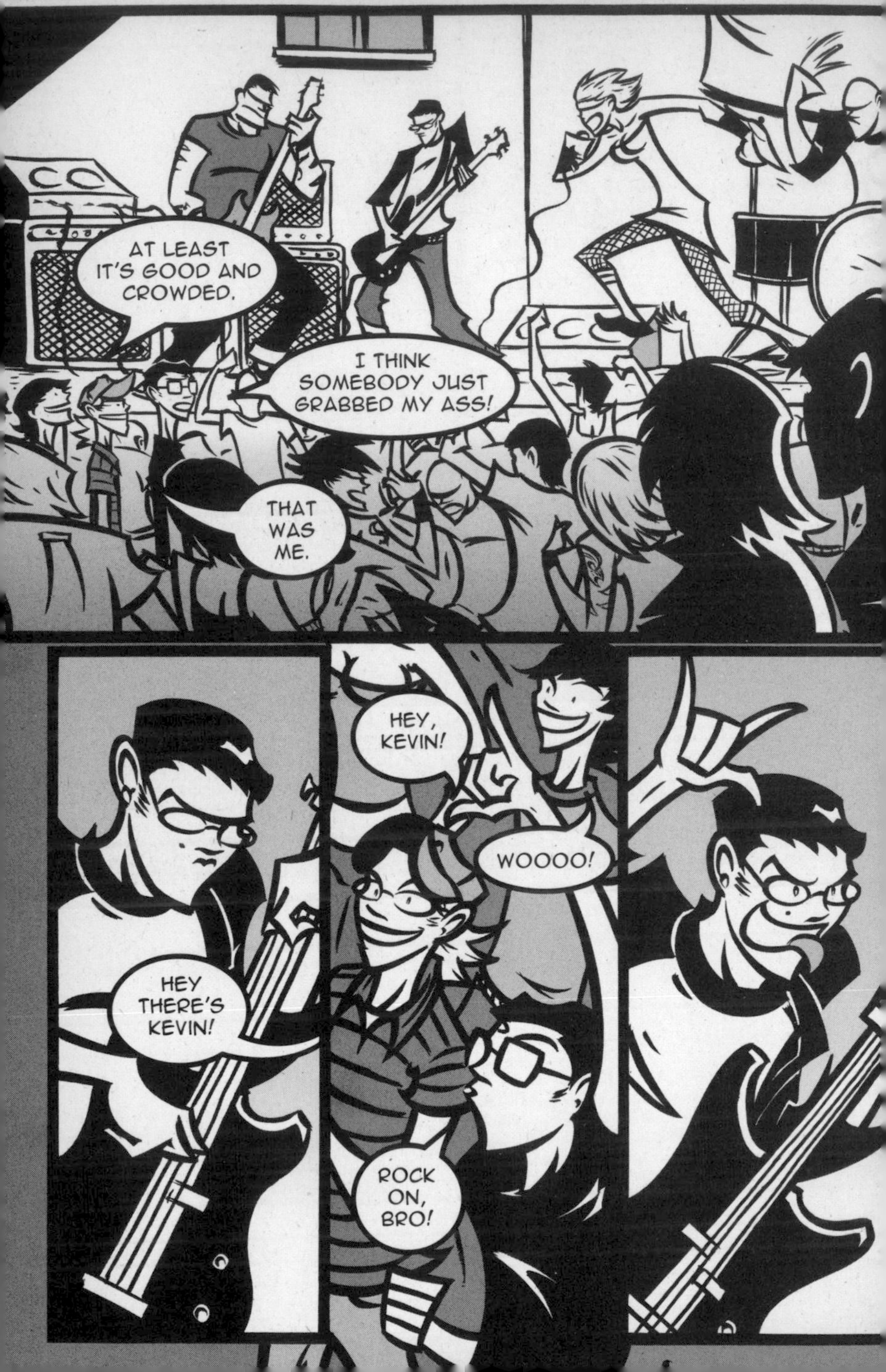
AT LEAST IT'S GOOD AND CROWDED.
I THINK SOMEBODY JUST GRABBED MY ASS!
THAT WAS ME.
HEY THERE'S KEVIN!
HEY, KEVIN!
WOOOO!
ROCK ON, BRO!

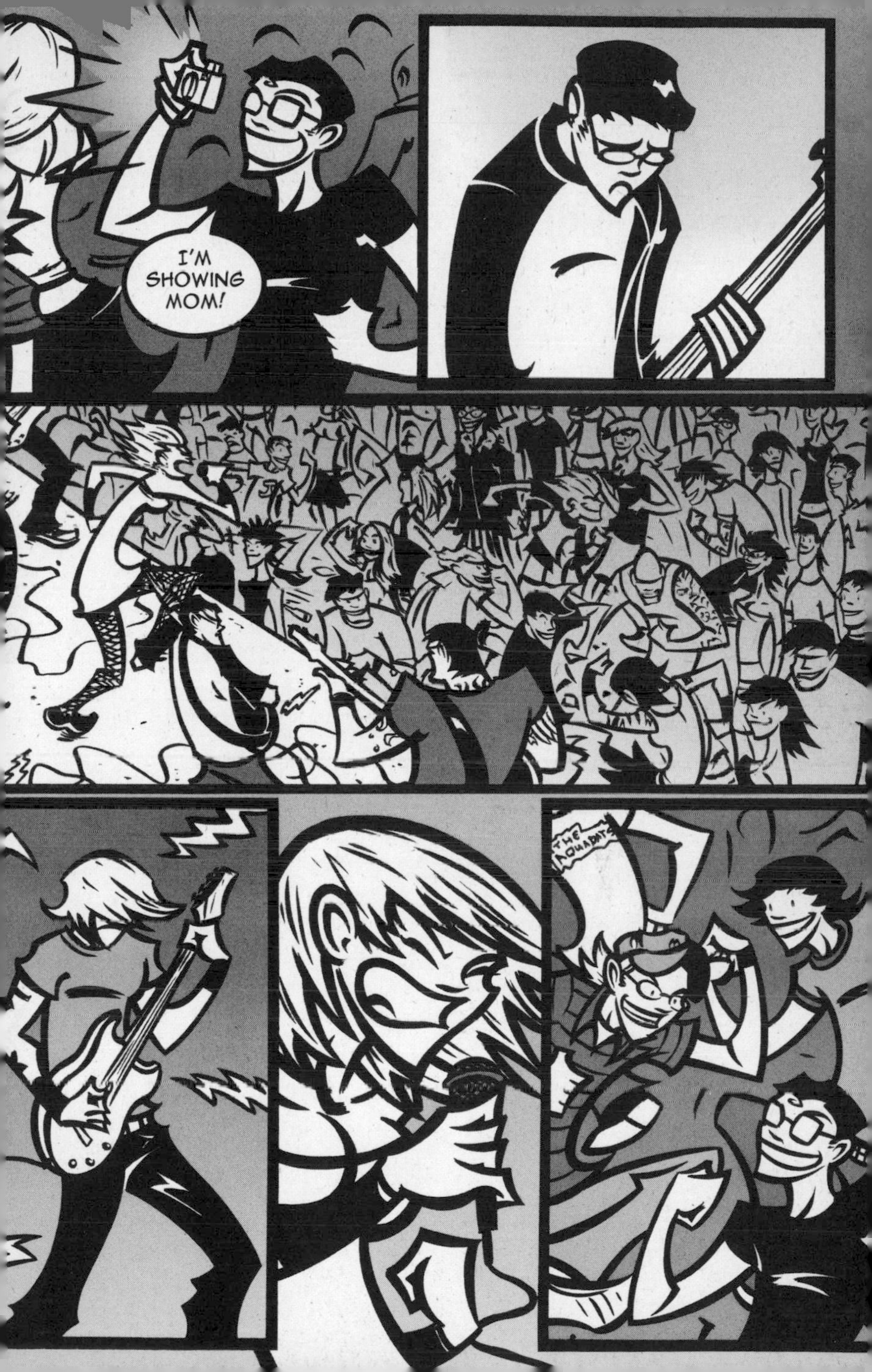
I'M SHOWING MOM!
THE AQUABATS

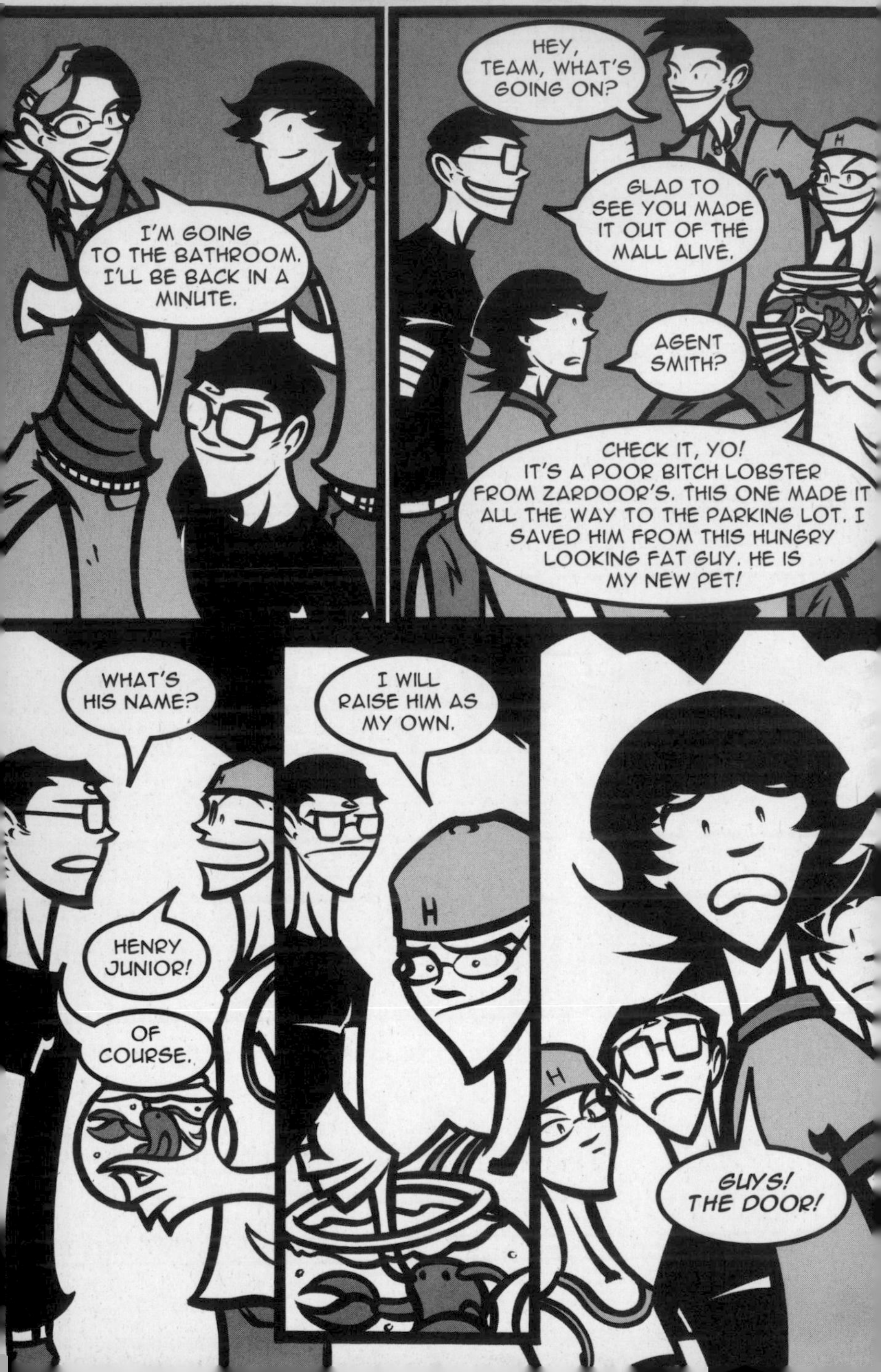
I'M GOING TO THE BATHROOM. I'LL BE BACK IN A MINUTE.
HEY, TEAM, WHAT'S GOING ON?
GLAD TO SEE YOU MADE IT OUT OF THE MALL ALIVE.
AGENT SMITH?
CHECK IT, YO! IT'S A POOR BITCH LOBSTER FROM ZARDOOR'S. THIS ONE MADE IT ALL THE WAY TO THE PARKING LOT. I SAVED HIM FROM THIS HUNGRY LOOKING FAT GUY. HE IS MY NEW PET!
WHAT'S HIS NAME?
HENRY JUNIOR!
OF COURSE.
I WILL RAISE HIM AS MY OWN.
GUYS! THE DOOR!

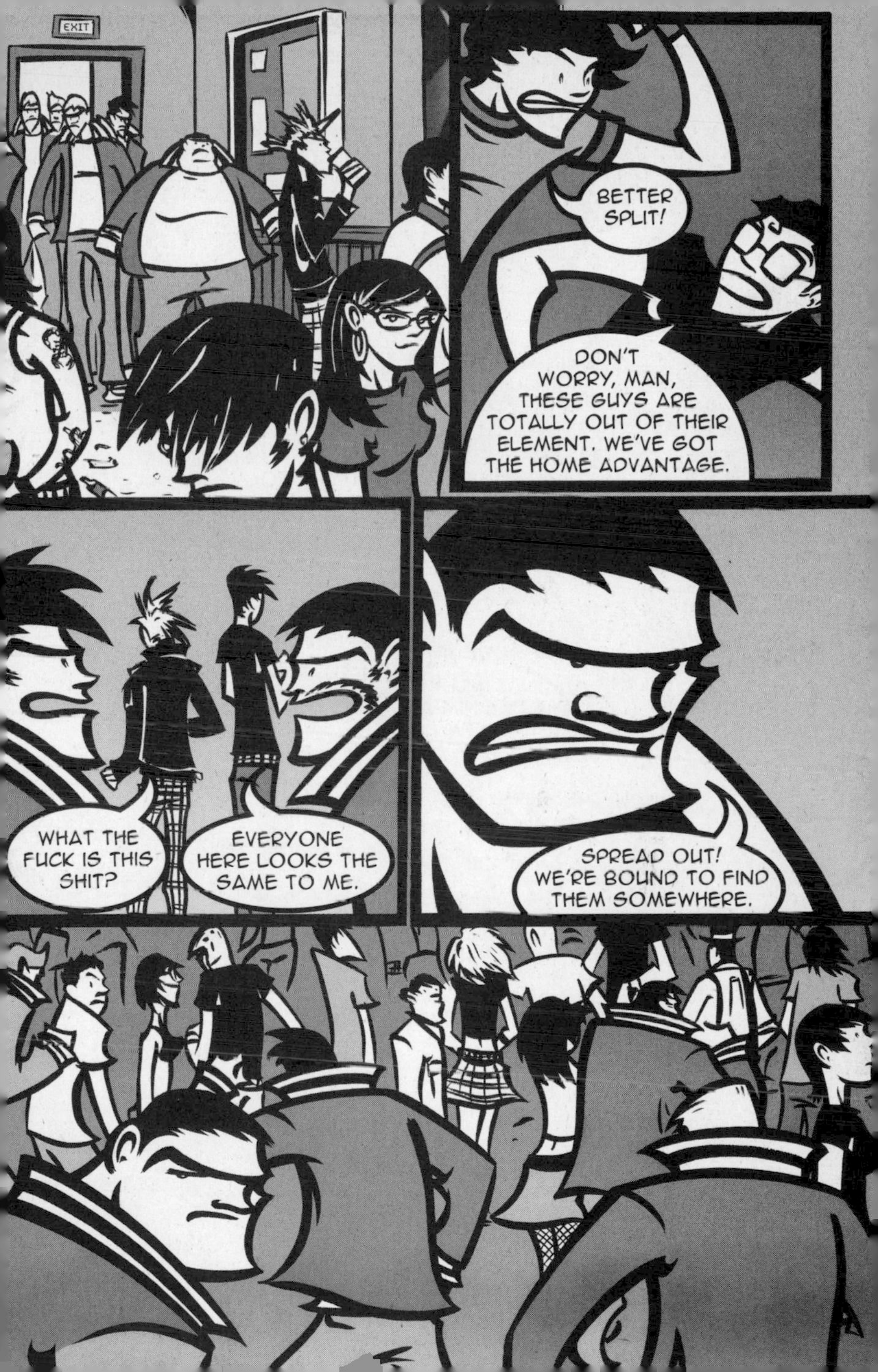
EXIT
BETTER SPLIT!
DON'T WORRY, MAN, THESE GUYS ARE TOTALLY OUT OF THEIR ELEMENT. WE'VE GOT THE HOME ADVANTAGE.
WHAT THE FUCK IS THIS SHIT?
EVERYONE HERE LOOKS THE SAME TO ME.
SPREAD OUT! WE'RE BOUND TO FIND THEM SOMEWHERE.

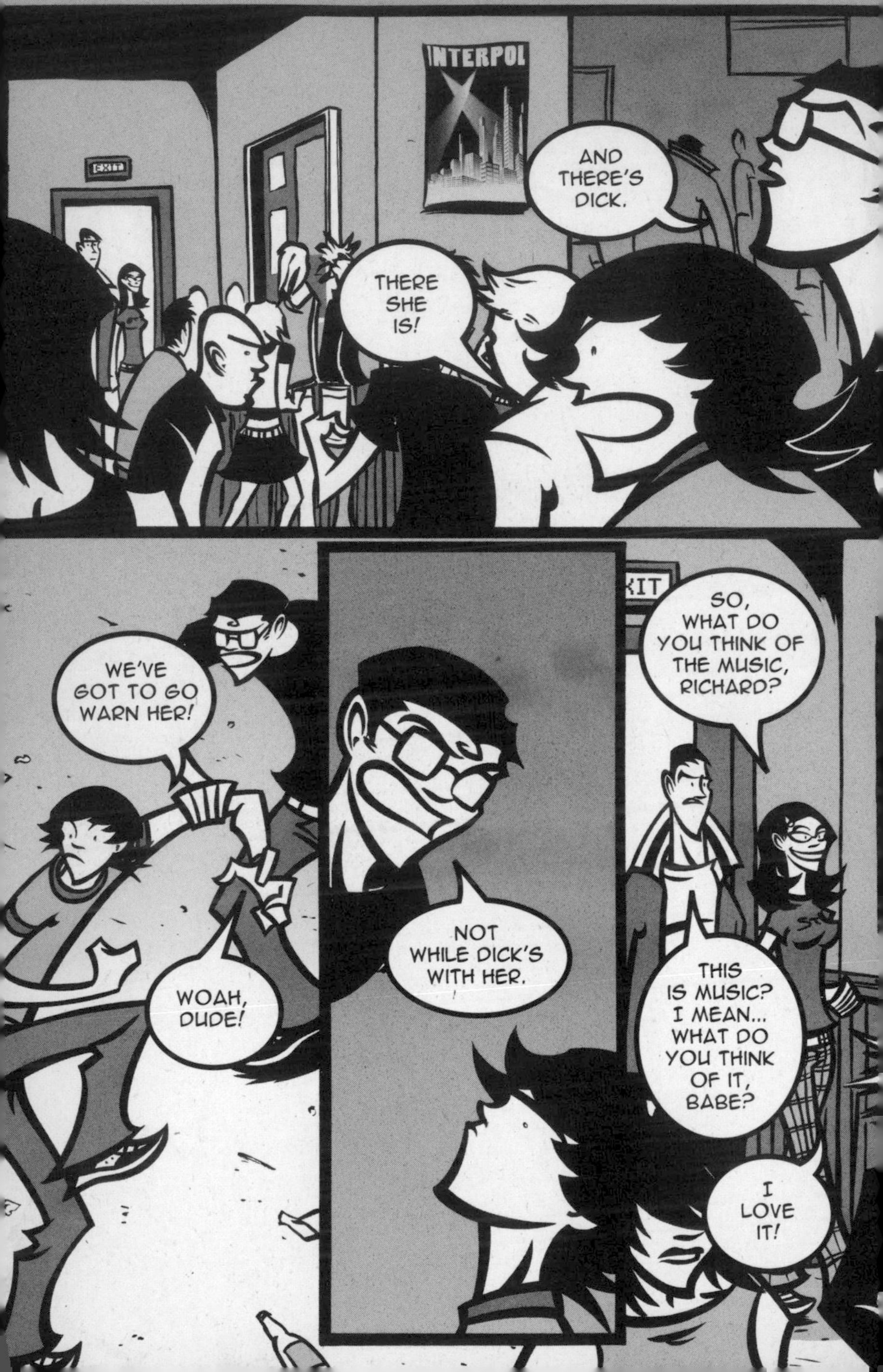
INTERPOL
EXIT
AND THERE'S DICK.
THERE SHE IS!
WE'VE GOT TO GO WARN HER!
WOAH, DUDE!
NOT WHILE DICK'S WITH HER.
EXIT
SO, WHAT DO YOU THINK OF THE MUSIC, RICHARD?
THIS IS MUSIC? I MEAN... WHAT DO YOU THINK OF IT, BABE?
I LOVE IT!

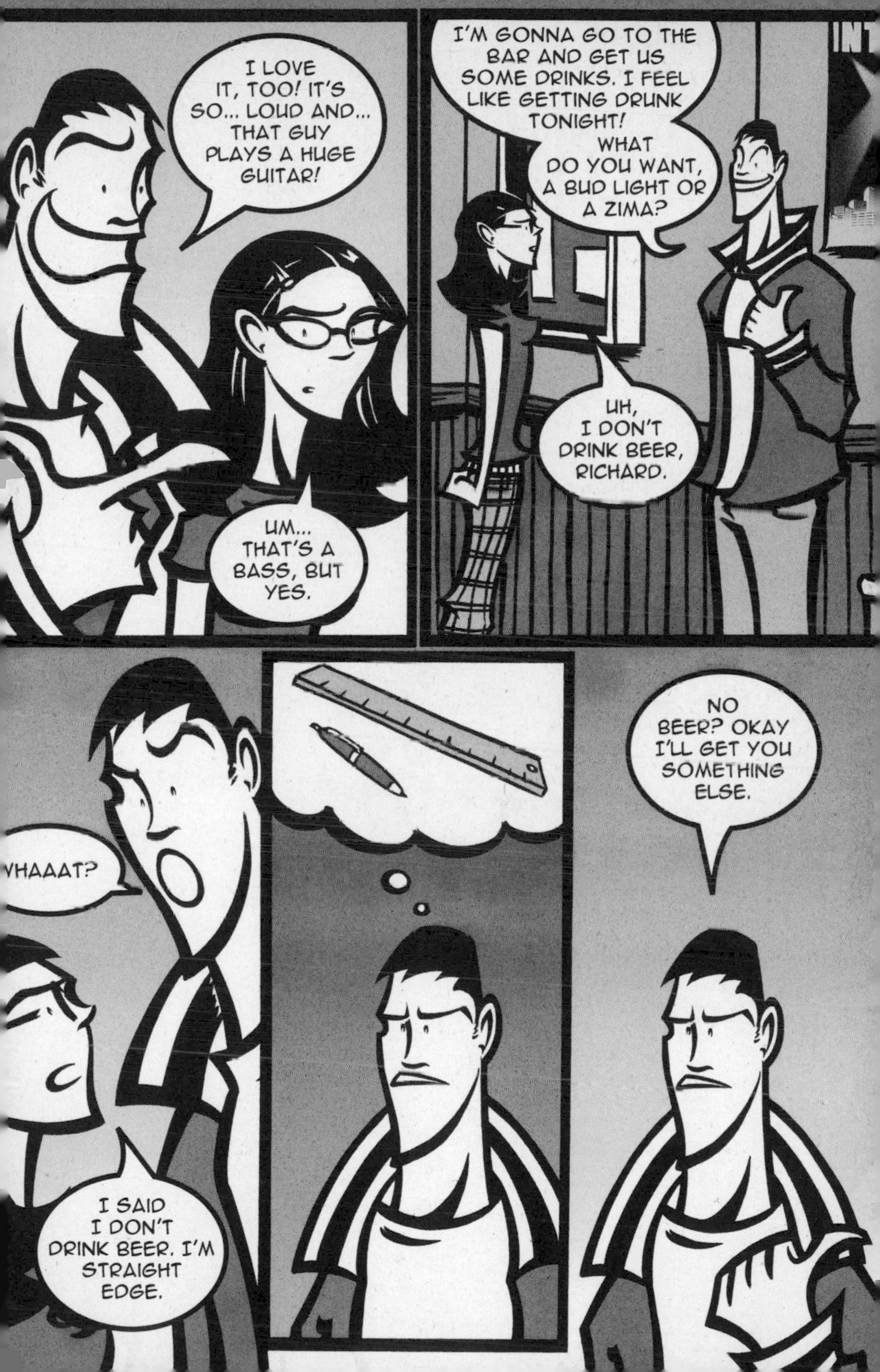
I LOVE IT, TOO! IT'S SO... LOUD AND... THAT GUY PLAYS A HUGE GUITAR!
UM... THAT'S A BASS, BUT YES.
I'M GONNA GO TO THE BAR AND GET US SOME DRINKS. I FEEL LIKE GETTING DRUNK TONIGHT!
WHAT DO YOU WANT, A BUD LIGHT OR A ZIMA?
UH, I DON'T DRINK BEER, RICHARD.
WHAAAT?
I SAID I DON'T DRINK BEER. I'M STRAIGHT EDGE.
NO BEER? OKAY I'LL GET YOU SOMETHING ELSE.

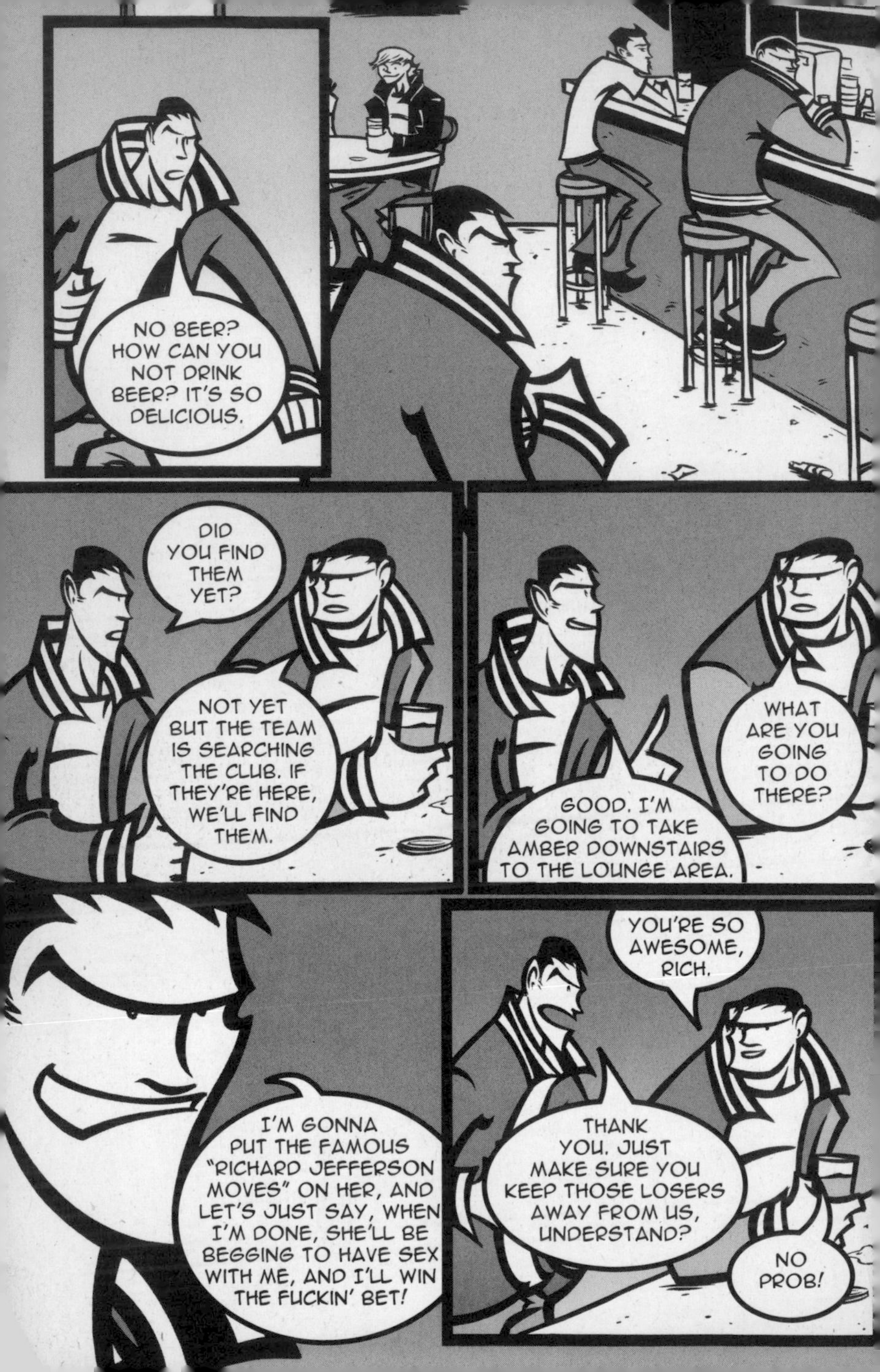
NO BEER? HOW CAN YOU NOT DRINK BEER? IT'S SO DELICIOUS.
DID YOU FIND THEM YET?
NOT YET BUT THE TEAM IS SEARCHING THE CLUB. IF THEY'RE HERE, WE'LL FIND THEM.
GOOD. I'M GOING TO TAKE AMBER DOWNSTAIRS TO THE LOUNGE AREA.
WHAT ARE YOU GOING TO DO THERE?
I'M GONNA PUT THE FAMOUS "RICHARD JEFFERSON MOVES" ON HER, AND LET'S JUST SAY, WHEN I'M DONE, SHE'LL BE BEGGING TO HAVE SEX WITH ME, AND I'LL WIN THE FUCKIN' BET!
YOU'RE SO AWESOME, RICH.
THANK YOU. JUST MAKE SURE YOU KEEP THOSE LOSERS AWAY FROM US, UNDERSTAND?
NO PROB!

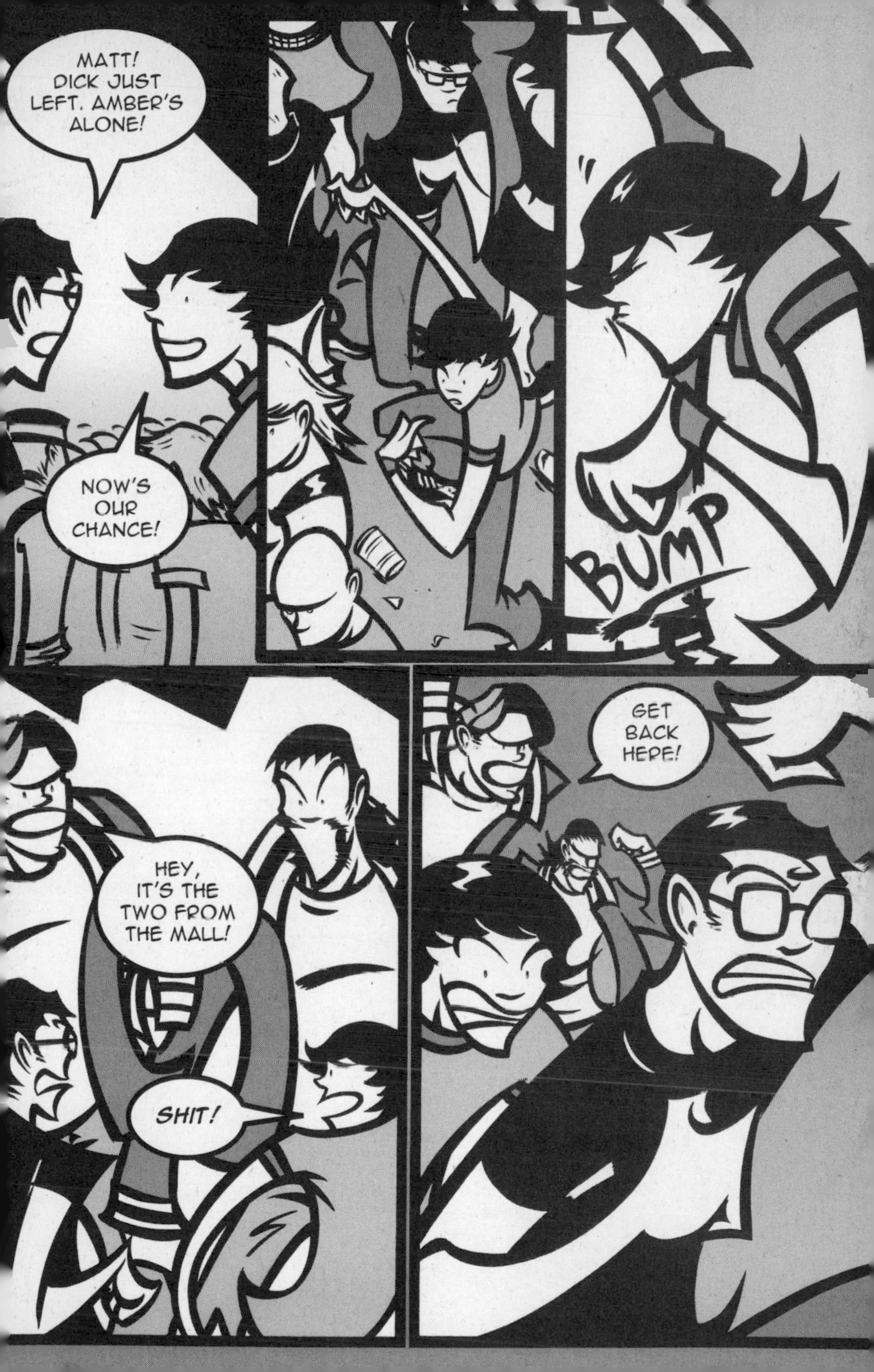
MATT! DICK JUST LEFT. AMBER'S ALONE!
NOW'S OUR CHANCE!
BUMP
HEY, IT'S THE TWO FROM THE MALL!
SHIT!
GET BACK HERE!

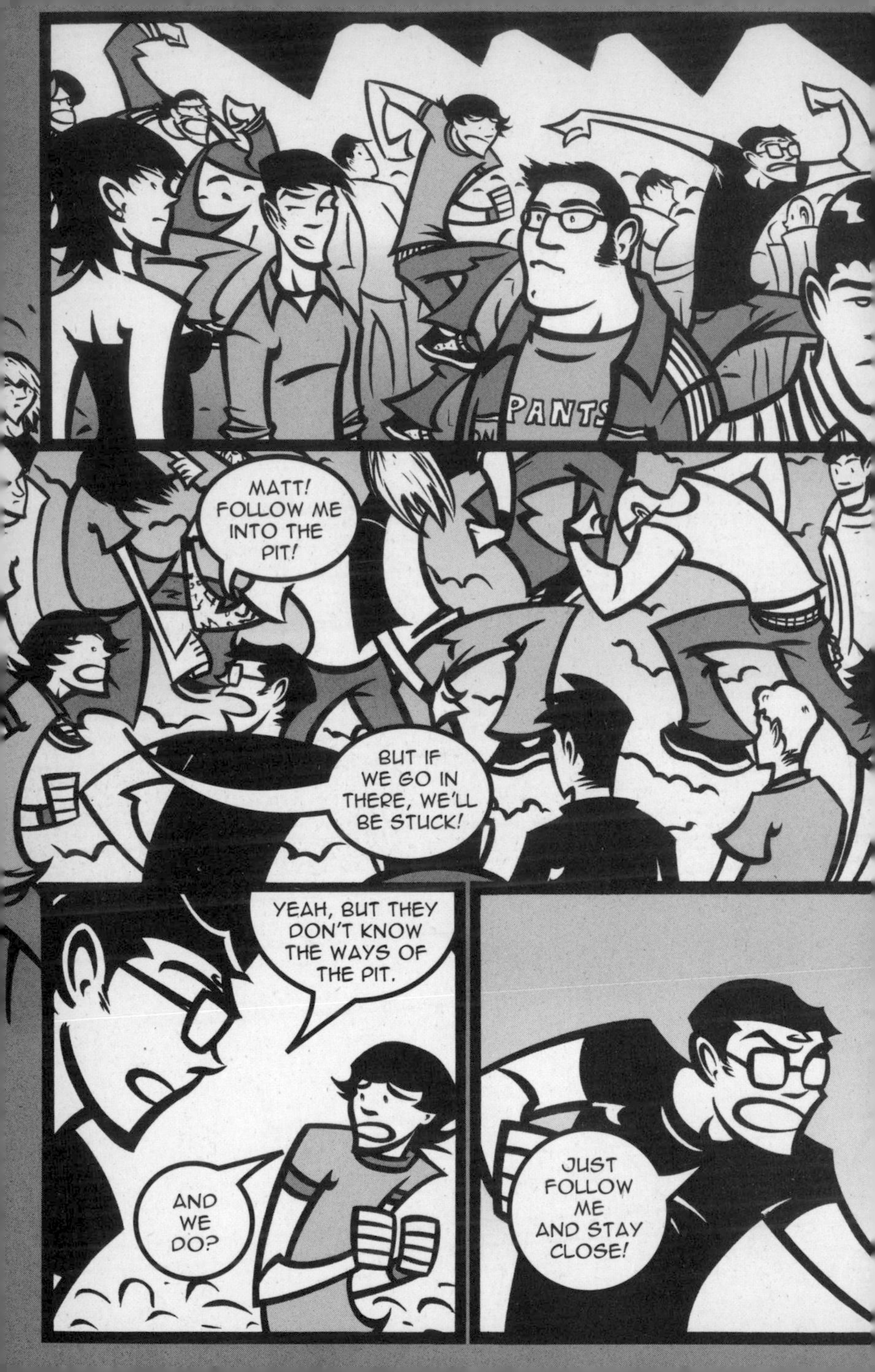
PANTS
MATT! FOLLOW ME INTO THE PIT!
BUT IF WE GO IN THERE, WE'LL BE STUCK!
YEAH, BUT THEY DON'T KNOW THE WAYS OF THE PIT.
AND WE DO?
JUST FOLLOW ME AND STAY CLOSE!

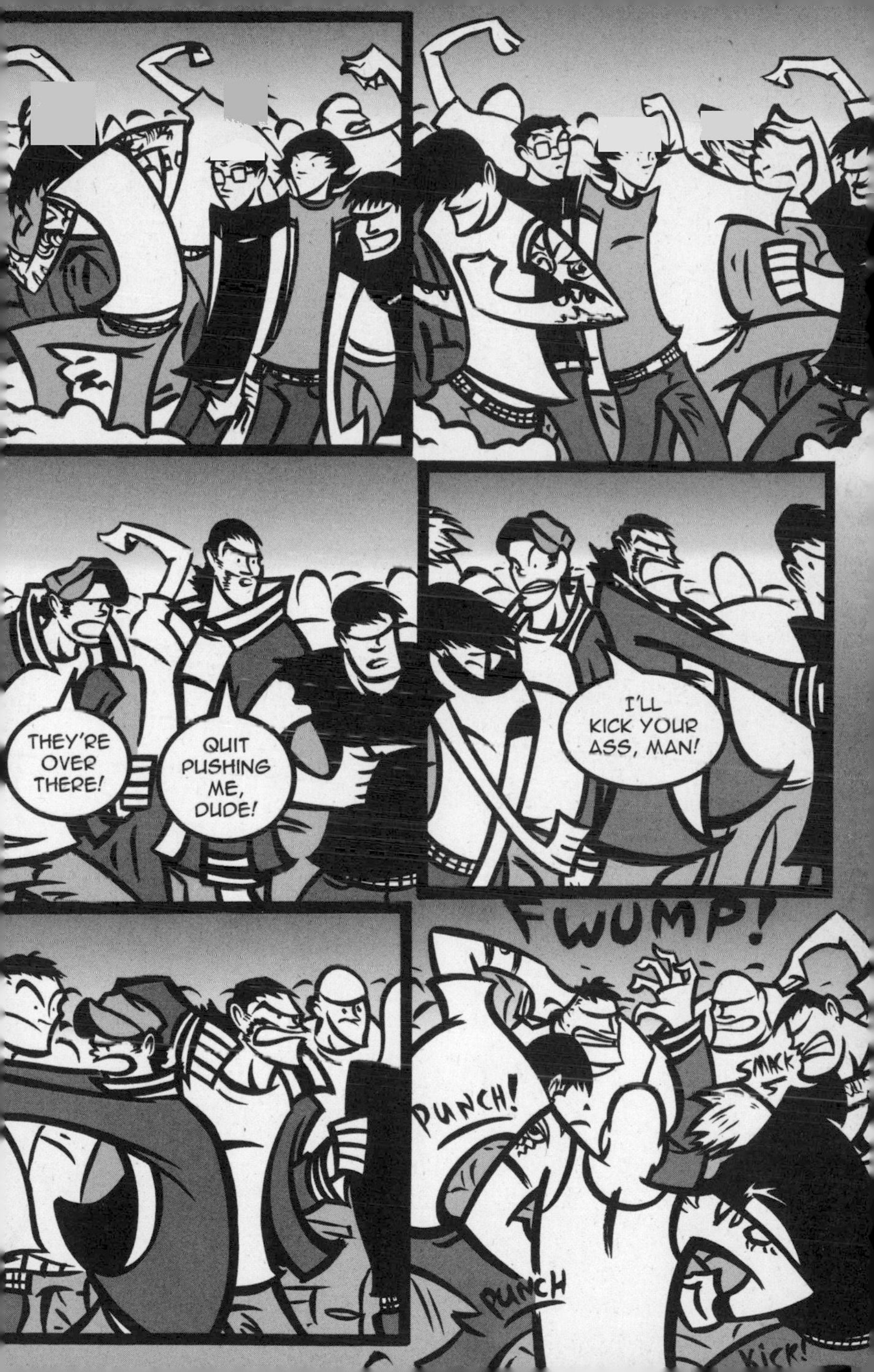
THEY'RE OVER THERE!
QUIT PUSHING ME, DUDE!
I'LL KICK YOUR ASS, MAN!
FWUMP!
PUNCH!
SMACK
PUNCH
KICK!

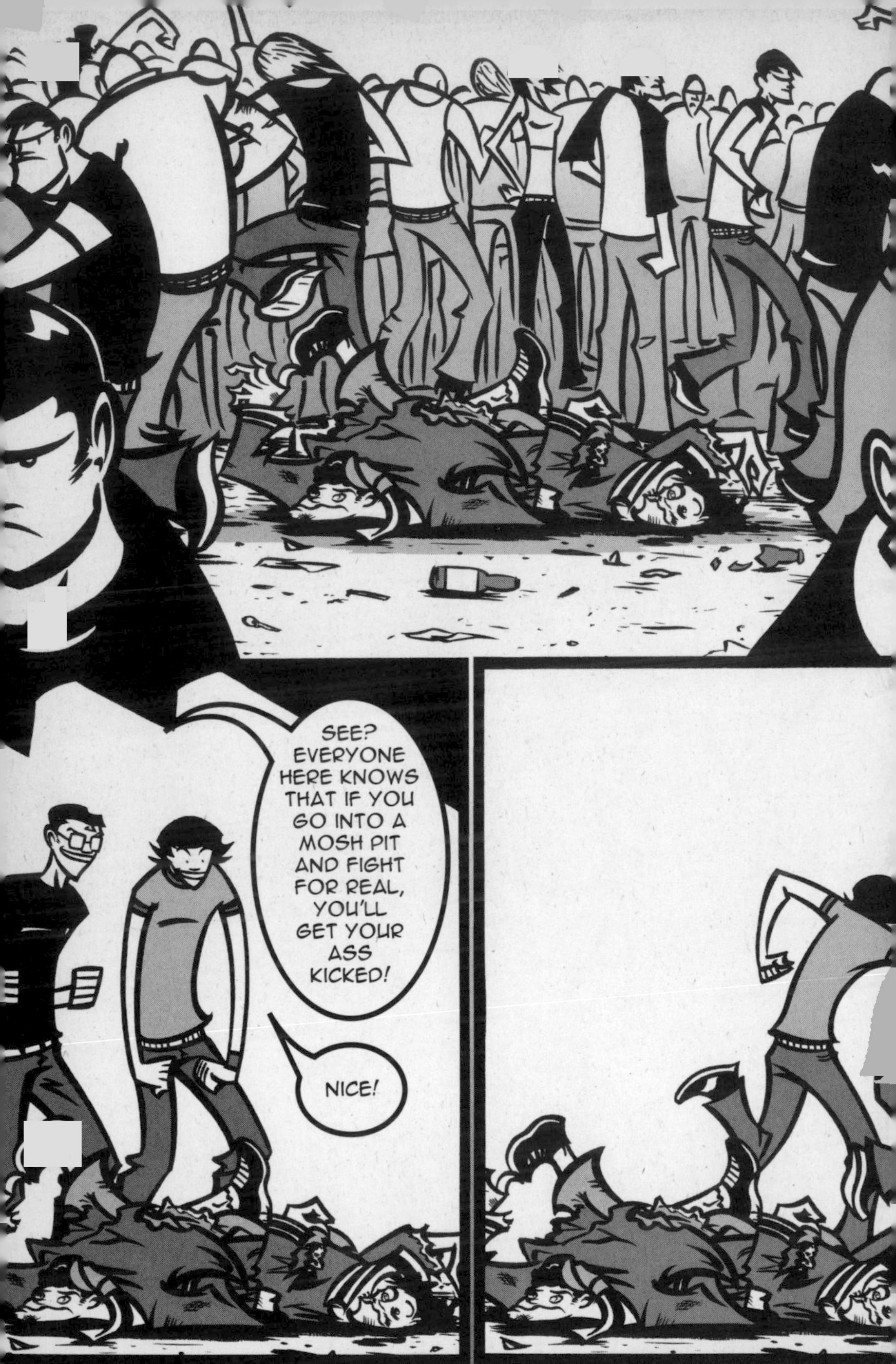
SEE? EVERYONE HERE KNOWS THAT IF YOU GO INTO A MOSH PIT AND FIGHT FOR REAL, YOU'LL GET YOUR ASS KICKED!
NICE!

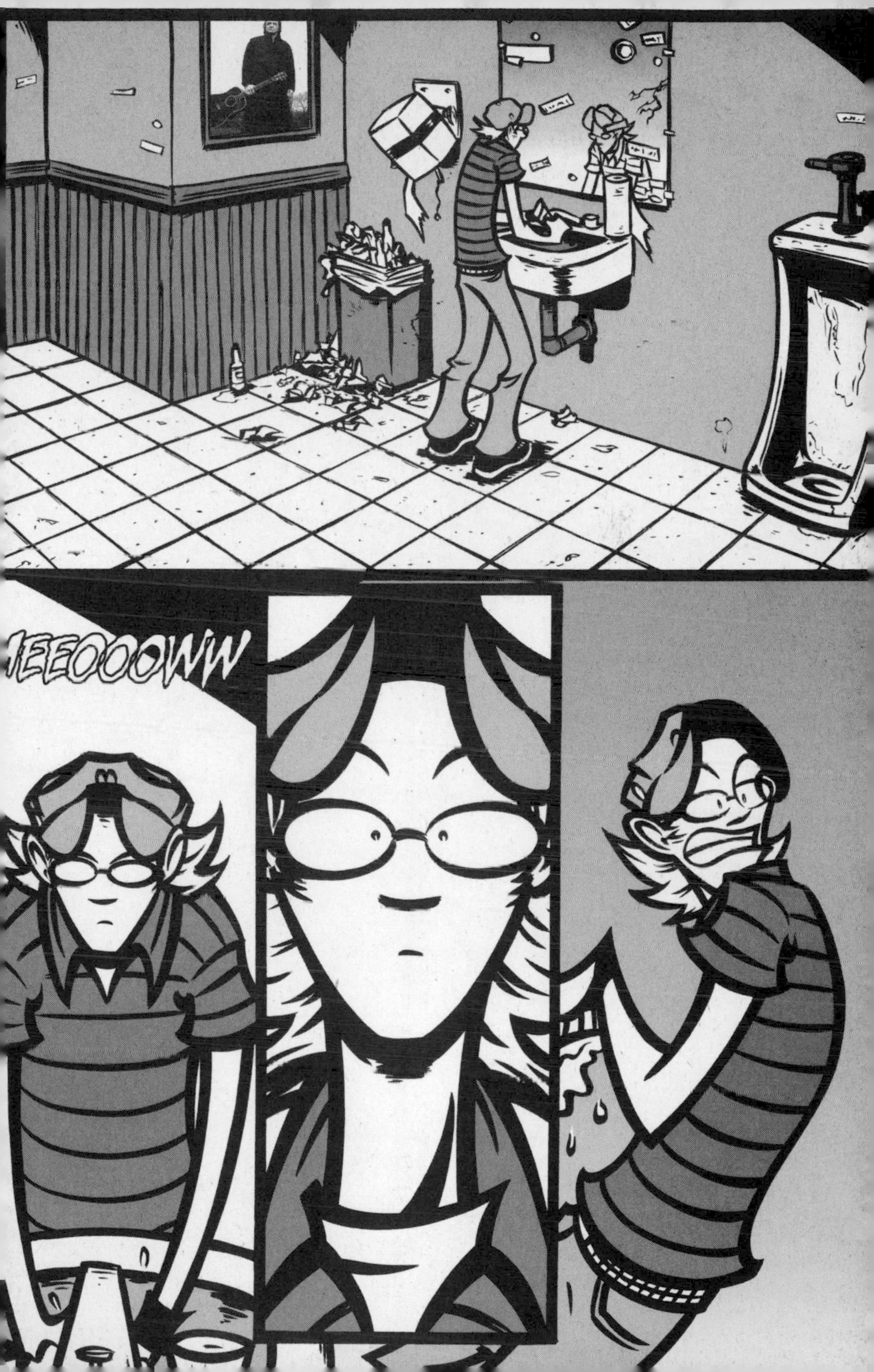
EEEOOOOWW

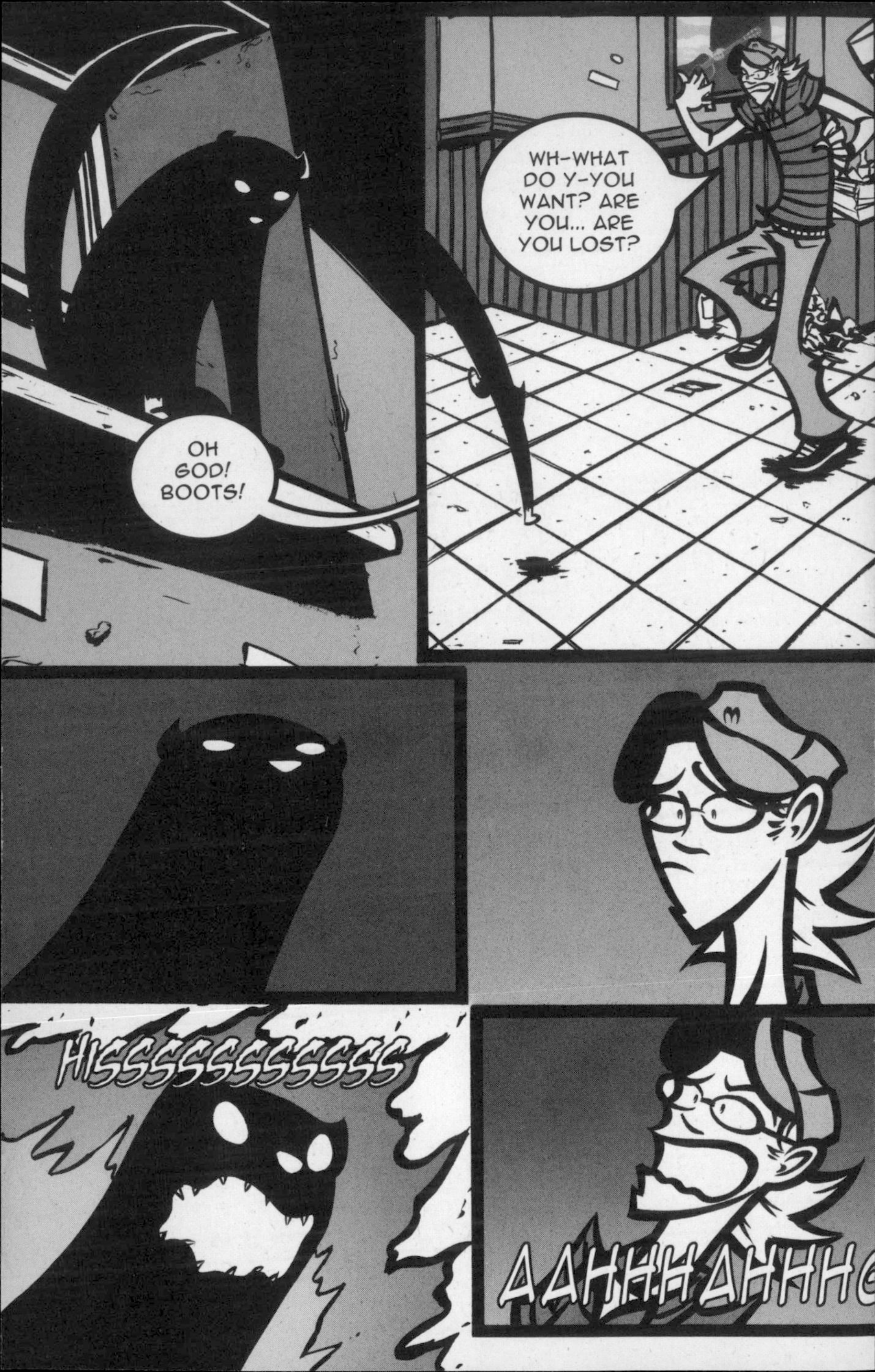
WH-WHAT DO Y-YOU WANT? ARE YOU... ARE YOU LOST?
OH GOD! BOOTS!
HISSSSSSSSSSSS
AAHHHAHHHG

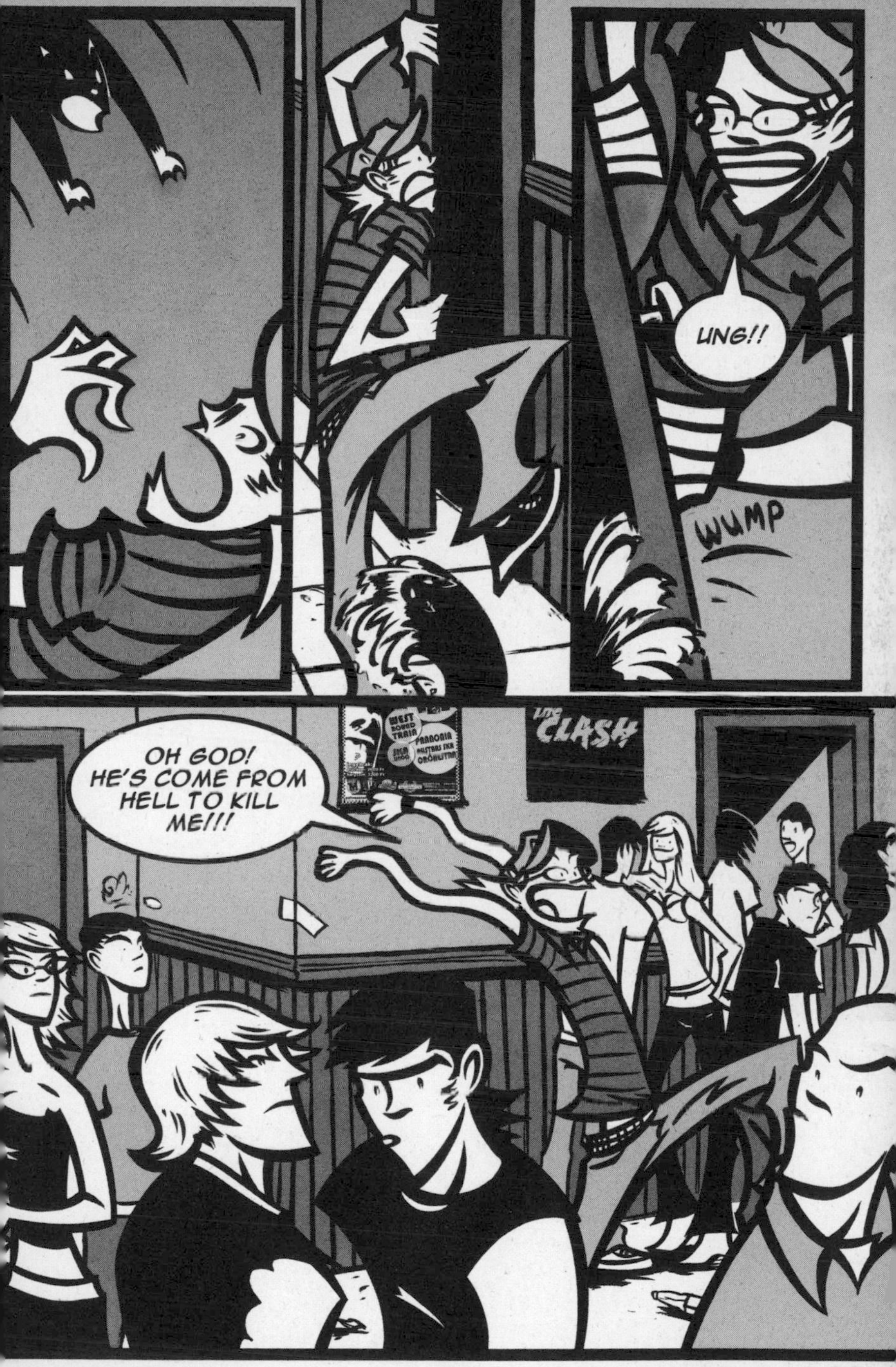
UNG!!
WUMP
OH GOD! HE'S COME FROM HELL TO KILL ME!!!
CLASH

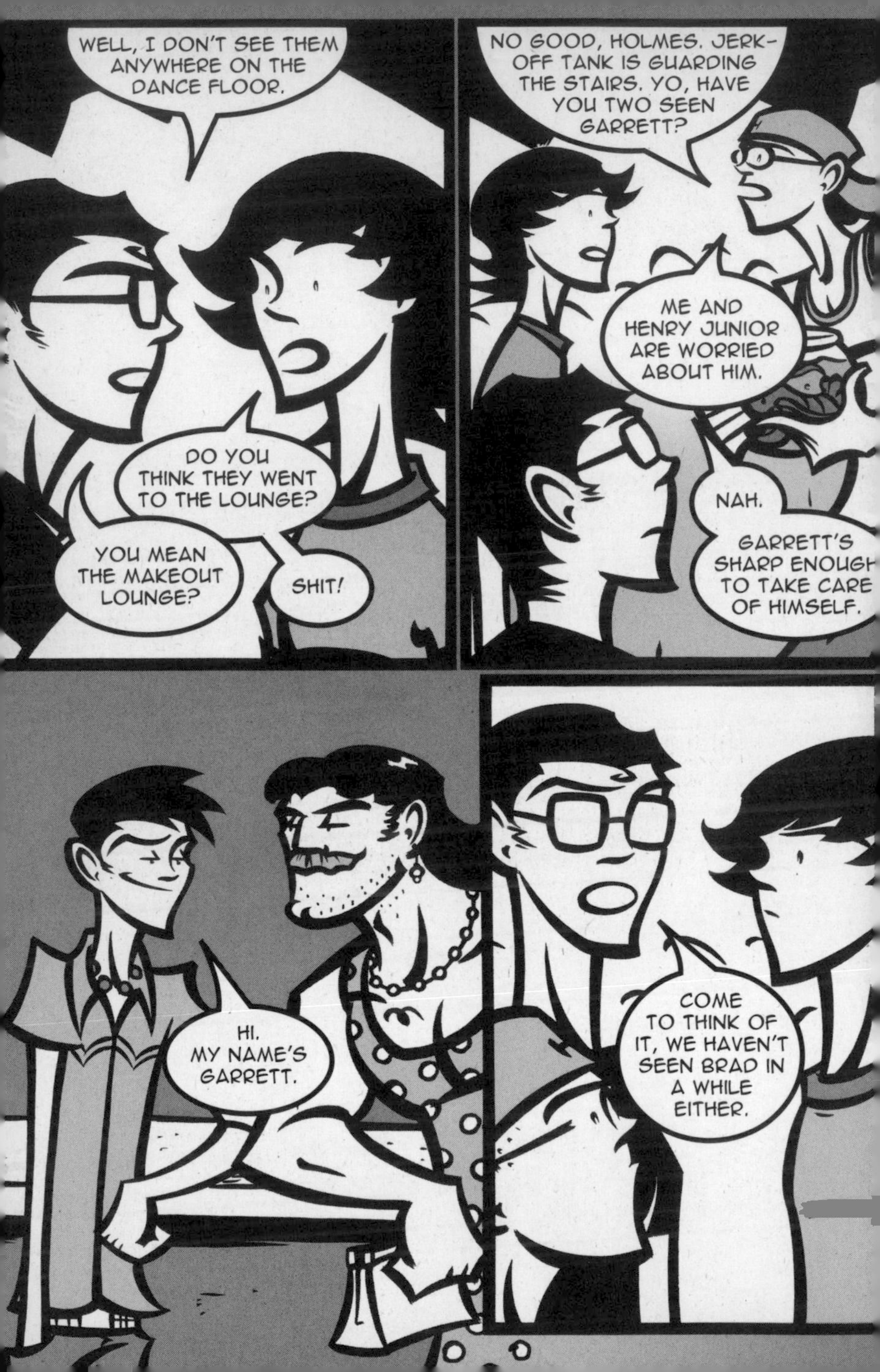
WELL, I DON'T SEE THEM ANYWHERE ON THE DANCE FLOOR.
DO YOU THINK THEY WENT TO THE LOUNGE?
YOU MEAN THE MAKEOUT LOUNGE?
SHIT!
NO GOOD, HOLMES. JERK-OFF TANK IS GUARDING THE STAIRS. YO, HAVE YOU TWO SEEN GARRETT?
ME AND HENRY JUNIOR ARE WORRIED ABOUT HIM.
NAH.
GARRETT'S SHARP ENOUGH TO TAKE CARE OF HIMSELF.
HI. MY NAME'S GARRETT.
COME TO THINK OF IT, WE HAVEN'T SEEN BRAD IN A WHILE EITHER.

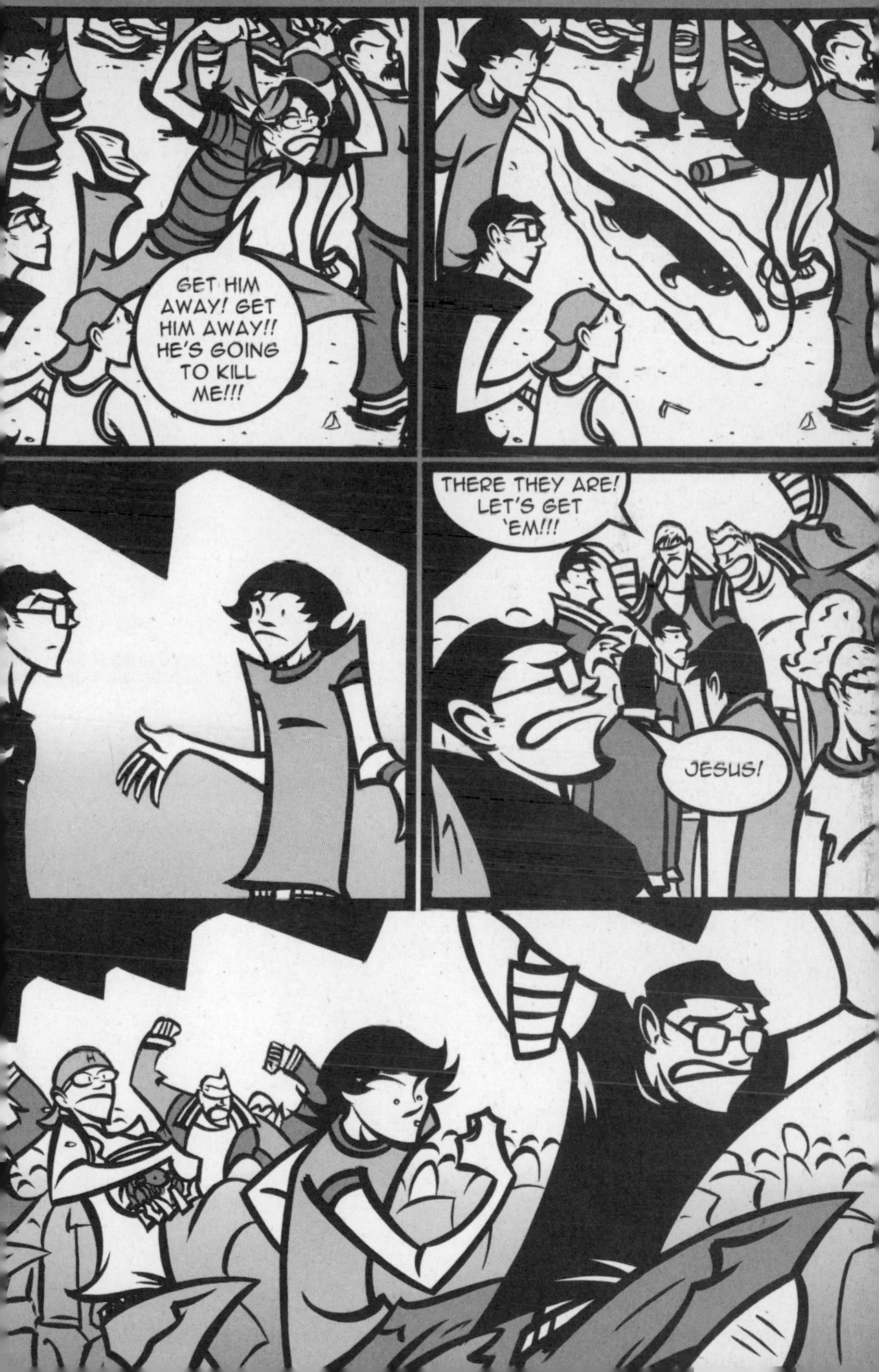
GET HIM AWAY! GET HIM AWAY!! HE'S GOING TO KILL ME!!!
THERE THEY ARE! LET'S GET 'EM!!!
JESUS!

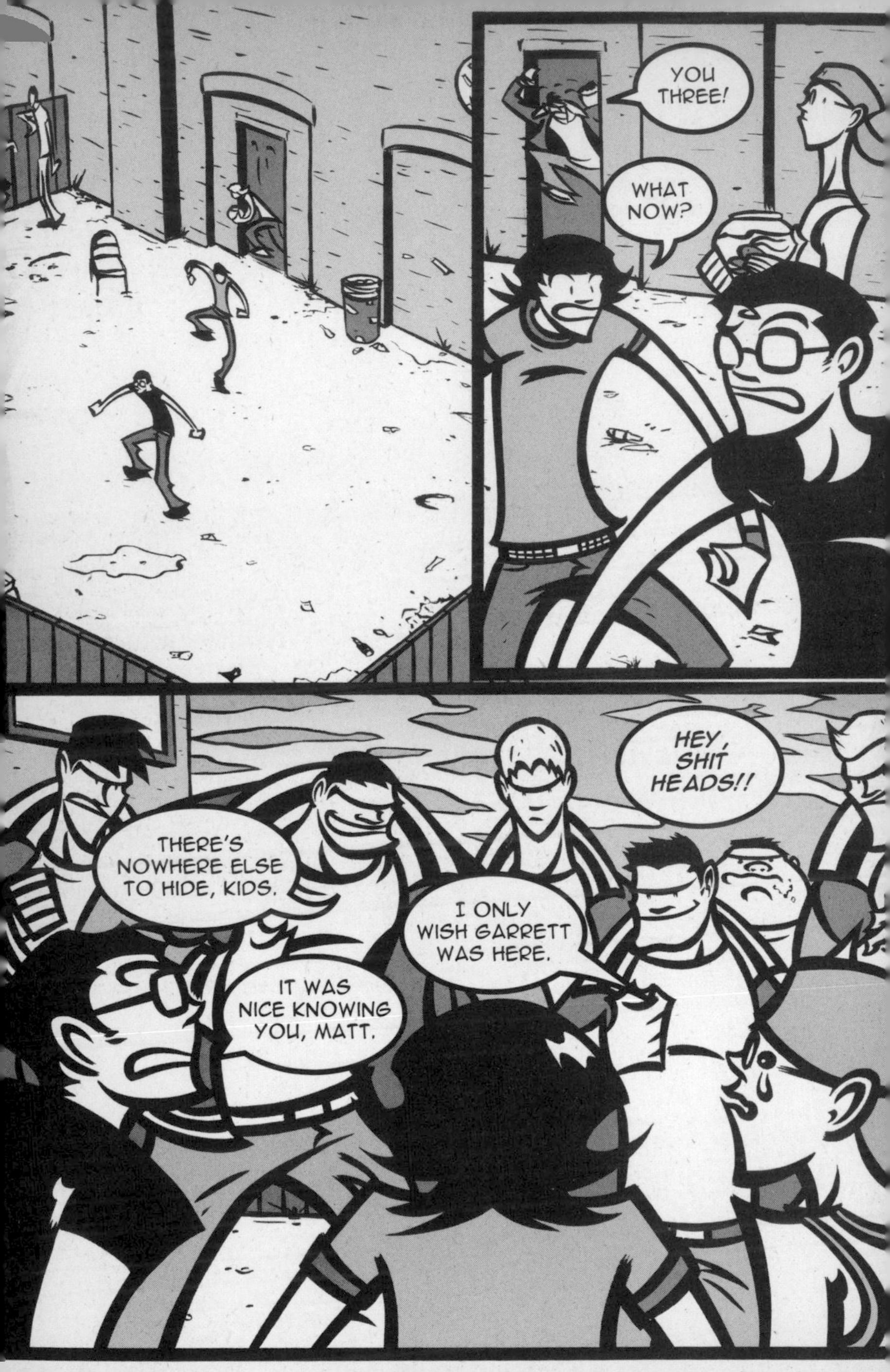
YOU THREE!
WHAT NOW?
HEY, SHIT HEADS!!
THERE'S NOWHERE ELSE TO HIDE, KIDS.
I ONLY WISH GARRETT WAS HERE.
IT WAS NICE KNOWING YOU, MATT.

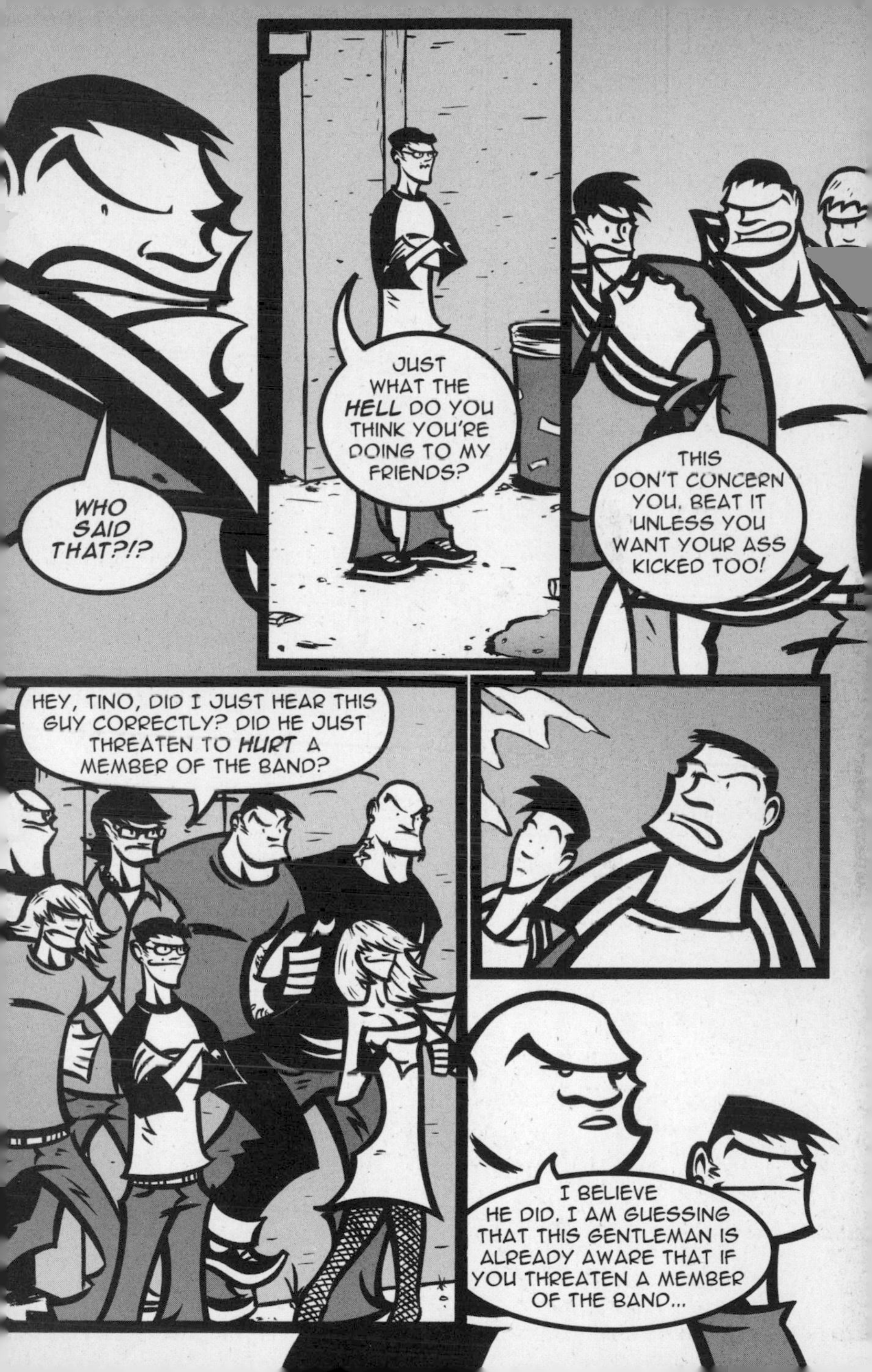
WHO SAID THAT?!?
JUST WHAT THE HELL DO YOU THINK YOU'RE DOING TO MY FRIENDS?
THIS DON'T CONCERN YOU. BEAT IT UNLESS YOU WANT YOUR ASS KICKED TOO!
HEY, TINO, DID I JUST HEAR THIS GUY CORRECTLY? DID HE JUST THREATEN TO HURT A MEMBER OF THE BAND?
I BELIEVE HE DID. I AM GUESSING THAT THIS GENTLEMAN IS ALREADY AWARE THAT IF YOU THREATEN A MEMBER OF THE BAND...

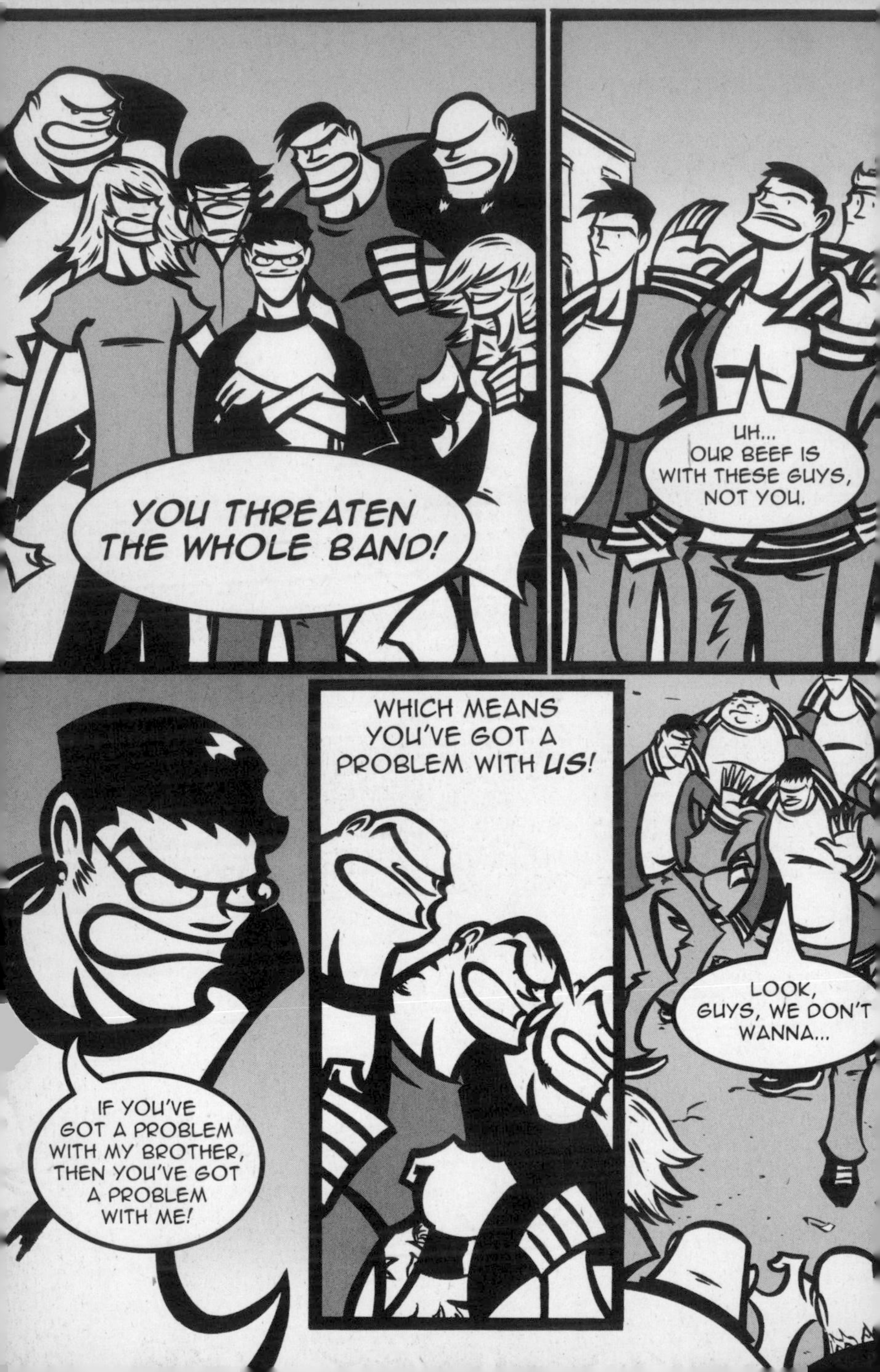
YOU THREATEN THE WHOLE BAND!
UH... OUR BEEF IS WITH THESE GUYS, NOT YOU.
IF YOU'VE GOT A PROBLEM WITH MY BROTHER, THEN YOU'VE GOT A PROBLEM WITH ME!
WHICH MEANS YOU'VE GOT A PROBLEM WITH *US*!
LOOK, GUYS, WE DON'T WANNA...

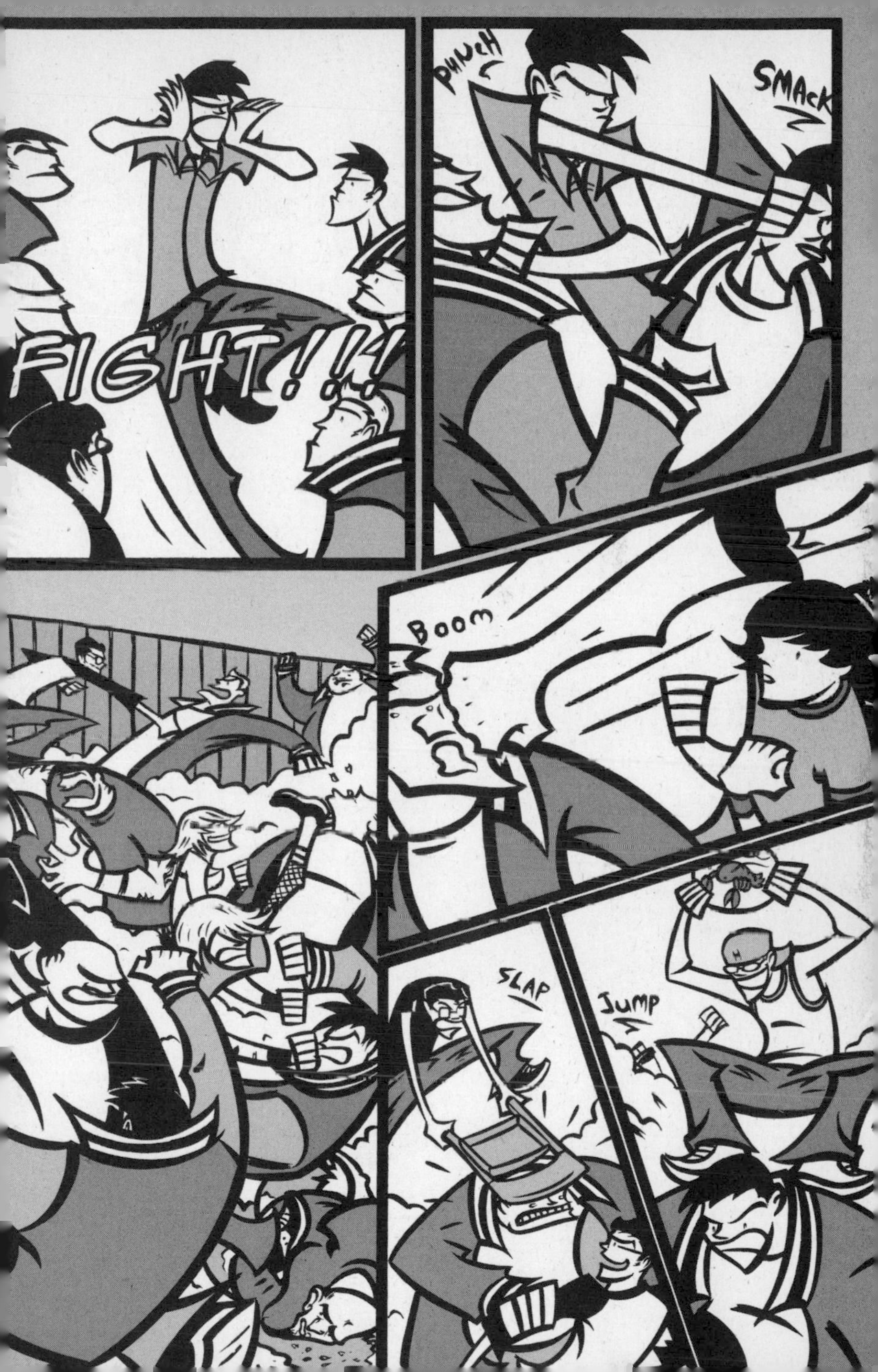
FIGHT!!!
PUNCH
SMACK
Boom
SLAP
JUMP

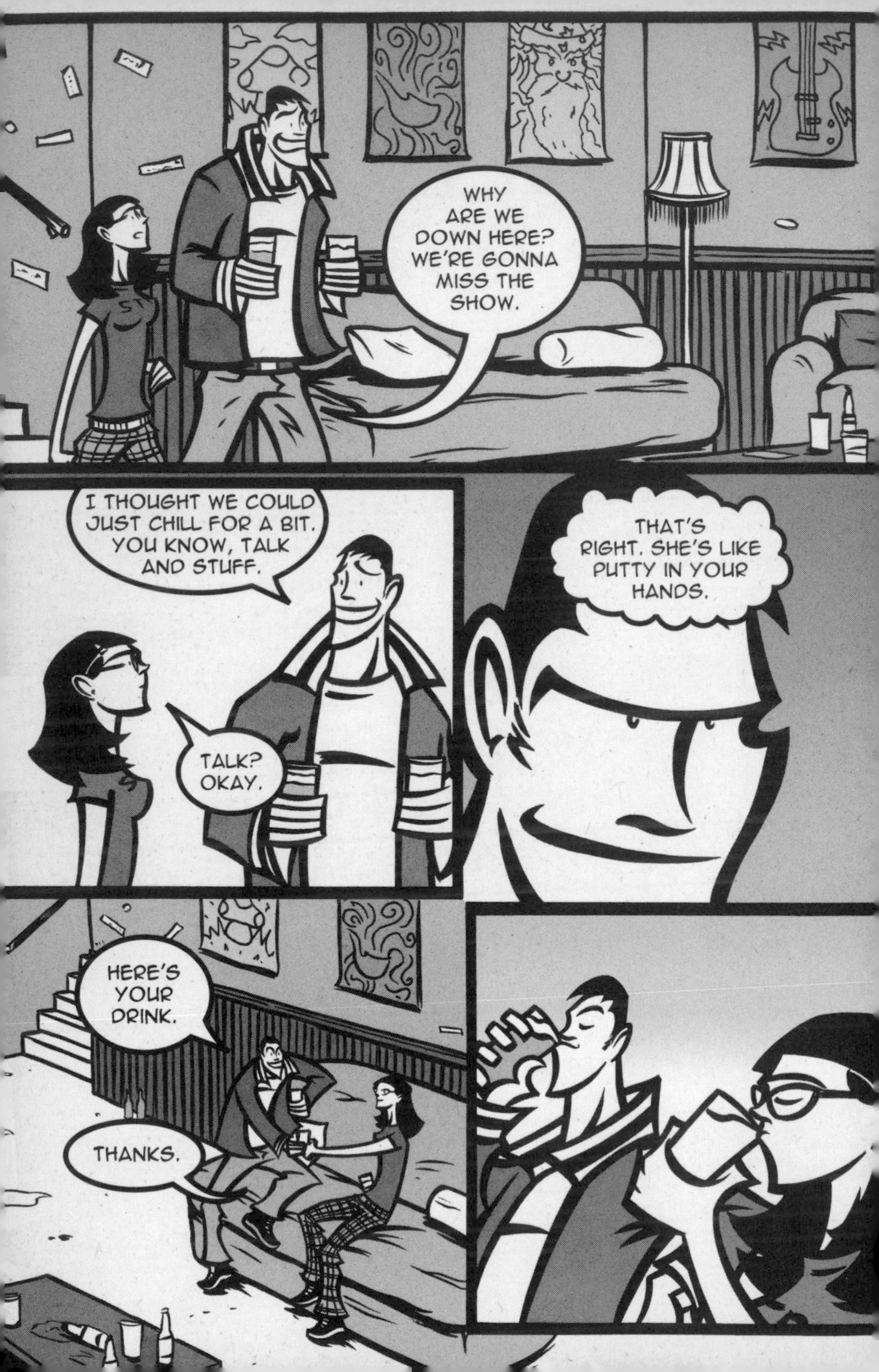
WHY ARE WE DOWN HERE? WE'RE GONNA MISS THE SHOW.
I THOUGHT WE COULD JUST CHILL FOR A BIT. YOU KNOW, TALK AND STUFF.
TALK? OKAY.
THAT'S RIGHT. SHE'S LIKE PUTTY IN YOUR HANDS.
HERE'S YOUR DRINK.
THANKS.

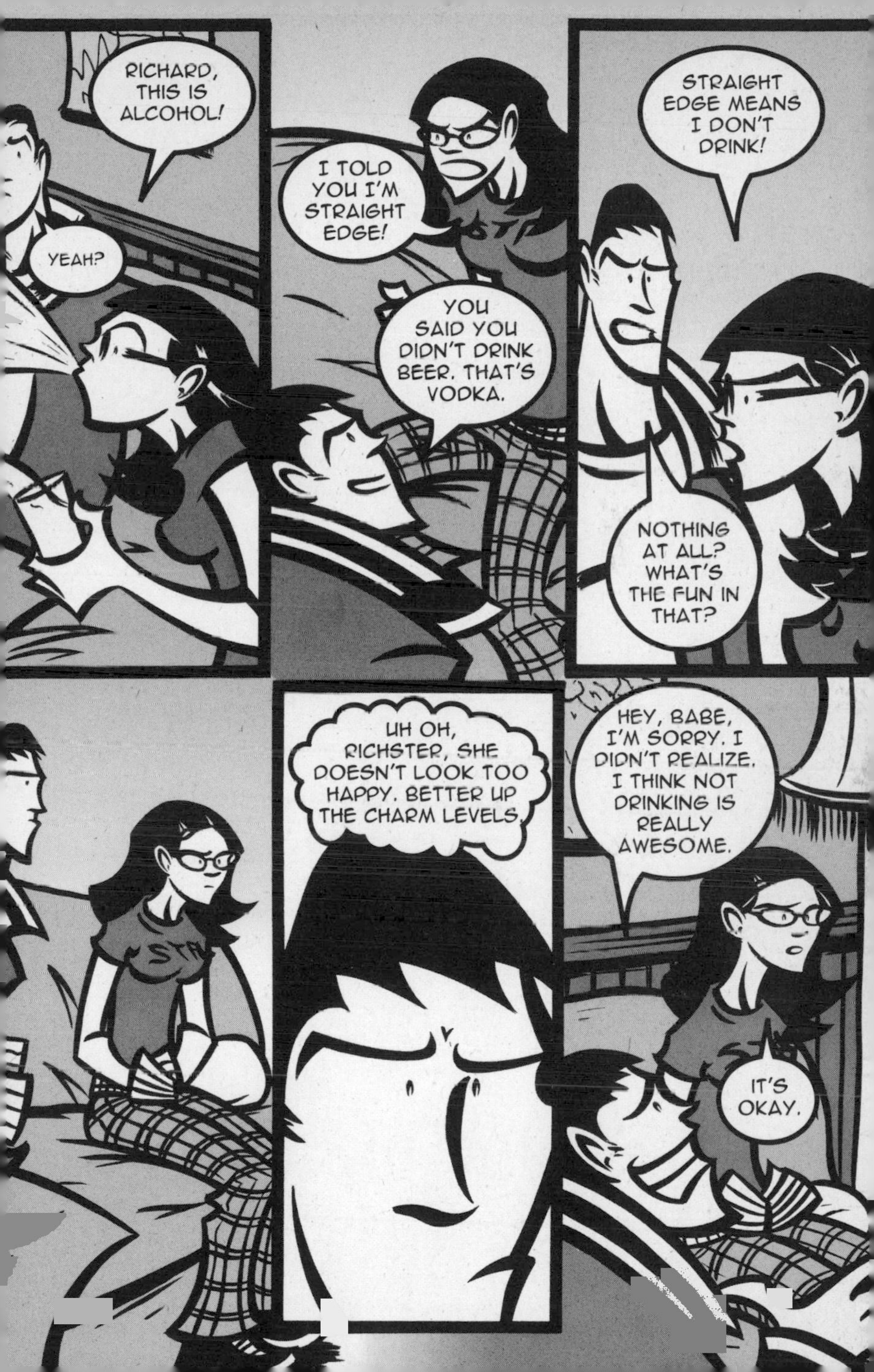
RICHARD, THIS IS ALCOHOL!
YEAH?
I TOLD YOU I'M STRAIGHT EDGE!
YOU SAID YOU DIDN'T DRINK BEER. THAT'S VODKA.
STRAIGHT EDGE MEANS I DON'T DRINK!
NOTHING AT ALL? WHAT'S THE FUN IN THAT?
UH OH, RICHSTER, SHE DOESN'T LOOK TOO HAPPY. BETTER UP THE CHARM LEVELS.
HEY, BABE, I'M SORRY. I DIDN'T REALIZE. I THINK NOT DRINKING IS REALLY AWESOME.
IT'S OKAY.

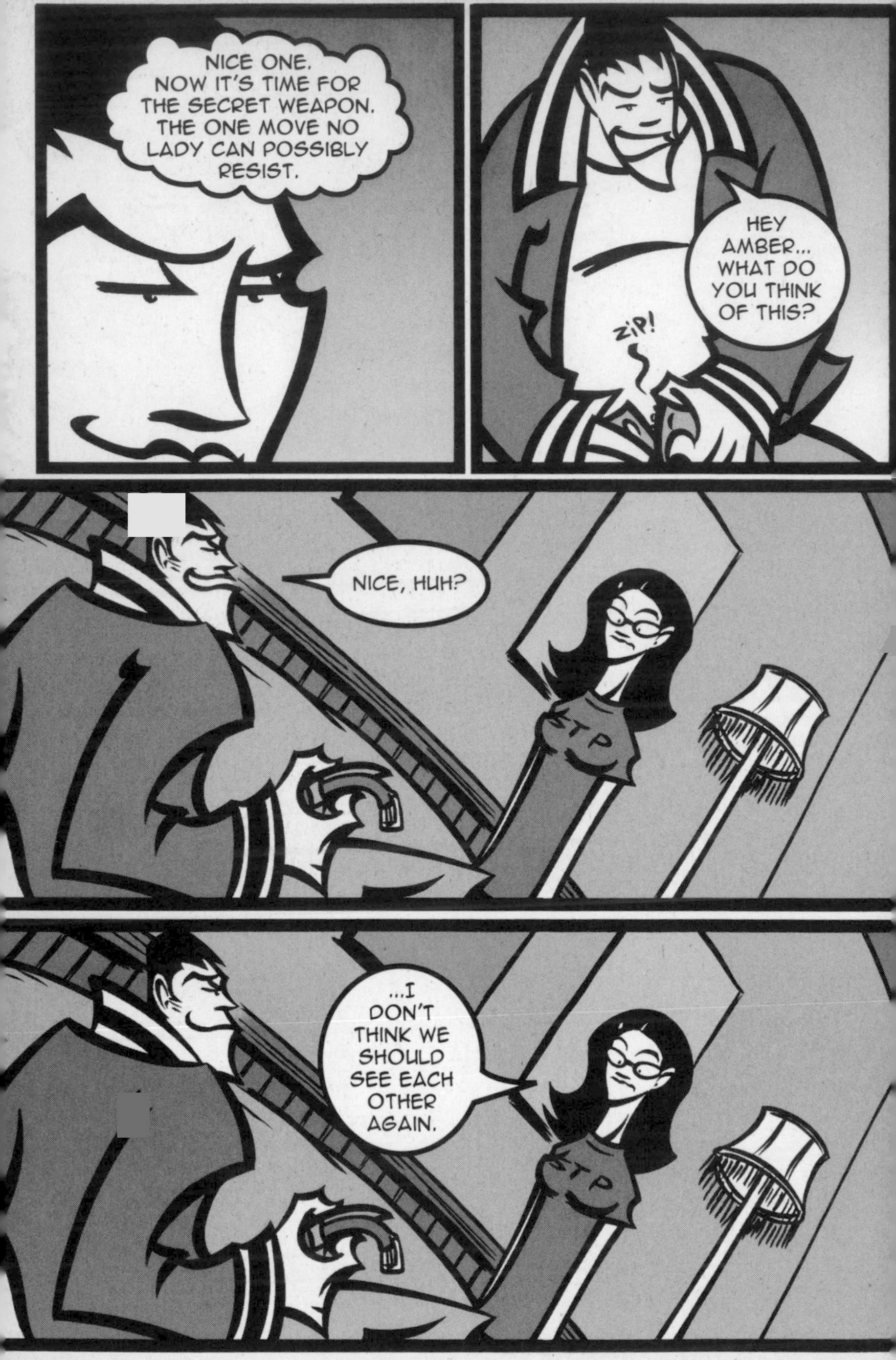
NICE ONE. NOW IT'S TIME FOR THE SECRET WEAPON. THE ONE MOVE NO LADY CAN POSSIBLY RESIST.
HEY AMBER... WHAT DO YOU THINK OF THIS?
ZIP!
NICE, HUH?
...I DON'T THINK WE SHOULD SEE EACH OTHER AGAIN.

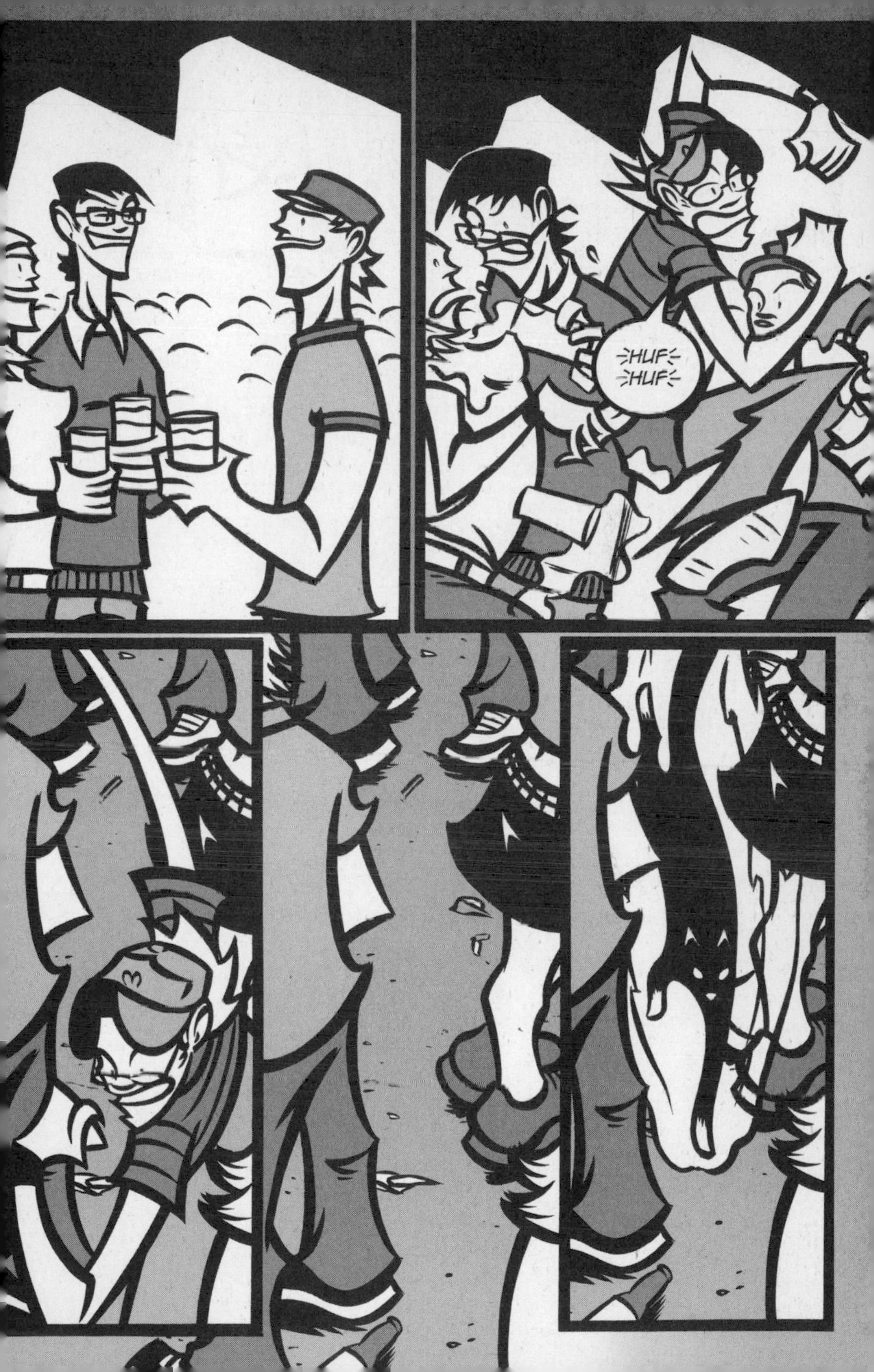
HUF HUF

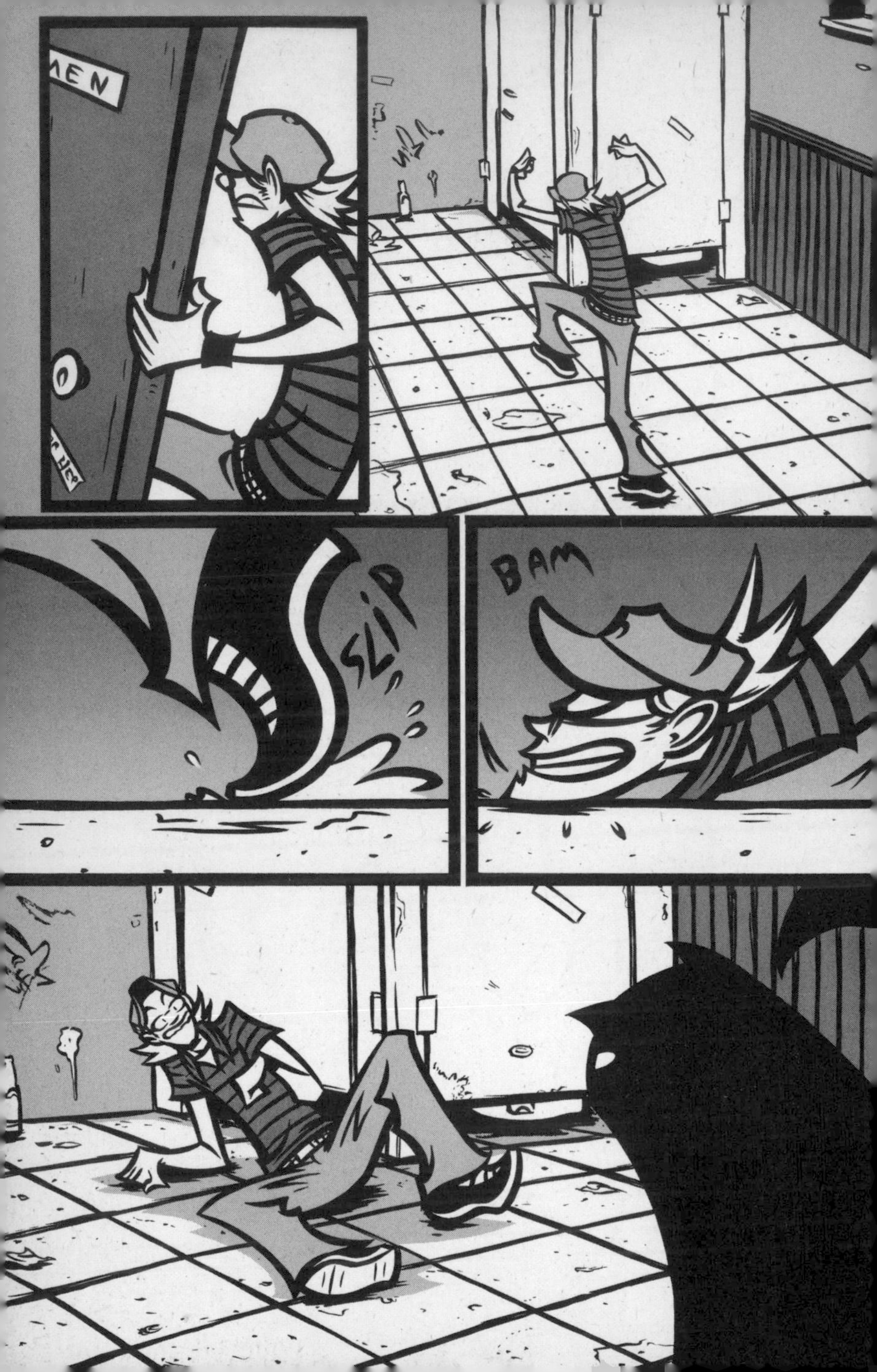
MEN
SLIP
BAM

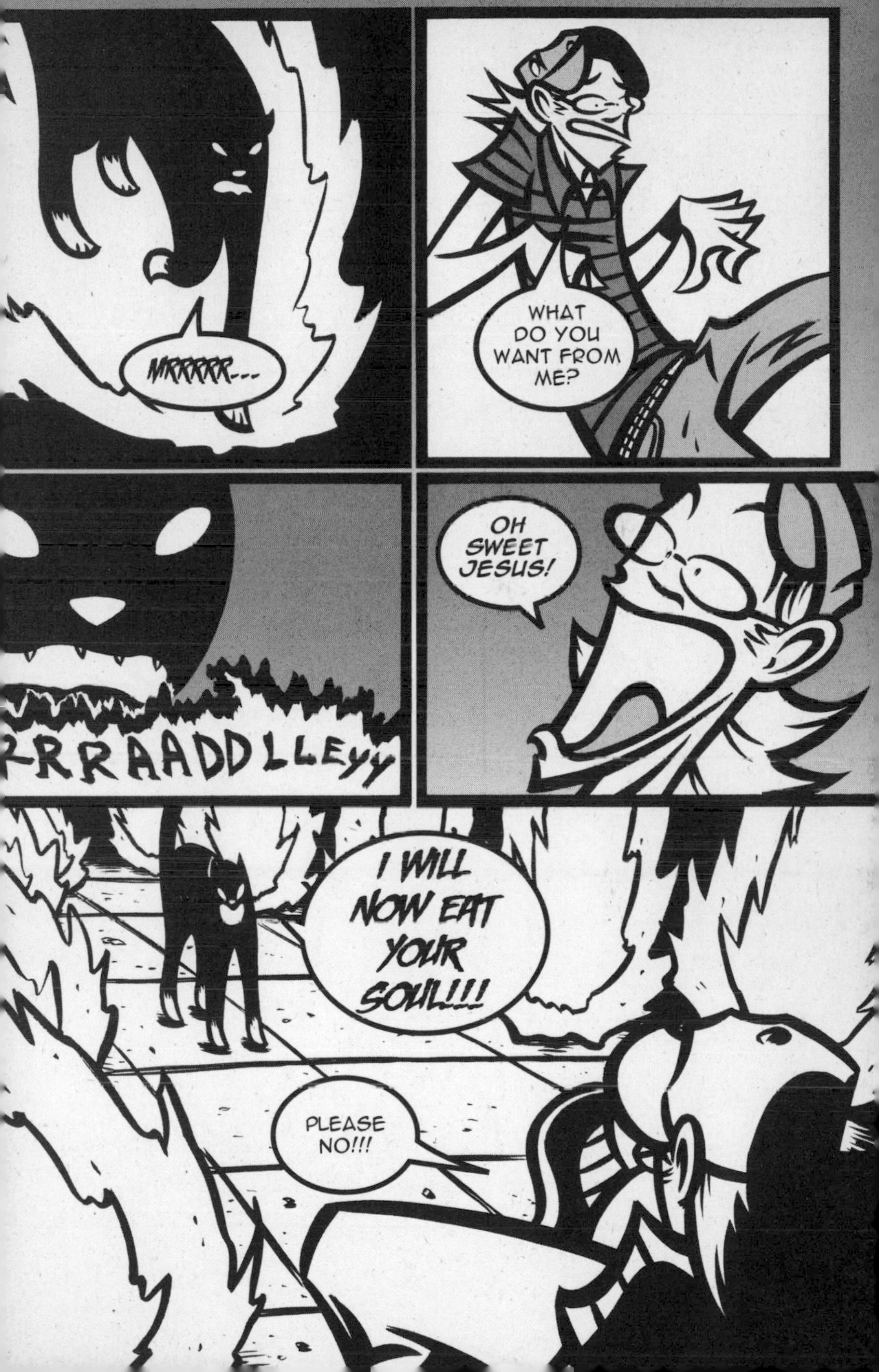
MRRRRR---
WHAT DO YOU WANT FROM ME?
RRRAADDLLEyy
OH SWEET JESUS!
I WILL NOW EAT YOUR SOUL!!!
PLEASE NO!!!

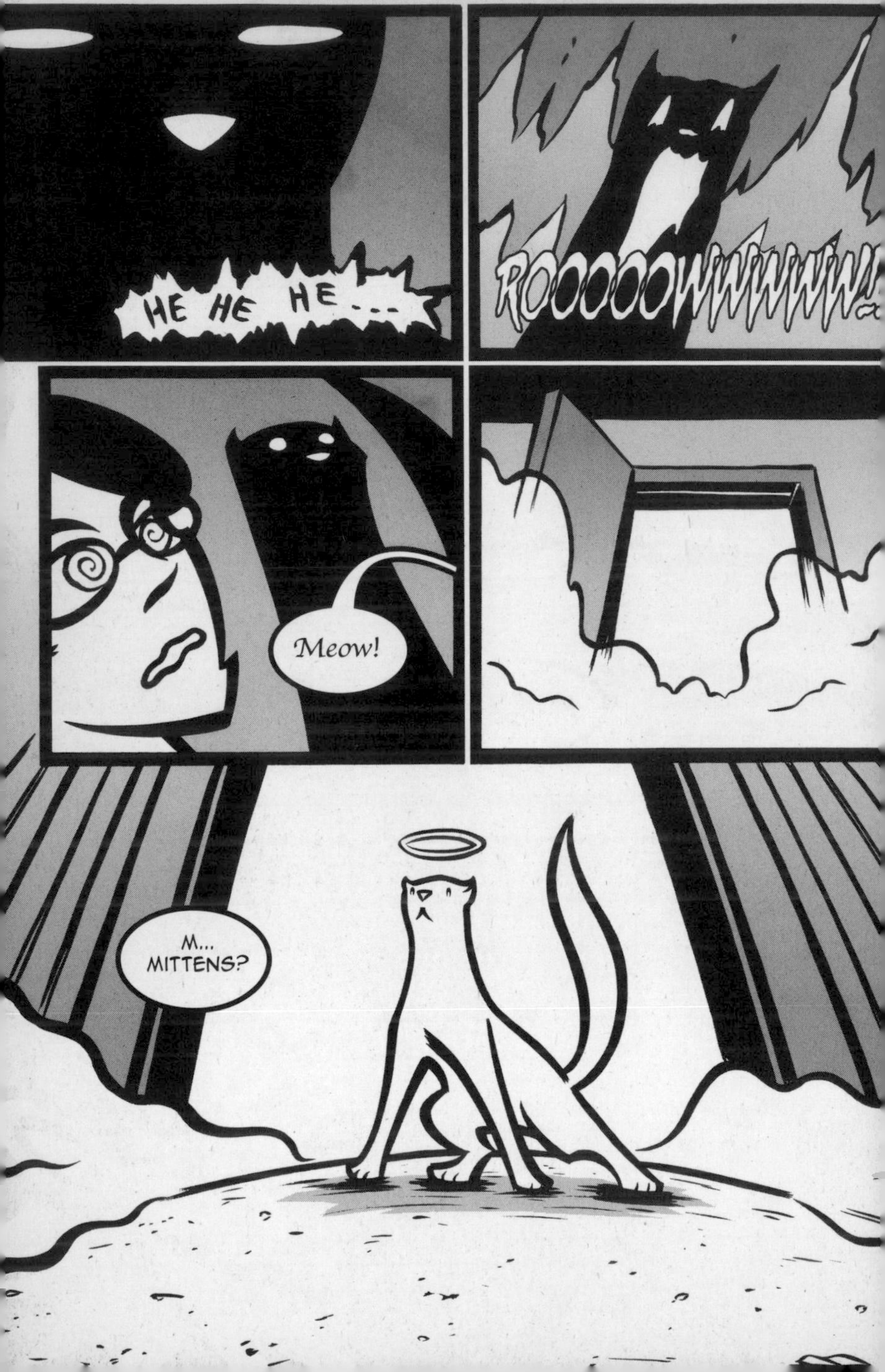
HE HE HE...
ROOOOOOWWWWWW!
Meow!
M...
MITTENS?

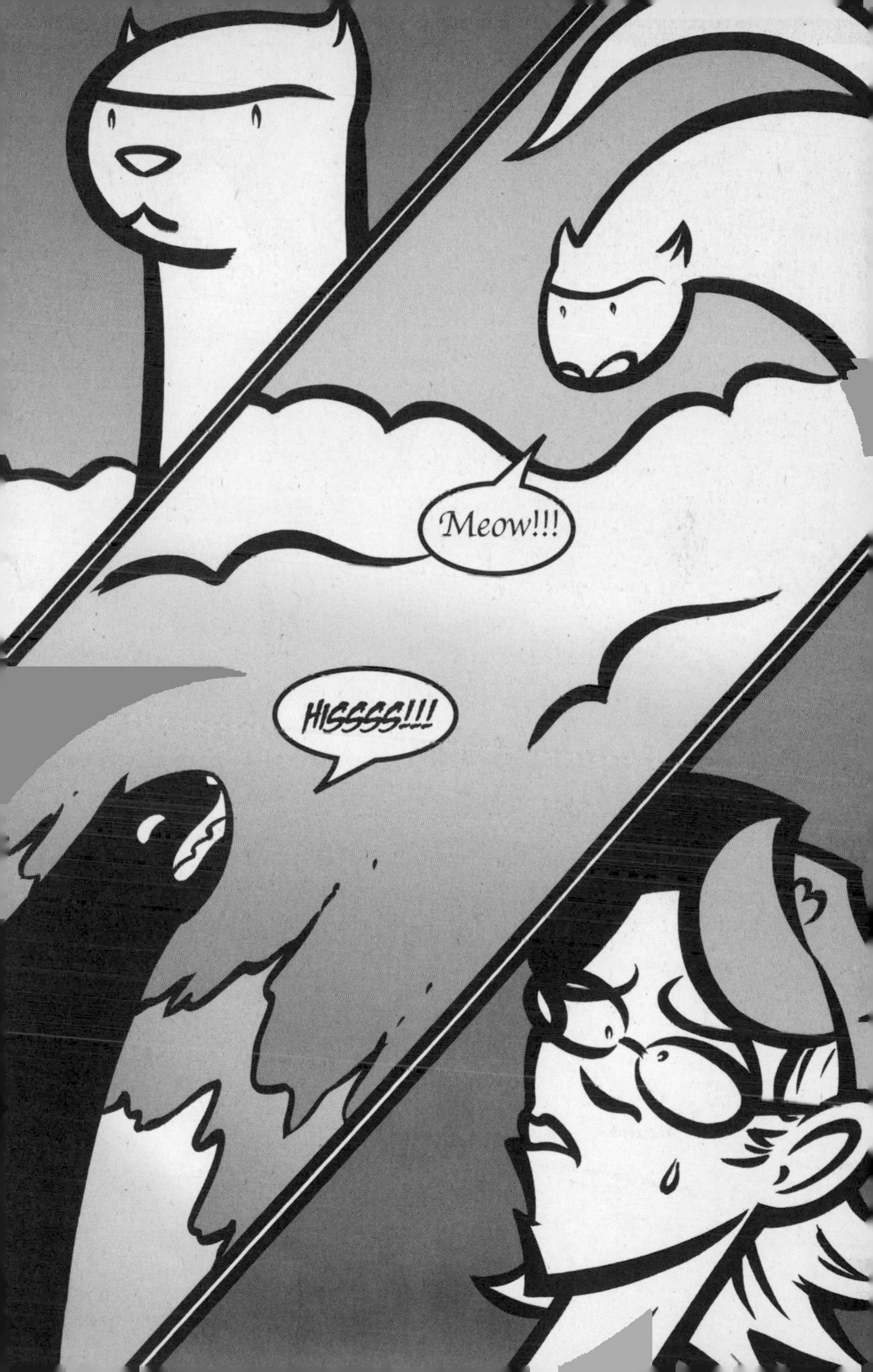
Meow!!!
HISSSS!!!

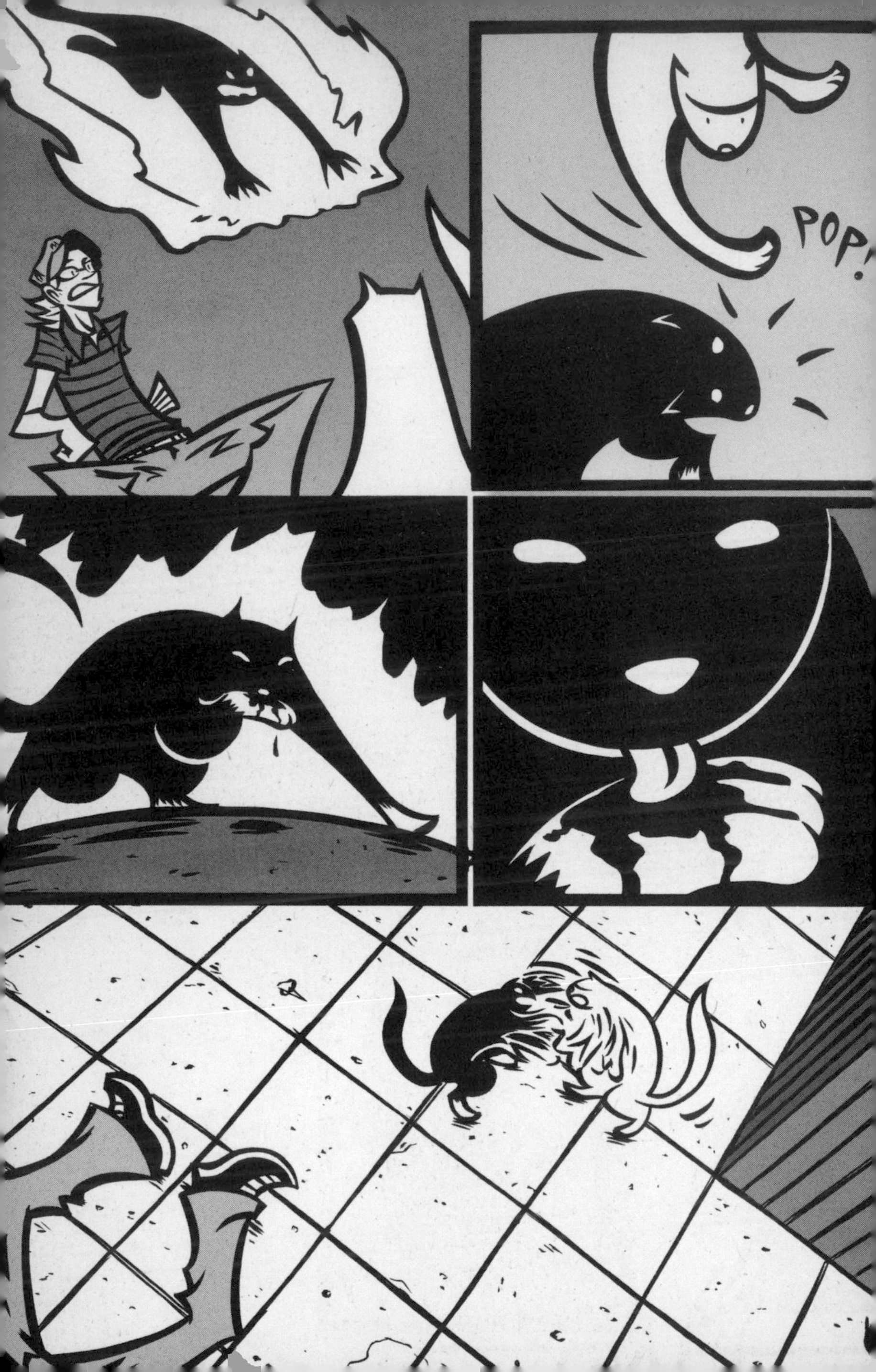
POP!

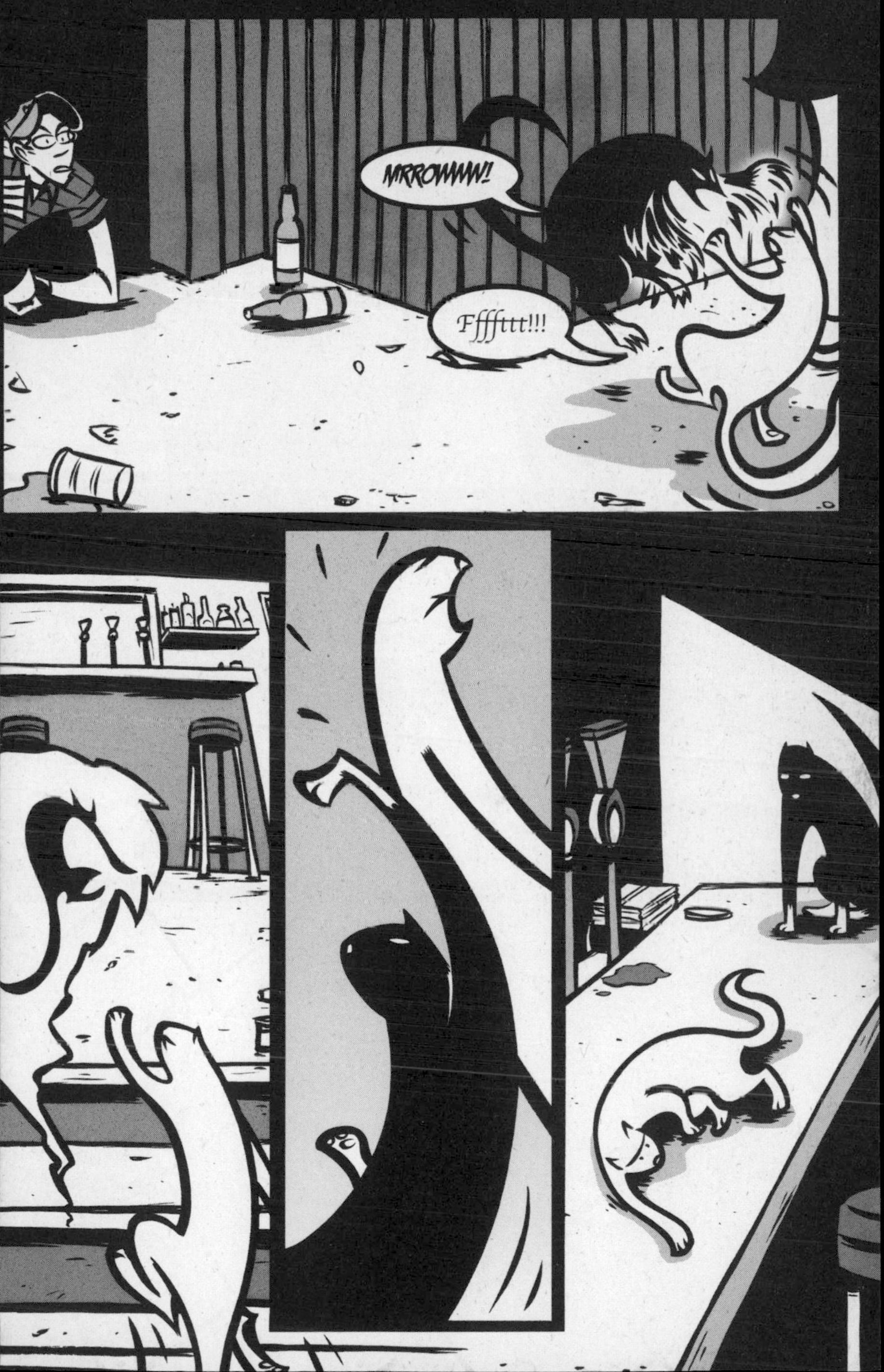
MRROWWW!
Fffftttt!!!

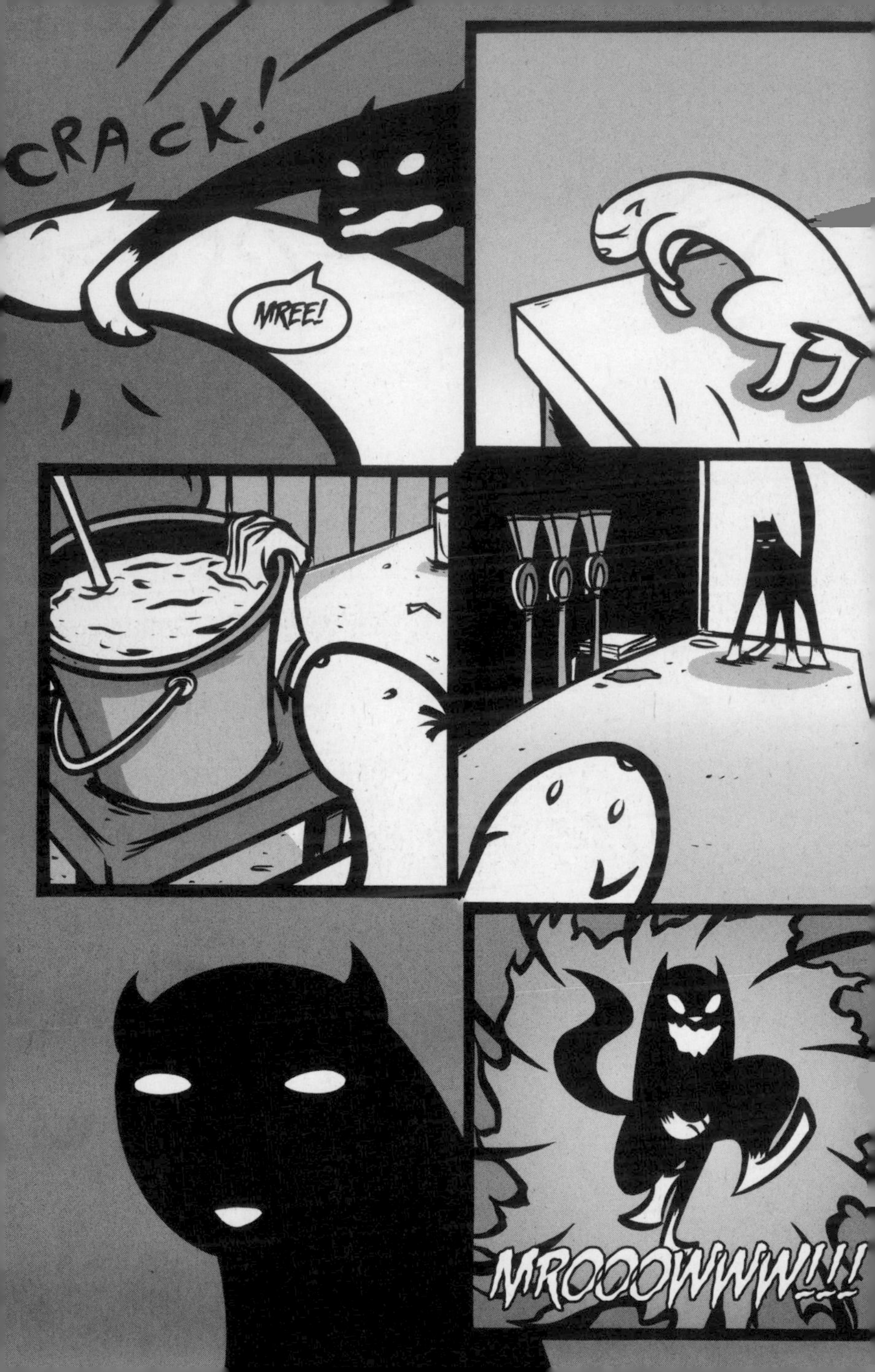
CRACK!
MREE!
MROOOWWW!!!

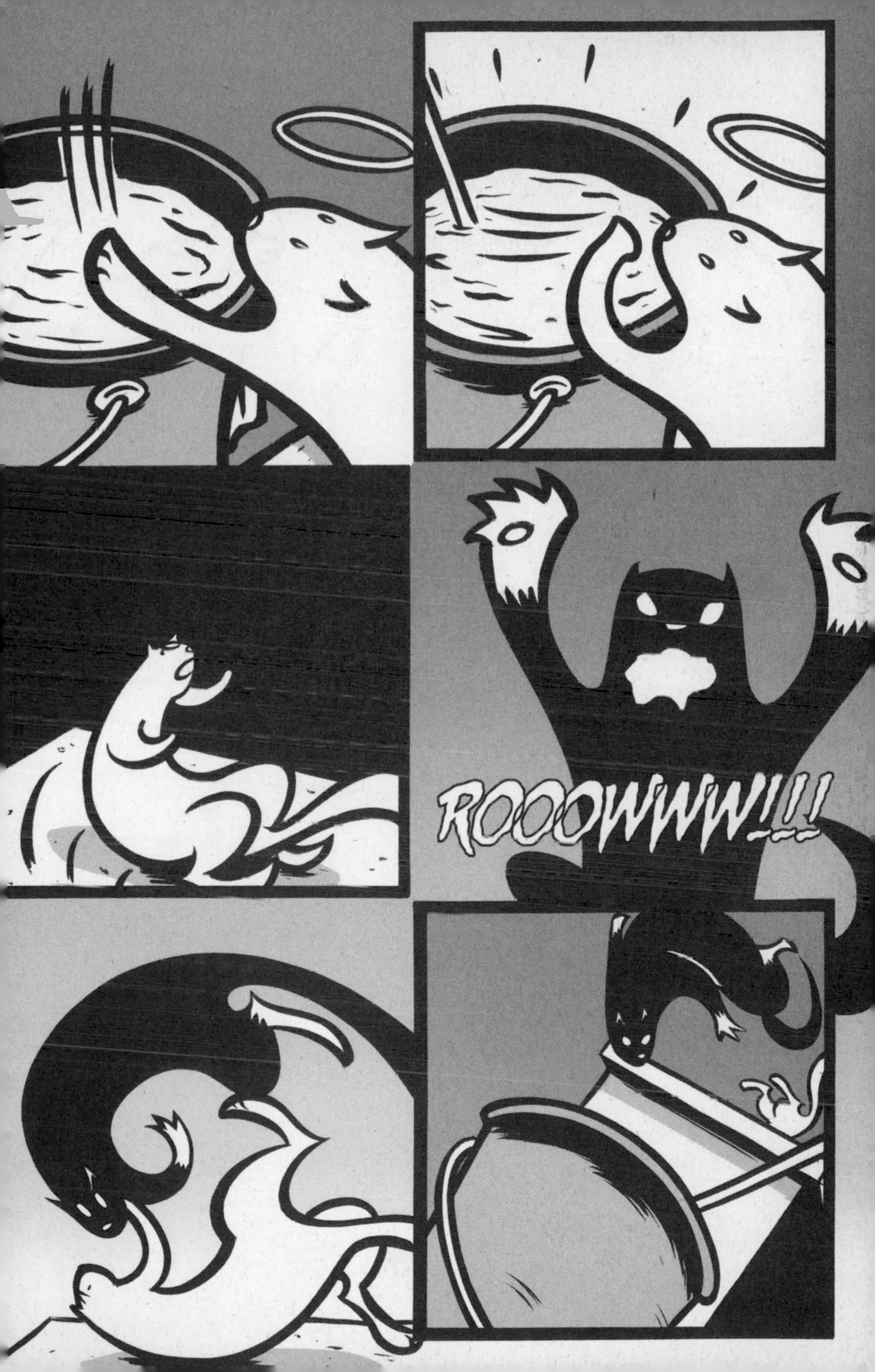
ROOOWWW!!!

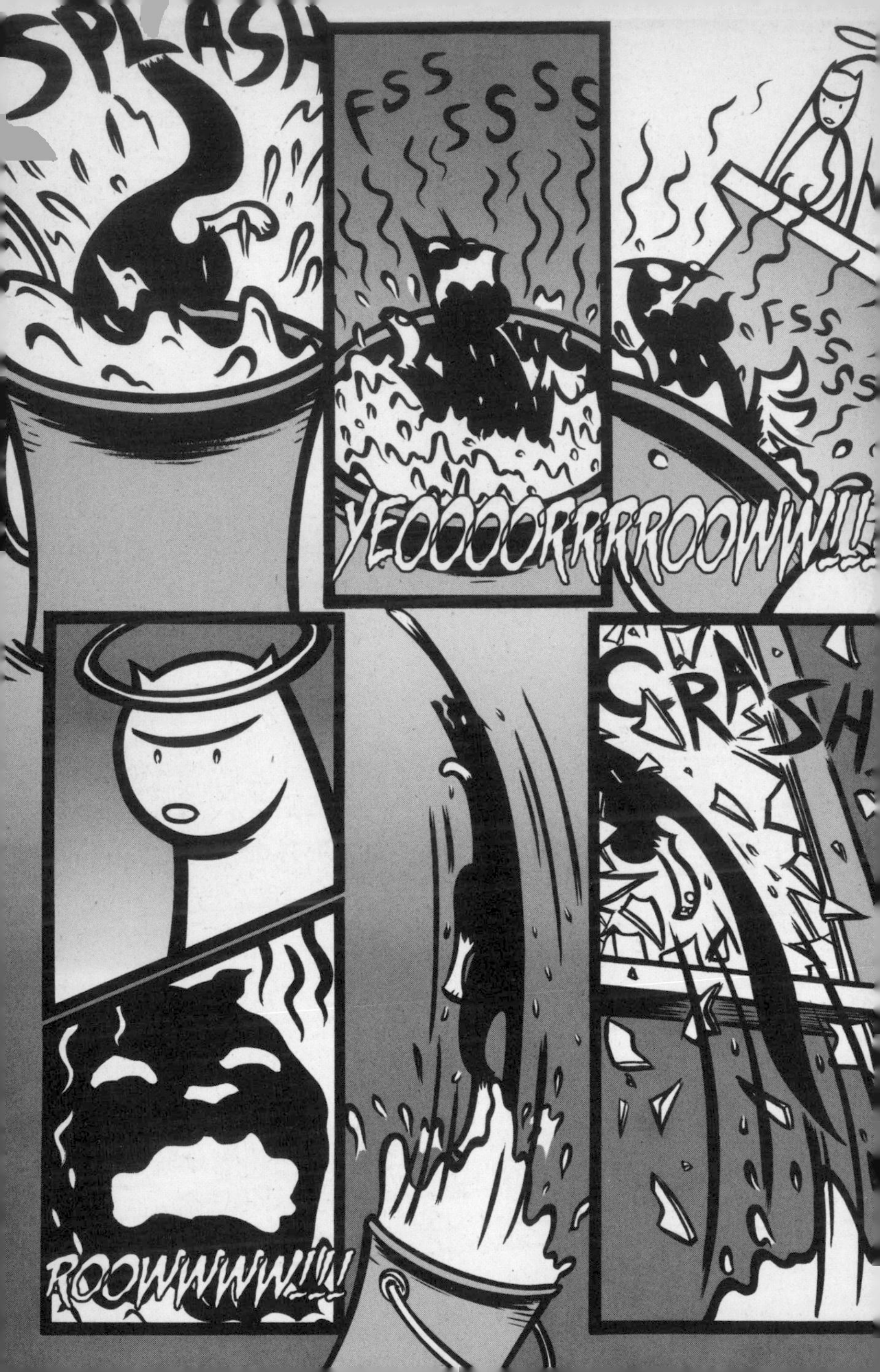
SPLASH
FSSSSSSS
FSSSSS
YEOOOOORRRROOWW!!
ROOWWWW!!!
CRASH

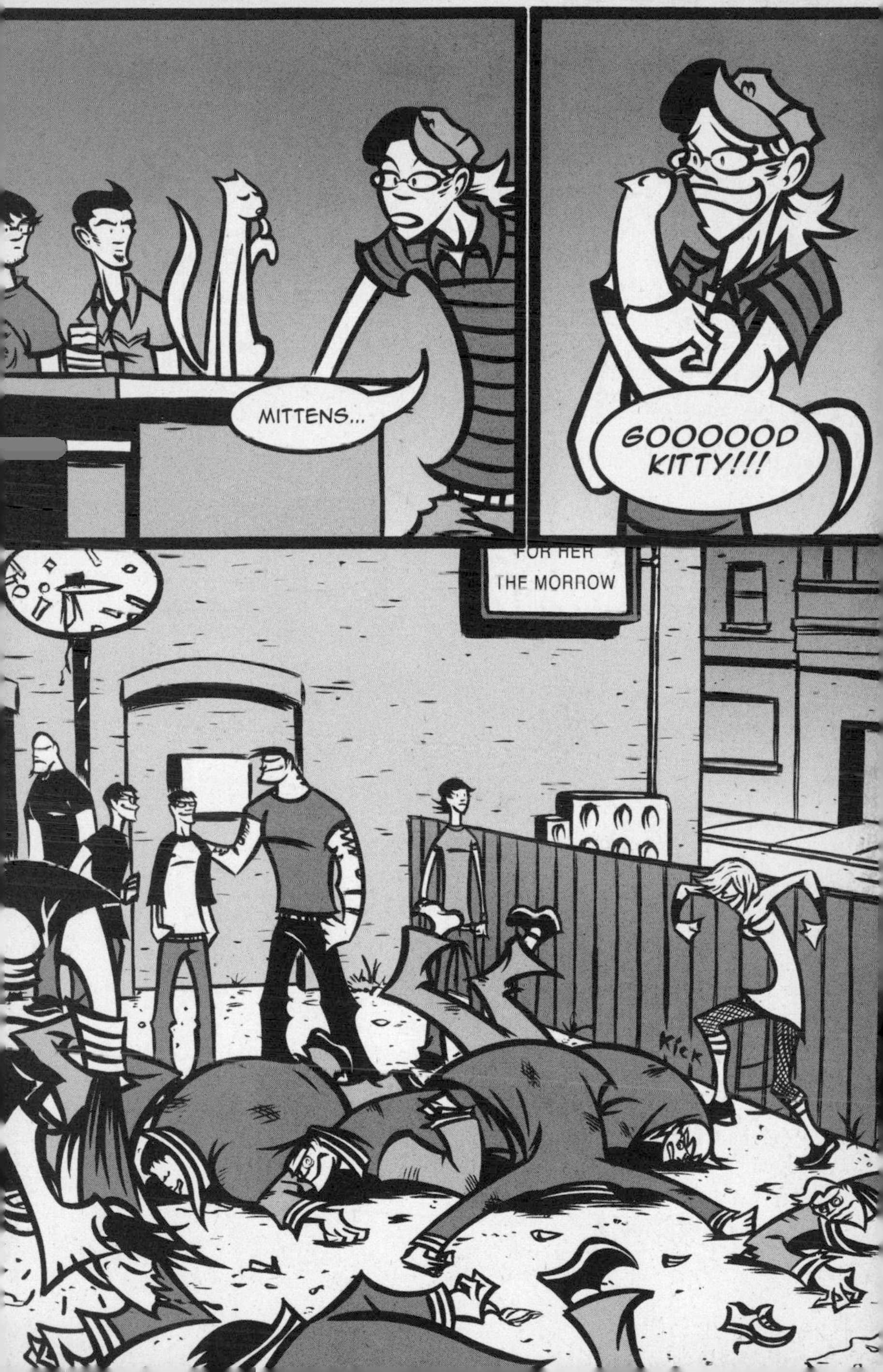
MITTENS...
GOOOOOD KITTY!!!
THE MORROW
Kick

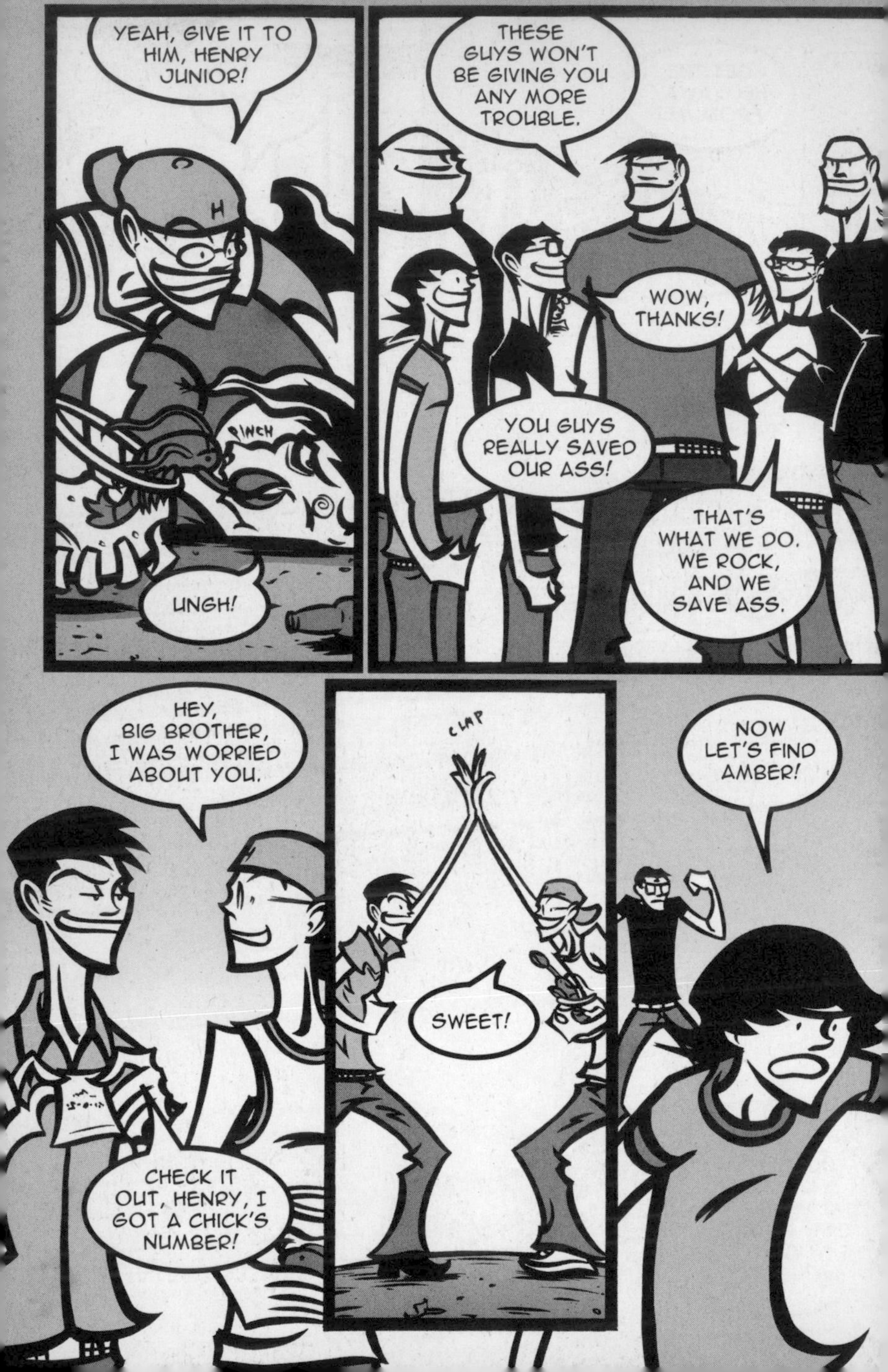
YEAH, GIVE IT TO HIM, HENRY JUNIOR!
PINCH
UNGH!
THESE GUYS WON'T BE GIVING YOU ANY MORE TROUBLE.
WOW, THANKS!
YOU GUYS REALLY SAVED OUR ASS!
THAT'S WHAT WE DO. WE ROCK, AND WE SAVE ASS.
HEY, BIG BROTHER, I WAS WORRIED ABOUT YOU.
CHECK IT OUT, HENRY, I GOT A CHICK'S NUMBER!
CLAP
SWEET!
NOW LET'S FIND AMBER!

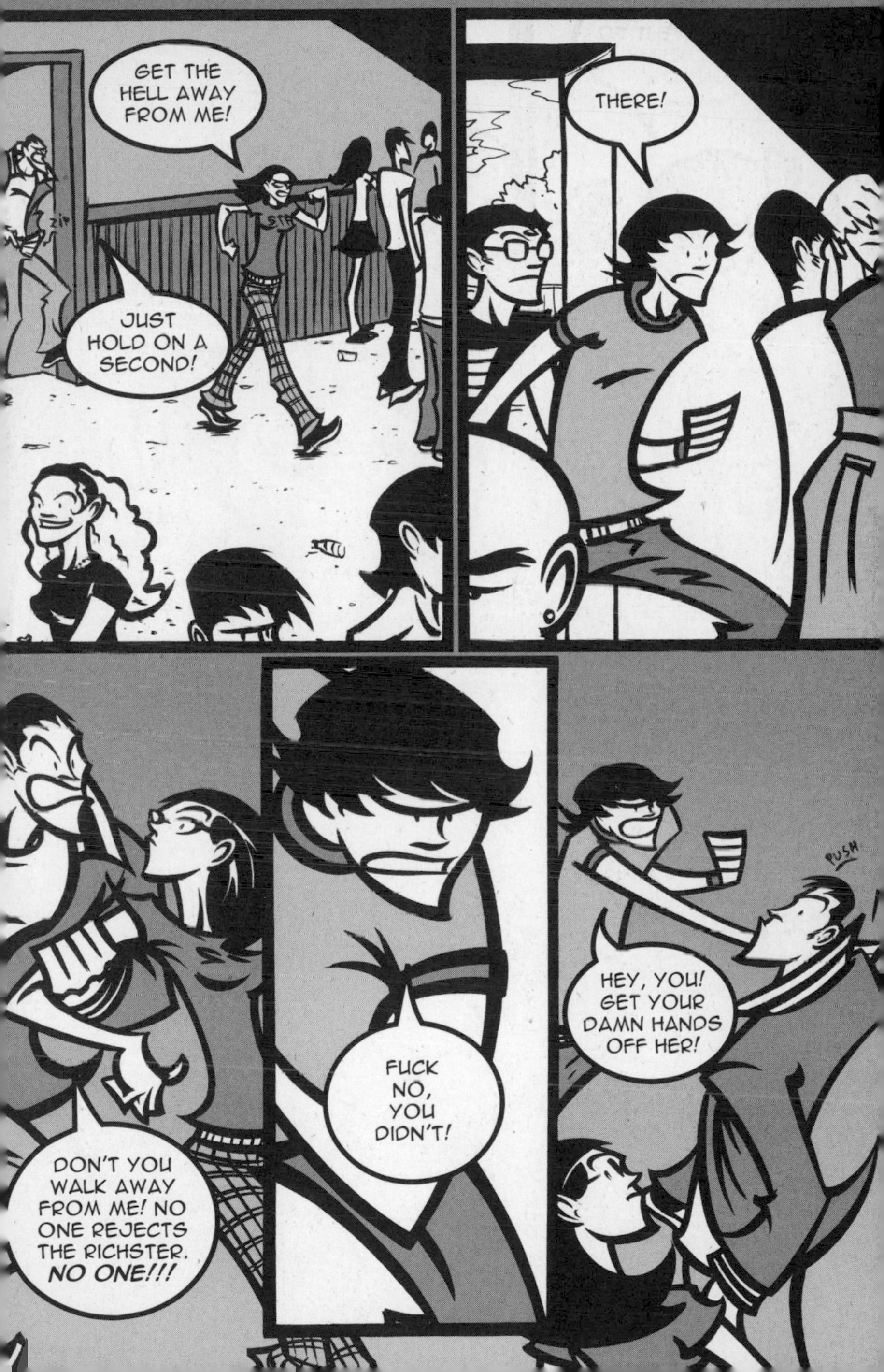
GET THE HELL AWAY FROM ME!
JUST HOLD ON A SECOND!
ZIP
THERE!
DON'T YOU WALK AWAY FROM ME! NO ONE REJECTS THE RICHSTER. NO ONE!!!
FUCK NO, YOU DIDN'T!
PUSH
HEY, YOU! GET YOUR DAMN HANDS OFF HER!

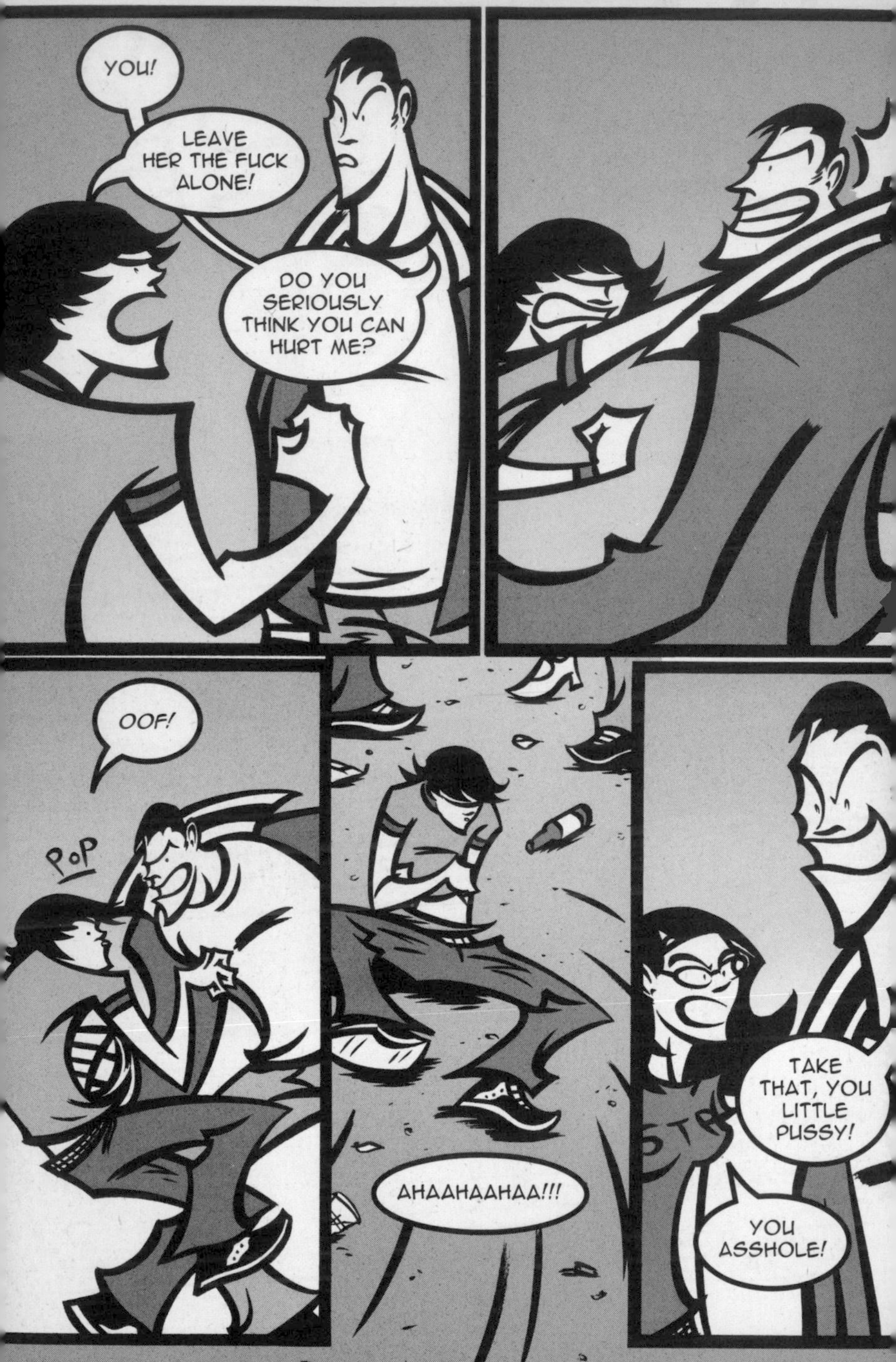
YOU!
LEAVE HER THE FUCK ALONE!
DO YOU SERIOUSLY THINK YOU CAN HURT ME?
OOF!
POP
AHAAHAAHAA!!!
TAKE THAT, YOU LITTLE PUSSY!
YOU ASSHOLE!

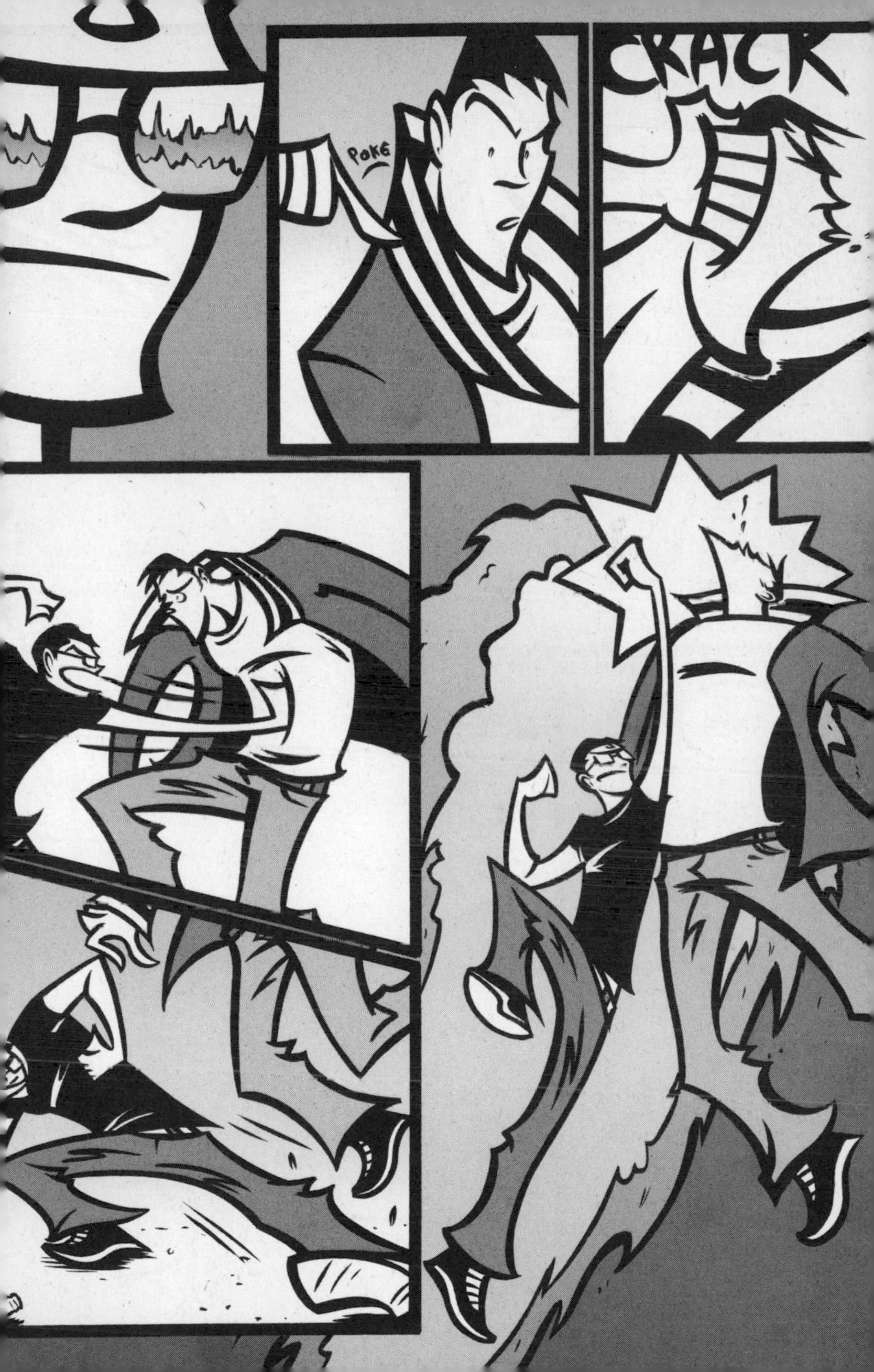
POKE
CRACK

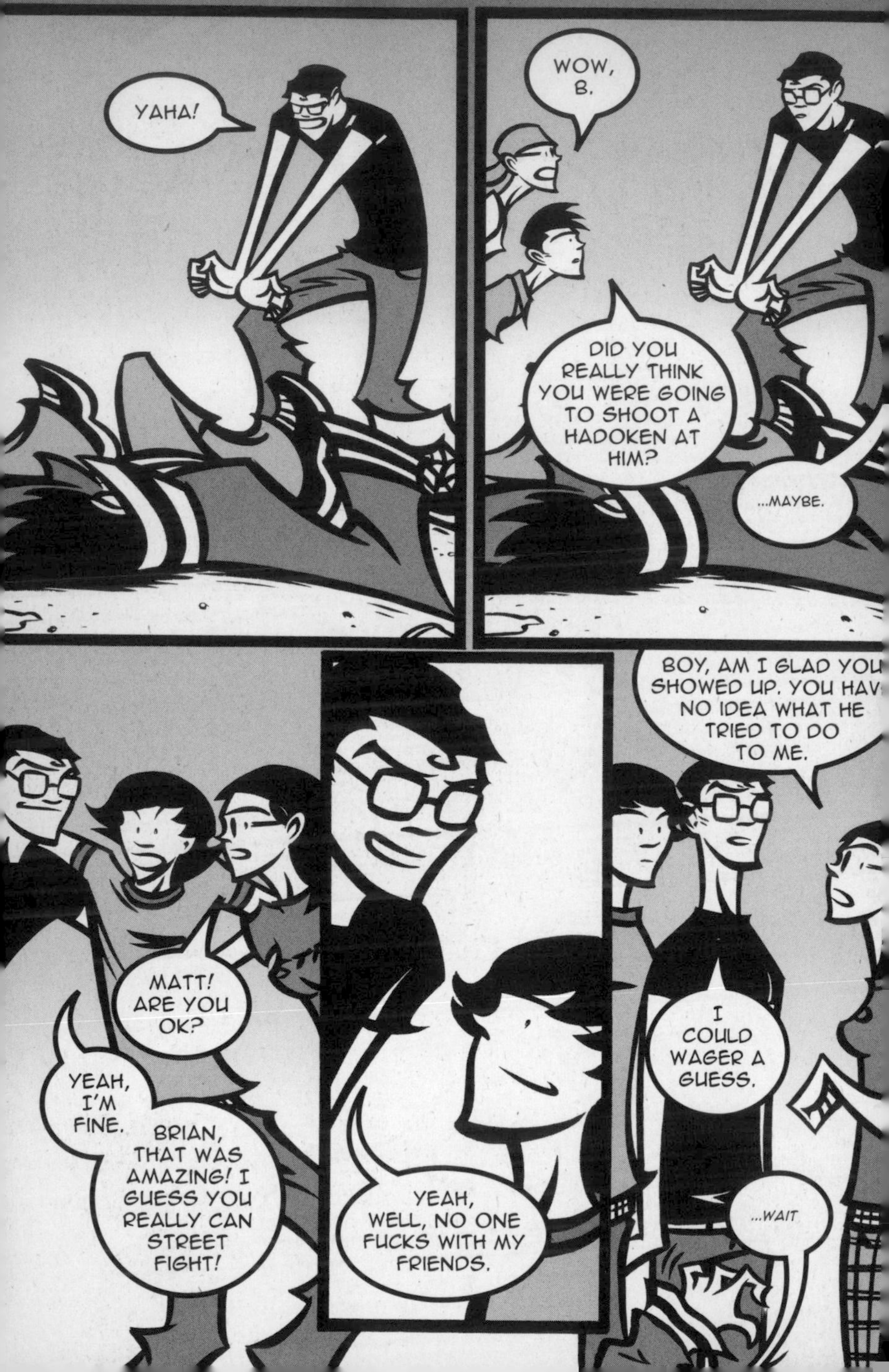
YAHA!
WOW, B.
DID YOU REALLY THINK YOU WERE GOING TO SHOOT A HADOKEN AT HIM?
...MAYBE.
MATT! ARE YOU OK?
YEAH, I'M FINE.
BRIAN, THAT WAS AMAZING! I GUESS YOU REALLY CAN STREET FIGHT!
YEAH, WELL, NO ONE FUCKS WITH MY FRIENDS.
BOY, AM I GLAD YOU SHOWED UP. YOU HAV NO IDEA WHAT HE TRIED TO DO TO ME.
I COULD WAGER A GUESS.
...WAIT

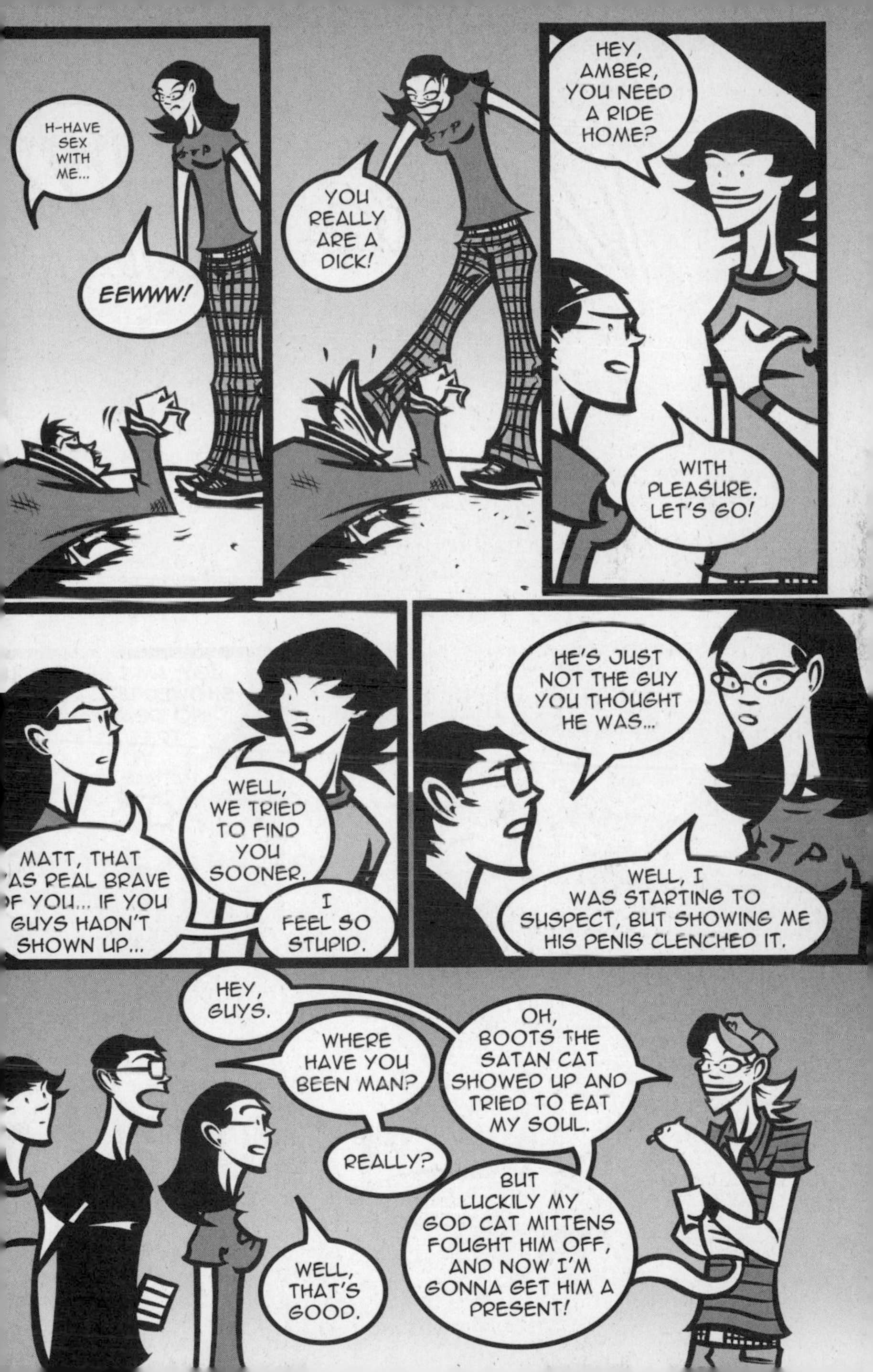
H-HAVE SEX WITH ME...
EEWWW!
YOU REALLY ARE A DICK!
HEY, AMBER, YOU NEED A RIDE HOME?
WITH PLEASURE. LET'S GO!
MATT, THAT WAS REAL BRAVE OF YOU... IF YOU GUYS HADN'T SHOWN UP...
WELL, WE TRIED TO FIND YOU SOONER.
I FEEL SO STUPID.
HE'S JUST NOT THE GUY YOU THOUGHT HE WAS...
WELL, I WAS STARTING TO SUSPECT, BUT SHOWING ME HIS PENIS CLENCHED IT.
HEY, GUYS.
WHERE HAVE YOU BEEN MAN?
OH, BOOTS THE SATAN CAT SHOWED UP AND TRIED TO EAT MY SOUL.
REALLY?
BUT LUCKILY MY GOD CAT MITTENS FOUGHT HIM OFF, AND NOW I'M GONNA GET HIM A PRESENT!
WELL, THAT'S GOOD.

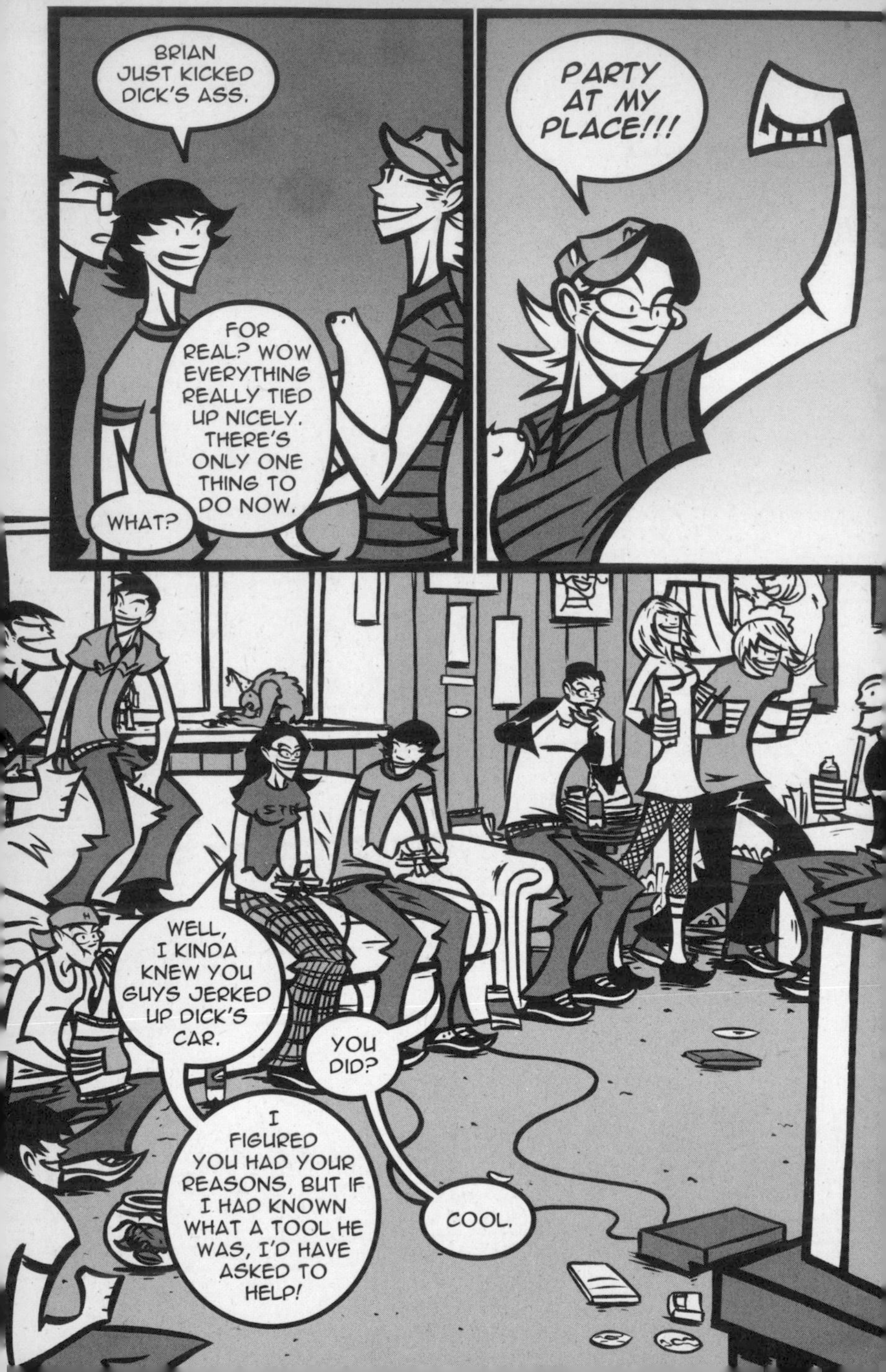
BRIAN JUST KICKED DICK'S ASS.
WHAT?
FOR REAL? WOW EVERYTHING REALLY TIED UP NICELY. THERE'S ONLY ONE THING TO DO NOW.
PARTY AT MY PLACE!!!
WELL, I KINDA KNEW YOU GUYS JERKED UP DICK'S CAR.
YOU DID?
I FIGURED YOU HAD YOUR REASONS, BUT IF I HAD KNOWN WHAT A TOOL HE WAS, I'D HAVE ASKED TO HELP!
COOL.

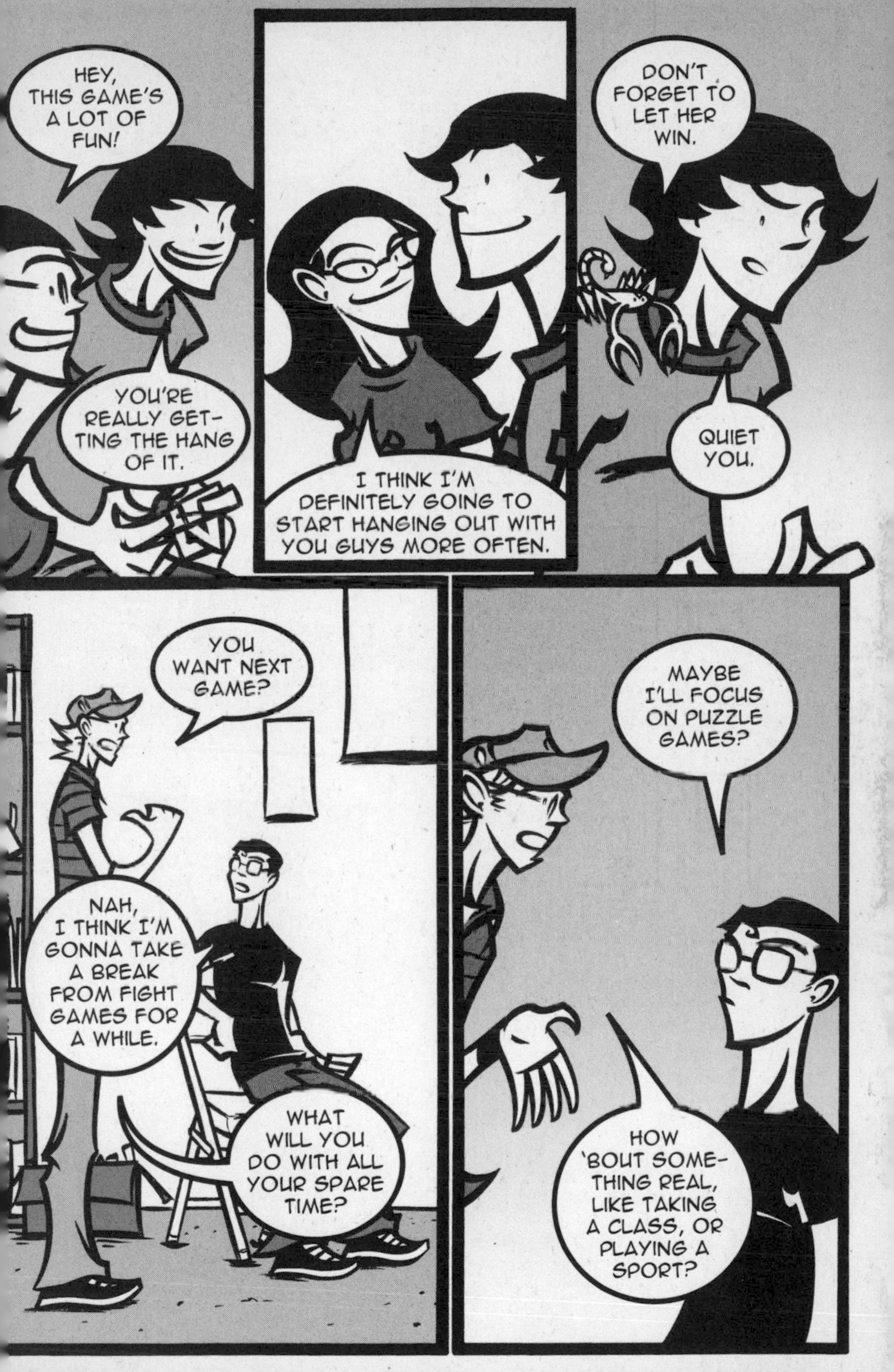
HEY, THIS GAME'S A LOT OF FUN!
YOU'RE REALLY GET-TING THE HANG OF IT.
I THINK I'M DEFINITELY GOING TO START HANGING OUT WITH YOU GUYS MORE OFTEN.
DON'T FORGET TO LET HER WIN.
QUIET YOU.
YOU WANT NEXT GAME?
NAH, I THINK I'M GONNA TAKE A BREAK FROM FIGHT GAMES FOR A WHILE.
WHAT WILL YOU DO WITH ALL YOUR SPARE TIME?
MAYBE I'LL FOCUS ON PUZZLE GAMES?
HOW 'BOUT SOME-THING REAL, LIKE TAKING A CLASS, OR PLAYING A SPORT?

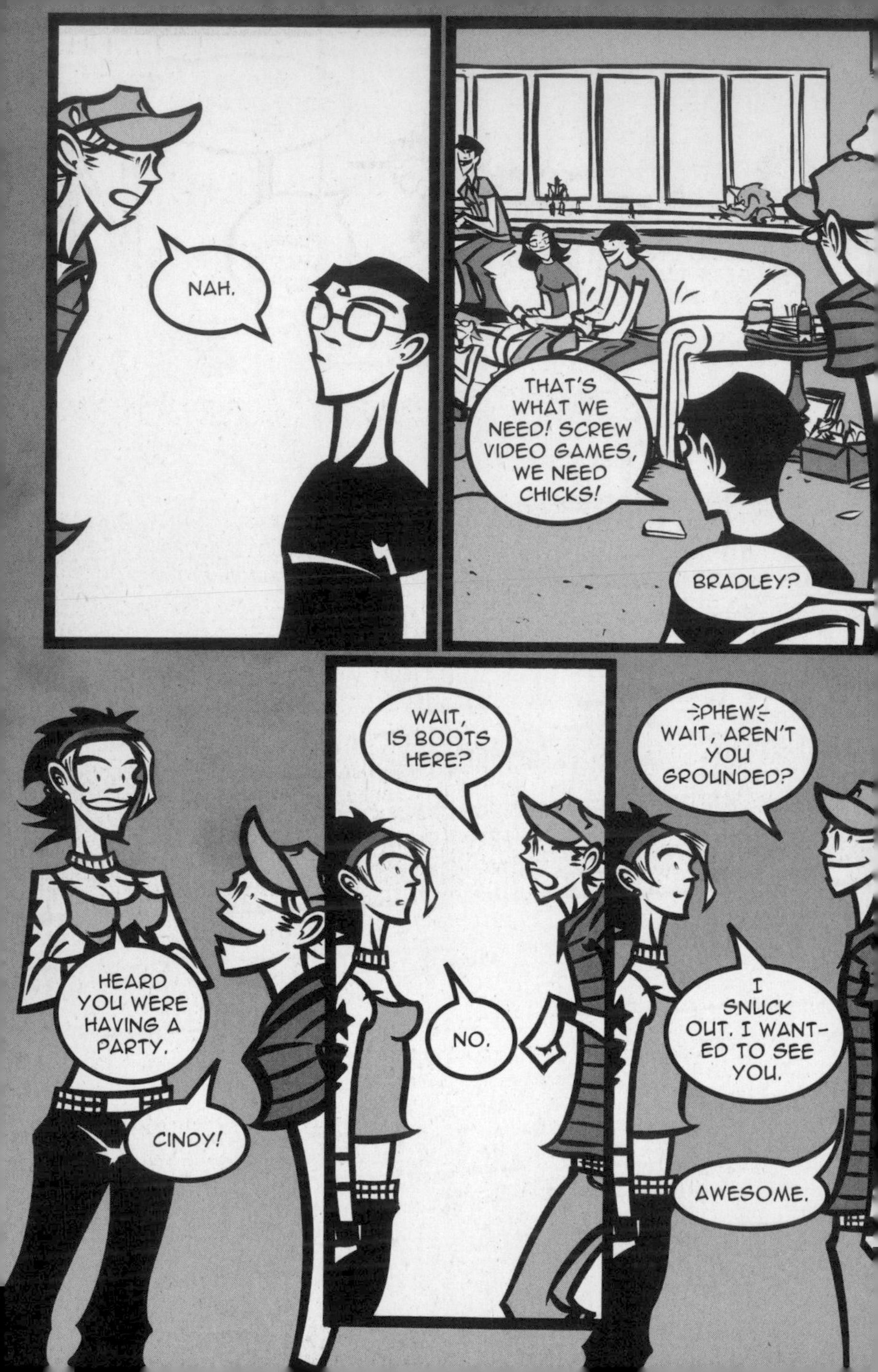
NAH.
THAT'S WHAT WE NEED! SCREW VIDEO GAMES, WE NEED CHICKS!
BRADLEY?
HEARD YOU WERE HAVING A PARTY.
CINDY!
WAIT, IS BOOTS HERE?
NO.
PHEW
WAIT, AREN'T YOU GROUNDED?
I SNUCK OUT. I WANTED TO SEE YOU.
AWESOME.

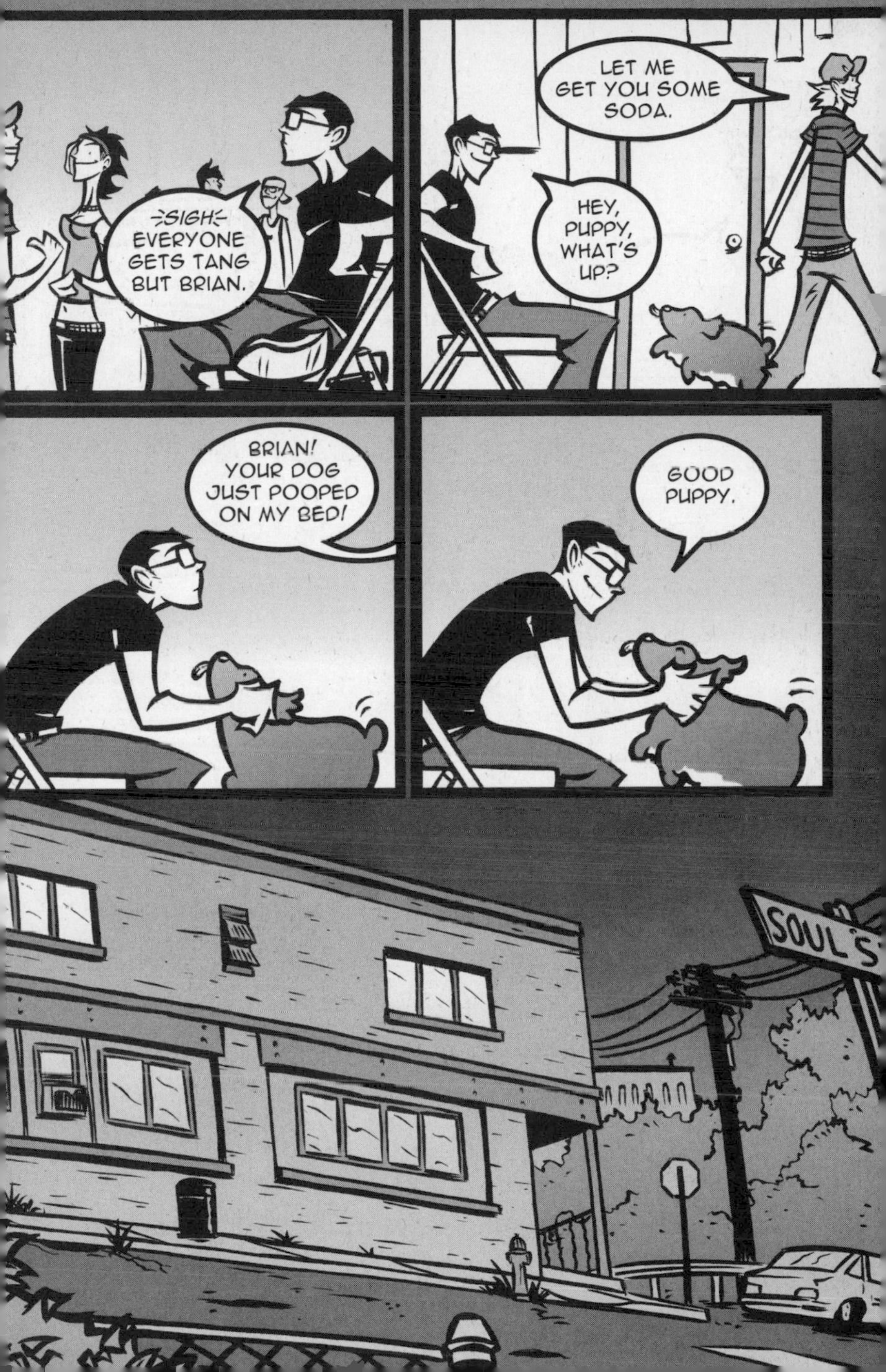

-SIGH-
EVERYONE GETS TANG BUT BRIAN.
LET ME GET YOU SOME SODA.
HEY, PUPPY, WHAT'S UP?
BRIAN! YOUR DOG JUST POOPED ON MY BED!
GOOD PUPPY.
SOUL'S

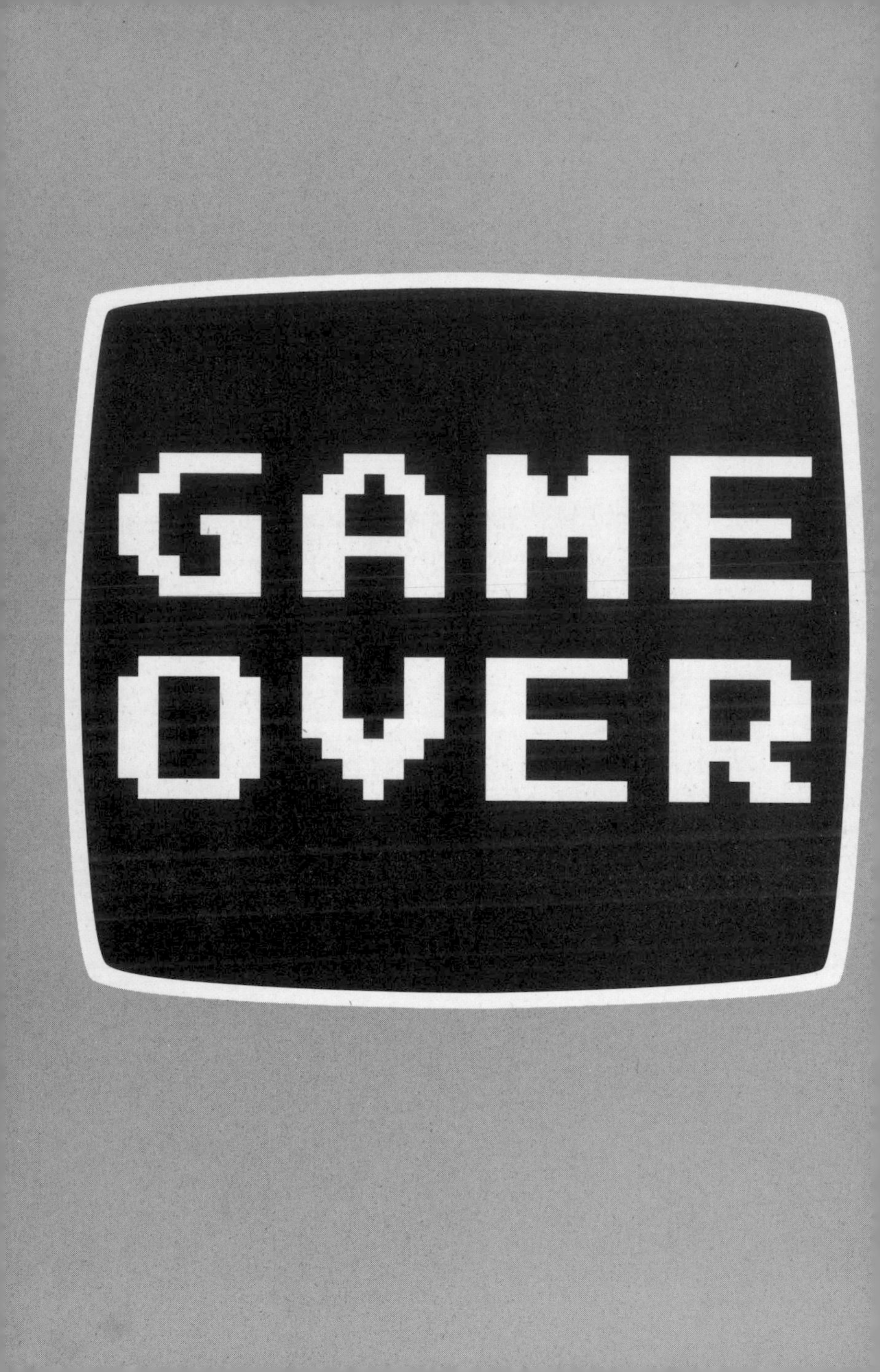
GAME
OVER

VERY SPECIAL THANKS TO...
MOM AND DAD
BRIAN S.
BRAD S.
KEVIN S.
ABBY
MIKE Z.
JON AND MATT R.
RAINA V DAVE
THOREN, TOM S.
    AND THE MAKE A FRAME ARMY
RANDY, JAMES,
    AND THE REST OF THE ONI TEAM.
AND EVERY ONE WHO
    SUPPORTED ME DURING THIS BOOK.
YOU ALL ROCK!

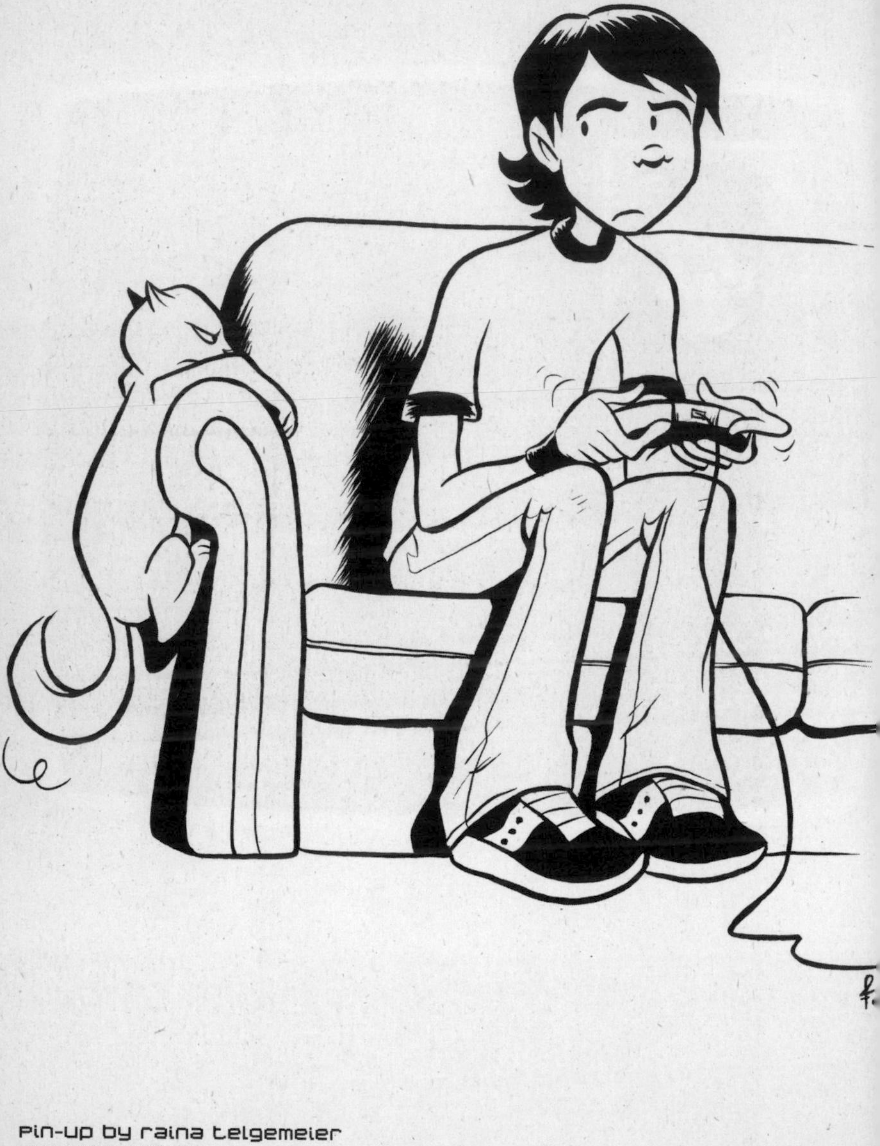

Pin-up by raina telgemeier
www.goraina.com

Matthew Loux grew up in rural eastern Connecticut. Matt's first video game system was the trusty ATARI 2600-acquired somehow by his brother Jesse. This began a life-long enjoyment (obsession) in video games. At some point between gaming sessions, Matthew managed to go to school. He eventually graduated from the school of Visual Arts in New York City, where his focus was split between his Playstation and his N64. Matt currently draws comics in NYC. Occasionally, he sneaks in a game or two when his editor isn't looking.

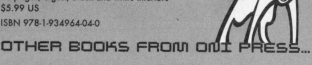

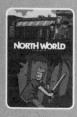